Darkness at Dawn

Darkness

The Rise of the Russian Criminal State

at Dawn

DAVID SATTER

Yale University Press / New Haven & London

Published with assistance from the Louis Stern Memorial Fund.

Printed in the United Stated of America by Integrated Book Technology.

The Library of Congress has cataloged the hardcover edition as follows:
Satter, David, 1947–
Darkness at dawn : the rise of the Russian criminal state / David Satter.
p. cm.
Includes bibliographical references and index.

1. Organized crime—Russia (Federation) 2. Russia (Federation)—Social conditions—1991– I. Title.
HV6453.R8 S27 2003
364.1'06'0947—dc21   2002015754

A catalogue record for this book is available from the British Library.

The paper in this book meets the guidelines for permanence and durability of the Committee on Production Guidelines for Book Longevity of the Council on Library Resources.

ISBN 13: 978-0-300-10591-9 (pbk. : alk. paper)

10 9 8 7 6 5 4 3

To the honest people of Russia

For nothing is hidden except to be known and nothing is secret except to be revealed.

—*Mark 4:22*

Contents

Preface

In *Darkness at Dawn*, I have tried to describe the rise of a business criminal elite and its takeover of the machinery of the Russian state, leading to the impoverishment and demoralization of the great majority of the population.

The book consists of narrative histories and personal stories. The histories show how criminal oligarchic power achieved its present dominance in Russia, while the stories of ordinary Russians provide a social context for the activities of this "elite." I have chosen to describe Russia with the help of stories because Russians experienced a spiritual crisis in the reform period as a result of being confronted with a new way of life for which their previous experience had not prepared them. To understand this spiritual crisis, facts alone are not sufficient. It is necessary to grasp the psychology of Russia, and this can be conveyed only through the stories of individual lives.

It is also not irrelevant that telling the stories of ordinary Russians is a way to help them. As the Danish novelist Isak Dinesen put it, "All sorrows can be borne if you put them into a story or tell a story about them."

Abbreviations and Administrative Delineations

CIS   Commonwealth of Independent States
FAPSI   Federal Agency for Government Communications and Information (formerly part of the KGB)
FSB   Federal Security Service
FSK   Federal Counterintelligence Service (predecessor of FSB)
GKI   State Property Committee
GRU   Main Intelligence Administration (military intelligence)
IMF   International Monetary Fund
KGB   Committee for State Security
MVD   Ministry of Internal Affairs
UVD   Directorate of Internal Affairs (subdivision of the ministry)
GUVD   Chief Directorate of Internal Affairs (principal subdivision of the ministry)
OMON   special police detachments of the Interior Ministry
RUBOP   (formerly RUOP) Regional Directorate for the Struggle with Organized Crime
SBP   Presidential Security Service

Krai   Best translated as "province" or "territory," a krai is a territorial subdivision that generally encompasses a large area, such as Primoriye in the Far East or the Krasnoyarsk region in Siberia.

Oblast   Often similar in size to an American state, an oblast has the same weight in the Russian administrative system as a krai.

Raion   A raion is a subdivision of a krai, oblast, or city and is responsible for most local administration, including the police and the courts.

Okrug   An okrug is an administrative subdivision of Moscow, created in the mid-1990s through the consolidation of groups of raions. It can also signify a Russian military district, for example, the North Caucasus military okrug.

Any call to personal discipline irritates Russians. Spiritual work on the formation of his personality does not present itself to the Russian as either necessary or interesting.
—*Nikolai Berdyaev,* Sudba Rossii (Russia's Fate)

Introduction

In 1991 Russia experienced a new dawn of freedom. The Communist party was dissolved, and Russia appeared ready to build a democratic future. The literary critic Yuri Karyakin spoke for many when he said, "For the first time in this century, God has smiled on Russia."[1]

Few at that time could have foreseen the outlines of what exists today. In the years that followed, many former Communist countries experienced a rebirth of freedom, but Russia came to be dominated by poverty, intimidation, and crime. The reason is that during the reform period, which witnessed a massive effort to remake Russian society and the Russian economy, Russia once again fell victim to a false idea.

The victory over communism was a moral victory. Millions took to the streets not because of shortages but in protest over communism's attempt to falsify history and change human nature. As a new state began to be built, however, all attention shifted to the creation of capitalism and, in particular, to the formation of a group of wealthy private owners whose control over the means of production, it was assumed, would lead automatically to a free-market economy and a law-based democracy. This approach, dubious under the best of conditions, proved disastrous in the case of Russia because, in a country with a need for moral values after more than seven decades of spiritual degradation under communism, the introduction of capitalism came to be seen as an end in itself.

The young reformers were in a hurry to build capitalism, and they pressed ahead in a manner that paid little attention to anything except the transformation of economic structures. "The calculation was sober," said

Aliza Dolgova, an expert on organized crime in the Office of the General Prosecutor; "create through any means a stratum in Russia that could serve as the support of reform . . . All capital was laundered and put into circulation. No measures of any kind were enacted to prevent the legalization of criminal income. No one asked at [privatization] auctions: Where did you get the money? Enormous sums were invested in property, and there was no register of owners. A policy similar to this did not exist in a single civilized country."[2]

The decision to transform the economy of a huge country without the benefit of the rule of law led not to a free-market democracy but to a kleptocracy that had several dangerous economic and psychological features.

In the first place, the new system was characterized by bribery. All resources were initially in the hands of the state, so businessmen competed to "buy" critical government officials. The winners were in a position to buy the cooperation of more officials, with the result that the practice of giving bribes grew up with the system.[3]

Besides bribery, the new system was marked by institutionalized violence. Gangsters were treated as normal economic actors, a practice that tacitly legitimated their criminal activities. At the same time, they became the partners of businessmen who used them as guards, enforcers, and debt collectors.

The new system was also characterized by pillage. Money obtained as a result of criminal activities was illegally exported to avoid the possibility of its being confiscated at some point in the future. This outflow deprived Russia of billions of dollars that were needed for its development.

Perhaps more important than these economic features, however, was the new system's social psychology, which was characterized by mass moral indifference. If under communism universal morality was denied in favor of the supposed "interests of the working class," under the new government people lost the ability to distinguish between legal and criminal activity.

Official corruption came to be regarded as "normal," and it was considered a sign of virtue if the official, in addition to stealing, made an effort to fulfill his official responsibilities. Extortion also came to be regarded as normal, and vendors, through force of habit, began to regard paying protection money as part of the cost of doing business.

Officials and businessmen took no responsibility for the consequences of their actions, even if those consequences included hunger and death. Government officials helped to organize pyramid schemes that victimized people who were already destitute, police officials took bribes from leaders of organized crime to ignore extortion, and factory directors stole funds marked for the salaries of workers who had already gone months without pay.

The young reformers were lionized in the West, but as the years passed and the promised rebirth of Russia did not materialize, debates broke out in Russia over whether progress was being prevented by the resistance of the Duma, by inadequate assistance from the West, or by the inadequacies of the Russian people themselves.

These arguments, however, had a surrealistic quality because they implicitly assumed that, with the right economic combination, it was possible to build a free-market democracy without the rule of law.

In fact a market economy presupposes the rule of law because only the rule of law can assure the basis of a free market's existence, which is equivalent exchange. Without law, prices are dictated not by the market but by monopolization and the use of force.

The need for a framework of law was especially acute in the case of Russia because for ordinary Russians, socialism was not only an economic system but also a secular religion that lent a powerful sense of meaning to millions of lives. When the Soviet Union fell, it was necessary to replace not only the socialist economic structures but also the "class values" that gave that system its higher sanction. This could be done only by establishing the authority of transcendent, universal values, which, as a practical matter, could be assured only by establishing the rule of law.

On May 10, 1997, the Greek police found in a shallow grave under an olive tree, two miles from the Athenian suburb of Saronida, the dismembered body of Svetlana Kotova, one of Russia's top models and a former "Miss Russia." It was learned that she had been the guest of Alexander Solonik (Sasha Makedonsky), Russia's number-one professional killer, who had himself been found strangled three months earlier in the Athenian suburb of Baribobi.

Svetlana's story evoked intense interest in Russia because of her youth and beauty and because there was something about the romance between a twenty-one-year-old beauty queen and a professional killer that was symbolic of the condition of modern Russia.

Svetlana met Solonik in a Moscow nightclub on New Year's night 1997 and traveled to Greece on January 25 at his invitation.[4] She was met at the plane with armloads of flowers and driven to Solonik's villa in a chauffeur-driven Mercedes. The rent on the villa was about $90,000 a year. Its amenities included a swimming pool, gym, basketball court, golf course, and gardens with sculptures. Beginning January 26, she called her mother every night. She said this was not life but a miracle.

The villa and Solonik's car contained a large quantity of firearms and other weapons, but it is not known whether Svetlana was aware of them. For five nights she lived as if in a dream, but on January 30, gangsters from the Kurgan criminal organization, a supplier of hired killers to the Russian underworld, arrived at the villa. While they were talking to Solonik, someone threw a thin cord around his neck and strangled him from behind. The visitors then came for Svetlana, who was on the second floor.[5]

When word of Svetlana's murder was released, the Russian newspapers were filled with pictures: Svetlana with flowing black hair in a long black gown with thin shoulder straps, Svetlana in a bathing suit looking out shyly from behind spread fingers, Svetlana with her head cupped in her hands, Svetlana in an evening dress with her hair in a bun off her forehead. No one, it seemed, could have been less prepared for the devilish game that she had fallen into.

Yet the fate of Svetlana Kotova had something in common with the fate of her nation, freely delivered into the hands of criminals during the period of reform. The rewards were quick and easy. There was a willful desire not to know.

It remains to be seen whether, in the long run, Russia will share Svetlana's fate.

But now he is dead; why should I fast? Can I bring him
back again? I shall go to him, but he will never come to me
again. —2 Samuel 12:7

1 *The* Kursk

SATURDAY, AUGUST 12, 2000

In the dim afternoon light of the Arctic summer, with pennants flying and amid the deafening roar of exploding missiles and torpedoes, the nuclear submarine *Kursk* moved into position to take part in the largest naval exercises in the history of the Russian Northern Fleet. The area where the exercises were taking place, 130 miles northeast of Murmansk in the Barents Sea, was a region of immense strategic significance for Russia. The Northern Fleet, the most battle-ready section of Russia's armed forces, operated in the Barents Sea and was the key to Russia's ability to challenge the West and to Russia's status as a great power.

The *Kursk*, one of eight active Oscar II class submarines, was the pride of Russia's Northern Fleet. In the event of war, its task was to cut NATO in half by severing the transatlantic sea link. Its Shipwreck missiles were capable of destroying an entire U.S. carrier group or transport convoy or, according to Russian naval sources, of being armed with nuclear warheads with a yield equivalent to that of 500,000 tons of TNT, sufficient to level Los Angeles or New York.[1] The mission of the *Kursk* was to demonstrate its two principal capabilities, destroying both aircraft carriers and submarines. First the *Kursk* fired its main weapon, the Chelomey Granit missile, codenamed "Shipwreck," which contained a 1,600-pound conventional warhead. It scored a direct hit against a Russian hulk target more than 200 miles away.

The *Kursk* then prepared to fire the 100 RU Veder torpedo, codenamed "Stallion," at a simulated submarine. The Stallion, a top-secret weapon, was

5

powered by a rocket booster that ignited underwater. Once the weapon was clear of the submarine, the booster sent it to the surface, and it homed in on its target like a missile. The Stallion to be fired by the *Kursk* was armed with a 220-pound warhead.

As the Stallion was fired, however, something went disastrously wrong. The torpedo's rocket motor exploded inside the torpedo tube, melting its metal walls in seconds and filling the forward weapon bay with flames. The warhead then detonated, blowing a hole in the *Kursk*'s reinforced hull. Icy water rushed into the ship but did not extinguish the fire, since the rocket booster was designed to burn without air. Flaming chunks of the booster were thrown into the forward weapons control room.

The submarine was pulled sharply downward, and in a little more than two minutes there was a second, gigantic explosion of the *Kursk*'s reserve torpedoes and torpedo-sized cruise missiles inside the torpedo compartment. The explosion ripped open the starboard side of the submarine back to the sail, an area the length of a school gymnasium. The force of the blast and a wall of seawater tore through the control room, destroying the switches, computers, and video screens that constituted the brain of the huge submarine. The living quarters forward of the reactor compartment were instantly flooded, leaving the sailors no chance to escape.[2]

At first Russian naval officers assumed that the explosions, which measured 1.5 and 3.5, respectively, on the Richter scale, came from the missile and torpedo that had been fired by the *Kursk*, but when attempts to establish radio contact with the submarine failed, an alarm was sounded and a massive search began. Finally, at 4:35 A.M. on Sunday, August 13, the *Kursk* was discovered on the sea bottom at a depth of 330 feet. At 7:00 A.M. President Vladimir Putin, who was vacationing in Sochi, was informed, and the navy began organizing an effort to rescue the crew.

Throughout Sunday the Russian authorities said nothing about the missing submarine. On Monday, August 14, Russian officials released the first information about the disaster. They said that problems had occurred on the submarine on Sunday and the *Kursk* had been forced "to lie on the sea bottom." A short time later they announced that communication had been established with the crew, that the *Kursk* was being supplied with electricity and fresh air, and that all of the crew were alive. All these statements, as events were to show, were untrue.

During the Cold War the Soviet Union had a rescue service that was considered to be as well equipped as that of NATO. In 1991 Russian deep-sea divers performed a rescue at a depth of 985 feet for which they received Star of the Hero of Russia awards. With the collapse of the Soviet Union, however, the rescue unit was disbanded. By 2000 the Russian navy was without deep-sea divers, and its minisubmarines, long used mainly for intelligence gathering, lacked trained rescue personnel. In the case of the *Kursk*, Russian officials justified the decision to dispense with a functioning rescue service by arguing that the submarine was unsinkable.

In the quiet provincial city of Kursk on Monday, August 14, people were caught up in the lazy rhythms of summer. There were few strollers on the street, and many of the factories were half empty.

The city, the scene of the battle of the Kursk Salient, which marked a turning point of the Second World War, is set in rolling hills and surrounded by fields of wheat, rye, and sunflowers. With the breakup of the Soviet Union, it lay only sixty miles from the independent country of Ukraine, but it remained a patriotic community that took pride in having given its name to Russia's most advanced nuclear submarine.

Valentina Staroselteva, whose son, Dmitri, was a sailor on the *Kursk*, was sitting at her desk in the medical unit of a ball-bearing factory where she worked as a physiotherapist. Instead of seeing patients, however, she occupied herself packing a parcel for her son. It included cookies, candies, pens, disposable razors, paper, and notebooks, all of which were in short supply in Vidyaevo, where Dima was based.

At 3:00 P.M. a news broadcast came on the television. Valentina paid no attention to it. Suddenly, however, she realized that the announcer was describing an accident aboard the *Kursk*. Valentina put down what she was doing and began listening more closely. Dima had written to her that he was leaving for three days of maneuvers. She realized that a disaster had befallen the *Kursk* and that her son was on the ship.

That evening the fate of the *Kursk* dominated the Russian television news programs. With each hour the information released by the navy press service changed. Quite soon the press service reported that radio contact had been lost and that the only communication consisted of tapping coming from the ship's interior. The figures for the number of people on board also changed, from 107, to 130, to "116 or 117," and finally to 118. Such shifts led to speculation that officials were trying to conceal the presence of civilian specialists on board.

As an armada of Russian ships gathered at the accident site in the Barents Sea, two rescue bells submerged repeatedly but were unable to latch on to the *Kursk*. Navy officials reported severe storms in the region and said that the rescue work was being hampered by the sharp angle at which the submarine was lying, strong underwater currents, poor visibility (about six feet), and silt that was being lifted from the bottom.

Britain, Norway, and the United States offered to assist in rescuing the trapped sailors. Both Britain and Norway had skilled deep-sea divers, and Britain offered to deploy its LR-5 minisubmarine, which is capable of resisting underwater currents and is equipped with a special joining hitch that allows it to attach to the hatch of a submarine regardless of the list. The Russian government, however, refused the offers. A spokesman for the Defense Ministry said that Russia had everything that was necessary to rescue the men, that the presence of foreign ships would only cause confusion in the zone of operations, and that the technical parameters of the NATO rescue vessels might not coincide with those of the Russian submarine.

Navy officials also began to suggest that the most likely cause of the accident was a collision with a foreign submarine. This possibility was rejected by the United States and Britain, the only powers with submarines in the area, but it was to be repeated continually by the Russian high command, deflecting attention, to a degree, from questions about incompetence in the handling of torpedoes aboard the *Kursk.*

Staroseltseva sat at home with friends. She found it impossible to eat or to sleep. The official information made no sense. What did it mean for a submarine to "lie on the bottom"? Had it sunk, or was it just resting there? If the rescue effort was proceeding "satisfactorily," why were the men still trapped? And why were the authorities refusing to accept foreign help?

The telephone rang constantly. The mother and stepfather of Alexei Nekrasov, a friend of Dima's who served with him on the *Kursk,* called from the village where they lived, twenty-seven miles outside Kursk. Alexei's stepfather, Vladimir Shalapin, a former submariner, told Valentina that on the basis of the existing information, there was reason to believe that their sons were alive. Staroseltseva also received a call from Valentina Budikina, chairman of the local Committee of Soldiers' Mothers. She said that she was in touch with the navy high command and that a trip to Vidyaevo was being organized for the relatives of the *Kursk* crew.

By Tuesday afternoon, August 15, the number of ships at the accident scene had increased from fifteen to twenty-two. They included the *Mikhail Rudnitsky,* which brought two minisubmarines, the *Priz* and the *Bester.* It was rapidly becoming clear, however, that the rescue effort was fundamentally flawed. The minisubmarines submerged repeatedly but failed to attach to the submarine's hatch. Navy officials said that the rescue vessels were having trouble attaching because the docking ring around the hatch had been severely damaged but that they continued to hear tapping coming from inside the submarine. At the same time, a diving bell took the first photographs of the *Kursk*. These showed that the entire nose section was gone, as if it had been cut off by a guillotine.

It was now clear that if there were survivors among the crew of the *Kursk*, they were in the rear compartments of the submarine, which were farthest from the explosion. But even there the sailors were threatened by the buildup of icy water and the rapidly diminishing supply of air.

The full horror of the situation of the trapped sailors was described in the evaluations of military doctors that were published in the press. Valery Matlin, a military doctor in Vladivostok who had participated in many rescue operations, said:

> The basic problems are cold, the absence of light, possibly of food and surplus air pressure, as a result of which the extremities become numb . . . with such low temperatures, this is practically not noticed and attributed to the cold. If the system of cleaning the air does not work, there will be a surplus of carbon dioxide and with this, there is a lowering of the motor functions and sleepiness and sweatiness, as a result of which the sailors are thrown from heat to cold. Besides, the metabolism slows disturbing the function of the intestines. As a result, there is constipation and sharp pain in the stomach.
>
> But the most terrible is the reduction in the resistance of the organism and complete unawareness of actions. The lads absolutely do not understand their condition. They experience euphoria. They leave this life without understanding this.[3]

Oktai Ibragimov, chief psychiatrist of the Pacific Fleet, said: "The situation is exacerbated by the low temperature at which the process of destruction of the psyche is accelerated . . . Of course, they are affected by the absence of light; people don't know how many hours in the day were passed in underwater captivity. Judging by everything, the sailors on the *Kursk* are completely disoriented. But nonetheless, I doubt that on board there is mass psychosis: there are probably very strong personalities."[4]

On Tuesday night the navy acknowledged for the first time the likelihood of fatalities. Vladimir Kuroyedov, the commander-in-chief, said that in light of the catastrophic damage to the nose portion of the submarine, some sailors had undoubtedly died. He said that an effort would be made to save the survivors, but, in sharp contrast to earlier, optimistic statements, he admitted, "I'm afraid the hope for rescuing the sailors is not great." In answer to reporters' questions, he said that much depended on the situation inside the submarine, but that he would preserve hope until August 18.

The news of the accident stunned ordinary Russians, who identified with the sailors trapped in an iron coffin at the bottom of the sea. Thousands went to churches to light candles and pray for the rescue of the men. Donations poured in from all over the country to a fund to aid the families of the crew. There were even donations from impoverished pensioners, some of whom could contribute no more than five rubles.

At the office of the Committee of Soldiers' Mothers in Kursk, relatives of the sailors gathered, with suitcases and bags of food, for the trip north. There were scenes of anguish and confusion. During the first few days of the crisis, many of the relatives had put their faith in the reassurances of the authorities, but as precious hours passed and the extent of the official misrepresentations became obvious, the level of fear steadily increased.

In an atmosphere of growing desperation, family members became openly suspicious of the authorities. Many could not understand why Putin was continuing his vacation in Sochi instead of flying to Vidyaevo. They also became suspicious of the continued refusal to accept foreign help. Some began to say openly that the real reason the authorities were refusing foreign assistance was that they were afraid of divulging military secrets even if it cost the sailors their lives.[5]

At the accident scene, the rescue bells and minisubmarines were submerging continually but could not attach to the Kursk. Navy officials, however, reported that there was "contact" with the submarine and that the rescue operation was proceeding "according to plan."

As Valentina helped Budikina organize the trip in the office of the Committee of Soldiers' Mothers, she listened to the radio and television. From the almost continuous reports it was clear that the whole world was riveted by the drama of the trapped sailors. In the United States, where news of the Kursk competed with the Democratic national convention, a State Department spokesman said, "We are very concerned about the fate of the crew of the submarine and hope that the operation to rescue them will be a success." Throughout Western Europe, broadcasts on all television channels began and ended with reports about the Kursk. The Times of London wrote: "Horrible—this is the best word to describe the condition of the sailors now on board the submarine Kursk. Accident lights are burning in the darkness, the air is difficult to breathe, and there is deepening cold and soul chilling fear.

The sailors are sustained only by the hope that rescue is possible and the conviction that they must, at all costs, hold on and wait for it."[6]

Finally, on the night of Wednesday, August 16, there were signs that the international reaction to the disaster was having an effect. The television news reported that after a call from President Clinton, Putin had ordered the navy to accept help from any source. When she heard this, Valentina felt a wave of relief. She was convinced that her son's fate depended not on the Russians but on the British and Norwegians.

At 4:30 on the afternoon of Thursday, August 17, Valentina, her daughter, Ina, and fourteen other relatives of the crew of the *Kursk* boarded the Simferopol-to-Murmansk train in Kursk. The family members wanted to travel together, and an extra car without compartments was attached to the train. The relatives were seen off by a large group of reporters and friends. As the train moved north across the heart of Russia, however, the passengers retreated into themselves, barely speaking to each other. Night fell, and the lights of rural stations flashed by in the darkness. Valentina asked Shalapin what he thought the chances were that their children would be saved. He hesitated for a moment and then said, "Fifty-fifty."

At 12:30 A.M. the train pulled into Moscow, but no one went outside to buy mineral water or to smoke on the platform. The last car of the train was now completely dark. The next morning the train stopped at Petrozavodsk, where a crowd of sympathizers was waiting on the platform. They brought food—including a bucket of steaming boiled potatoes—and shouted words of encouragement.

From that point on, sympathizers met the train at every station, offering food, money, and words of support. But these gestures did little to change the mood of the passengers, who had withdrawn into themselves and seemed to be in a daze. A conductress later told reporters that in their presence her blood pressure went up and she had trouble with her heart.

After a second night the train left the forest zone and entered an area of bare hills dotted with dwarf pines north of the Arctic Circle. Nadezhda Shalapina showed Valentina an issue of *Komsomolskaya Pravda* with pictures of their sons that she picked up before getting on the train in Kursk. "Here is my son, and beside him is his friend, Dima," she said. "I think our lads are not sitting on their hands. They are doing everything in order to save themselves. I believe my son will live." Valentina agreed, then closed her eyes and tried to rest. Two hours later the train arrived in Murmansk.

In the meantime two Norwegian ships, the *Seaway Eagle*, with Norwegian divers aboard, and the *Normand Pioneer*, which was transporting the British

LR-5 minisubmarine, were en route to the Barents Sea. The Norwegian divers were to prepare the *Kursk* for the arrival of the LR-5, which was then to lock on to the Russian submarine.

When the relatives got off the train in Murmansk, a naval escort met them and they were ushered to a bus and driven to a hotel in Vidyaevo. In Vidyaevo the sea was calm, and the weather was sunny, cool, and windy. One of the mothers remarked that the only thing that the relatives had got from God was this calm weather.

That night Valentina went to church and prayed for the life of her son. Family members were arriving from all over the country, and they placed their hope in the Norwegians, who, depending on which radio or television report one heard, had either begun or were about to begin the rescue. There were about thirty relatives of crew members at the service. Some of the men were attending church for the first time in their lives. The priest, Father Aristarch, said, "It's possible that some of the crew are dead and some are alive. We'll pray for those who are alive."

After the service Valentina and Ina returned to the hotel and listened to the latest television news report. Mikhail Motsak, the chief of staff of the Northern Fleet, said there was hope of finding survivors in the seventh, eighth, and ninth compartments. Valentina, however, could no longer maintain her faith. It was now seven days since the *Kursk* had gone down and four days since the last tapping from the ship's interior. It was almost too much to believe that the sailors were still alive. As she and Ina got up and walked to their room, she said to Ina, "Dima is dead. It's not necessary to fool ourselves any longer." With this, she burst into tears.

The *Seaway Eagle* and the *Normand Pioneer* reached the North Cape area of Norway on their way to the Barents Sea. To facilitate the work of the divers, the Norwegians had asked the Russians to send them information about the underwater currents and the angle of the submarine as well as drawings of the inner and outer hatches. Instead of official blueprints, however, the Russians sent handwritten drawings and notes that were almost useless. When the Norwegians complained that the drawings were inadequate and asked the Russians immediately to dispatch a naval team capable of explaining the *Kursk*'s operations to the Norwegian base at Vardno, the Russians said that there would be time for consultations when the ships arrived. Eventually the Russians did send a team to Vardno, but the information they provided, though more detailed, was inaccurate.

On Saturday, August 19, a full week after the explosion, the two Norwegian ships reached a point twenty miles from the accident and were stopped by the Russian navy. The news was relayed to Admiral Einar Skorgen, the heard of the armed forces for northern Norway, who called Admiral Vladislav Popov, the head of the Northern Fleet, and asked him what was going on. Popov explained that the Russians wanted to make one last attempt to rescue the crewmen themselves. Horrified and incredulous, Skorgen said that if the Norwegians were not allowed to proceed immediately, they would return home. The Russians then allowed the *Seaway Eagle* to proceed but continued to detain the *Normand Pioneer*.

On Sunday morning four Norwegian divers descended in a diving bell to the *Kursk*. They saw that working conditions were good and that, contrary to the claims of the Russian naval authorities, the underwater current was negligible. Later the divers would be able, without difficulty, to stand on the submarine's surface. The divers also saw that, again contrary to official Russian statements, the submarine was not resting at a sharp angle but had only a slight 10 percent to 20 percent list. This did not appreciably complicate the task of docking with the hatch and would have posed no problem to the LR-5 minisubmarine. They also saw that both the external stern hatch and the docking ring were completely undamaged. This meant that all conditions had long been in place for a successful rescue. As the Norwegians began work, they also noticed numerous marks on the body of the submarine where it had been repeatedly hit by incompetently maneuvered Russian rescue vessels.

The divers began by banging on the submarine in the region of the hatch for half an hour in the hope of getting a response from inside. The sound of their banging was audible through the cable connecting them to the diving bell in the *Seaway Eagle* above. When there was no answer, they set about the task of opening the external hatch. The Norwegians were delayed in opening the hatch because the Russians had told them that the operating wheel on its top needed to be moved in one direction, when in reality it should have been moved in the other. The Russians also wrongly informed the Norwegians how to open the pressure vent.

The diving continued all morning until, through a process of trial and error, the Norwegians succeeded in opening the external hatch. They saw that the airlock separating the external hatch from the internal hatch was flooded with water. The next step would normally have been to call in the LR-5, have it attach to the submarine, and pump out the water between the hatches so that rescuers could enter the submarine itself. But before doing this, it had to be determined whether the *Kursk* was flooded. If there was air in the rear compartments, there was still a chance that some of the sailors could be saved.

The divers could not enter the airlock in their bulky costumes, so a toolmaker on board the *Seaway Eagle* prepared a long tool with a key at the end. With its help, the lower hatch came to within a half-turn of being opened. At that point the divers used a robot to help push open the lower hatch. A residue of gas from the compartment escaped, and the divers saw that the compartment was completely flooded. They realized that there was no point in calling in the LR-5, because not a single one of the *Kursk*'s crew was alive.

On August 20 Valentina went to church four times. At the hotel, naval officers met with the relatives of the crew, and doctors went to each room and asked if they needed help. Everyone knew that news of the Norwegian rescue mission was imminent, and all waited anxiously.

At 6:00 P.M. the evening news came on. All the family members gathered around the television sets in the foyers of the hotel. The announcer said that he had news about the fate of the *Kursk*. The Norwegian divers had opened the stern hatches and found that the submarine was flooded. This meant that there was no longer any hope that any of the crew were still alive and the rescue effort would now be ended. After this announcement, Admiral Popov appeared on the screen and said that the circumstances were such that the majority of the sailors had not lived for more than three minutes. "We, trying to save people, did everything that was in our power . . . Forgive me that I could not protect your men."

The family members burst into tears. Tamara Annenkova, the mother of Yuri, one of the crew members from the Kursk oblast, fainted. The other relatives slowly went back to their rooms. As she walked the corridors, Budikina heard nothing but crying. It seemed to her that the walls of the hotel were black.

In the days that followed, representatives of the Northern Fleet came to talk to family members, ostensibly to answer their questions, but the encounters only generated more suspicion. The relatives asked how it had been possible to stage military exercises involving nuclear submarines without sufficient rescue equipment. They also asked why the authorities had waited to ask for foreign help. No one received an adequate answer.

During the week of uncertainty before the *Kursk*'s hatches were opened, the Russian naval authorities had claimed repeatedly that signals had been heard from the submarine and that some of the sailors might have survived until Friday, August 18, or even longer. Some officers had predicted that the oxygen in the submarine might last until August 25. With the rescue mission effectively over, however, the authorities made statements that all the sailors had died instantly and that there had never been any real possibility of rescuing them. Ilya Klebanov, the first deputy prime minister, asserted that the tapping had come not from the sailors but from broken equipment inside the submarine.

Some of the relatives began to leave Vidyaevo, but Valentina could not bring herself to do so. It was important for her to continue to see young sailors in the naval uniform that her son had worn. It somehow made her feel close to him.

On Tuesday, August 22, a large crowd of relatives gathered in the House of Officers, and at 1:00 P.M. Kuroyedov, Popov, Klebanov (who had been put in charge of a commission to investigate the accident), and Yuri Evdokimov, the governor of the Murmansk oblast, arrived to speak with them. There were 215 people in the hall, including 6 pregnant women.

For everyone, the issue of the delay in asking for foreign help was the most painful. When they saw the speed with which Norwegian divers opened the *Kursk*'s hatches, many of the relatives became convinced that had the Norwegians been called earlier, some of the crew could have been saved. In response to this, Klebanov said, "The earlier arrival of the Norwegian divers would hardly have changed the situation in that by the second half of August 14, there were probably no members of the crew left alive."

Sensing the skepticism in the hall, Kuroyedov asked, "Do you believe that the lads are alive?"

"Yes," came the reply.

"You don't trust the commanders of the fleet?"

"No!" came shouts.

"You and Popov should be put on trial," cried a woman. "You've disgraced yourselves before all of Russia."

A day of mourning for the crew of the *Kursk* had been declared, and this gesture inflamed the crowd further. "They declare a day of mourning and as a result stop all search efforts. We won't even receive the bodies."

Kuroyedov tried to respond but was interrupted.

"Why did the Norwegians leave? They would have saved our husbands!"

"Why didn't you call the foreigners sooner? What were you doing? Guarding military secrets?"

"I saved my son from Chechnya—sent him to the fleet! Thank you for protecting him!"

"You're a commander who cannot command. Take off your epaulettes!"

"Everything is hidden from us, and everything is hidden from the press."

Finally, everyone joined in a single cry: "Don't believe anything! They intentionally don't give us information! They are mocking us!"

Klebanov stood against the wall and was silent as Kuroyedov tried to respond to questions. Suddenly one of the mothers approached him, then grabbed him by the tie and, with a cry, began to try to strangle him. She was immediately removed and led away by two guards.

Many of the relatives were unable to believe that their husbands and sons were dead. They insisted that they were still alive somewhere in the only air bubble in the submarine, waiting for help. They refused to listen to any argument in defense of the authorities.

As Valentina watched, she felt sorry for Kuroyedov and Klebanov in spite of herself. As the hysteria mounted, she found that she could not take it any more, and she got up and left. The meeting with the commanders had been scheduled to last for ten minutes. In the end, it continued for an hour and a half.

That evening, Putin, who had arrived in Vidyaevo earlier in the day, also spoke to the family members. He stood on the dais in the assembly hall alongside Kuroyedov and Popov.[7] Putin expressed his condolences for this "appalling tragedy." "There have been tragedies. The thing is, it's hard to imagine and it's hard for me as well . . . You surely know that our country is in a difficult position and our armed forces as well, but I never imagined they were in such bad shape."

WOMAN (shouting): Why didn't they call the foreign specialists immediately? Why?!

PUTIN: I can answer that. The submarine was built at the end of the 1980s and was designed with all the rescue services for the sub built in. The Northern Fleet had these services at their disposal. Therefore, at my first question, [Igor] Sergeev called me on the 13th at seven in the morning . . .

MAN: The sub went down Saturday, and he calls on Sunday!

PUTIN: Just a second, I will answer. Contact was lost with the sub at 2300 on the 12th.[8] They began a search. At 4:30 A.M., they found it. On the 13th. In other words, I knew nothing about this. Nothing about what was going on. The defense minister called me on the 13th at seven in the morning and said: Vladimir Vladimirovich, there has been an emergency during a training exercise, contact has been lost with a submarine, we have located it, it is lying on the sea bed, we have identified it—it is our sub and rescue work is under way. My first question . . . Igor Dmitrievich, what is the situation with the reactor? What is being done to save the people on board? Do you need anything? Do you need any help from any ministry, department, or from the country? The whole country is ready to help. What must be done? We will do everything that is within our power. And if it is not within our power, then say what else is needed. We will act immediately. In other words, the answer was quite clear. But now it is clear. The military truly believed that they had all the means for rescuing the sub . . . As far as foreign aid is concerned, as soon as foreign aid was offered, on the 15th, then Kuroyedov accepted it at once . . .

(Noise in the hall.)

PUTIN: It's true, true. Television? They're lying. Lying. Lying. There are people in television who bawl more than anyone today and who, over the past ten years, have destroyed that same army and navy, where people are dying today. And here they are today leading the support for the army. Also with the aim of discrediting and collapsing the army once and for all! They have been stealing money to their heart's content over the last few years, and now they are buying everyone and everything! These are the laws they have made!

MAN: How is it that rescue vehicles . . . had been written off for scrap?

PUTIN: On the 15th, the first military attaches offered to help. On the 21st, they got into the hatch. On the sixth day. We believe that if our military had not immediately put their hope in the rescue services, if we had asked for help immediately, the Norwegians would have gotten into the sub on the 19th. So far as these rescue means are concerned, they broke down, there's not a damned thing left. There's not a damn thing left in the country! It's as simple as that!

SHOUTS IN THE HALL: So do they exist or not? You said yourself . . .

PUTIN: No, I said that these submarines built at the end of the '80s have special rescue services . . . which is why they said to me at once that we have all these means available. As far as diving equipment goes . . . We have it in the Black Sea and the Baltic, as far as I know. But they were not designed for rescuing these kinds of submarines. And that's all . . .

WOMAN (wailing): Where is my son?! Where is my son?!

ANOTHER WOMAN: How long will it take them to raise it, how long do we have to wait here? How long must I wait for my son?

PUTIN: As far as concerns . . . I understand you, and I understand that it is impossible to leave and it is impossible to sit and wait . . .

WOMAN: Do you believe them [the commanders]? You should put them behind bars! They have tricked you . . .

PUTIN: You can't say that they have tricked us . . . they told us the truth. These rescue resources existed, but didn't work.

PUTIN: They said that they had the equipment . . .

SHOUTS: In the '50s . . .

MAN: Are we to believe that the work with the rescue bells was completely legal?

PUTIN: Yes.

MAN: So everything that happened with the divers was an improvisation . . . ?

PUTIN: Yes . . . The regular rescue operation was unsuccessful.

MAN: So the day of mourning is announced and they count up the dead because we don't have the time or means?

PUTIN: For what?

SHOUT: For divers!

MAN: We didn't understand each other just now. I will . . . repeat the question: if officially we have allowed only for rescue bells and we have nothing else in Russia . . . It means that when they tell us that all means have been used—the very best we have—then that's because we don't have anything else.

PUTIN: We had counted on our equipment working.

MAN: All this equipment is intended for working on an even surface!

PUTIN: They were developed for . . .

MAN: They were not "developed" for the damage that was in reality!

SHOUTS: You let the emergency service fall apart!

WOMAN (shouting): Eight days. It was already clear on the second day that nothing was working. (Voice breaks.)

PUTIN: They didn't open it in eight days because there was a storm that hampered their work.

YOUNG MAN: The Norwegians got in in one hour!

PUTIN: The Norwegians came on the fifth day and got in on the sixth. The Norwegian government doesn't have these kinds of divers at their disposal; they were commercially hired.

SHOUTS: And what about the Norwegians?

PUTIN: The Norwegians did not lock on, they worked simply by hand. They used old-fashioned means. They simply came along and made a key. But they did not do what our equipment was meant to do, to dock with it and lock on.

A VOICE: And we couldn't do that. My God . . .

On Thursday, August 24, two days after the meeting with Putin, there was a memorial service for the crew of the *Kursk*.[9] "Wreaths over here! Don't toss your cigarettes!"

The buses with the family members came to a halt at the pier where the ship *Klavdia Elanskaya* was waiting to take them into the Barents Sea. "Oh," cried a grandmother hanging on to her grandsons. "He'll never come to us again."

"Our children are alive!" another woman cried, throwing a clenched fist upward. "Don't dare to bury them!"

Half of the relatives were reconciled to the deaths; half were not and did not want a funeral of any kind. The latter demanded a continuation of the rescue work and lived with the nightmarish conviction that their sons were alive, perhaps up to their throats in water and slowly suffocating.

The orchestra played a funeral march. Several women fainted. A woman in black was being held up by relatives. She clutched red carnations that looked like blood against the white robes of doctors waiting nearby. In a single night, the administration of the raion had obtained two thousand flowers, and the ramp leading to the ship was covered with them. "For the ceremonial march in memory of our heroically fallen comrades, line up! Line up in front of the monument." A grandmother fell and was caught.

At the docks were rows of submarines, half of them with their hulls underwater.

In front of the ship, they read out the names: "Lyachina!" "Dudko!" "Here."

"Sailor Sidyukin, mama and papa."

The hills in the fiord were violet, the water a bright turquoise. An enormous red jellyfish floated next to the ship. The local residents said that the water was normally gray or gray-green, but it changed its color to turquoise on the day the *Kursk* disappeared.

"Respected guests," announced the radio, "if someone needs medical help, appeal to the hospital." In the bar there were free coffee and tea. People could not stand. They were seated at the table and handed cups. It turned out that the ship would not travel to the site of the tragedy, a six-hour journey away; it would go only into the open sea. When the relatives learned this, they began to complain but were too demoralized to do much else.

Ivan Nidziev, the deputy commander of the atomic submarine division, explained to a reporter that the relatives were not being taken to the place of the accident because of doctors' orders. "They might try to jump overboard," he said.

A thunderous voice: "Ship—prepare for the laying of wreaths! Stop movement! Ship—to the place for the giving of honor to the heroic victms of the submarine of the Northern Fleet, *Kursk.*"

In complete silence, the Orthodox memorial service was led by Father Aristarkh. The Koran was read by the Imam-khatib; eight Muslims had served on the *Kursk.*

"Lower the flag! Wreaths on the water!" A siren sounded, and the flowers were cast into the sea. Near the railing stood a woman whose back was shaking. Everyone was weeping. The wreaths floated on the waves. There were wreaths from the Duma, from the government, from the raion; all floated past the ship. The last thing to be laid on the water was a woman's silk shawl.

For fifteen minutes the boat made a farewell circle around the wreaths. And then it became easier. "Be calm," said the mullah. "Do you see, on the horizon, it is raining. According to Islamic custom, this is a good sign. It means that a very good man is dying."

"Raise the flag! Head for the base!"

A light rain fell. Each of the relatives was given a plastic bottle containing water from the Barents Sea, which symbolically had touched their loved one's remains. The faces of people were calmer. For all its shortcomings, the ceremony gave the family members a sense of closure. Now—if only in their hearts—the bodies had been ritually put to rest.

"That's all, father," said one young woman. "Now we can go home."

After the memorial service, the relatives of the *Kursk* crew members began to return home. On August 24 Valentina left for Kursk. She had a feeling of emptiness and was overwhelmed by a sense of injustice that her only son had been taken from her. At home, three of her friends told her that they had dreamed that Dima was alive and asked her, "Why are they stopping the rescue?"

As the weeks passed, life returned to normal for relatives of the *Kursk* crew. A plaque to Dima was dedicated on the wall of Valentina's house stating that he had died "heroically" aboard the nuclear submarine *Kursk,* and a monument was dedicated in Kursk to the seven crew members from the oblast. Annenkova was given a new house to replace the shack in the village of Podazovka where she had lived for years without indoor plumbing.

Even those who accepted the crew members' deaths, however, were bothered by several questions. If it was clear from the beginning that all the sailors had been killed instantly, why were there reports of tapping from inside the submarine and the imminent success of the Russian rescue mission? If, on the contrary, there were indications that the sailors had survived the initial explosions, why had the Russian authorities waited five days to request foreign help?

For Valentina, there was no answer to these questions, but she became convinced that saving the lives of the crew had been very far from the government's first priority. Nonetheless, her understanding of what happened to the *Kursk* remained foggy—until she received a message, as it happened, from the dead men themselves.

In response to public pressure, Putin promised to retrieve the bodies of the sailors. Russian divers were sent to Norway for several weeks of intensive training. On October 20 a team of Russian and Norwegian divers descended to the submarine and began drilling holes in the external hull over the eighth and ninth compartments. On October 25, divers entered the submarine.

Such a recovery operation is not typical for the Russian armed forces, but the authorities apparently believed that, in light of the widespread anger over their handling of the *Kursk* incident, they had little choice but to make the attempt.[10]

During the next few days, before the operation was temporarily curtailed because of severe storms, four bodies were brought to the surface. One of the bodies was that of Lieutenant-Captain Dmitri Kolesnikov. In his pocket, wrapped in plastic, the divers found a note written between 1:34 and 3:15 P.M. on August 12. Kolesnikov said that at 12:58 P.M. all the sailors from the sixth, seventh, and eighth compartments had gone to the ninth compartment. "There are 23 people here," he wrote. "We made that decision because of an accident. None of us can get to the surface." He then listed the names of the survivors in the ninth compartment along with their military numbers. The note concluded with a message to his wife. The note began legibly but ended with the scrawled words "I am writing blindly."

Part of the message was read on national television. Kuroyedov's decision to make it public was greeted with gratitude and respect by Russian naval personnel, who said that Kuroyedov could have declared the message classified and thus prevented its contents from ever reaching the public. However, the naval authorities did not release the full text, on the grounds that part of the message was personal. Whether this was the real reason for the failure to release the full message could not be confirmed independently.

When the recovery mission resumed in early November, the bodies of eight more sailors were recovered from the *Kursk* before the effort was called off because of worsening weather and increasing risk to the divers trying to maneuver in the submarine's mangled interior. One of the bodies was that of Lieutenant-Captain Rashid Aryapov. On November 9 the deputy commander of the Northern Fleet, Vladimir Dobroskochenko, in a meeting with relatives of the crew, revealed the existence of a second note, found on Aryapov, written on a page torn from a detective novel, wrapped in polyethylene, and put in his clothing. However, nothing was said publicly about the existence of this second note.

For the family members, the news that at least twenty-three sailors had survived the explosion was emotionally devastating. Even those who believed that their sons or husbands had been stationed in a forward compartment were anguished by the thought of the survivors freezing and suffocating to death while Russian officials refused to ask for needed foreign help.

With the passing weeks, it became clear that the Russian navy could never have saved the trapped sailors on its own, because it lacked both divers and trained rescue personnel. Against this background, Klebanov's assurances that all 118 crew members had died instantly seemed like nothing but an attempt to cover up the indifference of the navy to its own sailors' lives.

At the same time, however, there was another question hanging over the disaster of the *Kursk:* What caused it?

During the crisis, claims by the Russians that the *Kursk* had been hit by a foreign submarine were brushed off by Western governments and sounded a discordant note against the background of the general tragedy. For most people, there was no issue more important than the failure of the navy to act quickly to save the surviving sailors. For many Russian military and political leaders, however, the question of why the *Kursk* sank was actually much more important. Lives were expendable, but incompetence in the handling of weapons discredited Russia's claim to be a great power. According to one account, the entire stockpile of torpedoes exploded inside the *Kursk* with a force equivalent to seven tons of TNT. Such a disaster had never before been recorded in any navy during peacetime.[11]

On October 25, as Lieutenant-Captain Kolesnikov's body was being brought to the surface, Kuroyedov, in prepared remarks, said that he was 80 percent certain that the reason for the disaster was a collision with a foreign submarine and that he would make up the remaining 20 percent and announce to the world which submarine it was. On February 26, 2001, however, *Izvestiya* reported the existence of the second note and said that in it Aryapov had blamed the disaster on the explosion of an experimental torpedo. Two days earlier, *Komsomolskaya Pravda* had quoted "Captain First Rank K.," the commander of another atomic submarine, who had seen the note, as saying that it contained a chronicle of the destruction of the *Kursk.* "Imagine," the officer told the newspaper, "that you are traveling in . . . a closed sleeping compartment without windows and the train begins to turn somersaults as the result of a derailment and you are writing everything down."[12]

Aryapov had served in the sixth compartment, where the ship's nuclear reactor was located. From there, he might have been aware of what caused the first explosion. After the second explosion, the sailors in the sixth, seventh and eighth compartments could have fled to the ninth compartment. Under these circumstances, Aryapov's note might well have confirmed that the *Kursk* had been destroyed by an explosion in the first compartment, the explanation that was least convenient for the authorities.

Though barely noticed at the time, the most plausible explanation of what happened to the *Kursk* was provided while the rescue drama was going on. On

Thursday, August 17, *Krasnaya Zvezda,* the official newspaper of the Russian Defense Ministry, published an article in electronic form suggesting that the blame for the *Kursk* accident could be laid to the government's decision to adopt a cheaper torpedo design. The article was quickly removed from the newspaper's server and did not appear in the printed version on Friday.

According to the article, in 1998 the *Kursk* had been refitted at the Sevmash shipyard in Severodvinsk to carry a new type of torpedo. Representatives of the Russian navy opposed their installation, but the manufacturer successfully lobbied for their use. The new torpedoes were difficult to store and dangerous to handle because they used cheap liquid fuel for propulsion instead of expensive silver-zinc batteries. This "economy" may have been what prompted Lieutenant Sergei Tylik to tell his mother, "We have death aboard," shortly before he set off on his fatal voyage.[13] In the 1980s the use of liquid fuel for the propulsion of new missiles in the Russian navy had been abandoned because it was considered too explosive.

The August 18 edition of *Krasnaya Zvezda* replaced the original article on the reasons for the accident with an article speculating that the *Kursk* had collided with an "unidentified object." Such a change could only have been the result of pressure from above.

As it happened, Klebanov had a vested interest in suggesting that the *Kursk* had sunk as a result of a collision: it was Klebanov who, as head of the defense industries, had promoted the use of the new torpedoes. Kuroyedov also had reason to prefer the theory of a collision, since he bore responsibility for not supporting the naval specialists who had objected to using the new, inexpensive but dangerous torpedoes.[14]

The Norwegian divers who examined the *Kursk* during the first rescue attempt saw that the damage had been caused by an explosion inside the submarine rather than by a collision with an external object.

On February 18, 2001, *Novaya Gazeta* reported that the commission to investigate the accident had concluded that there had been no collision with a foreign submarine but was reluctant to say so publicly. According to the newspaper, a detailed analysis showed that the *Kursk* had sunk as the result of a defect in its own weapons or the fatal mistake of an operator.

"What happened," the newspaper wrote, "was something that should not have happened under any circumstances. Scientists, shipbuilders, and naval officials assured us of this."[15] It was with this faith that the doomed crew of the *Kursk,* the most modern and powerful weapon in the Russian arsenal, had put to sea to help Russia challenge NATO—and the world.

"One can't believe impossible things."

"I dare say you haven't had much practice," said the Queen. "When I was your age, I always did it for half an hour a day. Why, sometimes, I believed as many as six impossible things before breakfast."

—Lewis Carroll, Alice in Wonderland

2 *Ryazan*

APRIL 2000

As darkness fell, traffic picked up in the circle in front of 14/16 Novosyelov Street, a twelve-story building on the outskirts of the city of Ryazan. Shoppers crowded into the new "Day and Night" grocery store on the first floor of the building, and residents returning home from work punched in the codes of their apartments and opened the new heavy metal door in the entrance.

Little about the scene suggested that on September 22, 1999, there might have been a gaping hole where the building now stood and that many of the people now hurrying about their business might have been buried under tons of rubble had not a miracle occurred that assured their survival.

The only trace of the incident was the metal door, which had been installed several months after a bomb was discovered in the basement of the building, forcing the evacuation of nearly 250 people. The bomb created panic in the city until the Federal Security Service (FSB) announced that it had been a dummy, placed there as part of a "test."

After the incident, residents of the building reported in television and newspaper interviews that they were suffering from heart problems and depression and their children were afraid to fall asleep at night. They also made clear they did not believe that they had been evacuated from their homes as part of a test. They were convinced that someone—possibly the FSB—had deliberately tried to blow them up.

A middle-aged woman entering the building said, "It's terrible to say this, but I believe that it was no training exercise."

"What should I believe," said Ivan Kirilin, a sixty-seven-year-old resident of the building, "what the government says or what was in the basement? You have to ask—who is responsible for the war? Who needed the war? The government, of course." (The day after the incident, the government, blaming Chechen rebels for apartment bombings in Moscow, Volgodonsk, and Buinaksk, began bombing Grozny.)

"The authorities are trying to hush it up and hide everything," said Tatyana Borycheva, another resident. "I think it's a big political game. They are fighting for power, and our lives are not worth a kopeck . . . [They] wanted to set up the Chechens to start a war and grab power."

Some of the residents said that they were considering filing suit against the FSB. Others were more cautious. "The general opinion is that we'd better not challenge them," said Tatyana Lukichyeva, "or next time, they will really blow us up."

The building at 14/16 Novosyelov Street was constructed in 1987 by the Ryazan Radio Factory, and most of the residents are factory employees. In general, they are patriotic citizens with little inclination to criticize the government. But as a result of the "exercise" and the events that followed it, they became convinced—in some cases for the first time—that their lives had no value in the eyes of the authorities. The process of enlightenment began on the night that the residents of 14/16 Novosyelov Street now consider to have been their second birthday.

At 8:30 P.M. on September 22, Alexei Kartofelnikov, a city bus driver, drove into Ryazan after spending the weekend at his dacha working in his vegetable garden. He parked his car in a lot a mile from the building and then proceeded home on foot. When he arrived, his attention was attracted by a white Lada parked in front of the entrance of the building with a male passenger in the back seat. The last two numbers on the car's license plates were covered with pieces of paper with 62, the code for Ryazan, written on them. A young blond woman was standing in the doorway of the building glancing around nervously.

In light of the bombing of four apartment buildings in the previous eighteen days in Buinaksk, Moscow, and Volgodonsk, the scene struck Kartofelnikov as suspicious. He went up to his apartment and dialed 02, the emergency number for the police.

In the meantime Vladimir Vasiliev, an engineer who lived on the eighth floor, returned home and also noticed the car. At this point the paper on the rear license plate had fallen off, revealing the number 77, the code for Moscow. Vasiliev noticed that the number on the rear plate was different from the number on the front. The blond woman who had attracted the attention of Kartofelnikov was now sitting with the male passenger in the car. Vasiliev took the elevator up to his apartment and also tried to telephone the police.

Kartofelnikov repeatedly dialed 02, but the number was continually busy. His daughter, Yulya, a twenty-three-year-old medical intern, went out onto the balcony to watch what was going on. She saw a second man emerge from the basement, check his watch, and get into the car. The car then pulled away with its three occupants. At that moment Kartofelnikov got through to the police.

Kartofelnikov described what he had seen, but at first the police refused to investigate. Kartofelnikov insisted, however, and finally the police agreed to come. Kartofelnikov and Yulya met the police in front of the building at 9:30. Yulya suggested that they go into the basement to make sure the occupants of the car had not left anything. Local derelicts had used the basement as a toilet, and the police did not want to go in; but Yulya insisted, and finally they went downstairs.

Seconds later, one of the officers bolted up the stairs shouting, "There's a bomb!" The two other policemen ran up behind him, and one of them told Kartofelnikov, "We've got to evacuate the building."

The building was soon engulfed in chaos. Police began going door to door telling people to leave. Residents took babies out of bathtubs, grabbed documents, and threw on overcoats. Those too ill or weak to leave the building were left behind. The police cordoned off the area, and the residents watched on the street as police, including Yuri Tkachenko, the head of the local bomb squad, entered the basement. The crowd became silent as people waited for the announcement that it had all been a false alarm. In the basement, Tkachenko disconnected a detonator and timing device and then tested three sacks of a white crystalline substance with an MO-2 portable gas analyzer. The substance in the sacks tested positive for hexogen, the explosive used in the bombings in Buinaksk, Moscow, and Volgodonsk. There now was no question but that someone had tried to blow up the building.

Police, fire engines, and rescue vehicles converged from all parts of the city, and, as word spread that a bomb had been found in the basement of 14/16 Novosyelov Street, residents of neighboring buildings also fled their homes in terror. In the end, nearly all of the 30,000 residents of the Dashkovo-Pesochnya area in which 14/16 Novosyelov was located spent the night on the street.

The police interrogated Kartofelnikov, his daughter, and Vasiliev and, on the basis of their descriptions, prepared identi-kit portraits of the suspects. In the meantime, 1,200 police officers were put on alert, the railroad stations and airport were surrounded, and roadblocks were set up on highways leaving the city. The police began stopping every white Lada and questioning its occupants.

Shortly before midnight, General Alexander Sergeev, the chief of the Ryazan FSB, arrived at 14/16 Novosyelov and met with the residents in front of building. "You can consider," he said, "that tonight you were born a second time." He promised that everyone would be allowed to go back into the building as soon as it was determined to be safe. An FSB agent questioned Kartofelnikov and, when he finished, told him, "You were born in a shirt" (a Russian expression meaning that someone has very good luck).[1]

At 1:30 A.M. the sacks and detonator were taken away by the FSB in a small truck. The residents continued to mill around in the cold until 3:00 A.M., when the Oktyabr movie theater, located across the street from 14/16 Novosyelov, opened its doors and the manager brought crockery from her home and served the residents tea. The refreshment, however, did little to restore the residents' shattered nerves. Ambulances continued to be called for people who had heart problems or experienced a sharp rise in blood pressure.

Many of those who crowded into the movie theater found it difficult to concentrate. They realized that someone had placed a bomb in the basement of their building, but the possibility that they and their families had come close to being killed was difficult for them to comprehend. At 5:00 A.M. a radio was turned on, and the residents listened to a bulletin on Radio Rossiya about the attempted bombing. The announcer described the incident and said that the bomb had been set to go off at 5:30 A.M. With this, silence spread through the theater as each person there realized that, had the bomb not been discovered, they would have had half an hour to live.

As morning arrived, Ryazan resembled a city under siege. The streets were full of reinforced patrols of police and students from local military institutes. Police wearing flak jackets and carrying automatic weapons blocked every exit from the city. Lines of cars and trucks many miles long formed on the roads while the police searched every car and trunk. Portraits of the three terrorists were pasted on virtually every post and tree.

At 8:00 A.M. Russian television networks reported the attempt to blow up a building in Ryazan and quoted officials in the Ryazan MVD to the effect that the explosive used in the bomb was hexogen. Sergeev appeared on Ryazan morning television to congratulate the residents of the building on being saved from a terrorist attack. A short time later Vladimir Rushailo, the minister of internal affairs, appeared on national television to announce that an attempt by terrorists to blow up a fifth Russian apartment building had been averted. Meanwhile, amid rumors that Ryazan had been singled out for terrorist acts because of the location there of the 137th Ryazan Paratroop Regiment, Pavel Mamatov, the head of the administration in Ryazan, ordered the sealing of every attic and basement in the city.

At 7:00 P.M., with the country steeling itself for new terrorist attacks, Prime Minister Putin appeared on the nightly news with an announcement that Russian aircraft had begun bombing Grozny. The message was clear: the terrorists could make an attempt on innocent lives, but their acts would be punished.

By the evening of September 23 the police dragnet was producing results. The white Lada was found abandoned in a parking lot. A short time later a call to Moscow was made from a telephone bureau for intercity calls, and the operator who connected the call stayed on the line long enough to catch a fragment of conversation. The caller said there was no way to get out of town undetected. The voice on the other end replied, "Split up and each of you make your own way out."

The operator reported the call to the police, who traced the number. To their astonishment, it belonged to the FSB.

A short time later the Ryazan police, with the help of tips from local people, arrested two of the terrorists. The detainees produced identification showing that they worked for the FSB. On orders from Moscow, they were soon released. Some type of explanation from the central FSB, however, was now inevitable.

On Friday, September 24, FSB director Nikolai Patrushev came out of a Kremlin meeting and told a reporter that the evacuation of the building in Ryazan had been part of a training alert and the bomb was a dummy planted by his agency. He said that the sacks found by the bomb squad contained nothing but sugar. The reading of hexogen by the gas analyzer had been an error. There had been similar exercises in other cities, but only in Ryazan had the people reacted promptly. He complimented the residents on their vigilance.

When Patrushev's remarks were reported in Ryazan, the population was dumbfounded. Everyone had assumed that the bomb was real. No one was more shocked than the residents of 14/16 Novosyelov Street, who for two days had lived in the belief that only a miracle had saved them from death.[2] In the next few weeks, life returned to normal for many of the residents of the building. The FSB held an awards ceremony in Ryazan at which Kartofelnikov and Vasiliev were given color television sets as a reward for vigilance, as was Nadezhda Yukhnova, the attentive telephone operator. The FSB spokesman, General Alexander Zdanovich, explained that the gas analyzer had given a false result because it had not been cleaned with alcohol—a hint that the alcohol had been used for drinking—and because Tkachenko had had hexogen on his hands after handling the explosive a week earlier.

The suspicion that the incident was not a test, however, did not disappear. The residents of the building wanted to know why, if the incident was a test, they had not been allowed to return to their apartments after the bomb was successfully neutralized and why they had not been told of the real nature of the incident for two days. They also wanted to know what right the FSB had to make them guinea pigs in an exercise—if, indeed, it was an exercise.

In the weeks after the incident in Ryazan, the Russian army entered Chechnya in an "antiterrorist action," and preparations for the presidential election campaign gathered momentum. As a result, for a time the puzzling incident ceased to be a focus of attention.

In February, however, Russian journalists began to reexamine the incident in Ryazan, and the information that they published almost completely discredited the FSB in the eyes of the residents of 14/16 Novosyelov Street.

The most important information was reported by Pavel Voloshin, a thirty-year-old reporter for *Novaya Gazeta* who arrived in Ryazan having earlier accepted the official version about a training exercise.[3]

Voloshin arrived in Ryazan in early February, checked into a hotel, and went to the city headquarters of the Ministry of Internal Affairs (GUVD), where he introduced himself to an officer from the GUVD press service and several investigators. He explained that he was investigating the recent exercise. To his surprise, the police seemed pleased to see him. "We have great respect for *Novaya Gazeta,*" said the press officer. "We sent back Canadian television and Japanese television, but we are ready to help you. You probably want to meet Tkachenko, the head of the bomb squad."

On the following day Voloshin was presented to a man in his thirties. "This is Tkachenko," said the press officer. The two retired to a room in the GUVD, and Voloshin interviewed the bomb expert for two hours.

Tkachenko insisted that the FSB version of events was not true. It was clear to him that the bomb planted in the basement of 14/16 Novosyelov Street was real. The detonator, including a timer, power source, and shotgun shell, was a genuine military detonator and obviously prepared by a professional. The gas analyzer used to test the vapors coming from the sacks clearly indicated the presence of hexogen.

Voloshin asked Tkachenko if the gas analyzer could have given a false result. Tkachenko said that this was out of the question. The gas analyzers were of world-class quality. Each cost $20,000 and was maintained by a specialist who worked according to a strict schedule, checking the analyzer after each use and making frequent prophylactic checks. These were necessary because the device contains a source of constant radiation. Tkachenko also pointed out that meticulous care of the gas analyzer was essential because the bomb experts' lives depended on the reliability of their equipment.

As for Zdanovich's claim that the gas analyzer had not been cleaned with alcohol, Tkachenko said that alcohol is never used to clean a gas analyzer. In response to Zdanovich's claim that Tkachenko had traces of hexogen on his hands after handling the explosive substance a week earlier, Tkachenko said that during that week he had washed his hands many times.

During the next few days in Ryazan, Voloshin interviewed the police officers who had answered the original call from Kartofelnikov. They also insisted that the incident was not an exercise and that it was obvious from its appearance that the substance in the bags was not sugar.

Drawing on these and other interviews, Voloshin published an article in the February 14–20 issue of *Novaya Gazeta* titled "Sugar or Hexogen? What Happened in Ryazan." In addition to describing the views of Tkachenko and others who had been on the scene, the article suggested that, to resolve the doubts in the matter, the FSB should publish the order for the exercise and give journalists access both to the material evidence and to the people who had placed the bomb in the basement.[4]

The article caused widespread discussion among the public, but there was little reaction from the government or the Russian press. The central FSB ordered Yuri Bludov, the head of the press service of the Ryazan FSB, not to comment on the events of September 1999 and issued similar orders to the Ryazan police and employees of the rescue service.

One afternoon after the original article was published, however, Voloshin received a call at the office of *Novaya Gazeta* from a woman who said she had some information for him concerning the Ryazan events. Voloshin and a colleague met her in the Lenin Library metro station. The woman was a forty-five-year-old teacher in a Moscow institute. She said that a girlfriend of one of her female students had met a soldier who bragged about guarding sacks of hexogen. The soldier's name was Alexei Pinyaev, and he was based in Naro-Fominsk, outside Moscow.

Voloshin decided to try to find Pinyaev. A few days after the meeting, he drove to the base in Naro-Fominsk. The entrance was heavily guarded, but he gained access to the base through a hole in the fence. He then walked into an administration building and found the personnel office, where he asked for Pinyaev, explaining that he was a friend of Pinyaev's relatives. Without asking any questions, a secretary directed Voloshin to Pinyaev's unit, and when Voloshin arrived at the unit, soldiers pointed out Pinyaev, who had just finished repairing a tank and was covered with fuel oil. Voloshin explained why he wanted to see him and gave him a pack of cigarettes. They then went to the soldiers' café, where Pinyaev told his story in great detail.

Pinyaev said that in the autumn of 1999 he had been sent from a base in the Moscow oblast to the base of the 137th Ryazan Paratroop Regiment, twenty miles from Ryazan, where paratroopers were prepared for fighting in Chechnya. After a period of shooting and parachute jumping, he was assigned to guard a warehouse that supposedly contained arms and ammunition. Guard duty was tedious, and Pinyaev and another soldier decided to look inside the warehouse. They opened the metal door and saw, instead of weapons, a pile of 50-kilogram (110-pound) sackcloth bags with the inscription "sugar" written on them.

Pinyaev said that they were puzzled as to why it was necessary to stand guard over bags of sugar, but, not wanting to leave empty-handed, they stuck a bayonet into one of the bags and poured some of the substance into a plastic packet. A short time later they made tea with it. The taste of the tea was revolting, and they feared that they had consumed some type of nitrate. They took the plastic bag to their commander, who called a bomb expert. The expert tested the bag and told the commander that the substance in the bag was hexogen.

Almost immediately, Pinyaev said, a group of high-ranking FSB officers arrived from Moscow, and he and the other soldier were relieved of their normal duties and began to be called regularly for interrogations. To his astonishment, Pinyaev and his colleague were berated not for stealing sugar but for "divulging state secrets." Their fellow soldiers advised them to prepare for long prison sentences. In the end, however, the matter was closed, and the FSB officers advised Pinyaev and the other soldier to forget about the warehouse and the "special sugar." A short time later Pinyaev was transferred to Chechnya, where an armored car ran over his foot. The accident occurred in deep mud, so Pinyaev did not lose his foot. But he was sent for treatment to Naro-Fominsk, where, after being released from the hospital, he continued to serve.

Pinyaev's story was published in the March 13 issue of *Novaya Gazeta* under the headline "Hexogen. FSB. Ryazan." The additional evidence appeared to increase the likelihood that the FSB had planned to blow up the building at 14/16 Novosyelov Street. For the first time, it was alleged not only that a gas analyzer had detected hexogen in the bags planted in the basement of the building (or that the detonator for the bomb was real) but that at the time of the Ryazan "exercise" a large quantity of hexogen was being kept under guard in a warehouse on a military base twenty miles from Ryazan in sackcloth bags that were labeled "sugar."[5]

Voloshin was interviewed at length by Russian newspapers and foreign correspondents. In the meantime, a group of deputies proposed to send to the general prosecutor a request for answers to questions regarding the incident in Ryazan raised by the *Novaya Gazeta* articles, including "Was any analysis of the substance carried out?" and "Who gave the orders to conduct these 'training exercises'?" The Duma voted 197 in favor of the motion and 137 against, but 226 votes, an absolute majority, were needed for passage, and the pro-Kremlin Unity party voted unanimously against.

The misgivings created by the *Novaya Gazeta* articles, however, were now so widespread that the FSB agreed to participate in a televised meeting between its top officials and residents of the building. The purpose of the program was to demonstrate the FSB's openness, but the strategy backfired. During the program, which was aired on NTV on March 23, 2001, Zdanovich could not explain why the "exercise" had been carried out without measures to protect the health of the residents, why the gas analyzer had detected hexogen, and why bomb squad members had mistaken a dummy bomb for a real one. When the program ended, the residents were more convinced than ever that they had been unwitting pawns in an FSB plot and had only through a miracle escaped with their lives.[6]

Three days after the broadcast, Putin, the former head of the FSB, was elected president of Russia.

At 14/16 Novosyelov Street, Vladimir Vasiliev reflected on the "training exercise" and its aftermath.

"When I think that this building could have been blown up and not only I and my family but many of the people I've known for years could have been killed, the idea just doesn't register."

I remarked that the victims of the bombings in Buinaksk, Moscow, and Volgodonsk also probably could not have imagined that they would be killed in their sleep.

"Who could imagine such a thing?" Vasiliev asked. "It doesn't conform to any human logic. But either someone was trying to blow us up or it was a test, and the claim that it was a test makes no sense. Does it make sense to test people for vigilance at a time when the whole country is in a state of panic?"[7]

"We thought about suing the FSB, but in order to file a case, each resident of the building would have had to write out his complaint individually. You need a lawyer for this, and someone has to pay for it. When people realized how much was involved, they gave up. After what happened, no one had the time or strength."

The building at 14/16 Novosyelov Street was an odd choice for a test of vigilance, because there was an all-night grocery store in the building, and residents could easily have assumed that someone unloading sacks of sugar was doing so for the store. At the same time, the effect of the test would have been minimal, because the building was at the edge of the city.[8]

As the target of a terrorist attack, however, the building was very well suited, especially if the goal was to claim the maximum number of lives. Like the building on Kashirskoye Highway in Moscow, 14/16 Novosyelov Street was a brick building of standard construction. In the event of an explosion, it would have offered little resistance, and there would have been little chance for anyone to survive. Moreover, since the building was on an elevation, it would also have hit the adjacent building with the force of an avalanche, and because of the weak, sandy soil in the area both buildings would probably have collapsed. The resulting tragedy in Ryazan would have eclipsed all the others.

With the people who planted the bomb as well as all the material evidence—the sacks and detonator—in the hands of the FSB, it is very difficult to establish the facts indisputably.

The mysterious Ryazan training exercise, however, is unlikely to be forgotten. If the bomb planted by the FSB in the basement of 14/16 Novosyelov was real and intended to murder 250 people as they slept, it seems very plausible that the successful bombings of the buildings in Moscow, Volgodonsk, and Buinaksk, in which hundreds died, were also carried out by the FSB. The implications of the events in Ryazan hang like a shroud over Russia and the entire Russian reform period.

*On the surface, everything appears new . . . New formulas
dominate life: those who were at the bottom are now at the
very top and those who were at the top have fallen to the
bottom; those who were persecuted now rule and those who
ruled are now persecuted . . . But try to penetrate beneath
the surface of revolutionary Russia to the depths . . . There
you will meet old, familiar faces . . . Behind the revolutionary struggle and revolutionary phraseology, it is not hard to
discover . . . snouts and mugs from out of a story by Gogol.*
—*Nikolai Berdyaev,* Iz Glubini (From the Depths)

3 The Young Reformers

"Alfred Reinholdovich, is there a book or isn't there?"

The interviewer, Vasily Ustyuzhanin of *Komsomolskaya Pravda*, was
speaking to Alfred Kokh, the former head of the State Property Committee
(GKI). Kokh had resigned in the wake of a scandal over a book on privatization for which he had been paid $100,000 by a Swiss accounting firm with
ties to Oneximbank, the victor in several of the most important—and bitterly contested—privatization auctions. Kokh and four other "young reformers," Anatoly Chubais, Maxim Boiko, Pyotr Mostovoi, and Alexander
Kazakov, had also been paid $90,000 each for chapters in another history of
the Russian economic reforms, published by Segodnya Press, which is 51
percent owned by Oneximbank.[1]

Ustyuzhanin: "On the 'Vremya' program, Sergei Dorenko showed a thin
pile of pages. Was this the entire [first] book?"

"*Mumu* [a children's classic by Turgenev] is also not a thick book. That
doesn't mean you have to drown Turgenev."

"But in your case? Is the book written?"

"Yes."

"How long is it?"

"More than 200 pages."

"You don't feel that you've broken the law?"

"What law?"

"According to the law on state service, an official does not have the right
to receive an honorarium for work connected with his official activities."

"I don't know about such a law. In general, the question of whether we violated such a law or not should be decided by a court."

"You don't feel pangs of conscience. Millions of people don't receive their salaries and you . . ."

"As far as conscience is concerned, I would say this. In the summer, I read the income statement of Boris Nikolaevich Yeltsin. He received for the book *Notes of the President* about $300,000. He bought a BMW. That is not an inexpensive automobile. In his case, there are no ethical problems. I always considered that if my boss allows himself something, so can I."

"You don't consider that you've done something reprehensible?"

"What are you talking about? This is generally accepted international practice."

"Are you upset about what happened?"

"I'm upset for my friends; for myself, a great deal less. I've already been slandered. The only thing left is to kill me."[2]

Shortly afterward, Kokh had another chance to explain his thinking. In a conversation with Chrystia Freeland, the Moscow correspondent of the *Financial Times,* he was asked whether it would be better if Russian cabinet members were paid salaries of $10,000 or more per month in order to avoid corruption.

"For me, that's too little," he said.

Freeland asked what sort of salary would have satisfied him. Kokh said nothing less than 3 percent of all the revenues he brought into the treasury as head of the State Property Committee. In 1997 this would have produced an income of close to $60 million.

Freeland said that she understood the attraction of money but she was under the impression that Kokh and the other young reformers were driven by other things: "market reforms, a commitment to the common good, a profound sense of personal honor."

"What do you mean by honor?" Kokh asked. "You won't get far on honor alone."[3]

Kokh was unusual in his frankness, but his views were typical of the morality of the "young reformers," a group of former Soviet advisers and academic economists who were put in charge of Russia's transition from communism to capitalism. Idealized in the West as resolute democrats, the reformers had actually been shaped by the psychological inheritance of communism. They cared little for individuals, seeing the transition as a scientific process ruled by the "laws" of the market economy. And without a sense of morality rooted in respect for the individual, there was little to prevent them, given the enormous temptations associated with a period of economic transition, from becoming corrupted themselves.

The original "young reformer," and the person responsible for creating the group that was to lead Russia into a new era, was Yegor Gaidar, a thirty-five-year-old economist who became the head of the first post-Soviet Russian government. In 1990, as the economics editor of *Pravda,* he contributed to the debate about the Soviet Union's future. At the time, however, he displayed none of the anticommunist fervor that he was to demonstrate a short time later. Instead he called for a gradual evolution to "communism with a human face" under the direction of the Communist party and warned against promarket radicalism. In late 1990 Gaidar left *Pravda* to establish the new Institute for Economic Policy, and, no longer subject to party restraints, his political position underwent a change. He began to work out radical economic reform proposals that focused on the Russian republic.

On August 20, 1991, Gaidar joined the crowd of pro-Yeltsin demonstrators outside the White House during the attempted coup. There he met Gennady Burbulis, a close Yeltsin aide, and the two discussed their conceptions of the Soviet Union's future. Burbulis agreed with Gaidar's emphasis on the fate of the Russian republic, and after the coup attempt failed, he introduced Gaidar to Yeltsin and arranged for him and his close associates to draw up a reform plan for Russia.

The group produced a plan calling for Russia to begin economic reforms, including the liberalization of prices and the creation of a freely convertible Russian ruble, without waiting for the other republics. Yeltsin liked this plan and took steps to act on it. Gaidar was appointed deputy prime minister and given authority to concentrate on the economy.[4] In November 1991 he was appointed minister of finance.

The appointment of Gaidar introduced a radical change in the style of Russian government. Gaidar had maintained close contact with free-market economists whom he knew from Soviet institutes and perestroika-era clubs, and they entered government with him. For the first time, a group of young people united by student ties was at the pinnacle of power. Bearded young men in jeans torn at the knee began to appear in the offices of the presidential administration, and supplicants, including ministers and factory directors, filled their waiting rooms from 7 A.M. until well after midnight.

Most of the young reformers had worked in Soviet ideological institutions where they had been expected to help "build communism." Holding strongly procapitalist opinions, they had constantly to express views that were the opposite of their true beliefs. The resulting moral degradation instilled a ruthless attitude toward the other functionaries of the Communist regime and toward the Russian people as a whole. Their disgruntlement was deepened by the fact that the party leaders distrusted them and denied them the prospect of brilliant careers.[5]

In the atmosphere of dual consciousness in which they worked during the Soviet period, the reformers developed a set of attitudes that were to shape the course of reform. These included social darwinism, economic determinism, and a tolerant attitude toward crime.

The reformers' social darwinism was, in many ways, a reaction against Soviet society's professed concern for the needy and helpless. It was expressed in a refusal to consider the effects of their policies on the Russian population. When, in one of the new government's first acts, price controls were lifted on almost all products, wiping out the savings of 99 percent of the population, Gaidar answered objections by saying that the money in people's savings accounts was not real because it did not reflect the quantity of available goods.[6]

The reformers' social darwinism was complemented by their economic determinism. It is an irony of the transition period that the reformers, intending to destroy socialism, preserved its most basic philosophical assumption, the belief that morality and law have no independent validity but are a function of underlying economic relations.

The reformers showed little interest in the sources of the legal framework that regulated the way in which the market economy in the West operated. In fact, conditioned by years of Marxist training, they dismissed moral idealism as "bourgeois thought," which was not based on anything real.

The consequences of social darwinism and economic determinism were greatly magnified by the most important practical effect of the worldview that the reformers brought to Russia's transformation. This was the reformers' indulgent attitude toward crime. Influenced by decades of mendacious Soviet propaganda, they assumed that the initial accumulation of capital in a market economy is almost always criminal, and, as they were resolutely procapitalist, they found it difficult to be strongly anticrime.

Because the bandits and black-market operators also wanted a free-market economy, the reformers began to see them as "socially friendly" and reacted to the criminals' growing wealth and property with equanimity and even approval, assuming that the gangsters would be able to hold on to their capital only as long as they were able to make it work "for the benefit of society."[7]

The combination of social darwinism, economic determinism, and a tolerant attitude toward crime prepared the young reformers to carry out a frontal attack on the structures of the Soviet system without public support or a framework of law. The result was a catastrophe for Russian society.

Russia in 1992, the first year of the reforms, was in need of fundamental change, but it was morally and psychologically unprepared for the rapid and apocalyptic transformation that the young reformers had in mind for it. The majority of Russians had a collectivist mentality and were not ready to be thrown into a competitive situation without social guarantees that they had long taken for granted. At the same time, the transition from a socialist economy to a market economy, in effect a transition from an economy of vertical ties to an economy of horizontal ties, was fraught with risk, since the horizontal ties that existed in the heart of the old structure and on which any new economy would have a tendency to be based were monopolized by the black market.

Despite the unpreparedness of Russian society for a sudden and rapid transformation, however, the reformers proceeded with maximum speed. In short order they freed prices, liberalized foreign trade, and removed import barriers. The money supply was compressed to fight inflation, and the ruble was made fully convertible. The effect of these measures, which were referred to collectively as "shock therapy," was to subject the planned Soviet economy to the full impact of market forces without normal market safeguards. The result was a sudden, catastrophic economic collapse that stemmed ultimately from an epidemic of theft.[8]

In postcommunist Russia, money was in the hands of gangsters, corrupt former members of the Soviet nomenklatura, and veterans of the underground economy.[9] Resources were controlled by government officials. In a society without moral or legal rules, these parties made common cause.

The temptations that the new system introduced were overwhelming. The salaries of officials were low, and a single official decision could make a businessman rich overnight. As a result, decisions began to be sold. A businessman seeking an export quota, the right to hold government funds in his bank, or a favorable privatization decision was told, "It would help your application if you could make a loan to the following offshore company."

Sometimes, particularly in the case of the city of Moscow, the transfer data for the offshore company were printed on cards for distribution. It was understood in such cases that the "loan" would not be repaid.

Bribery quickly became an integral part of the Russian way of doing business, and the expense of buying a government official was considered the most important part of a new enterprise's starting capital.

The young reformers were not the most corrupt members of the emerging Russian capitalist class. This honor belonged to the former members of the nomenklatura, particularly factory directors, who seized control of their enterprises and transformed them into "businesses." As the system of payoffs spread, however, the reformers' worldview undercut any inclination to crack down on corruption, for they assumed that abuses would eventually be corrected by the market itself. The reformers repeated to themselves that "all large capital was founded on dishonest money." Eventually, however, instead of eliminating the corruption, the reformers were captured by it. Many came to the conclusion that if there was no point in fighting the lawlessness, there was even less reason not to take advantage of it and to use their period in power—which they feared would be brief—to guarantee their own future and that of their children and grandchildren.

Those who tried to fight the corruption were soon overwhelmed.

"Floods of people came to the government offices," said Olga Sveridova, who worked for Burbulis.

> It was as if there had been an earthquake and the ground split and lava flowed up. They told us what was going on.
>
> From the beginning, the reports of corruption were serious. People said that officials everywhere were organizing private firms in the names of their relatives and then channeling government business to these supposedly independent firms.
>
> In the Sverdlovsk oblast, the oblast administration was granted a license to export goods to buy needed food and medicine for the population. Shortly after the license was issued, officials in the oblast organized firms run by their relatives, and these firms began exporting metal in uncontrolled quantities, particularly high-quality copper. They flooded world markets and caused a fall in world prices. I received information that among the imports supposedly for the needs of the population were French perfume and mink coats.
>
> In another incident, the Ministry of Fuel and Energy set up a private firm on the ministry's second floor. Anyone who wanted an export quota for oil had to pay for it through this firm. A company that wanted to export oil to Crimea

applied to the ministry for an export license on the grounds that oil sales to Crimea would strengthen Russia's position on the Black Sea. They were told that the ministry could not give them a quota but if they went to this private firm, they could get a quota for as much oil as they liked—for a price.

Some of the reformers were concerned about the growing criminality, but they said that the introduction of free enterprise is inevitably accompanied by an increase in crime. There were convinced that their time in office would be brief. They said that the changes would be a psychological shock and no one would love this government. They just waited to see how long they would last.

Nevertheless, at the end of February Burbulis created a commission to combat corruption which included all the heads of the law enforcement agencies.

At a meeting of the commission that I attended, Viktor Yerin, the minister of internal affairs, suggested checking the connections of officials' relatives. He explained that he could begin with the heads of administration in the oblasts and carry out detailed checks on the connections between government officials and newly formed commercial organizations. But he said that when he had first suggested this approach in the Ministry of Internal Affairs, he was warned by one of his subordinates that if he wanted to keep his position as minister, he should abandon the idea.

"Gennady Eduardovich," he asked [Burbulis], "can you give me a guarantee that I will be healthy and will work normally if I give an order through the police to carry out this inventory of the connections between officials and private firms?"

Burbulis said, "I can't give such a guarantee, but any material that you collect will be presented to the president." With that, the matter was dropped.

In December 1992, after only a year of work with the young reformers, Sveridova resigned her position in the government to join a think tank dedicated to humanitarian goals.

"I have respect for you," said Gaidar to Valery Chernogorodsky, the chairman of the Antimonopoly Committee, "but there is little need for an antimonopoly committee. The first priority is to carry out privatization." Chernogorodsky began to protest; it had taken weeks to get in to see Gaidar, and he needed his support. But Gaidar was unyielding. "Once a private sector has been created," he said, "there will be work for the committee to do."

Chernogorodsky left the meeting downcast and pessimistic. It seemed to him that the corruption of the reform process was becoming unstoppable.

The Antimonopoly Committee was founded on July 14, 1990, and Chernogorodsky was its first chairman.

The committee was at first considered to be nearly coequal with the State

Property Committee, and its approval was necessary for almost any economic reform measure. As a result, in the first six months of 1992, Chernogorodsky emerged as a serious obstacle to the plans of many former members of the nomenklatura to seize state assets.

There were several ways in which the members of the Soviet nomenklatura tried to use their connections to appropriate the country's wealth. One of the most common strategies was the attempt by factory directors to take over a large share of the assets of their factories as payment for their contribution of "intellectual property." Chernogorodsky regularly frustrated these attempts.

Another technique was for the director of a factory to consign the potentially most profitable parts of an enterprise to "daughter firms" controlled by his friends or relatives. The daughter firms were usually organized on the base of cooperatives that had been established inside the factory during the perestroika period, but the daughter firms' possibilities were much greater. Unlike the cooperatives, which were restricted to performing specific services, the daughter firms could control the majority of the enterprise.

At the same time, when a state enterprise was converted to a joint stock company, the government normally retained a block of shares, and officials frequently became directors. As a result, the boards of private enterprises—particularly those dealing with oil, gold, and diamonds—were frequently filled with powerful officials, sometimes on the level of deputy minister, who participated in the pillaging of the enterprise.

In January 1992 Chernogorodsky learned that the privatization plan for the Perm Rocket Factory in the Urals included a provision for giving an 80 percent share of the company, whose worth was estimated at $100 million, to the director and local officials because they had provided the enterprise's "intellectual capital." The plan had been approved by both the Ministry of Economics and the State Property Committee (GKI). The only approval that was still needed was that of the Antimonopoly Committee. Chernogorodsky, however, refused to agree to the plan. He protested to Valentin Stepankov, the general prosecutor, and then met with Chubais, who removed the deputy who had given his approval.

Sergei Stankevich, the former deputy mayor of Moscow, and Gavril Popov, the former mayor, organized Mosbiznesbank to handle the budget of the city of Moscow and named themselves as major shareholders on the grounds that they had contributed "intellectual capital." In the end, Stankevich left the board of the bank and Popov stayed, although he resigned as mayor.

In a conversation with Stankevich, Chernogorodsky said, "How can you, without knowledge, ability, or experience, run the city of Moscow? The reason is that no special knowledge is required."

Chernogorodsky's relative success, however, was possible only because of the unsettled political situation. The original economic reform program that had been approved in 1990 while the Soviet Union still existed called for the gradual introduction of the market with the continued existence of state enterprises until private capital appeared on the market as a result of the development of small business. This approach was opposed by Gaidar and Chubais, who argued that the most important priority was to create a class of private owners so that, once capital was in private hands, the market could work out the remaining economic problems automatically. The unspoken assumption in the Gaidar-Chubais argument was that it did not make sense to look too closely at the original accumulation of capital, which was likely to be criminal under any circumstances.

In April, however, Burbulis, who had supported Chernogorodsky, was removed as first deputy prime minister and replaced by Gaidar. Chubais became Gaidar's deputy. With the removal of Burbulis, the balance of power changed, and Yeltsin adopted the Gaidar-Chubais position. Beginning in June, fair rules of competition ceased to be even a remote priority. What mattered was the rapid creation of private capital.

By June 1992 Chernogorodsky's relations with his colleagues had undergone a serious change. Instead of working together, they began to treat him as an obstacle to the reform process. Conflicts with the Antimonopoly Committee began to occur daily. Chernogorodsky challenged attempts to take over enterprises and create daughter firms, but these began to be approved without his signature, in direct violation of the law. He tried to contact Gaidar, but Gaidar refused to come to the phone. Chernogorodsky wrote letters to Chubais but never got a reply.

As the country prepared for voucher privatization, Chernogorodsky saw that even the general prosecutor was not willing to take seriously violations of the law committed by the country's emerging capitalists. The Antimonopoly Committee had formed sixty-four territorial divisions, but the Supreme Soviet approved a budgetary measure making local authorities responsible for the financing of these regional divisions. This ended the effectiveness of the committee in the provinces.

As the abuses grew, Chernogorodsky could only object. He was convinced that, without guarantees of fair competition, reforms in Russia would lead to nothing but criminality. But his was a solitary voice, and there were increasing signs that his colleagues were losing patience with him. On July 18 he opened his mail and found a copy of a presidential decree freeing him from his post. With this, the internal government effort to regulate the reform process came to an end.

"Russians do not like abrupt change," said Vladimir Ivanov, a former member of the security service of the president. "For this reason, the appearance of the young reformers could only inspire resentment. The reformers talked about the 'Chicago school' [the University of Chicago school of free-market economics]. Many Russians took this to mean that they must have lived for a long time in Chicago, and if they had spent time in Chicago, they had probably been recruited there as foreign agents.

"The reformers also had strange last names. Chubais had a Baltic name. [Pyotr] Aven [the minister of foreign economic relations in the first Gaidar cabinet] and [Yakov] Urinson [director of the Center for Economic Ties and Prognosis] were Jewish. Koch had a German last name. Gaidar had an acceptable name, but he was fat, bald, and sweaty and spoke in jargon. None of them inspired love."

A former KGB counterintelligence officer, Ivanov served, after the fall of the Soviet Union, as an analyst in the security service of the president under General Alexander Korzhakov until disillusionment with all members of the Russian ruling establishment led him to resign and become the deacon of the St. Nicholas in Khamovniki Church.

Ivanov said that the attitude of ordinary people toward the reformers quickly got worse as the economic changes led to an upsurge in corruption.

Under the rules, the government privatization process was supposed to begin by privatizing unprofitable enterprises. The factory directors, however, began to "correct" the documents so that, after a few months, a profitable factory would look as if it were running at a loss and it were necessary to privatize it immediately. They then paid for an audit that confirmed that it was loss-making and either bribed the arbitrage court to eliminate tender bidding or else organized their own fictitious auction.

The State Property Committee had to approve these privatizations, and as a result the central GKIs and local GKIs turned into centers of bribery. We had agents in these organizations, so we knew that the process was being corrupted. Ordinary citizens also started writing to the presidential administration, and soon 10 kilograms of letters a day addressed to Yeltsin were arriving describing corruption. A whole staff was compiling summaries. The local branches of the FSK [Federal Counterintelligence Service] also dealt with corruption, so there was no shortage of information.

All these reports, however, had very little effect. Korzhakov sometimes took the information and reported it to Yeltsin. At other times we felt that he took the information and did not report it. Sometimes he came in and said, "I could not report what is happening." We asked him why not. He said, "I don't understand what you are writing. Write it again, once for me and once for the president in simple form."

When this problem was raised with the reformers, they said, "We are in the predatory stage of capitalism. All Western societies went through this stage, and we must go through it, too. Who were the ancestors of the Rockefellers? Bandits. Now they are normal people."

In this situation, I understood that my work was not necessary to anyone. We shared the information on corruption with the MVD [Ministry of Internal Affairs] and FSB, but they couldn't act on it either. I finally left the service in 1993.

The population degraded; that is, they lost moral standards. Such notions as honor, conscience, respect for law, patriotism, and self-sacrifice disappeared. Everything was for sale, even the courts. Theft, embezzlement from the treasury, bribes became normal, everyday occurrences; all those who were trusted to run the country pillaged it.—Sol Shulman, on Russia at the time of the first Romanov tsar, Vlast i Sudba (Power and Fate)

4 The History of Reform

At noon on December 31, 1999, the pale, puffy visage of Boris Yeltsin appeared unexpectedly on Russian television screens. For weeks, rumors had swirled around Yeltsin and his daughters in connection with possible corruption charges, and these reports gave rise to speculation that Yeltsin could not afford to surrender power.

It was this speculation that Yeltsin was about to dispel.

"Dear friends!" he said, speaking from behind his desk in the Kremlin in front of a decorated New Year's tree and the tricolor flag of the Russian Federation.

> Today, I am turning to you for the last time with New Year's greetings. But that's not all. Today, on the last day of the departing century, I am resigning . . .
>
> Russia must enter the new millennium with new faces, with new, smart, strong, energetic people. And we who have been in power for many years already, we must go . . .
>
> I want to ask for your forgiveness. For the fact that many of the dreams we shared did not come true. And for the fact that what seemed simple to us turned out to be tormentingly difficult. I ask forgiveness for not justifying some hopes of those people who believed that at one stroke . . . we could leap from the gray, stagnant totalitarian past into the light, rich, civilized future.
>
> Be happy. You deserve happiness. Happy New Year! Happy new century, my dear ones!

On the street, the news of Yeltsin's resignation spread quickly. Reactions ranged from relief that Yeltsin was gone to indifference based on the conviction that nothing would change.

In the early afternoon, Vladimir Putin, who only months before had been completely unknown to his fellow citizens, was appointed acting president at a Kremlin ceremony and given the nuclear codes. Putin then issued a decree granting Yeltsin and the members of his family lifelong immunity from prosecution. The decree was extremely broad. It shielded Yeltsin from searches, arrest, and interrogation and protected his cars, telephone calls, documents, luggage, and correspondence.

At midnight, the traditional message from the head of state was given by Putin, not Yeltsin. Putin announced that he was now the president and assured Russians that the armed forces, border guards, and law enforcement forces were working normally. "There will be no power vacuum," he said. "I want to warn that any attempt to exceed the limits of the law and Russia's Constitution will be decisively crushed."

The resignation of Boris Yeltsin and accession to power of Vladimir Putin marked the final act in the creation of a criminal oligarchic system in Russia. As a result of the first peaceful handover of power in Russian history, a small group who had used connections to carve up the wealth of the former Soviet Union were assured of the security of their possessions, and a new economic system was confirmed in which the animating principle was not productivity but theft.

The victory of a criminal oligarchy in Russia took place in two stages: the period from approximately 1992 to 1998, during which the system was created; and the briefer period in the late 1990s, when a nascent challenge to that system was successfully overcome. In both periods, what drove the process was not the determination to create a system based on universal values but rather the will to introduce a system of private ownership, which, in the absence of law, opened the way for the criminal pursuit of money and power.

The creation of an oligarchic system began during the perestroika period, but its untrammeled development started in January 1992 with the beginning of the post-Soviet reforms. The reforms were dominated by three processes: hyperinflation, privatization, and criminalization. Their interaction led to economic collapse, mass poverty, and the effective privatization of the Russian state.

The hyperinflation began on January 2, 1992, after the abrupt freeing of prices, and it quickly divided the population into a minority of the very rich and a majority of the hopelessly poor. Yegor Gaidar, the deputy prime minister, predicted that prices would increase three to five times and then begin to fall. In ten months, however, prices rose twenty-five- to thirtyfold, driving millions into destitution. Soon hawkers and peddlers were every-where as the members of the World War II generation took to the streets to sell their personal belongings. Within three months, 99 percent of the money held by Russian citizens in savings accounts had disappeared. Money that had been saved for decades to buy an apartment or a car or to pay for a wedding or a decent funeral was lost, causing psychological crises for millions of people.

The wiping out of citizens' savings was followed by the appearance of numerous commercial banks and investment funds, which were totally un-regulated. At a time when spiraling inflation pushed ordinary citizens to seek ways to conserve their incomes, these investment funds and many commercial banks, a large number of which had ties to high-ranking offi-cials, launched massive advertising campaigns, promising rates of return on investment of up to 1,200 percent. Most of these funds were pyramid schemes, and when they collapsed, more than 40 million people lost their savings a second time.

While millions were losing their savings, former Soviet government and Communist party officials used their connections to Russian officialdom to accumulate enormous wealth. The way had been well prepared. During the perestroika period, the Communist party apparatus had gone into business. Commercial organizations formed under the aegis of the Komsomol (Com-munist Youth League) were freed from taxes for five years and allowed to engage in foreign trade. Since there was otherwise a state monopoly of foreign trade, they were in effect allowed to set their own terms in satisfying nearly unlimited demand. The party, in the meantime, used party money, which at the time was indistinguishable from government money, to create commercial banks. And factory directors began to strip the assets of their factories. They did this by setting up cooperatives, usually staffed by their relatives, which became middlemen for factory business, charging exorbi-tant prices while performing no real service.

There were several ways of quickly accumulating vast, unearned wealth. One was to appropriate government credits. In 1992 inflation created a shortage of turnover capital, which paralyzed production and prompted the issuance of credits to Russian factories, whose value reached nearly 30 per-cent of the gross domestic product. With the inflation rate at 2,500 percent, these credits were offered at rates of from 10 to 25 percent. Instead of being used to pay salaries and purchase supplies, however, they were deposited in commercial banks at market rates, with the difference split between bank officials and the factory director.

A second way to acquire great wealth was to obtain permission to export raw materials. Although most prices in Russia had been freed from controls, energy prices, which at the beginning of the reform period were less than 1 percent of world market prices, continued to be regulated. Having abandoned the Soviet-era monopoly on foreign trade, the government began to allow anyone to export who could get a license; and since Russian raw materials were bought at the internal price for rubles and sold abroad at the world price for dollars, export licenses were akin to permission to print money. In Moscow they were frequently issued by the Ministry of Foreign Economic Ties, which functioned like a market, granting licenses in return for bribes, with the fee for the license insignificant in comparison to the size of the bribe.

A third source of wealth was subsidized imports. Out of fear that there would be famine in the country in the winter of 1991, the government sold dollars for the importation of food products at 1 percent of their real value, with the difference subsidized with the help of Western commodity credits. The products were sold, however, at normal market prices, with the result that the attempt to relieve the country's anticipated food crisis led to the enrichment of a small circle of Moscow traders. The value of import subsidies in 1992 came to 15 percent of the gross domestic product.[1]

In 1993 the impoverishment of the population and corruption of the reform process spawned a power struggle between the Supreme Soviet, the Russian parliament, and the executive branch of government which ended with the dissolution of the Supreme Soviet on October 4 and the creation of a new political system that greatly accelerated the growth of the criminal business oligarchy.[2]

The abolition of the Supreme Soviet left only one center of decision making in the country, the presidential apparatus; and its members, convinced of their impunity after the events of October, became ever more susceptible to bribery. At the same time, the Russian revenue system was put under the control of the president, and twelve banks, which had supported Yeltsin in his confrontation with the parliament, were "empowered" to handle government accounts. These banks, by delaying payments on government obligations and using budgetary funds to give short-term interbank credits at rates as high as 400 percent, reaped gigantic profits on the state's money. They were soon joined by regional banks that also acquired budgetary money and began to lend it out at interest. In the meantime, nonpayment of salaries began to be a permanent feature of Russian life.

Soon the leading Moscow banks became the core of financial political groups, each of which was tied to one or another leading political figure. As their power and wealth increased, the banks began to behave like states within a state, acquiring media outlets and establishing their own security services capable of spying on economic and political rivals as well as tapping the phones of thousands of ordinary citizens. With the resources of a former superpower at stake, the struggle for power between the financial political groups became the principal determinant of the policies of the Russian government.

The second process that contributed to the creation of Russia's criminal business oligarchy was privatization. Privatization both predated and survived the period of hyperinflation. The privatization that took place first is euphemistically described as "unofficial" privatization and consisted in the uncontrolled and illegal seizure of the economic infrastructure of the country. "Official" privatization took place in two stages: voucher privatization, from October 1992 to July 1994; and money privatization, which began in August 1994 and continued to the end of the decade.

Unofficial privatization began during the perestroika period as soon as government organizations were given permission to engage in commercial activity. Government officials, secretly and without any legal basis, began to take over their agencies and reorganize them as private enterprises. In place of ministries, they organized "concerns"; in place of the state distribution system, they created commodity exchanges; and in place of the state banks with their regional branches, they organized commercial banks. The new commercial enterprises used the same suppliers, the same buildings, and the same personnel. Only the name of the organization changed. But the assets of the organization became the property of its new "owners."[3]

Wild privatization was followed by voucher privatization, which began in October 1992. Each Russian was entitled to a voucher with a face value of 10,000 rubles (the monthly salary of an auto worker), which was redeemable for a share of Russian industry. The vouchers were of little use to most Russians, who were rarely paid dividends on them and had no say in management even when they invested their voucher in their own factory.

They were very useful, however, to those who could accumulate them in great numbers. This led criminal and commercial structures to buy them up as quickly as possible. In some cases, agents bought vouchers on the street from indigents and alcoholics, often for a bottle of vodka. In other cases, these groups organized voucher funds that advertised on television, promising high dividends, and then either did not pay the dividends or simply disappeared. In this way, criminal and commercial structures accumulated huge blocks of vouchers that they used to buy up the most desirable factories, often at giveaway prices.[4]

In the last days of voucher privatization, the federal property fund put more than a hundred of Russia's most valuable enterprises on sale at once, causing a sharp fall in the value of shares, which were then bought up by the voucher funds.[5]

When voucher privatization was succeeded by money privatization in the latter part of 1994, the population was already divided into a handful of groups that could participate in it and the vast majority of the population, which could not. The pressure to put property into private hands as quickly as possible, however, did not relent, and it led to the selling off of many of the country's remaining industrial enterprises, including the most desirable, at absurdly reduced prices.

The first step was to set a price for the concerned enterprise. Generally the factory director and officials of the relevant ministry decided on the price on the basis of an estimate of the cost of the buildings and equipment. These figures could be artificially lowered by using one- or two-year-old prices and writing off usable equipment. Or, to discourage outside investors, they could be artificially raised. Once a price was established, it needed to be approved by the local State Property Committee, which usually offered no objections.

If a powerful bank or commercial group was interested in the factory, the next step was to eliminate real or potential competition. Insofar as the auction was organized by the local property fund, which was subordinated to the governor, the party with influence in the region was in a position to manipulate the auction by falsifying documents or gaining information about the competing offer. In fact, many of the auctions took place only on paper. In cases in which auctions actually were held, competing bids often came from firms that worked for the victor. Only rarely did true competitive bidding take place and, in the event that a powerful group was outbid by an insistent competitor, the successful bidder could easily pay for his tenacity with his life.

The prices for which these enterprises were sold stunned Russian society; 324 factories were sold at an average price of less than $4 million each. Uralmash, the giant machine-building plant in Yekaterinburg, was sold for $3.73 million; the Chelyabinsk Metallurgical Combine also went for $3.73 million; and the Kovrovsky Mechanical Factory, which supplied the Russian army, the Ministry of Internal Affairs, and the security services with fire-arms, was sold for $2.7 million.[6] Telephone companies were sold for $116.62 per line, compared with rates of $637 per line in North America and $2,083 in Hungary. The United Energy Systems power-generating company was sold for $200 million. In Central Europe, a company with similar kilowatt production would have been worth $30 billion, and in the United States, $49 billion.

Russian oil companies sold tested oil wells for $.04 per realized barrel, compared with the North American price of $7.06 per barrel. The Murmansk trawler fleet, which consisted of 100 ships, each of which was less than ten years old and was worth $20 million when launched, was sold for $3 million. The North Sea Steamship Company was sold for $3 million.[7]

On September 9, 1994, the investor bulletin *Independent Strategy* reported: "The greater part of the basic productive funds of Russia are being sold for somewhere around $5 billion. Even if one considers that in Russia, the price of the basic means of production is equal to her gross domestic product [in the West, it usually is at least 2.6 times higher] . . . in effect, 300 to 400 billion dollars; the sum realized in privatization is minimal. For this reason, the agency recommends English investors not to miss the chance and to take part in the purchase of Russian enterprises."[8]

In late 1994 the Russian government, in response to pressure from the World Bank to reduce the rate of inflation to one percent a month and to balance the budget, ceased printing money to meet current expenses, including the payment of salaries. The situation became increasingly untenable, and to meet its obligations the government began to borrow money from commercial banks in return for shares in desirable, nonprivatized industries.

In theory, the "loans for shares" program provided for competition for the blocks of shares, with the winner determined by who could offer the largest credit to the government. In practice, however, the winner was the bank with the closest "informal" ties to the government, and the scheme, although it facilitated the handover of the most profitable Russian enterprises to the country's oligarchs, provided very little in badly needed revenue to the government. In 1995, for example, the total revenue from the mortgage auctions of twenty-one of Russia's most profitable enterprises was $691.4 million and 400 billion rubles.[9]

Once an enterprise had been "mortgaged," the proprietary bank was free to exploit it; and when the government failed to repay the bank loans—which, given the state's revenue shortage, was always the case—it was up to the bank that held the mortgage to organize the final sale of the enterprise. Unsurprisingly, the enterprises became the property of the banks that had provided the original loans.

In 1995 Oneximbank won control of 38 percent of Norilsk Nickel, the giant nonferrous-metals producer, in exchange for a $170 million loan to the government. Two years later, in August 1997, it paid $250 million to retain the stake. After its repayment of the loan was deducted, the government had gained a mere $80 million for a major share in the plant that produces 90 percent of Russia's nickel, 90 percent of its cobalt, and 100 percent of its platinum.

In the meantime Oneximbank was free to exploit the giant combine as it saw fit. Norilsk Nickel was one of Russia's leading earners of hard currency, but by the spring of 1997 it owed its workers 1.2 trillion rubles in back wages. It was common for workers to faint from hunger, and that year, for the first time in decades, the children of Norilsk were not sent out of the polar city for the summer. The failure of Norilsk Nickel to meet its obligations raised the question of what Oneximbank was doing with the money that it earned from the combine. According to *Obshchaya Gazeta*, the bank was involved in highly profitable projects that required enormous amounts of cash. One such project was paying early on promissory notes from the federal government to the regional administrations in return for 20 to 30 percent of the note's face value. Inasmuch as the government had a budgetary debt of more than 50 trillion rubles to employees, it was often unable to pay on these notes itself, and commercial banks used the income generated by their enterprises to buy these notes, leaving enterprises they controlled without enough money to pay salaries.[10]

In fact the empowered banks, which soon controlled roughly 50 percent of the economy of the country, began to feed continually off the state budget. They collected interest on budgetary funds, used the money to acquire the most valuable Russian enterprises, and then used the revenue from the enterprises to make huge profits by, in effect, lending money back to the government.

The loan-for-shares scheme changed the relationship between major financial institutions and the government. The banks had long enjoyed the protection of patrons in government, but now, for the first time, the banks were in a position to put pressure on the government. Officials had to go to the banks to discuss such issues as changes in interest rates and the size of the government's indebtedness. Having created powerful banks by entrusting them with the government's money, the government fell into dependence on them.

With the approach of the 1996 presidential elections, it became clear that the government not only would not be able to repay the loans it had taken but, on the contrary, would need new loans. This state of affairs led to plans to put some of the country's most valuable properties, such as the Perm Motor Factory, which produces aircraft engines, Aeroflot, and Svyazinvest, the telecommunications holding company, up for auction, with the banks that had received shares in the enterprises dictating the conditions.

The banks, for their part, acted to support the government that had enriched them, contributing a minimum of $170 million—and probably many times more—to the Yeltsin reelection campaign. The legal spending limit was $1.7 million. In this way, they helped to assure Yeltsin's victory.[11]

The third process that gave rise to Russia's criminal business oligarchy, and the one that left its stamp on the other two, was the process of criminalization.

As was the case with privatization, the modern stage of criminalization in Russia began during perestroika. The Gorbachev-era reforms started with the legalization of "cooperatives," which became the only privately run businesses in the Soviet Union. The cooperatives quickly prospered, but, viewed as ideologically illegitimate, they were left without police protection at a time when it was illegal to hire private guards. They therefore became tempting targets for coercion, and gangs began to be formed all over the country to extort money from them.

By 1992 nearly every small business or street kiosk in Russia was paying protection money to gangsters. As a source of wealth, however, shops and kiosks could not compare with the state budget, and when, after the beginning of the Gaidar reforms, criminal gangs saw that former Soviet officials were using their connections to acquire vast, unearned wealth, they began to use terror to take over the enterprises that the former officials had established. One sign of the gangsters' activities was the growing number of bankers and businessmen who fell victim to contract murders.[12]

The criminal terror against well-connected Russian businessmen, however, was short-lived. Soon the gangsters, businessmen, and corrupt officials began to work together. The gangsters needed the businessmen because they required places to invest their capital but, in most cases, lacked the skills to run large enterprises. For their part, businessmen needed the gangsters to force clients to honor their obligations. Before long, nearly every significant bank and commercial organization in Russia was using gangsters for debt collection.

The bandits' methods were simple. The debtor was contacted and informed that the gang knew his address and all his movements and that if he did not pay his debt by a certain date, he and his family would be killed. Usually this was enough to induce payment, in which case 50 percent of the money went to the gang. In cases in which the debtor was unable to make good the debt, he was usually murdered.

The partnership between business and crime did not stop with debt collection. It rapidly became clear that gangsters could be used for many purposes, from eliminating unwanted competitors to "persuading" potential business partners to soften their terms in contract negotiations. The most successful bankers and entrepreneurs became those with the closest ties to criminal structures.

Soon Russian commercial organizations consisted of businessmen whose principal skill was a talent for connections, corrupt officials who approved their projects in return for bribes, and gangsters who collected debts and eliminated competition. Increasingly, it became difficult to tell the difference between businessmen and gangsters. An unsuspecting Russian entrepreneur could easily find that in the event of a failure to agree on terms with a seemingly respectable businessman, his "partner" was ready to threaten his life.

By 1997 a ruling criminal business oligarchy was in place. A small group of bankers and businessmen, all of them previously unknown but with close connections to both gangsters and government officials, had gained control of the majority of the Russian economy. They included Boris Berezovsky, the head of the Logovaz car dealership; Vladimir Potanin, the head of Oneximbank; Vladimir Gusinsky, the head of the Most Bank; and Mikhail Khodorkovsky, the head of the Menatep Bank.

The ascendancy in Russia, however, of people who made their fortunes not through legitimate economic activity but through stealing led to economic collapse. In the period 1992–1999 Russia's gross domestic product fell by half. Such a drop had not occurred even under German occupation. Russia became a classic third-world country, selling its raw materials—oil, gas, and precious metals—in order to import consumer goods.[13] The value of investment in Russia fell every year for eight years, until in 1999 it was roughly 20 percent of its level in 1991.[14] Having acquired their money, for the most part illegally, Russia's newly rich declined to invest in Russia lest a future government confiscate their wealth. Money was moved out of the country in enormous quantities; estimates of the amount that left Russia illegally during the Yeltsin era range from $220 billion to $450 billion.[15]

The economic disaster was accompanied by a demographic catastrophe. In the years 1990–1994 male life expectancy fell by more than six years. In 1998 it was fifty-seven years, the lowest in the industrial world. In the late 1990s the Russian population overall fell by 750,000 a year, and the country faced epidemics of drug-resistant tuberculosis and HIV/AIDS.[16]

By 1998 the transition from capitalism to communism was more or less complete. The devastation that the reforms had wrought, however, led to steadily growing opposition, and it was the oligarchy's success in overcoming this opposition that constituted the second stage of its victory in establishing its power in Russia.

By the beginning of 1999 it was widely believed that, with the election of a new president in June 2000, a reassessment of the reforms, including a redivision of property, was inevitable. The expected settling of accounts with the ruling oligarchy, however, never took place because of a series of events unexpected by all but those at the highest level of Russian power.

In August 1998 Russia experienced a devastating financial crisis. Faced with spiraling obligations it could not meet, the government devalued the currency, defaulted on $40 billion worth of treasury bills, and announced a moratorium on commercial debt repayment. Prices rose sharply, and most people suffered a precipitous decline in their standard of living. The emerging Russian middle class was destroyed.

The economic crash had political consequences. Yeltsin's approval rating fell to low single digits, and the share of those who viewed him negatively rose to nearly 80 percent. As a result, Yeltsin felt under pressure to make concessions to his political opposition in the State Duma.

Five months earlier Yeltsin had fired Viktor Chernomyrdin, who had served as prime minister for five and a half years, and replaced him with Sergei Kirienko, the former minister of fuel and energy. In the wake of the August crisis, Yeltsin fired Kirienko and tried to rename Chernomyrdin, but the Duma voted down Chernomyrdin's candidacy twice, on August 31 and September 9. The Communists advanced the candidacy of Yevgeny Primakov, the foreign minister and former head of the Foreign Intelligence Service; and, rather than risk a third rejection of Chernomyrdin's candidacy and the prospect of new parliamentary elections, Yeltsin nominated Primakov, who was approved by the Duma by a margin of 317 to 63 on September 11.

The ascendancy of Primakov represented a break in the oligarchic system. For the first time since October 1993, when he had dispersed the Supreme Soviet, Yeltsin was faced with an alternative center of power.

Primakov quickly demonstrated that he wanted to win for the government a measure of political independence from the oligarchs and the presidential administration. To this end, he authorized an investigation of the affairs of the Yeltsin "family," the group at the pinnacle of power, which included Yeltsin's daughters, Tatyana Dyachenko and Yelena Okulova; Valentin Yumashev, the head of the presidential administration; Boris Berezovsky; Pavel Borodin, who was in charge of property management in the presidential administration; and other oligarchs and officials with close ties to Yeltsin.

The investigation began with Berezovsky, who in January 1999 was suspected of appropriating money belonging to the airline Aeroflot. Well before the Berezovsky-Aeroflot investigation, however, the general prosecutor, Yuri Skuratov, had been looking into the payment of possible kickbacks to Borodin from the Swiss firm Mabetex, in connection with construction and repair work on the Kremlin, a case that had implications for the Yeltsin daughters.

In the fall of 1997 Carla del Ponte, the Swiss prosecutor general, was given police reports showing that Russian organized crime controlled more than 300 firms in Switzerland and that a Swiss businessman of Albanian origin, Behgjet Pacolli, who headed Mabetex, was providing unexplained funds to Yeltsin and his daughters. In September 1998 these documents were forwarded to Skuratov.

On January 22, 1999, the Mabetex office in Lugano was raided, and records were discovered that showed payments of $600,000 on the credit cards of Yeltsin's daughters. It also appeared that Pacolli had paid kickbacks to Borodin and that a former copresident of Mabetex, Viktor Stolpovskikh, had received a commission of some $8 million from Pacolli, which he may have divided up among a large number of Russian officials.

Armed with del Ponte's report on the results of the search, Skuratov broadened his investigation into the Mabetex affair. He also intensified his investigation into the activities of Berezovsky. On February 2 and 4 heavily armed Federal Security Service agents raided Aeroflot and the private security firm Atoll, which was also associated with Berezovsky. It now appeared that a serious effort was under way to uncover corruption and that this included investigating the Yeltsin "family."

At about this time, however, Skuratov was secretly filmed in a sauna linked to the Solntsevo criminal organization engaging in sex with two prostitutes. Dyachenko showed the videotape to her father, and Nikolai Bordyuzha, the head of the Security Council, summoned Skuratov and asked him to resign. Skuratov gave his formal agreement but waited for the vote in the Federation Council, which, according to the constitution, must approve the removal of the general prosecutor. On February 17 the Federation Council refused to vote Skuratov out of office. Skuratov then ordered his staff to proceed with the investigation of Berezovsky.

After the Federation Council refused to dismiss Skuratov, representatives of the family secretly offered to let him prosecute Berezovsky in return for dropping the Mabetex investigation. Skuratov, however, refused. In March he received more detailed reports about Mabetex from the Swiss. A senior investigator, Georgy Chuglazov, said that 90 percent of the contents of the reports seemed to be true, and Skuratov commented that del Ponte's figure of $10 million for the value of Mabetex's bribes to highly placed Russians "seems to be a realistic estimate, although it has to be proved."[17]

On May 17 the Federation Council voted again on whether to remove Skuratov and again decided to leave him in place. A few days later the state television channel, RTR, showed the videotape of Skuratov having sex with the prostitutes on the prime-time news program. Yeltsin then appointed Vladimir Putin, the little-known head of the FSB, to take Borduzha's place as head of the Security Council (he remained head of the FSB). Under Putin's leadership, a criminal case was opened against Skuratov on the grounds that the sex acts in the video were actually bribes given in return for favors. On this basis, Yeltsin removed Skuratov and appointed an acting general prosecutor. The arrest order against Berezovsky was immediately revoked.

On the eve of the third vote on Skuratov in the Federation Council, Yeltsin lobbied the senators, promising liberal power-sharing arrangements with many of the regions. But the senators listened in closed-door session to Skuratov's report on high-level corruption and voted to support him by 79 to 61. For the Yeltsin "family," getting someone appointed permanently as prosecutor who would cut off the Mabetex investigation was now an urgent necessity.

At the same time, Yeltsin, whose behavior in office was inspiring indignation among the population, faced a vote on impeachment. There were five charges: that Yeltsin had illegally broken up the Soviet Union in December 1991; that he had acted unconstitutionally in dispersing the Supreme Soviet in October 1993; that he had violated the constitution in starting the war in Chechnya in December 1994; that he had weakened the Russian armed forces; and that he had carried out acts leading to the genocide of the Russian people.

The hearings on impeachment had been prepared for months. On May 12, the day before they began, Yeltsin fired Primakov and his government and installed as acting premier the interior minister, Sergei Stepashin. Primakov had become the most popular politician in Russia, and to Yeltsin his independence was becoming increasingly intolerable. At the same time, Yeltsin's readiness to fire Primakov was a signal to the deputies that in the event of impeachment, he might ban the Communist party and suppress the parliament by force.

Having defined the context, the Yeltsin "family" worked to head off the drive for impeachment.

MAY 15, 1999

A deputy from the Russian Regions faction in the State Duma was preparing to vote on the motion to impeach President Yeltsin when there was a knock on the door of his office, and a stranger entered and introduced himself as "a well-wisher who wants to offer you a very advantageous deal."

The stranger said, "You can receive big money, help yourself, and at the same time help us." He gave no indication, however, of whom he meant by "us."

Of the five accusations against Yeltsin, only one, unleashing the war in Chechnya, was believed to have a good chance of gaining the two-thirds vote necessary for impeachment. Accordingly, it was not a surprise to the deputy when the stranger explained that his principal concern was to prevent him from supporting the point of the indictment concerning Chechnya. "You can vote for impeachment," he said. "Just don't vote for the point concerning Chechnya. You can say that you supported impeachment but couldn't bring yourself to approve the charge concerning Chechnya because you did not think that the war was the responsibility of the president."

There was a pregnant pause, and the stranger said, "I can offer you $30,000."

The deputy got up and said, "I'm sorry, but I'm afraid that you have mistaken the door."

At about the same time, another deputy from the Russian Regions faction received a similar visitor who offered him $30,000 not to vote for impeachment. The deputy did not accept the $30,000 but expressed interest in a deal. He insisted, however, that he was going to vote for at least one point of the indictment against Yeltsin. His visitor asked him which one. The deputy said he would vote to convict Yeltsin of illegally dissolving the Soviet Union.

The visitor smiled. "We respect your choice," he said. They agreed on a payment of $52,000.

As Ksenya Kolbakova, a correspondent for ITAR-TASS, waited for the results of the voting on impeachment, these and other stories of attempts to bribe deputies circulated among the correspondents who crowded the corridor outside the press hall and were in constant contact with deputies and their staffs.

Although she had earlier believed that Yeltsin would be impeached on at least one of the five charges against him, Kolbakova now began to have doubts. There was obviously a well-coordinated effort under way to bribe the deputies into leaving Yeltsin in place, and, knowing the deputies from her work as a parliamentary correspondent, she had little faith in their will to resist.

The apparent reliance on bribery to save the Yeltsin presidency was all the more striking in light of the gravity of the issues at stake. The accusations touched on the whole history of Russia during the reform period.

The first day of the hearings began with a speech by Vadim Filomonov, the chairman of the Duma Commission on Impeachment, who slowly and self-confidently made the case for Yeltsin's removal from office.

He said that Yeltsin had not had the right under the constitution of the Russian Federation to dissolve the Soviet Union and, by concluding the Belovezhsky agreement, had done "colossal damage" to the security and defense capacity of the federation. In abolishing the Russian Supreme Soviet in 1993, he said, Yeltsin had seized power that belonged legally to the Supreme Soviet, and his actions had led to the deaths of a large number of innocent people. The war in Chechnya was illegal because the constitution did not give the president the right to decide on the use of force inside the country unilaterally, and Yeltsin's actions had resulted in enormous material damage and the deaths of tens of thousands of people.

In regard to the fourth charge against Yeltsin, that his actions had weakened the Russian armed forces, Filomonov said that the commission had found that the collapse of the Russian armed forces had been the result of "deliberate behavior of the president and his careless attitude toward his official responsibilities." Concerning the fifth charge, that Yeltsin had carried out acts "leading to the genocide of the Russian people," Filomonov said that even according to official data, the loss in population in Russia had been 4.2 million from 1992 through 1998. "Yeltsin consciously accepted the worsening of the living conditions of Russian citizens, with an inevitable rise in the mortality of the population and a decrease in the birthrate. All suggestions that the political course be changed were consistently refused."

Filomonov said that the special Commission on Impeachment had concluded that all the points in the indictment were justified. He closed by saying, "The blood of the murdered and crippled, the tears of the dying, degraded, and insulted beat in our hearts!"

Filomonov was followed by Viktor Ilyukhin, the chief accuser of Yeltsin and the chairman of the Duma's Committee on Security. He emphasized that Yeltsin's rule had been authoritarian and that therefore it was Yeltsin who bore responsibility for the tragedy of Russia. "The country is in a state of ruin and . . . this of itself renders impossible the further occupation of Yeltsin of his post. We hope that his removal will be the beginning of the process of the rebirth of the country. Our positive resolution of this question will be a serious warning for the present and future rulers of Russia."

The accusations against Yeltsin were answered by Alexander Kotenkov, the presidential representative in the State Duma. Yeltsin was not responsible for the breakup of the Soviet Union, he said, because at the time of the Belovezhsky agreement the Soviet Union no longer existed in its previous form. There were only seven republics left of fifteen, and so "Russia had nothing to withdraw from." The dissolution of the Supreme Soviet was justified, Kotenkov said, because the office of the president had greater popular legitimacy than the Supreme Soviet and the Supreme Soviet had resisted any attempt to eliminate its monopoly on power.

In reference to the third accusation, responsibility for launching the Chechen war, Kotenkov said that Yeltsin's decrees had not envisaged direct military action. The means used in carrying out Yeltsin's decrees on the disarming of the Chechen fighters had been chosen by the army. He also said that Yeltsin had tried to save the army from collapse and was not responsible for the "genocide of the Russian people," in that the population of Russia had been declining every year since 1960.

Each of the speakers then responded to questions from the hall, for the most part restating their positions.

In the meantime, crowds of demonstrators outside the building screamed, "Put Yeltsin on trial!" Reporters in the press hall watched the proceedings on television monitors and slept.

On the second day of the hearings there were speeches from the floor. Vladimir Zhirinovsky, the leader of the Liberal Democratic party, defended Yeltsin. "Just as Gorbachev deceived us," he said, "the Communists now want to do the same. You want to blame everything on one person . . . In 1917 you also found one person who was guilty of everything, the tsar. And he agreed with you. He even abdicated. And what did you do with him?"

Olga Beklemishcheva, a deputy from Nizhny Novgorod, said that during the investigation into the events of October 1993, it had been learned that the Moscow ambulances had been forbidden to give aid to the defenders of the White House. "Doctors were forced to ignore their professional obligation. Only doctor-volunteers from the Sechenov Academy helped the injured. Three of these volunteers were killed . . . I am going to vote for impeachment."

After several more speakers gave their views on various accusations, Viktor Benediktov, a doctor who had been invited by the Communists, was recognized. He brought with him a resolution of a recent congress of Russian doctors that spoke to the dire demographic situation in Russia. "Depopulation proceeds against the background of the worsening of the health of all age groups in the population," he said. "There is every reason to believe that the population of the country will be reduced to such a level in the twenty-first century that its preservation and replication will be impossible."

On the third day, Gennady Zyuganov, the leader of the Communists, said that 98 percent of the population of Russia was of one mind: "Yeltsin—go!"

Vladimir Ryzhkov, the leader of the Our Home Is Russia faction, said that his group would vote against impeachment, explaining foggily that "justice demands the movement to truth." Several more speakers from the opposition echoed Ilyukhin's remarks, and the session was then recessed for the voting and the counting of the votes.

As the debate came to an end, Sergei Zverev, the deputy head of the presidential administration, who knew the deputies well, began to tell journalists that he was sure that impeachment would not pass. Gleb Cherkassov, a correspondent for *Moscow News*, spoke to the assistants of deputies who had refused bribes. They told him that on Friday, May 14, the lobbyists had been offering $30,000 to vote against impeachment but that the price was going up.

Ksenya Kolbakova was disturbed by the physical appearance of the lobbyists, which suggested that they had just got out of prison. Many of them congregated in the buffet on the first floor, smoking heavily and drinking beer, creating a half-criminal atmosphere.

When the proceedings were adjourned for lunch, the parliamentary staff began to print ballots for each of the five points of the indictment, and the deputies were given until 3:00 P.M. to turn them in. Zyuganov told reporters that the accusation concerning Chechnya would get the 300 votes needed for impeachment and that the charge concerning the Belovezhsky agreement might also get the required two-thirds vote. His optimism was belied, however, by several events. In the first place, there were reports that scores of deputies were not taking their ballots. At the same time, journalists were being told by deputies and staff members in the Duma that the value of the bribes was continuing to rise. Lobbyists were contacting wavering deputies in their offices and offering them payments of from $50,000 to $70,000.

The Communists and the Yabloko faction were committed to voting for impeachment on the issue of Chechnya. The Russian Regions party also leaned toward impeachment, but its members were told that they were free to vote as they wished. The lobbyists concentrated their efforts on buying the votes of the members of this faction.

Kolbakova noticed that the Communist leaders had begun to meet behind closed doors and that when they emerged, they were taciturn and grim, in sharp contrast to their earlier optimistic demeanor. Finally, Alexander Kravetz, the party's secretary for ideology, entered the Duma press room and took his place behind a microphone at a table on the stage. The crowd of reporters became silent and leaned forward as he began to speak. "Deputies are being bought," he said. "The starting price is $30,000. If a deputy agrees to vote against all points of the indictment, there can be a lot more."

The votes were still being counted, but in the wake of Kravetz's statement, all tension was gone. No one any longer expected that Yeltsin would be impeached.

At 5:30 the counting commission announced that, on the critical vote on Chechnya, 283 deputies had voted in favor of impeachment. This was a large majority but 17 short of the necessary two-thirds vote. The other counts of the indictment received even fewer votes.

After the totals were announced, the Communists appeared stunned. Filomonov found it difficult to speak. Zyuganov told reporters, "This was all bought." He promised to begin an investigation on the following day.

With the defeat of the impeachment motion, Stepashin set about trying to organize a pro-Kremlin party capable of pushing aside the burgeoning Fatherland–All Russia movement being organized by Yuri Luzhkov, the mayor of Moscow, which had recruited Primakov. On August 23 Luzhkov promised that if Primakov, the most popular politician in the country, should run for president, he would support him.

As the economic situation in Russia got steadily worse, Yeltsin's approval rating dropped to 2 percent, and an awareness spread among people closely connected to the Yeltsin regime that their positions and wealth were in jeopardy.

The law on privatization, passed in 1992, established general procedures and was not designed to be applied to specific acts of privatization. These were carried out on the basis of presidential decrees. All the big oil companies and the financial industrial groups had been created by decree, as had the public television station, ORT. The sale of industrial enterprises under the loans-for-shares program had also been carried out by decree. What had been created by decree, however, could be eliminated by decree, and with the election of a new president, it was increasingly likely that many of the results of privatization would be undone with the stroke of a pen.

At the same time, the investigations of Berezovsky and Mabetex demonstrated that, in the event of an election victory by people opposed to Yeltsin, those who had amassed wealth illegally during the Yeltsin years—and this was virtually the entire new elite, including members of the Yeltsin family—were in danger of losing not just their property but also their freedom and even their lives. For this reason, the people around Yeltsin were determined to keep him in office or secure the presidency for his hand-picked successor at virtually any cost.

At first it was hoped that Stepashin would be the person to defeat Primakov. It soon became clear, however, that he was ill suited for that role. He seemed to have no enthusiasm for making visceral attacks on Primakov and Luzhkov, and there were reports that he had rejected schemes for introducing a state of emergency and canceling the presidential elections for fear of setting off a civil war.

According to an article on July 22 in *Moskovskaya Pravda,* which was based on leaked documents, one of the schemes mooted in the Kremlin was to cause chaos in Moscow by organizing terrorist acts, kidnappings, and a war between rival criminal clans.[18] The plan, known among insiders as "Storm in Moscow," was never implemented, but an even greater crisis emerged to change the course of history and, against all expectations, save the Yeltsin regime.

On August 5, 1999, a Muslim force led by Shamil Basayev, a Chechen guerrilla leader, and Khattab, a guerrilla leader believed to be a Saudi citizen, entered western Dagestan from Chechnya with the purpose of starting an anti-Russian uprising. On August 9 Stepashin was dismissed, and Vladimir

Putin took his place.[19] On August 22 the force withdrew into Chechnya without heavy losses.

The incursion provoked indignation in Russia, but there were also immediate suspicions that the invasion was a provocation intended to prepare the public for a new war in Chechnya. The internal forces assigned to guard the border had been withdrawn shortly before the Chechens invaded, so the force led by Basayev and Khattab entered Dagestan without resistance. For two weeks, while the invaders fought with the local police, the Russian army made no move to attack them. The invaders then withdrew from Dagestan in a convoy of 72 Kamaz trucks without interference. Commenting on the invasion, Vitaly Tretyakov, the editor of *Nezavisimaya Gazeta*, which is owned by Berezovsky, wrote that the Chechens had been lured into Dagestan in an operation organized by the Russian intelligence services.[20]

Alexander Zhilin, a prominent military journalist, wrote that he had spoken to high-ranking officers in the general staff, the Ministry of Defense, and the Interior Ministry and that all were in agreement that the invasion was a preparation for another preelection Chechen war. "In this connection," he wrote, "all my interlocutors without exception stressed a not unimportant point: the FSB and the Security Council were headed simultaneously by the present head of the government, Vladimir Putin."[21]

Despite concern that it was a provocation, the invasion of Dagestan refocused the attention of the country on the northern Caucasus. In late August, the Russian armed forces began land and air attacks on villages in Dagestan controlled by Wahhabi Muslims in apparent retaliation for the earlier incursion. On August 31 a powerful explosion ripped through the underground Manezh shopping center next to the Kremlin, killing one person and injuring thirty.[22] This event unsettled the political atmosphere, but the tension had to reach a qualitatively new level before the population was sufficiently galvanized to support a second Chechen war. This occurred as a result of developments over the next few days.

The events unfolded as if according to plan.

At 9:40 P.M. on September 4, a car bomb exploded in Buinaksk, a city in Dagestan, demolishing a five-story apartment building housing Russian military families. The death toll from the explosion was 62, with nearly 100 people injured.

On September 9, shortly after midnight, an explosion destroyed all nine stories of the center section of the building at 19 Guryanova Street in the Pechatniki section of Moscow. Several bodies were hurled into the surrounding streets. Fires raged for hours under the smoldering rubble. By the end of the first day, the death toll had risen to ninety-eight.[23]

Russian officials immediately blamed the Guryanova Street bombing and the bombing in Buinaksk on Chechen terrorists seeking revenge for their "defeat" in Dagestan. A spokesman for the FSB identified the explosive used in the bombing as a combination of hexogen, a military explosive, and dynamite. According to Yeltsin, terrorists had "declared war on the Russian people."

The residents of Moscow now began to fear being blown up in their beds. Yeltsin ordered Luzhkov to have all 30,000 residential buildings in the city searched for explosives, and residents organized round-the-clock patrols. The police received thousands of calls from city residents reporting suspicious activity, and a building near the scene of the explosion on Guryanova Street was evacuated in a false alarm.

On September 13 a massive explosion reduced a nine-story brick apartment building at 6 Kashirskoye Highway in Moscow to a smoldering pile of rubble. The bombing took place at 5:00 A.M., and Muscovites awoke to graphic television footage showing emergency workers feverishly going through the debris. A rescue worker asked, "How can anyone tell how many people are dead if we find them in small pieces?" The death toll in the Kashirskoye Highway explosion soon reached 118.

On September 16, with funerals for the first bombing victims still going on, a truck bomb ripped off the facade of a nine-story apartment building in the southern Russian city of Volgodonsk, killing at least seventeen and injuring sixty-nine. The psychological shock of the explosion, which, like the explosion on Kashirskoye Highway, took place at 5:00 A.M., was so great that afterward hundreds of people were unwilling to sleep in their homes and insisted on spending the night outdoors.[24]

In the aftermath of the explosion, Putin appeared on television and said that it was necessary to "wipe [the terrorists] out in their toilets."[25]

With the bombings, the psychological preconditions had been created for a second Chechen war.

Russians have always referred to Hitler's "treacherous attack" on the Soviet Union, and it was anger over that attack that helped to mobilize the Soviet Union in the first days of World War II. The bombings played a similar role. For the vast majority of Russians, the Chechens had carried the war to the Russian people and now had to be made to pay a price even if that meant going to war.

Almost from the beginning, however, there were doubts as to whether the bombings were really the work of Chechen terrorists. Both Aslan Maskhadov, the Chechen leader, and Basayev denied that Chechens had anything to do with the bombings.[26] More disturbing than such denials, however, were the circumstances of the bombings themselves, which made the claims that they were the work of Chechen terrorists increasingly implausible.

First, all four bombings had the same "signature," as attested by the nature of the destruction, the way the buildings' concrete panels collapsed, and the volume of the blast. In each case the explosive was said to be hexogen, and all four bombs had been set to go off at night to inflict the maximum number of casualties.

Second, to do what they were accused of having done without expert assistance, Chechen terrorists would have needed to be able to organize nine explosions (the four that took place and the five that the Russian authorities claimed to have prevented) in widely distant cities in the space of two weeks. They would have had to be able to act with lightning speed. In the case of the bombing on Kashirskoye Highway, the police checked the basement where the bomb was placed three hours before the blast.

Third, the Chechens also would have needed to penetrate top-secret Russian military factories. Investigators said that each bomb contained 450 to 650 pounds of hexogen, which was produced in Russia in only one factory, a plant in the Perm oblast guarded by the central FSB. Its distribution was tightly controlled. Despite this, the presumed Chechen terrorists were supposedly able to obtain the hexogen and transport tons of it to locations all over Russia.

Finally, Chechen terrorists would have had to demonstrate technical virtuosity. In Moscow, the bomb on Guryanova Street caused an entire stairway to collapse. On Kashirskoye Highway, an eight-story brick building was reduced to rubble. In Volgodonsk, the truck bomb that killed seventeen people damaged thirty-seven buildings in the surrounding area. To achieve this kind of result, the explosives had to be carefully measured and prepared. In the case of the Moscow apartment buildings, they had to be placed to destroy the weakest, critical structural elements so that each of the buildings would collapse like a house of cards. Such careful calculations are the mark of skilled specialists, and the only sources of such specialist training in Russia were the *spetsnaz* (special assignment) forces, military intelligence (GRU), and the FSB.[27]

Another troubling aspect of the apartment bombings was the timing. The bombings were explained as a response to the Chechen-led Muslim invasion of Dagestan earlier in the month (regarded by many as a Russian provocation). A careful study of the apartment bombings, however, showed that it would have taken from four to four-and-a-half months to organize them. In constructing a model of the events, all stages of the conspiracy were considered: developing a plan for the targets, visiting the targets, making corrections, determining the optimum mix of explosives, ordering their preparation, making final calculations based on the makeup of the explosives, renting space in the targeted buildings, and transporting the explosives to the targets.

If these calculations were even approximately correct, planning for the apartment bombings would have had to begin in the spring and so could not have been in retaliation for the Chechen invasion of Dagestan. They might, however, have been part of a plan that included the Chechen invasion of Dagestan, the Russian bombing of the Wahhabi villages in seeming retaliation, and the bombings in Buinaksk, Moscow, and Volgodonsk as seeming revenge by the Chechens. But such a plan could only have been implemented by elements of the Russian government in cooperation with the FSB.[28]

At first these inconsistencies troubled only a small number of people familiar with terrorist operations and the capacities of the FSB. But on the night of September 22, six days after the bombing in Volgodonsk, the "training exercise" incident took place in Ryazan, and the "terrorists" captured there were found to be members of the central FSB.[29] A short time later, after weeks of insisting that the explosive used in the bombings in Buinaksk, Moscow, and Volgodonsk was hexogen, the FSB suddenly changed its explanation and announced that the explosive was a combination of aluminum powder and ammonium nitrate, which can be found on any collective farm.

Many Russians did not want even to consider that the FSB might have been behind the apartment-house bombings, but these two events increased suspicion. The notion that a fake bomb had been put in the basement of the apartment building in Ryazan as part of a training exercise was more than many people were ready to believe. At the same time, the change in the identity of the explosive appeared to be an attempt to negate the impact of the fact that a gas analyzer in Ryazan had detected hexogen and that the only factory in Russia that produced hexogen was guarded by the FSB. The police had already arrested one person whose hands showed traces of hexane, a chemical similar to hexogen.[30]

These suspicions, however, did not create serious problems for the FSB. In the cases of both the Ryazan "training exercise" and the change in the identity of the explosive, the FSB's claims, though implausible, were difficult to refute. The sacks found in the basement of 14/16 Novosyelov Street in Ryazan were in FSB custody, and outside access to them was prohibited. At the same time, there was no way to prove that hexogen had been used in the bombings, because the bombing sites were cleared within days of the explosions, destroying the crime scenes. On Guryanova Street, the rubble was cleared away in three days.[31]

In the aftermath of the bombings, Russia launched a new invasion of Chechnya, which now enjoyed overwhelming popular support. Putin was identified as Yeltsin's designated successor, and preelection propaganda on his behalf got under way at the same time as Russian troops moved across the northern Chechen plain toward the Terek River. In a country tired of criminality and chaos, the state-run television helped Putin project an image of competence, energy, and determination, and within weeks he went from having virtually no support in the country to being by far the leading candidate for president.

As both the Chechen war and the presidential campaign progressed, however, fears that the events leading to the war had been orchestrated became increasingly widespread. Some political observers in Moscow noted that events were unfolding in a manner that matched the conditions described by Harold Lasswell, a University of Chicago political scientist, as being optimal for successful propaganda. In a book describing Allied propaganda during World War I, Lasswell said that a propagandist's success is limited by the tension level of the subject population, which he described as "that condition of adaptation or mal-adaptation, which is variously described as public anxiety, nervousness, irritability, unrest, discontent, or strain." According to Lasswell, "the propagandist who deals with a community when its tension level is high, finds that a reservoir of explosive energy can be touched off by the same small match which would normally ignite [only] a bonfire."[32]

There was no question that Putin's prosecution of the Chechen war was taking place in a society whose tension level after the September bombings had increased dramatically. When Voloshin began to investigate the Ryazan incident, he was advised to read Lasswell's book by friends who were aware of the popularity of American political science literature within the FSB. After doing so, Voloshin became convinced that events were being played out according to a scenario written by Lasswell.

At the same time, although the bombings were supposed to have a Chechen "trail," there was no proof of Chechen involvement, and for the Chechens the bombings made no sense.[33] Having won conditional independence in the first Chechen war, the Chechens knew that they easily could lose it if Russia were sufficiently provoked. If it is assumed that the Chechens understood the danger of an invasion but—out of sheer hatred—bombed the apartment buildings anyway, it would have been logical for them to launch new acts of terror once the invasion took place. But none occurred. At the same time, by blowing up apartment buildings in impoverished, working-class neighborhoods while ignoring targets of strategic or symbolic significance, the Chechen terrorists appeared to be declaring war on the Russian people, a response that would have been completely illogical if their goal was to protest the actions of the Russian state.

There may never be conclusive proof of who organized the apartment-house bombings. Definitive evidence bearing on the Ryazan incident is in the hands of the FSB and presumably will never be made public. However, the political situation at the time the bombings took place, the level of preparation, organization, and expertise demonstrated in their execution, and the suspicious nature of the "training exercise" in Ryazan all suggest that the bombings were organized not by the Chechens, who had nothing to gain from them, but by those who needed another war capable of propelling Putin into the presidency in order to save their corruptly acquired wealth. These could only have been the leaders of the Yeltsin regime itself.

In October 1999 Yeltsin's entourage helped to organize Unity, a pro-Kremlin political party that was identified with Putin. At the same time, Fatherland–All Russia, the party organized by Luzhkov and Primakov, was subjected to merciless attacks in the "family"-controlled press.[34] In the end, although Unity had no ideology, it took 23 percent of the vote on December 17, finishing slightly behind the Russian Communist party, which had 24 percent. Fatherland–All Russia, which had been expected to do well, received only 13 percent of the vote.

In light of the results, Luzhkov and Primakov withdrew from the race for president, clearing the way for Putin. The only remaining question then became when to hold the presidential elections. The Chechen war continued to go well, and Putin's approval rating remained high, but there was no guarantee that this situation could be maintained until the scheduled election date in June 2000. If Yeltsin resigned immediately, however, Putin would become acting president, and elections could be held in three months, giving him an enormous advantage. Yeltsin's entourage persuaded him to agree, and on New Year's Eve, Yeltsin resigned, handing over the reins of power.

The elections were set for March 26, and Putin eschewed serious campaigning and avoided even explaining where he stood on the major issues facing the country. As a result, the Russian people elected someone about whom they knew nothing, which allowed them to invest him with hoped-for characteristics.

With the help of the September bombings, the anger of the population was redirected from the criminal oligarchy that had pillaged the country to the Chechens. And since it appeared that the war was being prosecuted successfully, Putin was the recipient of the public support that would have otherwise gone to those trying to fight the death grip of criminals on Russian society.

The result was that Putin won with 54 percent of the vote. Gennady Zyuganov, the Communist leader, received 30 percent, 2 percent less than in the first round against Yeltsin in 1996.

MAY 7, 2000

At just before noon, Putin entered the Andreevsky Hall of the Grand Kremlin Palace and walked down a red carpet toward the podium where Yeltsin was waiting for him. The two men then stood together under the golden double-headed eagle while banks of video cameras recorded what was described as the first peaceful, democratic transfer of power in Russian history.

Yeltsin said that he had not expected to feel such strong emotions. Pronouncing his words slowly, as if he was having trouble reading the teleprompter, he said, "Now we have something to be proud of . . . We did not allow the country to fall into a dictatorship. We preserved a dignified place for Russia in the world community . . . and opened the path to providing normally for the needs of the people."

Addressing Putin, Yeltsin said, "Take care of Russia."

As Yeltsin's political rivals, Zyuganov, Luzhkov, and Grigory Yavlinsky, the chairman of the Yabloko party, looked on, Putin placed his right hand on a copy of the constitution and took the oath of office, promising to guard the rights and freedoms of citizens and the integrity of the government and to follow the constitution.

Putin then began his speech, which he appeared to have memorized. "We are obliged to do everything," he said, "so that the authorities chosen by the people will work in the interests of the people, defend Russian citizens everywhere, in our country and beyond its boundaries, and serve society." He described how, during the election campaign, he had met with people on the street and they had told him, "Please, at least, don't deceive us." Putin promised to work "openly and honestly."

But standing in the splendor of the Andreevsky Hall, Putin also gave the audience to understand that he had established tsarist goals for himself. "In Russia," he said, "the head of the government was always and will always be the person who answers for everything."

In this way, a potential challenge to the criminal oligarchical system in Russia was defeated. The Putin era picked up where the Yeltsin era left off. Alexander Voloshin, Yeltsin's chief of staff, was retained as head of the presidential administration.[35] Mikhail Kasyanov, Yelstin's finance minister, was appointed prime minister, and both he and a majority of his key ministers had close ties to the "family."

Perhaps most important, the Yeltsin family appeared to dictate the choice of the new general prosecutor. On May 16, 2000, the Federation Council discussed the candidacy of Dmitri Kozak. On the following day, however, Putin proposed another candidate, the acting general prosecutor, Vladimir Ustinov. According to the newspaper *Segodnya,* this change of heart occurred after Kozak's candidacy was rejected by Voloshin. The problem, according to the newspaper, was that Voloshin was not sure that Kozak would not continue to dig into the Aeroflot and Mabetex cases.

In nine months, the situation had changed to a degree that many would have not thought possible. With grants of immunity from prosecution for Yeltsin and his family, and a new government that looked very much like the old, the members of the ruling oligarchy no longer had to fear criminal prosecution, and all talk of a reexamination of the distribution of property during the privatization process—the largest corrupt giveaway of state resources in history—disappeared.

You get free cheese only in a mousetrap.
—Popular Russian saying

5 *The Gold Seekers*

On a hot day in April 1995, a long queue formed on a busy St. Petersburg street outside the firm Russian Real Estate. Shabbily dressed people waited patiently for the office to open its doors.

Vera Mozzhilina, the first person in line, had lost 5 million rubles when Russian Real Estate went out of business and had been waiting for seven hours, since 7:00 A.M., with her son, Vasily, to meet with a representative of the firm. Mozzhilina and her husband lived with Vasily and his wife, their daughter, and her daughter in a small, three-room apartment, and they wanted to construct an additional dwelling to relieve the overcrowding. The Mozzhilins had already tried to build one house, but hyperinflation had wiped out their savings, and they could not afford to finish it. To earn money for the new house, Mozzhilina's husband, a truck driver, had gone to the Orenburg oblast to help with the harvest, working sixteen hours a day hauling grain. When he had returned, he and Vera had had the money they needed, but she had persuaded him to invest his earnings in Russian Real Estate until the spring, when the necessary construction materials would be available.

In fact, Russian Real Estate was the hope of many. In 1993 the firm began to saturate the Russian airwaves with advertisements promising to pay 6 rubles a day on an investment of 1,000 rubles, and this launched a gold rush.

Almost overnight, Russian Real Estate organized 46 regional branches and 1,100 sales points in 280 cities. No one knew what Russian Real Estate's exact business was, but the advertisements had a hypnotizing effect. Long queues formed outside the offices of the firm, many of which were set up in rural post offices, and the sight of them lured further crowds of investors.

In fact, Russian Real Estate did not own real estate or anything else. It was a shell company. In January 1995 the firm closed its doors, assuring shareholders that they would receive their money at a later date. The result was panic. Investors again formed lines outside the company's offices, only this time they were waiting no to invest their money but in the vain hope that some small part of it could be saved.

Vera had visited the firm four times to demand that it honor its contract with her. The first three times the staff had said that they could not tell her anything. At her fourth meeting, they had said they would give her her money if she came back a fifth time. Encouraged, she ordered the materials for the house in order to build it that summer.

As they waited, Vera gave her son her raincoat but kept a tight grip on her shopping bag. Vasily had no idea that inside the shopping bag was a glass bottle filled with gasoline.

At a little before 2:00 PM. Vasily left to stand in the shade of a nearby tree. As the hour struck, the office opened its doors, and Vera walked in. Suddenly Vasily heard a thin, child's cry followed by horrible screaming. The queue erupted in panic. Vasily ran in through the crowd. In the corridor there was a sharp smell of something burning, and on the floor of the office he saw, to his horror, the blackened body of his mother. "At least they give money for funerals," she said. Mozzhilina was rushed to a nearby hospital but died there three hours later.

Commenting on the incident, the newspaper *Trud* wrote, "We live in constant stress. We are afflicted with woes to which we are not accustomed. And among them is inflation, which forces many to tempt fate. In fact, the majority of those who put their rubles in Russian Real Estate knew, or at least guessed, that they were taking a risk. But where could one put them in order for them to be safe? We are accustomed to the fact that the government deceives us, but that a person undertook an obligation, promised to make good on it, issued a document, and then cheated us . . . this is hard to accept."[1]

In the months that followed, Vasily tried to learn the exact circumstances of his mother's death. He was sent back and forth between the police and the local prosecutor. In the meantime, the rumor spread in Koltushi, Mozzhilina's village, that her death was a case of murder, not suicide. The village was full of people who had lost money in Russian Real Estate, and they said that the firm had organized the murder of Mozzhilina, a laboratory assistant who had recently taken a job as a house painter to earn a higher pension, to frighten others who had bought shares and now were demanding their money.

The materials of the investigation were finally obtained by a reporter for *Trud*. They confirmed that the death of Mozzhilina was a suicide. Witnesses told investigators that Mozzhilina had been received by M. A. Ingre, the deputy director of the firm. He had told her that he could not give her her money but that after several months she would be able to get it at the post office where she had bought her shares. Mozzhilina had said that she was not leaving until she received her money and then took the bottle she was carrying out of her shopping bag, doused herself with gasoline, put a match to her clothes, and burst into flames.

The beginning of reform in Russia signaled the dawn of hope not only for ordinary citizens but for a new class of swindlers who realized that, under conditions of hyperinflation and in the absence of any type of legal protection, it would be possible to organize dummy firms, collect enormous amounts of money from the population, and disappear.

The generation that came of age during perestroika had watched party and Komsomol functionaries grow rich by appropriating state assets, and it became fashionable among many of Russia's talented youth to work out ever more subtle schemes for deceiving ordinary citizens or stealing their property. Alexander Konanykhine, a graduate of the Moscow Physical Institute who organized a network of profitable businesses, socialized during these years with other graduates of the institute. Lacking opportunities in science, many of the graduates now planned to make careers in business, and Konanykhine was struck by their complete cynicism. A frequent topic of conversation, for example, was the behavior of Russian gangsters, who were criticized not for brutality but for ineffectiveness. At one party attended by Konanykhine, it was suggested that instead of sending hoodlums to threaten every businessman in a certain area, it would be more effective simply to stuff leaflets into mailboxes advertising insurance against fire, vandalism, and theft. Anyone not buying the insurance could then be targeted for arson or physical attack. This idea was later put into effect in various parts of Moscow.

In late 1991 the Russian Exchange Bank began to pay 20 percent on deposits. This rate was several times higher than the interest paid by other commercial banks, and the offer was publicized with the help of professional advertising. Almost immediately deposits began to pour in. For the first time, the market saw that it was possible to attract huge amounts of money with high interest rates. This lesson was learned best of all, however, by unscrupulous operators who found that the possibilities for using high interest rates to attract money from a population with no experience of prudent investment were practically unlimited, particularly if there was no intention to pay.

From 1992 through 1994, 800 dummy firms defrauded nearly 30 million Russians of 140 trillion rubles in what became known as the "theft of the century."

The techniques used by swindlers were designed to take advantage of the weaknesses and gullibility of Russian citizens that had been created by decades of Soviet life.

First, Russians were exposed to an avalanche of false advertising by banks and financial companies. Under the Soviet regime, Russians had been conditioned to put absolute faith in television and the printed word. As a result, when the press filled with advertisements promising enormous returns on investment, Russians tended to trust the promises. They said, "Of course it's true. It was in the newspapers."[2]

The advertising campaign was followed by reports that early investors were making enormous profits. These reports galvanized the country. With the inflation rate at 300 percent, the various pyramid schemes were paying from 1,000 to 10,000 percent. Ordinary citizens began to hear: "Uncle Vanya received three million rubles, and you sit like a fool. Why don't you invest?" People began to think, "I really am a fool, sitting and not investing."

Soon there developed a reliable pattern. The higher the promised dividends and the more active the advertising campaign of a given firm, the more intense was the flood of investors and the faster the rise in the income of the company. Unfortunately, the period during which the firm honored its commitments was correspondingly brief. In the case of the most aggressive companies, it was usually about three months.[3]

By the time many Russians finally caught on to what was happening, they had been left completely impoverished, a condition that, in many cases, would persist for the rest of their lives.

On July 27, 1994, Tamara Tyukalova, a Moscow astrologer, left work early to buy a hundred shares in the MMM investment company. Like millions of other Russians, she already owned shares in the company, whose stock, in just a few months, had increased in value 125 times. Tyukalova took a metro to the Dynamo station and began walking to the MMM office on Leningradsky Prospekt. In the past there had always been free access to the office, but on this occasion she was surprised to see a line of people waiting on the sidewalk outside.

"Are you buying?" she asked a woman in the line.

"No," the woman replied, "I'm selling."

"Why are you waiting?"

"They have no money, so we have to wait."

Tyukalova had not sensed the slightest danger in her investment in MMM. Now, for the first time, she began to feel uneasy. She left the queue, took the metro to the MMM office on Bogdan Khmelnitsky Street, and found a line there, too. The situation was the same at two other MMM offices: people were standing in line to sell their shares and being told that there was no money. Tyukalova forgot about returning to work and rushed home to sell her shares.

Tyukalova had invested in MMM because she needed money to publish the journal *Hermes*, which she edited with a group of other astrologers. The journal increased its circulation as Russians turned to astrology for help in surviving in a new and unfamiliar economic environment. When their savings were wiped out by hyperinflation, many of Tamara's friends became deeply depressed. Having grown up in a country with fixed prices, they had not realized that such a thing was possible. As the purchasing power of salaries was cut in half and the value of pensions fell by two-thirds, millions of people were forced into petty trade, which in Moscow centered on the metro stations. Pensioners began to sell their possessions. Many elderly women bought cigarettes from kiosks and sold them at a markup or sold bread after the stores closed at 8:00 P.M. After work, factory workers bought goods in wholesale warehouses and took them to sell. Even pregnant women participated in the trading. One such woman, Tamara's neighbor, bought heavy lamps after work and stood for hours in an underground corridor trying to sell them to passersby.

Tamara's mother wrote to her that she regretted not having died before the Soviet Union collapsed and people became completely helpless.

It was in this situation that newly organized commercial banks and investment companies began to engage in massive advertising in the newspapers, on radio, and on television. Of the ads, the most engaging and the most ubiquitous were those for the joint stock company MMM. In February 1994 shares in MMM went on sale for 1,000 rubles, and the walls of the metro stations began to be plastered with pictures of three M-shaped butterflies and the words "Flying from the Shadow into the Light." A serial advertising the company began running every night on prime-time television, featuring episodes in the life of Lenya and Katya Golubkov, who invested in MMM. The serial described how Lenya and Katya bought and then sold their shares in MMM, always at a big profit, and finally achieved their dream of buying a house in Paris. Local offices of MMM opened throughout Russia; nearly a hundred opened in Moscow alone. The value of shares in MMM rose dramatically. Ordinary citizens saw that it was possible to buy shares in MMM and sell them a week later for three times the price.

In the meantime the saga of Lenya and Katya continued every night on television. MMM took out full-page ads in the major newspapers showing how much investors could expect to earn in three months, six months, or a year. The firm also sponsored soccer matches and treated Moscow residents to a day of free rides on the Moscow metro. Anyone who called 100 to get the correct time heard the words "MMM—no problem," the latest price of MMM shares, and finally the time.

Russia was swept with MMM fever, which was also referred to as "mani, mani, mani" (a rough approximation of the English word "money"). Tyukalova, who began to buy shares in MMM in March, noticed that the share price was being discussed everywhere: in stores, on the metro, and in cafés. Several newspapers tried to investigate the mechanism allowing purchasers of shares in MMM to realize such phenomenal profits, and there were warnings on the radio about the dangers of the new investment companies, particularly MMM; but these notes of caution were drowned out by the volume of the promotion unleashed on a population that had never been exposed to professional advertising before and by the fact that early investors in MMM were realizing profits of nearly 7,500 percent.

As millions bought shares in MMM, no one bothered to ask how the shares were backed. There were rumors that the company had invested in giant military factories that were hidden underground. But no one possessed details on this or any other investment. At the same time, there was a willful determination not to ask questions and, in that way, to destroy the impression of a magic formula for producing money that allowed everyone to become rich overnight. Few could imagine that 90 percent of the revenues of MMM were being spent on advertising and that, in reality, MMM was investing its money with the sole purpose of enriching a small group of directors and the corrupt officials who protected them.

Throughout the spring, as millions of people were caught up in the cascade of unearned wealth, there was a subliminal realization that no investment could increase in value 125 times in a few months. But millions of Russians, who had never heard the term *financial pyramid*, were mesmerized by the increase in the value of their shares, which, as it later transpired, rested on nothing but the willingness of new gamblers to enter the market and was determined by no one but MMM's directors, who continually raised the quoted price.

Once the spell was broken, however, panic began immediately.

On July 28 Tyukalova rose early to get to an MMM office. She first went to the office on Leningradsky Prospekt, but after seeing a line there stretching around the block, she left for the MMM headquarters on Varshavsky Boulevard. There shareholders from all over the city overflowed the sidewalks and filled the normally busy street. Desperate to redeem their shares, they surged forward, beat on the locked doors of the building, and smashed the windows. Soon thirty OMON militia with clubs, bulletproof vests, and automatic weapons arrived to protect the building, and the people outside formed a long queue to sell their shares. Officially the shares were worth 125,000 rubles each, but no one was sure how much they would receive for them. The progress of the queue was minimal. The area in front of the headquarters was soon filled with dust, dirt, mounds of plastic bottles, cigarette packs, and banana peels. But during the long hours of waiting, well-dressed people entered the building with suitcases full of shares and left with sacks of money.

As night fell, shareholders carrying their certificates in purses, in briefcases, and inside their clothing slept on the sidewalk and on benches and windowsills, converting the barren industrial district where the MMM headquarters was located into a vast outdoor encampment for people whose only capital was hope.

On the following day, new arrivals from the provinces replenished the crowd, and as the hours passed, the shareholders grew restless in the heat. Announcements were periodically broadcast from the building reassuring investors that they would be able to sell their shares for the full price.

Finally there was an announcement that MMM would begin by paying war veterans, invalids, and pensioners. "Please write out statements explaining your situation, and you will get your money," the announcer said.

With this, people of all ages began writing out statements and turning them in under the eyes of the police. Tamara wrote out a statement asking for money on the grounds that she was an invalid and a pensioner.

During the long hours of waiting, the shareholders were buffeted by contradictory rumors. One elderly woman told Tamara that she had heard over the radio that on the following day all the MMM sales points in Moscow would be open. Another woman said over a megaphone that on August 2, shares in MMM would go on sale for 150,000 rubles. Other rumors concerned people who had been suffocated with polyethylene bags for failure to repay loans and people who had committed suicide. Tamara talked with people who had sold their cars and apartments to buy shares in MMM and were now desperate. They had never dreamed that they could lose everything.

Later in the day there was an announcement that MMM would sell new shares, which they called "tickets," for 1,000 rubles apiece. MMM employees began to distribute fliers with tables that demonstrated how, in three months, investors would double their money. This announcement of the tickets inspired a new wave of activity as people unable to sell their original MMM shares fought to get into the queue to buy the new certificates, which featured a picture of Sergei Mavrodi, MMM's founder, and were quickly nicknamed "mavrodiki."

Tamara bought 100 of the new shares after standing in line for three hours. Fights broke out as some people tried to jump the queue, and there were bitter arguments in the crowd.

"They fooled you once, and you want to be fooled again," skeptics said.

"It's none of your business," was the usual reply.

The purchase of mavrodiki, however, did not settle the question of what would happen to the shares that were still held by millions of people. On Saturday, July 30, the MMM headquarters was closed although thousands of people remained in front of the entrance. Militia still guarded the building. As the day wore on, there were periodic announcements to the crowd over the loudspeaker that there had been no change in the value of MMM shares.

People in the part of the crowd where Tyukalova was waiting for news discussed the situation. An elderly woman predicted that by evening the shares in MMM would be selling for 90,000 rubles. Others decided that when trading resumed, the value of each share would be 150,000. The discussion was interrupted by the voice of the announcer.

"Respected shareholders," she said. "I ask for your attention. When I said that the value of your shares was unchanged, I was guided by the quotes for yesterday. If you would like the share price for August 1, I would like to hear some applause." The crowd applauded weakly.

"Thank you," she said. "The value of shares in the joint stock company MMM on August 1, 1994, is as follows: selling—1,195 rubles, buying—1,130 rubles." Gasps rose from the crowd. It was now clear to everyone: the pyramid had collapsed.

Mavrodi, however, had taken steps to shield himself from the fury of his investors. Since the previous winter he had declined to pay taxes and refused to meet with representatives of the tax police. He even demanded of the Ministry of Finance that he be left alone and threatened that, if he wasn't, he would unleash the fury of his shareholders on them.

With MMM tottering on the brink of ruin, he refused to pay a fine levied by the tax inspectorate, and late at night on August 4 he was arrested at his home and charged with "large-scale tax evasion."

The arrest made it possible to offer an alternative explanation for the collapse of the MMM pyramid—that Mavrodi had intended to meet his obligations but was prevented from doing so by the interference of the government. The strategy had its intended effect. Shareholders, desperate to believe that they might eventually get their money back, rallied to Mavrodi's defense. On August 5 a "union of shareholders," organized from people in the crowd outside the main MMM headquarters, began to demand Mavrodi's release. They sent a letter to President Yeltsin that said, "In the half year of its operation, MMM never once deceived us . . . However, as a result of the attacks on MMM by government organs, there was a panic among shareholders that led to a disastrous fall in the shares' value. As a result, we lost the money that we invested in MMM, which, for many of us, was our last money."

The shareholders began to demand that Mavrodi be freed in time for his birthday in late August. The appeal was published in the newspapers, and Tamara in this way learned Mavrodi's birthday. She immediately went home and did his horoscope. She saw that he was the type of Leo who used his powers to take advantage of people and that it was impossible to trust him.

In the meantime Mavrodi, though still in prison, decided to run for a seat in the State Duma from Mytishchi, a town north of Moscow, which had been vacated as a result of the murder of Andrei Aizderdzis, a local businessman. Not coincidentally, as a deputy Mavrodi would have immunity from prosecution.

To run his campaign, Mavrodi's associates recruited people who had been ruined in the collapse of MMM, beginning with invalids and pensioners who had requested the return of their money on grounds of hardship. The length of time that investors had to wait before supposedly being paid was tightly connected to their "activism," which was measured with the help of a system of points. Several women whom Tamara had met in the crowd in front of the MMM headquarters called her to say that they were going to work for Mavrodi and urged her to join them. This time, however, she was not ready to be fooled. "There are enough swindlers in the Duma already," she said.

On October 13 Mavrodi was released from prison, and as the campaign gathered momentum he gave the following explanation of why MMM had been created. "Through MMM," he said, "there takes place a natural redistribution of the free resources of the society in favor first of . . . socially defenseless groups: pensioners, the poor, and the unemployed." Mavrodi promised that contributions to his campaign would help make it impossible for the government in the future to interfere in the operations of MMM under any pretext.

In the end, people decided to vote for Mavrodi for various reasons—in the hope that he would return the money he had stolen from them but also because they believed that anyone clever enough to fool the whole country would make an excellent deputy. There were even those who argued that Mavrodi would make a good president. On October 30, Mavrodi was elected a deputy. In the meantime, Tyukalova learned that many of those who had lost money in MMM had died of heart attacks or strokes.

Once Mavrodi became a deputy, the case against him for nonpayment of taxes was dropped, and although the government had stated that it intended to collect fines from him amounting to nearly 50 billion rubles ($25 million), this money was never paid.

Mavrodi had also violated the securities legislation, which made him vulnerable to a charge of large-scale swindling. The financial broker's license that governed the public sale of stock in MMM did not give management the right to set the share price themselves.

In March 1995 a case was finally opened against Mavrodi on charges of swindling, but it was assigned to a team of three investigators, two of them students, who were burdened with other work. Not a single high-ranking executive of MMM was interrogated, there was no serious audit of the company, and no effort was made to find missing financial documents. At the same time, only a small number of victims of the pyramid scheme were interrogated, although by the most modest estimates the losses suffered by victims exceeded 10 trillion rubles.

Mavrodi did not attend Duma sessions or the meetings of the Foreign Affairs Committee to which he was assigned. Finally, in January 1996, he was deprived of his deputy's mandate for absenteeism, and the investigation for tax evasion was renewed.

But again the case against Mavrodi went nowhere. The investigators had two financial audits with different estimates of the amount of money on which Mavrodi should have paid taxes. Rather than order a third audit, they decided that the case should be dropped.

The lax attitude of the law enforcement agencies toward Mavrodi was explained by many as the result of the desire of government officials who functioned as "silent partners" of Mavrodi to avoid having their role in the construction of the MMM pyramid exposed. It was not until early 1997 that Mavrodi was finally charged with swindling. But by this time, he had disappeared. Several months later, in September 1997, more than three years after the collapse in share prices, the MMM joint stock company was declared bankrupt. In theory, this meant that those who had lost money in the pyramid could demand repayment after the liquidation of the company's assets. But all traces of MMM's assets were now also gone.

When Tyukalova heard that MMM had been declared bankrupt and there was no trace of the company's assets, she took it as further proof that Mavrodi had been protected by high officials in the government. But Tyukalova did not give in to bitterness. She had slowly rebuilt her fortunes, working long hours as an astrologer. Now she was determined to put the past behind her and to move on.

Viktor Veryutin waited calmly as the man who was chain smoking in front of him gathered his courage. They were standing in the deserted stairwell of an office building near Taganskaya Square in Moscow, and the man looked around constantly to make sure that no one was listening.

"The apartment was near the Hotel Budapest," he said. "It was an old communal apartment. One of the rooms was rented under the name Futurum Rus. Between May 1994 and February 1995, the directors of First FSK [First Financial Construction Company], Igor Peterikov, Alim Karmov, and Alexei Shelekhov, visited the room regularly. They brought money in leather sacks, suitcases, and paper bags. They then left by train for the Czech Republic. Each day money was brought in and taken out."

Veryutin now realized how First FSK had operated—and how thoroughly he and thousands of others had been fooled.

Veryutin was a retired colonel in the KGB, who had worked for FAPSI, the section of the KGB engaged in eavesdropping. During the hyperinflation he had lost his life savings of 9,000 rubles, accumulated over thirty-two years. At the same time, the purchasing power of his pension decreased by 70 percent.

Viktor had never been wealthy, but as a KGB officer he had had a good apartment and earned enough to meet his needs. Now he had to economize even on food. After breakfast, he did not eat for the rest of the day. In the evening, he had a meal of tea and bread.

In this situation, Veryutin began to notice advertisements for investment companies and commercial banks. Like many former KGB officers, his knowledge of capitalist investment was limited to what he had learned by eavesdropping on Western embassies. But he was attracted by the advertisements for First FSK. The company was engaged in the reconstruction of buildings on Trubnaya Street in the center of Moscow. It promised investors a return of 240 to 270 percent, which, given the rate of inflation, was a moderate figure. The company was endorsed by city officials, including Mayor Yuri Luzhkov and Vladimir Resin, the deputy mayor for construction. Resin had even said that although some companies cheated people, Muscovites would be well advised to invest in First FSK.

Viktor went with his wife, a high school teacher, and six other former KGB agents to the work site on Trubnaya Street, where he saw a row of three- and four-story nineteenth-century buildings being reconstructed. This tangible proof that the company was involved in a serious project impressed Viktor. He and the other members of the group decided to invest in First FSK.

Veryutin and his wife had no money, but they had a gold watch, a gold necklace, and gold earrings, all of which he could sell for cash. Viktor decided to organize an investment for himself and the others who had gone with him to Trubnaya Street. He contributed 4 million rubles (about $2,000) of his own along with the money of the other retired agents.

For a number of months, First FSK operated normally. In its main office on Miusskaya Street, several dozen operators sat at computer terminals receiving deposits from citizens while, in another part of the hall, tellers paid out dividends. Even when other financial companies collapsed, advertisements for First FSK appeared on television regularly showing an ancient Russian knight on a horse announcing in a stentorian voice, "It's time to receive dividends, gentlemen!"

In late October, however, Viktor received a telephone call from one of his colleagues, who said First FSK had stopped paying dividends and had put a hold on the cashing in of investments. Seized by fear, Viktor at once took the metro to the First FSK headquarters, where a crowd of investors had gathered in front of the entrance.

After several hours, Peterikov came out and addressed the crowd. He said that he was waiting for cash and that the investors' money was safe. He insisted that dividends would be paid.

Peterikov's assurances, however, did nothing to stem the panic. On the following day, 20,000 people filled the courtyard and the nearby street. There was widespread hysteria, but some people held on to hope that they would get their money because First FSK had been endorsed by the city government.

Peterikov came out again, insisted that investors would get their money, and announced that he would receive investors who were experiencing "particular hardships." One of those who was received was Veryutin. Peterikov told him he would get his money in two days. When Viktor returned, however, the doors were not being opened for anyone.

The crash of First FSK stunned investors. Initiative groups of investors were organized in Moscow and twenty-nine other cities. The archway leading to the offices of First FSK was papered with lists bearing thousands of signatures. None of this, however, relieved the anguish of the investors. In 1994–95 the death rate for investors in First FSK was between 15 and 20 percent. Persons calling investors for meetings were frequently told that the investor had just died of a heart attack or stroke.

Delegations from the initiative groups went to the Department of Economic Crimes of the police, the FSB, and the general prosecutor to demand that a criminal case be started against First FSK. Everywhere they were told that payments were being made or were delayed only because of temporary difficulties. The standard reply from the prosecutor of the Tverskoi district was "First FSK made payments and is doing so at the present time . . . there is no basis for starting a criminal case."

In February 1995, during a hearing of the Moscow Arbitrage Court, evidence emerged that the investors' money had been taken out of the country. The investors in First FSK had presumed that their money was being held in the Kalita Bank and that First FSK was one of the bank's founders. Testimony at the hearing, however, established that First FSK was not a founder of the bank, that the money paid to First FSK by investors had never been deposited in the bank, and that in fact First FSK owed Kalita Bank 84 million rubles. On May 11 Peterikov fled Moscow and was never seen again. At the same time, Veryutin learned from one of his former colleagues who was still working for FAPSI and had been monitoring Czech radio broadcasts that a fund calling itself Futurum Aurum was beginning to solicit investments from citizens in the Czech Republic through an advertising campaign similar to the one in Moscow on behalf of First FSK in the summer of 1994.

In early June Veryutin went to the last functioning office of First FSK on Baumanskaya Street and sat quietly in the waiting room, pretending to read the company's brochures.

An elderly couple came in and asked for their money so they could pay for a gravestone for their son, who had been killed in Chechnya. The woman who received them said that the company had no money to give them.

After the couple left, the women in the office began to talk among themselves, unaware that they were in the presence of a professional eavesdropper. They said that it was ironic that First FSK had gathered money from the Russian population to help rebuild a section of Moscow but had actually given it to the Chechens. From the conversation, Viktor realized that the investors' money had been used by Chechen gangsters to buy arms for the breakaway government in Chechnya.

Veryutin put down his brochure and asked them: "Girls, how is it possible that you collect money and give it to Chechens so they can kill our soldiers? Why don't you inform the FSB or the police?"

"What business is it of ours? They pay us money."

"And if it was your fiancé who was killed in Chechnya?" Viktor asked one of the younger women.

"I don't know anything," said the woman. "The person who knows everything is Oleg Boldirev." To Veryutin's surprise, one of the women then gave him Boldirev's telephone number.

For the next three months Veryutin called Boldirev repeatedly in an effort to persuade him to meet. Boldirev invariably refused, but he was always polite and, it seemed to Veryutin, not without sympathy for the investors. Finally, in the summer of 1995, Boldirev agreed to meet him. Boldirev now worked for a private security firm, and he met Veryutin on the street near the Taganskaya metro station. "If I give you any information," he said, "they'll kill me. I've been warned."

Veryutin said, "You know where to find Peterikov. You know perfectly well that our money went to Chechnya."

"They'll kill me," he said. "I really can't tell you anything."

Finally, Boldirev agreed to talk to an officer of the Ministry of Internal Affairs, but only if he was summoned officially.

The police, however, showed no interest in talking to Boldirev. Veryutin contacted Nikolai Neno, the head of the Department of Economic Crimes, who assured Viktor that he would call Boldirev, but did not. Viktor continued calling Neno, but finally Neno stopped even coming to the phone; his secretary said he was "on a business trip."

Viktor called Boldirev and said, "We have to meet again." Boldirev hesitated at first but finally agreed, and they met in a deserted stairwell, where Boldirev described to Viktor how millions of dollars had been shoved into suitcases and taken to a communal apartment at One Petrovskiye Linii near the Hotel Budapest. When Boldirev finished speaking, Viktor for the first time felt that he understood the low esteem in which the Moscow authorities held ordinary Russian citizens. The money that thousands of trusting people, acting on the city authorities' recommendation, had turned in to First FSK had never been deposited in any bank. It had been shoveled into suitcases, taken to a conspiratorial room in a communal apartment and then smuggled out of the country to Prague. Viktor felt he had been spat upon as well as robbed.

Viktor went to One Petrovskiye Linii and knocked on the door of apartment 301. A middle-aged man opened the door. Viktor said that he needed to speak with the people who had previously rented the apartment. The man gave him an address near the Krasniye Vorota metro station. There, at a second-floor apartment, he was greeted by a man about twenty-five years old. "You had an apartment on the Petrovka, and there was a room there where people brought money," Viktor said.

"How do you know this?"

"This is the money of our investors," Viktor said. "It's money that is being used to kill our soldiers in Chechnya."

The young man quickly became cooperative. He described how men had come and gone from the room with bags of money at all hours. He also agreed to talk to the police. Veryutin gave the man's name to the Department of Economic Crimes, but no one called the young man, and no one called Boldirev.

Veryutin was now convinced that he would never get any help from Russian law enforcement authorities, who he suspected were being paid off by the swindlers. But he recalled the Czech broadcasts, which were monitored by his FAPSI colleagues. It occurred to him that he might be able to get help from the Czechs. He called the Czech embassy and asked for a meeting, explaining, "Those who robbed us are robbing you."

To his surprise, he was given an appointment with an economic attaché. At the meeting, Viktor told the Czech diplomat what he knew about the export of investors' money to Prague. The information was duly recorded and apparently made an impression. Several days after Viktor's visit to the embassy, Nellie Pavlaskova, the Radio Liberty correspondent in Prague, visited the office of Futurum Aurum, acquainted herself with the company's documents, and confirmed that the company was established as an affiliate of First FSK in Moscow. The Czech Ministry of Internal Affairs began an intensive investigation of Futurum Aurum.

On March 9, 1996, Alim Karmov, who had not been seen for months in Moscow but was now the director of Futurum Aurum in Prague, called a press conference at which he read a statement addressed to the company's Czech investors. "All these years," he said, "I deceived you and did not speak one word of truth. I did this in order to cheat you out of your money and give it to others. Having fallen into this hole, it was impossible to get out of it and to tell the truth was terrible. I am ashamed to look in the eyes of the people to whom I did harm. You are people, and I am an animal—what's more, a Russian animal."

Immediately after the press conference, Karmov fled to Malta. But he returned to Prague a short time later and was arrested. This led to speculation that he had returned to avoid being killed. In his statement, Karmov had not only stated that he had taken the money of Czech citizens to "give it to others" and that "to tell the truth is frightening"; he had also claimed to be "a Russian animal." As his documents were to demonstrate, however, Karmov, though born in Nalchik in the Kabardino Balkar Autonomous Republic, was a Chechen.

After the arrest of Karmov in Prague, Veryutin and a group of other investors renewed their efforts to persuade the Russian police to investigate the case of First FSK. They met with Pyotr Yuzhkov, the assistant to Kolemikov, the deputy minister of the MVD, and urged him to send an investigator to Prague. Yuzhkov's only reply was "If you want to investigate, go to Prague yourself."

In November 1995 an investigator from the Department of Economic Crimes was finally appointed to the case, but he was replaced, as were his successor and his successor's successor. By May 1997 the department was on its sixth investigator, and like all the others he was hampered by a lack of funding. Many investors, physically ill and emotionally exhausted, began drifting away. Only Veryutin and a few others continued to search for the stolen money despite daily evidence of the indifference of the authorities and the fact that their hope was gone.

On November 25, 1994, Svetlana Osipova was watching the midnight news on NTV when the anchor, Lev Novazhenov, said, "This just in. The morgue has received the body of Vladimir Rachuk, the founder of the Chara Bank. He was found hanged in an office. More information at the end of the broadcast."

Hearing these words, Osipova felt as if she had been hit by a car. She had invested in the Chara Bank, which had just closed its doors. For weeks she had prayed that her money would be returned to her. She had had faith in Rachuk, who, in his frequent television interviews, had emphasized that Chara was a civilized bank whose principal goal was to promote Russian culture. But now it was clear that there would be no promotion of culture and no money for the tens of thousands of people who, impressed by the bank's image, had invested their savings. It occurred to Osipova that she would now have to sell her body organs in order to survive.

Osipova worked as a dispatcher in an apartment building and lived with her husband, a cab driver, and their three children in a three-room apartment. When the free-market reforms began in 1992, the hyperinflation wiped out the family's savings of 10,000 rubles. Even so, she and her husband managed to pay for the funerals of his grandmother and stepfather. Currently they were responsible for three elderly people, her mother and father and her husband's mother, all of whom were in failing health.

The psychological stress caused by the reforms had led to a soaring death rate, and Svetlana frequently heard stories of the indignities visited on the dead. Many people died at home, and while commercial hearses refused to take a body without payment, the municipal hearses were so overburdened that the dead sometimes lay where they had died for two or three days. In this situation, Svetlana feared that in the event of another death she would not be able to assure even that her family members were buried with respect.

In early 1994, advertisements for banks and financial companies offering high rates of return on investment began to appear in the newspapers and on television. It occurred to Svetlana that this might be the way out of her financial dilemma. Unfortunately, she had nothing to invest. Her only possession of any value was the family's three-room apartment, and she felt that she could not risk the family's home.

As the financial pressure grew, however, Svetlana began to reconsider. She pondered advice in the press that capital should not sit dormant but should be made to work. Her apartment was the family's capital. Perhaps it was only logical to turn it into cash and make an investment.

Of the investment companies and commercial banks that were sprouting up, the most appealing to Svetlana was the Chara Bank. Rachuk, the president, was the son of a high official in the Soviet film industry, and the bank had established an oversight committee that was chaired by the film director Nikita Mikhalkov. The bank had sponsored the production of two films and was endorsed by some of the best-known members of the Russian cultural elite.

Rachuk became a well-known figure. He appeared on television and discussed the bank's investment plans. There was a photo of him, his wife, and his children in the newspapers, and Svetlana took it as proof of his honesty that he was not afraid to show his face publicly.[4]

With prices rising every day, people all over Moscow were soon discussing financial companies and where to get the best return on investments.

Finally, Svetlana and her husband decided to sell their three-room apartment on Ramenki Street and invest the proceeds. The family of five began to live with her mother-in-law, occupying a single room of her two-room apartment on the Frunzenskaya Embankment. Osipova received 97.5 million rubles ($75,000) for her apartment and deposited the money under five separate agreements with the Chara Bank. In each case, the contract was for six months, and she was to receive a return of 15 percent a month.

At first, nothing troubled Svetlana. Every time she went to the headquarters of the Chara Bank on Second Tverskaya-Yamskaya Street, she was impressed by the bank's popularity. Outside, people queued up to invest their money, often standing in pouring rain for four or five hours. As they waited, prospective investors spoke about what they would be able to buy in three or six months when their agreements expired. One said he would buy a refrigerator, another furniture. One person wanted to sell an old car and then buy a new one. There were people who needed money for lifesaving medical operations. People spoke constantly about their investments, and it seemed to Osipova that she was participating in the dawn of a new way of life.

The Chara Bank met its commitments reliably, and many people who had invested for six-month periods did not withdraw their money when their deposits matured but reinvested for another six months. Soon nearly 85,000 people had made deposits.

On October 18, 1994, however, Osipova received a call at home from a friend who told her that Chara had stopped paying on its contracts. It was 8:00 P.M., but despite the late hour Osipova took the metro to the headquarters of the bank, where she saw an enormous crowd. Everywhere, terrified people were pushing and crying. Representatives of the bank opened a window and began to address the crowd through megaphones. They said, "There are temporary difficulties. We'll resume work soon." The voice of Marina Frantseva, Rachuk's wife and the bank's cofounder, came over a loudspeaker. "Everyone will be paid in February," she said, "plus four months of interest."

The assurances, however, did not convince Osipova. She felt a sense of panic when she saw the anguished faces in the crowd. For the first time, she had the feeling that the Chara Bank's concern for culture was nothing but a facade.

All that night, Tverskaya Street was blocked by thousands of depositors.

Several of them began compiling lists of names. Svetlana gave her name. When the car of a "new Russian" who was trying to navigate through the crowd knocked over two old women, the driver was saved by the police from enraged investors who wanted to tear him to pieces.[5]

The next day Svetlana joined other investors and went to the local police station. She had assumed that banks were somehow regulated by the government and it was not possible for them simply to take the citizens' money and not account for it. The police, however, told the investors that the Chara Bank was a commercial structure, not a government structure, and that officials of commercial structures did not fall under the criminal code.

When the investors realized that they were unlikely to get any assistance from the police, they flooded into the Tverskoi municipal court, where they tried to file suit against the bank. At first no one wanted to deal with them. Some of the judges were openly hostile. They said, "It's your own fault. You trusted them and spent crazy money." But as the crowds in the halls grew into thousands, paralyzing normal activity, the court started accepting the complaints demanding that Chara honor its contracts.

As the days passed, the area in front of the Chara Bank became a meeting place for depositors, and Svetlana began to go there once a week in the hope of getting news. She prayed that Frantseva had been telling the truth and that in four months she would be able to withdraw her money.

On the night of November 25, however, when she learned that Rachuk was dead, her hope disappeared.

On November 26 there was a huge crowd outside the headquarters of the bank. Rachuk's death was being discussed everywhere, and nearly all the depositors were convinced that he had been murdered. Many suggested that he had been killed because he had wanted to give the depositors their money.

Later that day, Rachuk's body was cremated. The official cause of death was listed as a heart attack. The few investors who managed to attend the cremation tried to get a look at Rachuk's body but were not successful. They wanted to see if there were marks around his neck that would indicate hanging. After the cremation, Frantseva addressed the depositors and swore on her husband's body that she would return their money to them. A short time later, however, she also disappeared.

In the months after Rachuk's death, Osipova tried to recover from her feelings of helplessness and humiliation. Her life, however, had been completely transformed. She and her family survived on meals of potatoes and macaroni and slept five to a room. When Svetlana thought about the likelihood that she would never again be able to afford a home of her own, she could barely speak.

Svetlana had little taste for political action, but to avoid despair she joined a group of Chara investors who picketed the offices of the general prosecutor every Tuesday, calling on him to uphold the law. And, as she spoke to others, she came to understand better the giant conspiracy of which her personal victimization was a small part.

When the Chara Bank closed its doors, it owed its depositors 500 billion rubles. The first question asked by the investors was how much of this money the bank still controlled. As the search began for answers, it became clear that the people who had appropriated the savings of tens of thousands of depositors enjoyed the protection of some of the most powerful people in the country.

After October 18, 1994, the Chara Bank ceased paying on contracts, but it continued to operate. As investors met every week in the courtyard in front of the bank, lights burned in the windows.

Some of the initiative groups of investors began to demand that the bank's license be canceled so that it could be declared bankrupt and new management named. Despite these demands, however, the bank's license was not revoked, and it continued to give credits to dozens of dummy structures that were then liquidated or declared bankrupt. The bleeding of the bank's resources stopped only in March 1996, when the bank's license was revoked by the Central Bank. Shortly afterward, shots were fired through a window into the apartment of Sergei Dubinin, the Central Bank chairman. By the time the Chara Bank was declared bankrupt and new management was named on July 17, 1996, its coffers were empty and almost all its records had been destroyed.

In October a liquidation commission was established, and the Moscow Directorate of Internal Affairs organized an investigative group under the direction of Major Mikhail Larin to uncover the bank's hidden assets. Despite the fact that it was beginning its work two years after the bank closed its doors, the group achieved some significant success in locating property that had been purchased with the money of the bank and legally belonged to the investors.

On April 1, 1997, Larin arrested Frantseva, who had unexpectedly returned to Moscow from exile in Spain, and interrogated her in the Sailor's Silence Prison, where, according to the newspaper *Segodnya*, "he learned much that was interesting." On April 25 an auction was held of ten apartments in two buildings in the center of Moscow—one on Prechistinka Street, the other on Bolshaya Serpukhovskaya Street—that had been traced to the Chara Bank. Already living in the buildings were several generals in the Ministry of Internal Affairs and Sergei Medvedev, President Yeltsin's former press secretary. The apartments in these buildings were sold for 9 billion rubles, and the money was used to begin to reimburse the bank's investors. When the Committee on Municipal Housing refused to transfer title in the apartments to the purchasers, the Tverskoi municipal court launched a criminal case against the committee for nonfulfillment of a court decision.

The investigative group soon also identified Chara Bank property registered to dummy firms on Sretenka Street, in the city of Mitino, and on Lomonosovsky Prospekt.

Hope spread among the investors, including Osipova. On May 23, however, she picked up a copy of *Segodnya* and, with a feeling of horror, read the headline. It announced: "The Keeper of the Chara Bank's Secrets Is Killed: Not One of His Colleagues Believes the Version of Suicide." Larin had been found dead in his father's apartment, shot in the head with his own gun, which was found in his hand. The article said that no one who had known Larin accepted the idea of suicide. Rather, the manner of his death suggested that the murder had been carried out by professional killers who might have gained entry to the apartment by wearing police uniforms. The gun could have been put in Larin's hand after he was shot.

In the days after the killing of Larin, Osipova changed her attitude to the loss of her money. Whereas before, she and other investors had turned to the government in the faint hope that the authorities would try to help them recover some of their savings, she now saw that the forces that had cheated her were themselves part of the government. There was no hope for her, because her exploiters had nothing to fear from the official enforcers of the law.

What does man gain by all the toil at which he toils under the sun? A generation goes and a generation comes, but the earth remains forever.—Ecclesiastes 1:3–4

6 *The Workers*

"One of our women has been diagnosed with leukemia," said Lyudmilla Tikhonova, the leader of the free trade union in the Golubaya Oka Textile Factory, to Viktor Buryakov, the director, as they spoke in his office. "She needs money for food and medicine. I implore you to give her her back pay."

Outside, in the dying light, the snow was turning into dirty slush as it accumulated on the street. Buses and trucks poured exhaust into the frigid night air, and pedestrians who had just got off work crowded the sidewalks where women from the factory were selling the shirts produced by the factory from makeshift stands.

"There is nothing I can do," Buryakov said. "There are many people in difficult situations. We can't help all of them."

"This is not a common cold. This is a serious illness. If your mother or sister had this disease, how would you react?"

"As soon as there is money, we'll give her help."

Lyudmilla got up to leave. She had little faith in Buryakov, but she was still shocked by his cynicism. In that moment she saw how little the workers were worth in the eyes of the directors of the factory. They would not release a gravely ill woman's back pay even to save her life.

The Golubaya Oka factory, a three-story brick building on a busy street not far from the ancient Ryazan Kremlin, employed 500 people and produced men's shirts, sheets, military tunics, and camouflage. Its employees were mostly young single women, many of whom who had grown up in orphanages. Salaries in the factory were low, but for a time they were paid regularly. In 1996, however, there was a cut in orders from the Ministry of Defense, the factory's biggest customer, and the directors stopped giving workers their pay.

At first the directors said the delay would be temporary, but they did not say when the workers would receive their salaries. At the same time, the managers offered to pay the workers in shirts. Some workers accepted the offer and spent five days a week sewing the shirts and the rest of the time trying to sell them. Others refused and insisted on waiting for their back pay. Three years later, they were still waiting.

Through the spring, summer, and fall the women survived with the help of relatives in the countryside, who shared the food they raised on their private plots. As the cold weather set in, however, it became obvious that the women were becoming ill. They lost weight and appeared frail. They developed nosebleeds and fainted. Doctors who arrived at the factory after calls to the ambulance service said the workers were suffering from emaciation and malnutrition.

Finally, in February 1997, after eleven months without pay, the women decided to go on strike. On the last day of the month a free trade union was organized, and Tikhonova was elected chairman. The women then went to their machines and refused to work.

The action by the normally docile employees made an impression on management. The bosses circulated among the workers and tried to persuade them to give up the strike. "Work, be patient," they said. "We have been patient," the women answered.

The strike continued for two months despite repeated threats from the managers. In late May the factory director, Lyudmilla Andreeva, was replaced by Buryakov. Shortly before his arrival on May 31, the workers halted the strike. In return, Buryakov paid each worker 50 to 100 rubles, enabling many to make their first food purchases in months.

For the rest of 1997 the workers received partial payments, enough to induce them to continue working. Among other things, the factory received an order from an American prison, and the women began sewing flannel pajamas for American convicts. To the women's amazement, the pajamas were of high-quality material and had to be sewn with buttons, pockets, and decorative details.

In February 1998, however, the payment of partial salaries ceased. Buryakov explained that the factory did not have the money to pay them, a statement that was greeted with incredulity by the workers.

In fact, the managers of the factory did little to conceal their corruption. The workers saw that the directors took expensive foreign trips at factory expense and that space in the factory was being rented out to stores and the revenue did not appear in any records. They also saw that equipment was disappearing, including imported sewing machines and the factory's cars and trucks, and that apartments belonging to the factory and intended for workers were being sold on the side with no record of what had happened to the money.

Under these conditions, the workers again went on strike. The pattern was the same as before: the women went to their machines but refused to work.

The strike infuriated Buryakov, but the women, despite verbal abuse, refused to yield.

It was in this atmosphere that Tikhonova approached Buryakov about help for the seamstress with leukemia and was refused.

The refusal to deliver back pay for a leukemia victim shocked the women and initially stiffened their resolve. Finally, however, events undermined their will to resist.

In March, a loader, in despair over his inability to feed his family, hanged himself in his home, leaving an invalid wife and two children. Shortly afterward Viktor Purikhov, an electrician, was diagnosed with lung cancer. Lyudmilla appealed to Buryakov to give Purikhov his back pay so he could buy medicine. Buryakov refused. A short time later, Purikhov's ulcer burst, and he died.

The two deaths struck fear into the workforce. Many of the workers began to think that if they did not return to work, they would not be able to count on help from management for anything. In late April the strike was abandoned. In a mood of deep resignation, the workers returned to work hoping that once the factory began to produce shirts again, they would be paid enough to survive.

The condition of the seamstresses at the Golubaya Oka Textile Factory was typical of the situation of workers in Russia. Privatization, which put 80 percent of Russian industrial enterprises in private hands by 1996, was supposed to make workers "co-owners" of their factories, but instead it made it possible to exploit workers in a manner that, in some respects, was worse than the exploitation that had existed under the Soviet Union.

The liquidation of state property removed Russia's factories from the control of the government but did not alter the working relationships inside the factories, leaving the directors, who were the last representatives of the Soviet regime following the dispersal of the Communist party committees, in complete administrative control.

In formal terms, ultimate authority was vested in the shareholders, but in reality the shareholders were not in a position to impose their will on the director. Because the director decided on hiring, firing, and promotions and controlled all information, he could dominate the shareholders' meetings even if he owned only a small number of shares. It was he who decided what information to make available to the shareholders, and with the share-holders' names printed on the ballots, the consequences of voting against him ranged from demotion to dismissal.

In a few short years there was a change in the character of Soviet-era factory directors.[1] Men who had been dedicated to meeting the targets of the economic plan and often knew little else began to strip the assets of their factories.

One technique used was to withhold necessary payments, including salaries, and deposit the funds at interest. The director typically established close personal connections with a local bank, making it dependent on the factory, and thus on him. The factory's income was then deposited in the bank at high interest or invested, with the director and bank officials splitting the income.

Another technique for stripping assets was to create "daughter firms" that functioned as middlemen, charging exorbitant prices for inconsequential services. Finally, as a result of their access to shops and warehouses and control over transport and security guards, the directors were able to organize the theft of equipment, raw materials, and products, which, following privatization, began to disappear in large quantities from Russian factories. In the first years of the reform period, huge lines formed at Russian border crossings as trucks headed for foreign ports with materials stolen from factories at the behest of their directors.[2]

Faced with the rapacity of the directors and their own vulnerability as a result of the collapse of industrial production, the workers often sank into a helpless passivity, which was reflected in letters to Russian newspapers.

"I work at the machinery factory, where our pay is being withheld," wrote a woman in Lipetsk in a letter to the newspaper *Lipetskiye Izvestiya*. "I am supporting a sick son. My pay is extremely low, and even this I don't get. Not long ago, they paid us for February. I begged to be paid for March, but my application is lying on the desk of the chief bookkeeper. I am tired of having to go and ask for the things that I'm entitled to."

The newspaper's "family lawyer" replied: "You can change your place of work, but where are you going to find a factory with vacancies . . . ? You could appeal to the labor board and the courts. But will this really help you get your money? The best advice I can give you is to ask to meet . . . with the director, and maybe, as an exception, he'll agree to satisfy your request."

This incident, described in a bulletin of the IRA-SOK news agency, inspired a brief comment from the editor of the bulletin. "It would be better, of course, not to go to this director but to crawl. You will then impress him with your defenselessness. In this country, they love the humble and submissive."[3]

In fact, it was the defenselessness of Russian workers that, amid the rise of a class of criminalized factory directors and the impotence of the official trade unions, gave rise to the first workers' protests. These protests were crushed ruthlessly, but they demonstrated by their futility the real condition of workers in the post-Soviet era.

YAROSLAVL, DECEMBER 26, 1995

"You have the right not to go to work in a state of hunger. If they accuse us of breaking the law, we have to ask: Who is going to accuse them of violating the constitution, which states that there is a duty to pay for work?"

The speaker was Vladimir Dorofeev, the head of the independent trade union Unity. He was addressing 1,000 workers of the Yaroslavl Heating Equipment Factory who had gathered under an overcast sky in the courtyard of the plant. The managers had warned that anyone participating in the demonstration would be fired, and they videotaped the protestors from the windows of the factory's upper floors. The demonstrators, however, were not intimidated. They cheered Dorofeev's remarks and carried signs reading "Only Slaves Work for Free."

When the meeting concluded, the workers returned to their shops. In some shops, the workforce was divided between those who were ready to operate their machines and those who were not. But in the fuel injector shop, the shop of precision details, and the shop of body details, workers disconnected the electricity, bringing production in the plant to a halt.

The problems in the Yaroslavl Heating Equipment Factory started with the fall of the Soviet Union. Thereafter orders and supplies declined sharply, causing production to fall by more than half. At the same time, hyperinflation destroyed the life savings of the workers, causing mass demoralization. In some cases the savings were as much as 15,000 rubles, which had previously been enough to buy a three-room apartment. Within a few months, it sufficed to pay for a pair of boots.

As living conditions worsened, the local authorities gave the workers parcels of land from the state and collective farms. The workers had little experience in agriculture, but as delays in paying salaries reached one month and began to be regular, many workers started to raise their own food.

In the summer of 1992, throughout the countryside outside Yaroslavl workers were putting up sheds or little houses on tiny plots and digging wells. Each weekend the electric trains leaving for the countryside were filled with people carrying construction materials and pails. Once the harvest began, the trains were so crowded that people had to ride on the steps, grasping the handrails on the outside of the cars.

Dorofeev also took a plot and began spending his weekends growing potatoes and vegetables.

The delays in paying salaries soon reached two months, and the factory began to give workers part of their pay in the form of meals in the factory buffet. The food was of prison quality, but the workers accepted it eagerly, often bringing it home for their children without eating anything themselves.

After the factory was privatized, conditions became worse. Part of the production as well as truckloads of spare parts disappeared. Metal cutting machines were removed and sold on the side. Materials were taken from the construction site of a future sports complex and used to build three- and four-story dachas for the factory management.

By mid-1994, malnutrition and financial uncertainty had led to a deep social crisis. Families broke up as men found it impossible to support their children. Workers who became ill could not afford medical care and died prematurely. There were the first suicides. One day in the factory, a woman stopped Dorofeev and said to him, "Do you know what I'm forced to feed my daughters? Animal feed. I take cow feed, mix it with pearl barley, cook it, and serve it." Dorofeev recalled that the last time people had been forced to eat animal feed was during the siege of Leningrad.

In this situation, Lev Sokolov, the director of the factory, organized daughter firms to sell the factory's products, bypassing the factory's sales department. Soon there were fifteen such firms, all of them run by friends of Sokolov.

One of the daughter firms was Intra-Center, which offered to buy up the workers' shares in the factory for 10,000 rubles each. In response to this offer, Dorofeev tried to calculate the real value of the shares, taking the value of the factory's buildings, raw materials, and equipment and dividing the total by the number of shares. He concluded that the real value of one share was 1,500,000 rubles. On this basis, he tried to persuade workers not to sell, but many, desperate for extra cash, did so anyway.

Soon Intra-Center owned 25 percent of the shares in the factory. A short time later, Sokolov sold the factory's garage to Intra-Center for a nominal price. The factory also liquidated its repair shop and, seven months later, transferred the equipment to Intra-Center. In this way the directors of Intra-Center, a shadowy group of entrepreneurs connected to Sokolov, took over the factory.

For months, as the crisis worsened, the workers were unwilling to take any action over the nonpayment of salaries for fear of losing their jobs. In June 1995, however, Dorofeev and Nikolai Volosyuk, a metalworker, began going from shop to shop, recruiting members for a new, free trade union to fight for the workers' back wages. "Before they ask a slave to work," Dorofeev argued, "they feed him. But here they don't even consider us slaves." On June 4, at a meeting of a hundred workers in the conference hall of the factory, the free trade union was born. It demanded the liquidation of wage arrears and an investigation into the daughter firms that had been set up by Sokolov. Warning strikes were held in several of the shops. In the free trade union's first show of strength, a crowd of more than 1,000 workers gathered in the courtyard of the factory for a meeting. The demonstrators carried signs reading "Who Will Feed Our Children?" and "The Bosses Belong in Prison, Not in the Canary Islands."

Shortly after the protests began, Sokolov resigned, ostensibly for reasons of ill health. With his resignation, the delay in payment of salaries increased to nearly three months.

Alexander Pirozhkov, Sokolov's deputy, was elected director in July. In September Sokolov left for Cyprus on a vacation paid for by the factory, and a few days later he drowned while swimming in the Mediterranean.

The news of Sokolov's death stunned the factory. Both workers and managers were convinced that someone had helped him drown. Sokolov knew about the financial machinations in the factory, and his knowledge would have been dangerous to his former colleagues, particularly at a time when the workers were demanding their back pay. At the same time, hiring a killer in Cyprus, with its large Russian population, would have presented no difficulty.

Sokolov was given a grandiose funeral with a limousine, police escort, sea of flowers, and marble gravestone with a huge portrait made at the factory's expense.

The new director promised to pay all back salaries, but instead the delays in paying wages grew even longer. Workers in several shops staged a wildcat strike on July 22, and Pirozhkov closed down the factory. The lockout ended two weeks later, but Pirozhkov still made no move to pay salaries.

In response, the whole factory struck. Pirozhkov finally agreed to liquidate half of the three-month arrears in wages, and the workers returned to work, but soon afterward the factory again stopped paying salaries.

As the cold weather set in, the workers survived by doing odd jobs and borrowing from each other. Many were attracted by fascist splinter groups and anti-Semitic conspiracy theories. On November 16, 1995, the newspaper *Severny Krai* reported that an epidemic of mental illness had been provoked in the Yaroslavl oblast by the effects of unemployment, uncertainty about the future, poverty, and the loss of money in pyramid schemes and banks. "The latest evidence suggests that one in five [residents of the oblast] is not all there mentally."

Throughout the fall the workers worked without pay. In December, after the mass demonstration addressed by Dorofeev, they struck, bringing work to a halt. The strike lasted for two weeks, until Pirozhkov promised to pay the wage arrears. But the wages never materialized, and indeed the lag in payments increased further. By May 1996 the workers were owed six months of salary, and many, overwhelmed by a sense of helplessness, gave up fighting for their pay.

Dorofeev, however, was determined to continue the fight. With the help of a few managers who secretly sympathized with the workers, he began to gather information about the corruption at the factory.

As a trade union leader, Dorofeev had the right to review the factory's financial records, and he soon made several discoveries. One of them was that although the factory was not giving workers their salaries, Pirozhkov had been paid 48.5 million rubles between December 1995 and June 1996. He also discovered that the factory had paid 391 percent interest on credits of 3.5 billion rubles from Credprombank, although the highest interest rate being charged for such credits during that period was 200 to 240 percent. At the same time, the factory's taxes were not paid directly to the government but to Credprombank so that the bank could first collect interest on the money. Payments had been delayed by two weeks for at least a year and a half. Dorofeev took this information to the prosecutor, and the police arrested the Credprombank executives responsible for the Leninsky raion.

By June the lag in paying salaries had reached eight months, and the workers survived only because they raised potatoes and other vegetables on their dacha plots. Every Monday they arrived at the factory exhausted after a weekend of hard work.

Dorofeev began a campaign to shake the workers out of their lassitude. Using the information he had gathered, he spoke at meetings every day in various shops of the factory describing how the bosses had been stealing the factory's resources while the workers waited in vain for their pay. The workers' indignation was rekindled, and on June 26 they again went on strike.

After the strike began, Pirozhikov met with Dorofeev and promised that the workers would be paid if they began to work. "We have workers fainting from hunger," Dorofeev responded. "If someone fainted into a machine, there would be nothing left of him. It would be like going through a meat grinder. Is that what you want? Our position is simple: first pay, then work."

The strike continued into August. Dorofeev, however, soon found that his success in rallying the workers was affecting his own security. He began to receive phone calls in the middle of the night. Sometimes he heard only heavy breathing; sometimes he was asked, "Did you order a woman?"

On August 26 hundreds of workers marched to the headquarters of the oblast government and demanded that the factory be declared bankrupt; such a declaration would have led to the appointment of new management.

Soon after the demonstration, five men came to Dorofeev's apartment building and asked the neighbors about him. Finally, they came to Dorofeev's apartment when his wife, Nina, was at home. They told her they were "friends from the Caucasus"—an expression that would be taken to mean members of a criminal organization—who needed Dorofeev for a "business conversation." Their appearance threw Nina into a panic. Dorofeev appealed for help to the head of the local FSB, and for a time the visits ceased. Soon afterward, however, Dorofeev's son was shot during an argument, arrested in his hospital bed, charged with attempted murder on the basis of a souvenir knife that was found in his pocket, and later sentenced to five years in prison.

In the meantime the factory increased financial pressure on the workers. In September the workers returned to work and received their salaries for September and October. In November, however, all payments ceased, and by the spring of 1997 the lag in paying salaries had reached nine months.

Dorofeev continued to try to rally support for collective action, but the workers' will to defend their rights had evaporated. The managers began firing workers outright or cutting their salaries (which were not being paid in any case). Finally, Dorofeev himself began to feel overwhelmed by the difficulty of defending the rights of thousands of workers who wanted nothing more than to be paid their salaries.

One night, shortly before May Day 1997, Dorofeev was at home watching television when he heard the sound of bottles in another room. He got up and found his wife lying across their bed in an unnatural pose. He called an ambulance, and she was rushed to the hospital, where the doctors pumped her stomach and saved her life. She had taken sleeping pills. Vladimir found a suicide note, which summed up the impotent anguish of the entire work-force of the Heating Equipment Plant. It read: "Damn you, Pirozhkov."

CHEREPOVETS, DECEMBER 23, 1997

"If you consider yourselves to be cattle, you can work," said Lyudmilla Ivanova, a leader of the free trade union in the Severstal steel mill, to a group of crane operators and metal cutters in the converter shop. "But if there are no cattle here, we have to strike."

The men formed a tight circle around Lyudmilla. "She's right," one of the workers said. "You have to force them to respect you. What happens here is really a disgrace. The pay is miserable, and they don't pay that."

Suddenly the shop was flooded with guards wearing black berets and carrying automatic weapons. They were accompanied by the shop manager. "We'll fire you all," the manager said. "If you don't like it here, get out." The workers, however, held their ground. They had removed the keys from the giant cranes that transported slabs of steel in the shop, and all work was paralyzed. The leader ordered a woman to search Lyudmilla. But five work-ers grabbed a gas-powered cutting torch and turned it on the guards.

"No!" Lyudmilla shouted. "We don't need blood."

Lyudmilla and Anatoly Kosmach, another leader of the free trade union, agreed to leave. "Hold on, lads!" Lyudmilla shouted as she was being led away. She was convinced that the workers would now join the strike.

The Severstal steel mill employs 50,000 people and is one of the two largest in Russia. In 1992, shortly before the privatization of the factory, Yuri Lipukhin, the general director, appointed Alexei Mordashov, the son of a close friend, financial director of the plant. When the mill was subsequently privatized, Mordashov founded a daughter firm called Severstal-Invest, 24 percent of which belonged to the factory and 76 percent to him. The starting capital of Severstal-Invest was 100,000 rubles ($50 in 1993).

The daughter firm soon came to play a key role in the life of the factory. Although the factory had an official sales department, people seeking to buy steel from Severstal were told that they had to make their purchases through Severstal-Invest, which kept 20 percent of the proceeds. As a result, the firm, which employed five people, quickly became a wealthy organization and one of the two biggest taxpayers in the Vologda oblast.

The privatization of the steel mill also led to the birth of a free trade union, which had 2,000 members within six months. The free trade union was small compared with the 38,000-strong official trade union, which distributed vacation packages and apartments, but because its members worked in key parts of the combine, it was a potentially serious force.

In 1993 and 1994 world demand for steel was high, and the workers at Severstal lived well; unlike workers elsewhere in Russia, they were highly paid and were paid on time. In 1995, however, there began to be delays in paying salaries. Because the steel mill was highly profitable, the workers at first assumed that the delays were temporary. But the lag increased to two months and caused serious hardship. Workers borrowed money from each other and put off making basic purchases, including food and clothing.

At this time a shadowy firm called Partner, which was later found to be an affiliate of Severstal-Invest, opened offices in the factory administration building and offered to buy the workers' shares in the factory. The workers, seeing little way to cope with the financial pressure, began to sell.

In September 1995 the free trade union organized picketing to protest the delay in paying salaries, and the lag was temporarily eliminated.

Meanwhile the managers of the factory engaged in large-scale theft, looting the warehouses, writing off high-quality metal as waste, and sending shipments of metal to fictitious destinations. In some cases, entire forty-car trains disappeared.

The thefts, which were publicized by sympathetic managers in anonymous leaflets that circulated in the factory, infuriated the workers, and membership in the free trade union rose to nearly three thousand.

In April 1996 elections were held for a new director. Lipukhin suggested Mordashov. Severstal-Invest had purchased thousands of shares in the factory through Partner, so Mordashov controlled a large block of votes. He was elected without opposition.

Lipukhin, a former worker, had been respectful toward employees, but Mordashov, who had always worked in administration, treated them with contempt, referring to them as "cattle." He traveled everywhere with armed guards. When workers complained about the hiring of new administrators at a time when they were not getting their salaries, Mordashov replied, "Why should I pay you just to move dirt from place to place? I'll pay the managers who sell our production."[4]

The financial empire of Mordashov meanwhile continued to expand. He purchased shares in a number of large factories and became the head of the Metallurgical Commercial Bank (Metcombank), from which Severstal took credits at exorbitant rates of interest. He also purchased newspapers and television stations and soon exercised decisive control in the Cherepovets city duma and the Legislative Assembly of the Vologda oblast.

As the situation at the factory deteriorated, Lyudmilla, who worked as a reporter for the newspaper *Voice of Cherepovets,* wrote sympathetically about the workers. Vladimir Marakasov, the head of the free trade union, invited her to edit their newspaper. A short time later she was invited to be deputy chairman of the free trade union. In December 1996 Marakasov resigned, and Yelena Vinogradova, who worked in the factory's house of culture, was named to replace him. In this way, two women became the leaders of the free trade union.

As the nonpayment of wages became chronic, the factory put pressure on members of the free trade union, warning them that they would be fired for the slightest violation. Nonetheless, the free trade union maintained its membership and in January 1997 organized a demonstration of several thousand in front of the factory administration building to protest the nonpayment of wages.

After the demonstration the factory resumed paying salaries, and then, as in the past, there were new delays. From June through August no salaries were paid.

The atmosphere in the factory was becoming critical. The workers could not understand why they were not being paid if the factory was profitable. The steelworkers pressed for a meeting of free trade union members from all the shops. On November 27 the workers finally met and gave the bosses until December 20 to satisfy their demands for a collective contract, payment of all arrears in salaries, and an end to harassment of the free trade union. The union sent Mordashov a letter describing a plan to avoid accidents at the steel mill during the strike, but Mordashov refused to discuss it.

By mid-December the delay in paying salaries stood at fifty-three days, and it was clear that a strike was inevitable. Lyudmilla and Yelena worked out a plan for shutting down the factory's shops in stages, and activists were assigned to rouse their fellow workers.

On December 19 Mordashov barred the free trade union leaders from the factory. The guards were given a list of twenty-five people who were not to be allowed onto the grounds, and the activists were intensively shadowed. Despite the ban, however, on December 20 Lyudmilla slipped into the factory through an opening in the wall and went to the railroad shop, where she incited the workers to support the strike.

On the evening of December 21, Vinogradova left home with a friend's passport, which she presented to the guards outside her apartment who were waiting to detain her. They allowed her to pass, and she got on a train for Moscow to seek support from human rights organizations.

Later that night, Lyudmilla entered the factory in a truck disguised as a worker's wife who had come to take a shower because the plumbing had broken down in their dormitory. She hid inside until morning, when she joined Sergei Rybkov, another trade union leader, and began going from shop to shop, inciting workers to strike. In the shop that prepared freight cars for intrafactory transport, 300 people stopped working. Part of the metal-shaping workforce also joined the strike. By evening, eight of the principal shops in the factory had stopped work.

Despite the extent of the strike, however, word of it spread slowly, because Mordashov controlled the local press. When a crew from Vologda Television tried to film the strike, the factory guards arrested them and destroyed their videotape. Only national press coverage of Yelena's speech at the House of Sakharov in Moscow partially overcame the information blockade in Cherepovets.

On the night of December 22, Lyudmilla slept at the apartment of a friend. The next morning she entered the steel mill in workers' clothing and went to the converter shop. Her appearance led to the incident in which the workers almost turned a cutting torch on the factory security guards. She was detained until evening.

After leaving the factory, Lyudmilla appealed for help to Tamara Gusnyak, the Cherepovets prosecutor. Gusnyak warned Mordashov that the harass-ment of the trade union leaders was illegal. Gusnyak's warning, however, was ignored, and after the strike Gusnyak received threats against her children and was forced to resign.

Other activists also continued to enter the factory grounds, usually through openings in the wall. There they hid from the guards and met with workers in the shops. As soon as the guards discovered them, they seized the activists, beat them, forced them into cars, drove them into the countryside, and threw them out into the bitter cold.

While this was going on, other union leaders gathered at the factory entrance and asked whether management was ready for negotiations. The answer was "No one is going to talk to you."

As the strike entered its fourth day, other shops joined the protest. In the shop for cold rolled iron, workers halted the cranes and refused to unload the product. They also refused to remove steel that was dipped in vats of sulphuric acid for cleaning, creating the danger of an explosion. Lyudmilla and Karpov arrived at the entrance of the factory and demanded to be allowed to talk to the workers. When the guards refused, Karpov said that the union bore no responsibility in case of an accident. Finally, the guards allowed them to call the shop and tell the workers to resume operating the cranes.

With much of the combine paralyzed, the management quickly began giving workers their pay. By the fifth day of the strike, the workers had been paid for October and part of November, and the time lag had been reduced from fifty-three days to eight.

The flow of money had an effect: although workers continued to join the strike, a large number returned to work.

The fate of the strike now depended on the railway shop, which had not joined the strike but sympathized with it. The shop was responsible for the railroad that linked every shop in the factory; a shutdown there could paralyze the operations of the entire plant.

On December 26 Lyudmilla and seven other trade union leaders again slipped into the factory and entered the railroad shop, where about 100 workers were waiting for them. "We ask you to join the strike," they said. "Mordashov has met only one of our demands." After the activists left, however, Mordashov called a meeting of the shop and promised to raise salaries by 25 percent. He also offered a bonus of 1,000 rubles to each worker not to join the strike.

On December 27, the railroad shop workers met at 6:30 A.M. Lyudmilla, Karpov, and Rybkov urged them to join the strike. Igor Kachalnikov, the chairman of the official trade union in the shop, told the workers that it would be suicidal to do so. The workers in the shop were angry about the years of nonpayment, but one by one they offered the opinion that the strike was doomed. Lyudmilla, who had barely slept for a week, had no strength to argue with them. After forty minutes, they returned to their jobs.

With this decision by the workers in the railroad shop, the strike was broken. Slowly workers in the other shops returned to their jobs, and on January 3 a decision was taken to end the strike.

The suppression of the strike marked the end of the effort by the Severstal steelworkers to defend their rights. A short time after the strikers returned to work, the Severstal management announced plans for layoffs and for closing the giant Martinovsky shop, with its twelve blast furnaces. This news left the workers unwilling to risk fighting further. As the weeks passed, the delay in paying salaries began again to lengthen.

In a discussion of the situation at the plant on Vladimir Posner's television program, it was stated that the factory had made a profit of 1.5 trillion rubles in 1997 but that only 8 percent of that sum had been for salaries. Mordashov, however, gave interviews in which he blamed the failure to pay salaries on alcoholism among the workers.

After one such interview, a handful of pickets gathered in front of the factory administration building to protest. The demonstrators carried signs reading: "We demand that you apologize for your words." Mordashov was rarely seen by the workers, but on this occasion he came out to talk to the pickets. "I'm not going to apologize," he said. "I'm right. The workers do drink."

NEFTEYUGANSK, JUNE 26, 1998, 8:45 A.M.

As the traffic on Oil Workers Street built up and the hazy morning sun promised another sweltering day in the Siberian swamplands, Anatoly Shiryaev, the leader of the free trade union, entered the waiting room for a meeting with Vladimir Petukhov, the mayor of Nefteyugansk. Suddenly a guard ran into the room, disturbing a group of petitioners who were standing together looking over their documents. "They killed someone in the alley," he said.

At that moment, three more guards ran into the room.

"What happened?" Shiryaev asked.

"Two gunmen just shot the mayor."

Shiryaev went outside and joined the crowd that was gathering in the square. Next to the mayoralty was the headquarters of Yugansk Neftigas, the regional oil company now owned by the energy conglomerate Yukos. Only four days earlier, Petukhov had ended a hunger strike to protest the policies of Yukos.

The crowd soon grew to 5,000. Finally, shortly before noon, Viktor Tkachev, the first deputy mayor, arrived and announced that Petukhov was dead. The people in the square had only one explanation for the mayor's death. He had been murdered by Yukos.

Yukos was a vertically integrated company created in 1993 by the Russian government. It consisted of two oil-drilling companies, Yugansk Neftigas and Samara Neftigas; three oil-processing plants; and twelve companies for the sale of oil products.

On December 8, 1995, in an auction held as part of the loans-for-shares program, the controlling interest in Yukos was purchased by Mikhail Khodorkovsky, the thirty-six-year-old chairman of the Menatep Bank and, with a personal fortune estimated at 2.4 billion dollars, one of the richest men in the world. Menatep organized the auction and was represented by the two permitted bidders. A bid from a third firm acting for a consortium of Alfa Bank, Inkombank, and Rossiisky Kredit was rejected for "the absence of properly filled out banking documents."

With no competition, Khodorkovsky purchased the controlling packet of shares in Yukos—the second-largest oil company in Russia, with an estimated 2 percent of the known oil reserves in the world—for $159 million, $9 million above the starting price.[5]

In 1995 Petukhov was the head of Debit, a firm created out of the Department of Drilling and Capital Repairs of Yugansk Neftigas. The firm became a creditor of Yukos, which ran up an enormous debt to Debit for completed work. Debit filed suit against Yukos, which responded by accusing Petukhov of financial irregularities, including concealing half of Debit's profits. Petukhov started to have problems with the tax police. In order to avoid these problems and to force Yukos to pay him, Petukhov decided to run for mayor of Nefteyugansk.

Petukhov waged an openly anti-Yukos campaign. The incumbent mayor had allowed Yukos to pay its local taxes with nonliquid promissory notes, many issued by dubious companies, and Petukhov attacked Yukos for exploiting the region. In addition, the oil workers felt hostility toward Khodorkovsky, openly doubting that so young a man could have amassed such an enormous fortune honestly.

During the campaign, a group of Petukhov's employees sent him a letter accusing him of financial machinations. But Yukos was believed to be behind the letter, and because of the sharply negative attitude in the city toward the conglomerate, it only boosted Petukhov's popularity. Unexpectedly for both Petukhov and Yukos, Petukhov was elected mayor.

The election results set the stage for a confrontation between Yukos and the workers of Nefteyugansk. The new mayor demanded that Yukos pay its taxes with money instead of with promissory notes or property. Yukos, however, paid its tax debt with promissory notes and with a transfer to the city of the airport, with its huge maintenance costs, agricultural installations, and asphalt factory.

In 1998 the price of oil fell from twenty dollars to nine dollars a barrel, and Yukos, which had to pay off debts and foreign credits, paid local taxes only in the first part of 1998 and amounting to only 63 percent of what it had paid during the equivalent period in 1997. The result was that the city had no money to pay the salaries of police, teachers, and doctors.[6]

At the same time there began to be delays in paying oil workers, who now had to wait up to two months for their wages.

Nefteyugansk had always enjoyed full employment and well-stocked stores. Now, for the first time, indigent people appeared on the streets. They were effectively hostages in the city because the oil industry was the only place to work.

In April 1998 Yukos announced pay cuts of 60 to 70 percent and a program of restructuring.[7] Of the 38,000 people who worked in Yugansk Neftigas, 26,000 worked in fifty-one organizations that serviced the oil wells. These organizations were declared independent and left to negotiate with Yugansk Neftigas, which took advantage of its monopoly position in setting prices for their work.

Oil workers, who had always spent money freely, were now impoverished, and the abrupt change in their situation led to an explosion of hatred.

Yulya Korshakevich, an aide to Petukhov who had arrived in 1967, explained the reasons. "The city was an island, surrounded by hundreds of miles of swamps," she said. "In the winter, there were subzero temperatures and perpetual dusk. During the summer, it was difficult to breathe because of the swamp gas. But this was the path to the first oil. We built the first oil well, the first apartment building, all in the most difficult conditions. Now, it's all done, and Khodorkovsky buys it for nothing and throws people out into the street. People have a right to live well. They lost their health in this gasified swamp."

Petukhov began to rally the population against Yukos. At his suggestion, Shiryaev, a worker in the subsidiary enterprise Yugansk-Frakmaster, organized a free trade union, and on May 27, the day of the Yugansk Neftigas shareholders' meeting, the union staged a massive demonstration in front of the Yugansk Neftigas headquarters.

There was a mood of desperation in the crowd. Thousands had not received their salaries or their vacation pay and were unable to take their children out of the city for the summer. There was also an undercurrent of fear. Some of the oil workers did not participate lest they be photographed and fired. The workers who did take part carried signs reading: "Yukos—Bloodsuckers," "Yukos—Get out of Holy Russia," and "A Hungry Teacher Is a Disgrace to the Country."

In his speech to the crowd, Petukhov called Yukos a criminal organization that was growing fat on the sale of oil produced by the people of Nefteyugansk.

On June 2, in another demonstration, more than 25,000 people, one-quarter of the population of the city, filled the central square and demanded the immediate payment of back wages. Petukhov was the main speaker. "No one should dictate to us," he said; "not Yukos, not the center."

After Petukhov finished speaking, demonstrators surrounded the Yugansk Neftigas building, trapping Sergei Muravlenko, a high official of Yukos, inside. The standoff lasted until Yukos agreed to make a partial payment of its debt to the city. From the point of view of the crowd, Petukhov had wrung a concession from the "monster" Yukos.

A short time later, Vladimir Dubov, the deputy chairman of Rosprom-Yukos, arrived in Nefteyugansk and met with the local tax authorities. They announced that the debt of Yukos and Yugansk Neftigas to the city was about 80 million rubles but that the debt of the city to Yukos was nearly 228 million rubles. Petukhov staged a hunger strike, which ended eight days later when a commission was created to verify the results of the audit. In the eyes of the oil workers, this was Petukhov's second victory over Yukos.

Three days later, however, while crossing an empty lot on the way to his office, Petukhov was killed.

As news of the killing spread, the crowd in the square swelled to 30,000. Over the entrance to the mayoralty, signs appeared reading: "Yukos-Menatep —Murderers!" and "This Blood Is on Your Hands!" Speakers from the crowd said, "We know who killed our mayor. This was done on orders of Khodorkovsky." The crowd demanded that deputies in the city duma who had formed the opposition to Petukhov submit their resignations. A petition began to circulate demanding an "end to the looting of Russia." It called for the resignation of Yeltsin and the State Duma and the withdrawal of the license for Yukos to exploit the mineral resources of western Siberia.

When dusk fell, the square was lit by thousands of candles, and funeral music was played over loudspeakers. Meanwhile demonstrators halted traffic on the bridge crossing the Ob River, and someone set fire to the front doors of the apartments of three deputies who were in conflict with Petukhov and suspected of complicity with Yukos. Immediately afterward, nine of the twelve deputies in the city duma fled.

The police did not share the conviction of the crowd that Yukos was responsible for the murder of Petukhov. They gave greater credit to the possibility that Petukhov had been assassinated for his action in closing the city market, which had been run by Chechen gangsters. But the hatred of Yukos in Nefteyugansk was so great that alternative explanations for Petukhov's murder were not considered.

On June 30, Petukhov's funeral was attended by 70,000 people. In the foyer of the local house of culture, where Petukhov's body was lying in state, many people cried openly. From the house of culture, the cortège went to the mayoralty and the Church of Saint Panteleimon before departing for the cemetery. The entire route was covered with flowers.

The emotional outpouring united the city as all ages and nationalities mourned the fallen mayor. Immediately afterward, however, Yukos accelerated its promised restructuring. The oil workers continued to accuse Yukos of the murder of Petukhov, but as fear of unemployment gripped the oil fields, their will to challenge the conglomerate disappeared. There was also a growing sense of foreboding over what would happen to the region when the Caspian Sea oil came on line. In many ways, in mourning Petukhov, Nefteyugansk seemed to be mourning for itself.

"You know, when I buried my father and mother, I did not cry," recalled Viktor Pushkarenko, a deputy in the city duma, "but here, when Petukhov was put in the ground, I could not hold back tears."

My police are my protectors.—Vladimir Mayakovsky

7 Law Enforcement

A light wind lifted the cellophane wrappers and papers in front of the Kuznetsky Most metro station. In front of the double glass doors of the metro, a man was kicking a prone figure repeatedly in the face. The victim, whose face was covered with blood, moaned and shuddered each time he was struck.

Jonas Bernstein, an analyst for the Jamestown Foundation *Monitor*, and I entered the metro and went to the police station, where a police officer was sitting at his desk going through some papers. "There's a man being beaten outside on the sidewalk," I said. "He needs help."

The policeman gave no sign that he had heard me.

"He's being kicked in the face," I said.

The policeman continued to leaf through his papers.

Under the law, the police must register any report of a crime, even if it is made verbally. Officers assigned to a metro station cannot leave their posts because the metro is considered of special importance, but in the case of an assault in progress, they are supposed to report the attack to the nearest police station, which should react immediately. This policeman, however, made no move to do anything.

I prepared again to try to get his attention, but now Jonas intervened. "You did your best," he said. "Now let's get out of here. The next thing you know the bandits will go after you."

With that, we gave up, leaving to his fate the person being beaten on the sidewalk outside.

The encounter at the Kuznetsky Most metro station was not an isolated incident. People in danger in Russia are frequently ignored by the police, and many ordinary citizens have paid for the indifference with their lives.

There are several reasons why the police often do not make a serious effort to defend ordinary citizens. In the first place, the Russian police, as in the past, are organized to support the political authorities against society. They do not have a psychological predisposition to defend individuals. In this respect, the situation is little different from what it was in the nineteenth century, when the marquis de Coustine noted that police in Russia harass the innocent but, in a crisis, do not rush to offer aid.

Also as in the past, the Russian police are judged according to a quota system that rewards a low crime rate and a large number of "solved crimes." This system induces the police to avoid anything that will ruin their statistics. As a result, they avoid accepting complaints from citizens who have been the victims of difficult-to-solve crimes. If a citizen's apartment is robbed, they may try to persuade the victim not to report it by saying, "Nonetheless, we won't find them." They also may avoid classifying a person who has disappeared as missing or an unidentified corpse as the victim of foul play because, in both cases, they may become involved in efforts that threaten their record for solving crimes.

Perhaps most important, the police in postcommunist Russia do not want to defend ordinary citizens because they regard it as an unproductive use of their time. After the fall of the Soviet Union, many of the best law-enforcement professionals left the intelligence services, the Interior Ministry, and the Office of the Prosecutor General to work for private security bureaus at fifteen times the pay. Many of those who were left were incapable of getting a job elsewhere. These officers saw that government officials all around them were using their positions to obtain illegal wealth and, following their example, began to use every opportunity to solicit bribes.[1]

In time, the police began to resemble just one more criminal gang, and their obsession with making money left them with neither the time nor the energy to enforce the law.[2]

The most common forms of police corruption became well known.

Many police officers extort payoffs from street vendors. Thousands of people sell cigarettes, newspapers, flowers, and novelties on the street in Moscow and other Russian cities, and all of them are vulnerable to pressure from the police.

The usual approach is for a policeman to ask a vendor if he has a license to trade. If the vendor can produce a license, the policeman informs him that he is in a place where trading is prohibited even if dozens of people are trading all around them.

Formally, illegal trading is punished with confiscation of the item and a fine, but the police are usually open to negotiations. "At two o'clock the cops seized our goods—we were selling leather jackets," explained a street trader. "We went to the station in a paddy wagon with a grating in the back. They told us that the court would determine our punishment. We sat in a cell for four hours and then began to bargain intelligently. We settled on 500 rubles."[3]

Another form of corruption is extorting bribes from drivers on the highway. In Moscow, each traffic policeman (GAI) is expected to fine nine drivers and three pedestrians a day.[4] Once his quota is filled, however, he can fine drivers without bothering to turn over the proceeds to the state. A policeman will stop a car, preferably a late-model foreign car, and explain to the driver that he has violated the traffic laws. The driver may not have been guilty of any violation. But since he has little way of proving his innocence against the word of a traffic policeman and the required payment is always less than the fine for his supposed crime, the incident almost always ends with the payment of a bribe.

In one exercise carried out by the Ministry of Internal Affairs to assess the level of corruption among the Russian traffic police, a truck with a shipment of liquor traveled from Vladikavkaz to Rostov-on-Don, passing twenty-four GAI posts. Only two posts refused to waive the inspection in return for a bribe.[5]

In June 1995, Chechen terrorists in a convoy of covered trucks were able to bribe their way past twenty-two GAI posts without being checked as they traveled to stage a raid on the southern Russian city of Budyennovsk.[6]

The type of corruption most likely to affect ordinary citizens, however, is the shaking down of persons during routine identity checks.

According to the law, the police can check a citizen's documents if there are reasons to suspect that he has committed a crime or is preparing to commit one. There is a list of reasons why a person may be stopped, for example, if he is not dressed according to the season, if his fists are injured, or if there is blood on his clothes. In practice, however, the police stop whomever they want. It is enough to look a police officer in the eye and quicken one's pace or, on the contrary, slow down. The police are particularly disposed to stop anyone from the Caucasus, but they are also on the alert for new arrivals in the capital. That is why it is risky to ask a police officer for directions.

Once a person is stopped, if he is not carrying his passport or, in the case of a visitor to Moscow, if he did not get a registration stamp, he will be detained.

The police also detain persons who are drunk or have been caught urinating in public.

All of these persons are taken to holding cells in local police stations that are called "monkey cages" and from which the fastest way out is to pay a bribe.[7]

One evening V. was walking in the center of Moscow when an attractive young woman approached him and asked if he knew where to find a store that sold foreign books. V. had heard of the store but did not know the exact address. Nonetheless, he started a conversation with the woman and continued it for as long as possible. Finally, however, the woman left, and V. headed for the metro.

At that moment he was stopped by two police officers who demanded to see his documents. V. showed them his identification as a member of the union of journalists, but one of the officers demanded his passport. V., who knew his rights, insisted on presenting it only in a police station. He was taken to the police precinct in a nearby metro station, where he handed it over and the officer copied his information on a sheet of paper.

"What were you talking to the girl about?" the policeman asked unexpectedly.

"That's my business."

"So you won't admit anything?"

"I have nothing to admit."

The police officer rubbed the tips of his fingers with his thumb.

"You wanted to fuck her, didn't you."

"Listen, I showed you my passport. What more do you want?"

"We want to know more about the woman. She had a nice body. Why don't you slip us her telephone number?"

V. was silent.

"All right," said the police officer. "I'll detain you on suspicion of committing a crime."

"What crime?"

"We've got several murders connected with narcotics. And a few on sexual grounds too. We'll see what fits, and then you'll be sent out of here in a prison convoy."

V. tried to understand what was happening. It seemed to him that this was all a terrible dream.

The police officer took V. from the precinct in the metro to the police station that served the local area. V. was brought before the duty officer, who was obviously bored but had a friendly expression. He asked V. whether he had been drinking and whether he had urinated on the wall of the metro station. To both questions, V. answered no.

V. was next put in a monkey cage, which was full of other people detained on the street. Most of his fellow prisoners were being held because they had not been carrying their passports or had been caught relieving themselves in public. In each case, the police had asked how much money the offender had and then imposed a fine equal to this amount. No receipts had been given and none requested.

The arresting officer arrived and took V. to a room on the third floor for interrogation. As questioning proceeded, police officers carried on frank conversations from a telephone on an adjoining table about payoffs with the relatives of arrested persons.

The interrogation continued for hours. The arresting officer did not ask for a bribe directly. But as the questioning wore on and he painstakingly went over every one of V.'s movements in the course of the day, it became clear to V. that this was what he was waiting for.

Finally, the officer said he would charge V. with a crime. "You resemble a wanted rapist," he said, "and we've got a wagonload of cooperative witnesses."

"You are not afraid?" asked V.

"Of what?"

"That you'll go too far. As far as I know, prosecutorial oversight has not been abolished."

"That's a trifle," said the officer. "The law is the taiga and the prosecutor is only a bear." V. was taken to be fingerprinted and then was put in a cell where he was told that he would spend the night.

At 11:00 the next morning, V.'s arresting officer appeared and again tried to intimidate him into giving a bribe, telling him that he was about to be charged. V., however, continued to refuse to offer a bribe. Finally the police officer arranged for V. to receive his passport and let him go.

At first V. was relieved to be free, but after some time passed, he vowed to take action against the police officers who had humiliated him. His friends and relatives, however, managed to dissuade him, arguing that he would only be destroyed. With great difficulty, V. finally accepted their advice.[8]

Yekaterina Karacheva, a reporter for *Kriminalnaya Khronika*, also ended up in a police holding cell.

Karacheva was looking for Karbyshev Street and approached a policeman for directions. Instead of helping her, he demanded her documents. She handed him her press card identifying her as a correspondent for *Kriminalnaya Khronika*.

"Did you spend a long time drawing this?" he asked, and then, without waiting for an answer, demanded her passport.

Karacheva said she did not have her passport.

"That's what I thought," he said. "Get in the car. We're going to the station."

"Can I take a look at your documents?"

"No, you can't."

"Why not?"

"You should have asked when I asked to look at yours."

"But I want to know who arrested me."

"You'll find out in the station, and, in general, shut your mouth."

Karacheva was taken to the police station for the Khoroshovo-Mnevniki district and put in a holding cell with seven other people. She was not searched, so the police did not find the notebook and pen that she was carrying, and after the police left she began taking notes. One of the occupants of the cell asked her what she was doing.

"I'm gathering material for an article," she said.

"If you want," he said, "I'll describe for you how our valiant police stop people and put them in the monkey cage."

"Why only you?" the others asked.

One of Katya's fellow inmates said that he worked as a peddler. Often while resting on a bench he was approached by the police, who asked for his documents. The next question was "What's in the bag?" The police then checked the bag that contained his wares. "Aha, goods! You're trading in an unauthorized place."

The peddler then had a choice. He could pay a "fine," which was negotiated on the spot, or he could insist that he was not violating the law and refuse to give the police anything. In the latter case he was arrested, taken to the station, and put in the monkey cage, where the police could forget about him for the rest of the day. It was easier just to pay the "fine."

Another inmate described how he had been standing with two friends drinking beer near a metro when the police arrested them. They were taken to a police station and put in a holding cell with other slightly inebriated persons. The police waited for four hours and then released them at 2:00 A.M., taking a payoff from each.

The men left the police station and went back to the metro, where they encountered another patrol and were again arrested. They were taken to the same station and again put in the monkey cage, where they were recognized by a policeman who had worked the previous shift. "What are you doing here?" he asked. They explained what had happened, and he released them without demanding a fine. "Get out of here," he said, "and make sure I don't see you again."

The men returned to the metro station. It was nearly 4:00 A.M., so they had no choice but to wait until the metro began running. They went to an all-night store, bought some beer. and chatted with the saleswomen. The guard, however, called the police, and they were again arrested and taken to the police station. This time they were not put in the holding cell. The men asked the police for a discount as "regular customers." A duty officer promised that the next time he saw them, he would give them a lesson in good behavior with the help of a nightstick, and let them go.

Before long a police officer took Karacheva to the boss of the station. He gave her a lecture about the need to carry a passport and then apologized. She had spent only forty minutes in the monkey cage, but she later told friends that that was enough to give her an idea of the operations of the police.[9] She signed a paper stating that she had no complaints about her treatment by the police and was released.

The atmosphere of physical insecurity created by the ineffectiveness of the police pervades Russian society, undermining the very notion of rule by law. Russians have come to think of their world as completely lawless and to assume that, in dealing with crime and intimidation, they are completely on their own.

The vulnerability of ordinary people was demonstrated in innumerable concrete cases.

On a wintry day in late 1998, Svetlana Lebedeva returned home to her Moscow apartment after a lengthy hospitalization to find workmen milling about and the furniture gone. Her jewelry, shoes, and clothing were also missing.

When Svetlana asked her husband, Boris, what had happened, he said that he had removed some things from the apartment while it was being repaired. A short time later, however, he filed for divorce, and Svetlana, an invalid who could not work, found that her bank account, to which Boris had access, had been emptied.

Some of the couple's neighbors told Svetlana that Boris had a lover and that the furniture, clothes, and jewelry could probably be found at the woman's apartment. They even provided the address. In his filing for divorce, Boris asked for the question of the division of property to be dealt with in the future. This meant that the issue could be postponed indefinitely. Svetlana, whose pension was 500 rubles, was left with no way to survive.

Svetlana did not know where to turn. A friend mentioned the legal aid clinic of the Moscow Helsinki group, and she appealed to the staff there for help. With the assistance of Anna Gusarevo, a legal student who worked with the group, Svetlana filed a motion asking for alimony and an immediate division of property. She and Anna went to the 75th district police station on Kutuzovsky Prospect and presented a statement to the local beat officer, describing the theft. The statement included the address of Boris's lover and suggested that this was where the police would be able to find the missing property.

After the two women handed in Svetlana's statement, the beat officer read it and turned it over in his hands. Finally, he said, "I don't have the right to take this statement. You should give this to the office of the Ministry of Internal Affairs. It's only fifteen to twenty minutes away on foot."

When Svetlana and Anna reacted with surprise, he said, "Of course, I can accept your statement, but you understand that if I take it, I'll send it by post. It will take at least a week to get there, and then it will lie there for two weeks before it is taken by an investigator. Do you realize how much time you'll lose? If you take it there yourself, you'll save three weeks."

Anna felt that something did not make sense, but she thanked the officer and left with Svetlana for the office of the Interior Ministry, which had responsibility for several of the local police stations.

When the women arrived at the ministry, a duty officer studied the statement. The conflict of thoughts was written on his face. Finally, he said, "You are addressing this statement to the wrong boss."

"I can change the name," Anna said.

"No, no," he said. "This is an official document. You have to rewrite it entirely and bring it back tomorrow."

Anna had no desire to come back on the following day, which was a Saturday, but she rewrote the statement and returned with her husband but without Svetlana, who was ill. This time the duty officer took her statement and disappeared for forty-five minutes. When he returned, he said, "You don't have the right to make such a statement. Where is your victim? She is the one who should submit this statement." Anna said that Svetlana was ill and explained that she was turning in the statement at her request.

"I was at your office yesterday for an hour, and a duty officer promised to take this statement," Anna said.

The officer told her to wait for a minute and then went upstairs. It was obvious from his manner that he did not want to deal with the situation. As Anna waited, the police shouted at prisoners, most of them apparent vagrants, who were standing behind a metal separation. Finally the police officer returned with an investigator.

"You understand that this is Saturday," he said. "There is no one available right now. Come on Monday."

"If you don't want to take my complaint," Anna said, "please explain in writing that you don't accept it and list the reasons."

"I can't give you a statement."

"Then take *my* statement."

The investigator was now furious. "What's wrong with you?" he shouted. "Don't you see that we're extremely busy?"

"You're behaving very aggressively," Anna said.

"How should I behave with you?"

"You should behave decently. You have no right to shout at a law-abiding citizen."

"OK," the investigator said finally. "We'll take you to our chief."

Anna was taken up some stairs to the office of a senior police officer. He asked Anna when the theft had occurred. She said that this was written in the first line of the statement. He asked her where the victim was, and Anna repeated that Svetlana was ill.

"The victim should come and bring her passport."

"Svetlana Lebedeva has given me her power of attorney, and I have described the events as she related them to me."

"You need to sign a statement that you won't give false testimony," the senior police officer said.

"All right then," Anna said. "I'll sign a statement that I won't give false testimony."

The senior officer now had no way out.

"Your power of attorney is written on a computer," he said, after some hesitation, "and your behavior inspires doubt that you're really connected with this affair. Nonetheless, we'll react to your statement."

After four hours, Anna felt that she was finally getting somewhere, and she called the officer's attention to the address where Svetlana believed her things were located.

The senior officer now said that the police would go with Anna to talk to Svetlana, and a group consisting of Anna, her husband, two beat officers, and the investigator went to Svetlana's apartment. At the apartment, Svetlana confirmed the facts in the statement and said that she had asked Anna to help her.

"You see," Anna said. "I am the representative of this woman. Will you now take the statement?"

"No," the investigator said. "You describe what happened very briefly. You need to write what happened in more detail. Explain the incident word for word and bring in the statement on Monday."

At this point Anna no longer had the strength to argue. She also feared that her husband would lose his temper, so they left.

On Monday Anna brought a complaint written by Svetlana to the local office of the Interior Ministry. In it Svetlana described every detail of what had happened, and the police at last accepted the statement. A week later, Anna called the ministry and asked who was working on the case. She was transferred from one person to the next. In the course of a week, Anna called more than two dozen times to ask what action had been taken without getting an intelligent response. Finally, she wrote a complaint to the raion office of the Ministry of Internal Affairs. When she got no reply, she wrote again, and again got no answer.

Anna finally complained to the Moscow headquarters of the Ministry of Internal Affairs and then to the prosecutor for the Dorogomilovsky raion. She received no answer from the Moscow office, but she and Svetlana did get a response from the prosecutor. He invited them to his office and told them that he had studied the materials of the case and had ordered the police to investigate the theft of Svetlana's belongings and report on their findings by June 28.

Anna now decided to find the police officer who received the order from the prosecutor. After many telephone calls, she located him and went to the station where he was working. When she asked him what he had done in Svetlana's case, however, he looked at her blankly.

"The prosecutor has demanded an answer by June 28," she said.

"June 28," he repeated. "Why is it so urgent?"

The deadline came and went, and with little hope Anna left Moscow for the summer intending to resume the search for law enforcement in the fall.

On January 25, 1998, at 5:00 P.M, Tatyana Teterina, a twenty-five-year-old single mother, left the apartment of her aunt, Anna Tsaryapova, promising to return in an hour. An hour passed, and she did not return. Several hours later, there was still no sign of her.

At about 11:30 a man walking his dog found Tanya's body under a tree. Her head was swollen, apparently the result of being struck with a blunt object. The passerby called the police, and Tanya's body was taken to a nearby morgue. Tanya had no documents, and the police could not identify her.

The next morning, however, Anna called the police and explained that her niece was missing. The fact that a young woman's body had been discovered the previous night had been noted in the morning incident report. Nonetheless, when Anna asked for help in finding her niece, the duty officer said, "If she's still missing in three days, come in and write a statement."

Anna felt a stab of panic. But she prepared to wait three days to make an official report. It did not occur to her to demand that the police begin an immediate search. Instead, she began searching for Tanya herself.

Tanya's parents, Mikhail and Galina Romanov, were able to leave their apartment for only brief periods because Galina was caring for Tanya's four-year-old daughter, Dasha, and Mikhail had just been operated on for cancer. So Anna began calling Tanya's acquaintances.

Soon Anna reached a woman who had been with Tanya the previous night. The woman said that she and Tanya had spent an hour on Parkovaya Street, ten minutes away, chatting and smoking. At about seven Tanya had run out of cigarettes and said that she was returning to her aunt's apartment. This was the last that the woman had seen of her.

Anna called Tanya's friends and went to the homes of those who did not have telephones, but none had any idea what had happened to her.

At home, Galina sat on her knees before an icon and prayed. "God," she said, "it's all in your hands." Dasha, who realized from the adults' conversation that her mother was missing, at first said nothing and then, without warning, suddenly began crying and said, "I'll never see my beautiful mother again."

Anna went back and forth between her apartment and that of Tanya's parents, which was in a neighboring courtyard, and tried to imagine what could have happened to her niece. Tanya had been despondent about her divorce and the absence in her life of a man, and she was given to erratic behavior, having once passed out at a drunken party. But it was inconceivable to Anna that she could have disappeared for more than twenty-four hours if she had not been harmed.

The following afternoon, Galina took Dasha for a stroll and several times saw women who, from a distance, resembled Tanya. Dasha ran up to the women and each time returned and said, "It's not Tanya."

On the morning of January 29, Anna went to the police station and wrote a statement declaring that her niece was missing. To Anna's surprise, the duty officer asked Anna what Tanya had been wearing and then left to check some records. When he returned, he said, "Let's go to the morgue." Anna was driven to the morgue in the nearby city of Fryazino, where she was shown the body that had been found in Schelkovo. It was Tanya.

"Galya," she said, speaking over the phone in a hysterical voice moments later, "our Tanya was murdered." For three days while her family agonized, Tanya's body was lying in a morgue only a few miles from her home.

Tanya's funeral was held a week after the murder. No one was surprised that the police had ignored Anna's original inquiry, even though the body of a female murder victim had been found in the area. "We have become accustomed to the idea that if a body is found without documents, the police will make no effort to seek the relatives," said Nastya Perfilyeva, a friend of Tanya's. "If someone disappears, we have to call around to the morgues, because no one will look for them."[10]

They were also not surprised by indications that the police had no intention of seriously investigating the case.

After Tanya's body was identified, the police interviewed Anna, Tanya's parents, and her friends. But the interviews were perfunctory, and no one was interviewed twice. A relative of Anna's who worked for the Ministry of Internal Affairs in Moscow called the Schelkovo police several times and on each occasion talked with a police officer who described some work that was being carried out in connection with the case. But he said that he had the impression that if it had not been for his calls, the police would have made no effort to investigate the murder at all.

The case was not easy to solve. There was no apparent motive, and there were few clues. A police officer told Anna that Tanya was probably killed by a drug addict whom she may have asked for a cigarette. A half-smoked cigarette was found near her body.

At the service to mark the fortieth day after Tanya's death, Anna realized that Tanya's killer would probably never be found. She was left with only one hope—that her niece's killer would eventually be arrested in connection with another crime.

At 8:30 P.M. on January 13, 2000, Tatyana Zelinskaya left the train station in the village of Yudino, crossed a pedestrian bridge, and began walking toward her apartment a short distance away.

It was a mild evening, and the surrounding forest was covered with a blanket of snow. Tanya turned down Krasnaya Street, a well-lit thoroughfare lined on both sides by one-story wooden houses. Other people who had gotten off the train were walking nearby, and she could see her apartment building in the distance. Suddenly something struck her painfully in the back. She turned and saw a man in his twenties wearing an oversized jacket and holding something near his stomach. He fired two more shots; one grazed her abdomen, and the other missed. She fought to keep her balance, but blood began running down her legs. She took a step and fell.

Tanya had married Vladislav Bezzubov in 1994 and divorced him in September 1997. At that time Bezzubov, who was deep in debt as a result of a series of unsuccessful commercial ventures, demanded that Tanya sign over their joint property to him. Bezzubov continued to live in the same apartment with Tanya and her sister, Nina, and the two women's daughters, and he began to threaten both women. On one occasion when Tanya was absent, Nina and Bezzubov got into an argument, and Bezzubov beat Nina savagely.

After her sister was beaten, Tanya went to the Yudino police department and wrote out a complaint. In response, Bezzubov was picked up, held for three days, and released without being arrested.

In November 1998 Bezzubov moved out of the apartment but made harassing phone calls, sometimes simply breathing into the phone and at other times making threats. "For $200 or $300," he told her, "I can arrange to have you killed. No one will look for you, and no one will care." Despite the pressure, Tanya refused to sign over her share of the property. Instead, she tried to expedite court hearings, which, at Bezzubov's insistence, were continually postponed.

In July 1999 at 8:00 A.M., Nina left home in Yudino to catch a train to meet Tanya in Moscow. As she neared the station, she was attacked by two men in leather jackets, one of whom beat her with a metal pipe, knocking her unconscious. She was picked up off the rails, carried to the platform, and taken to the Odintsovo hospital. Several days later Bezzubov called Tanya and said, "You've received your first warning. If you don't respond, there will be a continuation."

Tanya went back to the Yudino police. She said that her ex-husband had called her and admitted his connection to the attack on Nina. The police, however, declined to take action against Bezzubov. They said that the dispute was a family matter and needed to be resolved at home without the interference of the authorities.

On October 29, Nina, who had suffered a skull fracture, broken jaw, and concussion, prepared to return to her job. On her way to work, however, she was attacked again, this time by a young man in a ski mask who beat her with an iron bar. Her body was thrown on the railroad tracks where an express train was due in five or six minutes. A man walking his dog saw Nina lying on the rails covered with blood and pulled her to safety. A short time after the attack, Bezzubov called Tanya again and said, "Did you see what happened to your sister? Next time, it will be even worse. We'll kill her."

Tanya was now frantic. She went again to the Yudino police and wrote out a statement in which she described Bezzubov's call and his admission of responsibility for the nearly fatal attack on Nina. The police took the statement but did not call her. She finally went to the station and asked why Bezzubov had not been arrested. The duty officer said that they had decided not to open an investigation because "we have only your word."

Tanya now decided to try to defend herself in a different way. A friend of hers told her about Your Rights, an organization that gave legal advice and material assistance to the families of former prisoners, and she appealed to them for help.

Vladimir Singayevsky, the chairman, listened to Tanya's story, and at his request Sergei Shashurin, a deputy in the State Duma, wrote to the Yudino police and asked why no criminal case had been opened in connection with the attack on Nina. Alexander Chernikh, the chief of the Yudino police, wrote back that the police had declined to open a criminal case because Bezzubov, who was mentioned in Tanya's complaint, had been out of town when the attack occurred. Yet in their statements to the police, neither Tanya nor Nina had claimed that Bezzubov had carried out the attack on Nina himself. They had said only that he had taken credit for the attacks and had threatened the women afterward.

Tanya continued her daily routine, but she lived in fear. In the meantime Bezzubov intensified his campaign of harassment and threats, calling her at all hours, ridiculing her, and making repeated references to the fate of Nina, who was still in the hospital.

Finally Singayevsky sent two members of the group to warn Bezzubov that they were following the case and to tell him not to harass Tanya. On January 13 Tanya was shot in the back as she returned home.

Immediately after the shooting, a crowd of people formed around Tanya, an ambulance was called, and she was taken to the hospital in Odintsovo. The doctors there pronounced her out of danger, and an investigator from the Yudino police took a statement from her as she lay in her hospital bed. Despite the shooting and Bezzubov's history of threats, the police still declined to start a criminal investigation against him.

Tanya now decided to concentrate all her efforts on obtaining an official ruling on the division of property in the hope that once the matter was settled, there would be no reason to terrorize her. A hearing on the matter was scheduled for February 3, 2000.

At the hearing, Tanya, accompanied by a representative of Singayevsky's office, told the judge that her life was in danger and a decision on the division of property needed to be taken immediately. The judge, however, postponed the case until April, noting that Bezzubov had told the court that he was ill.

In April the four apartments that Tanya and Bezzubov had owned together were divided between them. But the harassment continued. Anonymous callers advised Tanya to "guard her health." Bezzubov also called, although when Tanya heard his voice, she hung up.

In June someone set fire to the car belonging to a friend who had agreed to live with Tanya and Nina in order to provide protection. Thoroughly frightened, Tanya went again to the police. A duty officer took her in to see Chernikh, who told her that the police were fed up with this "domestic scandal." When Tanya told him that she had already been shot and now was afraid of being killed, Chernikh offered a suggestion. "Why don't you use the same methods against him that Bezzubov is using against you?"

Tanya returned home and realized that, in the jungle in which she lived, Chernikh was probably right. She could either hire bandits to eliminate Bezzubov or sell her belongings and move to some place where Bezzubov would not be able to find her. Tanya's parents lived in Ukraine, and they could help Tanya and her sister find a place to live there.

One morning in October, Tanya asked me what I thought. Bezzubov and an unknown man had followed her menacingly after a court hearing that denied Bezzubov's appeal of the decision on the division of property. I told Tanya that, given the lack of protection, the best thing for her and Nina to do would be to leave for Ukraine as soon as possible.

A Russian naval officer lays wreaths on the water during the
memorial ceremony of August 24, 2000, for the crew of the nuclear
submarine *Kursk*, which sank following an explosion during a
training exercise, killing all aboard. *Izvestiya*

The *Kursk* at port. *Murmansky Vestnik*

Moscow mayor Yuri Luzhkov (left) speaks to journalists at the site of the bombing of an apartment building on Guryanova Street on September 9, 1999. The government attributed the bombing to Chechens but this was never proved. Vladimir Novikov

The aftermath of the bombing of the apartment building on Guryanova Street.

The remains of the Samara police headquarters after a devastating fire on February 10, 1999. The fire has officially been called an accident, but many believe that it was arson.

Police investigate the murder of a young woman who is assumed to have been the victim of a contract killer.

Shareholders in MMM wait outside the investment company's central office in
Moscow on July 24, 1994, in the hope of getting some of their money back after
the collapse of the share values. Alexander Ivanishin

Former president Boris Yeltsin (right) and Vladimir Putin leaving the Kremlin Palace after Putin's inauguration as president. Dmitri Astakhov

The site of an apartment building in Volgodonsk that was bombed in September 1999. The government also attributed this bombing to Chechens.

Relatives and friends mourn victims of the Volgodonsk apartment bombing.

Andrei Klimentiev is released from prison on April 21, 1997, after serving eighteen months, pending a new hearing on charges that he stole $2.4 million in currency credits. While awaiting the hearing, Klimentiev successfully ran for mayor of Nizhny Novgorod, but the election results were overturned, and he was sent back to prison in May. Nikolai Moshkov, ITAR-TASS

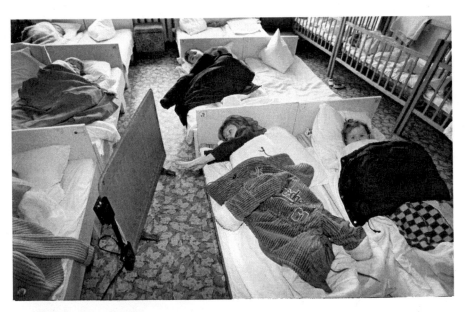

Children in a Vladivostok kindergarten huddle for warmth around an electric heater. Vladimir Sayapin, ITAR-TASS

Anatoly Bykov, the chairman of the board of directors of the Krasnoyarsk Aluminum Factory (KRAZ), denouncing his former ally Alexander Lebed, governor of the Krasnoyarsk krai, at a press conference, December 8, 1998. Vitaly Ivanov, ITAR-TASS

Evgeny Nazdratenko, who as governor exercised near-dictatorial power in alliance with organized crime in the Primorsky krai. ITAR-TASS

Viktor Cherepkov, the mayor of Vladivostok who fought the corruption of the krai governor, Nazdratenko, at a rally of his supporters.
Vladimir Sayapin, ITAR-TASS

Svetlana Kotova, the former Miss Russia who was killed when the man she was living with, Alexander Solonik, Russia's leading professional killer, was murdered by rival organized crime members.

Выписка
...ла №1 учредительного съезда
...ластной общественной организации
...политический союз "Уралмаш".

Members of the Uralmash criminal organization celebrate the founding of their "social political union" in a Yekaterinburg restaurant. *Argumenti i Fakti*

A depositor in the Chara Bank expresses his feelings in the wake of the bank's collapse. Mikhail Klimentiev

If you live with wolves, learn to howl.—Russian proverb

8 Organized Crime

SAMARA, FEBRUARY 10, 1999

Shortly after 5:00 P.M. in the Samara police headquarters, several employees on the third floor noticed the smell of smoke. At first they assumed it was coming from a garbage fire in the courtyard. As the smell became stronger, however, they left their offices and went into the corridor. At that moment, fire flashed along the wall, the corridor filled with smoke, and the lights went out in the entire building.

By the time the first firefighters arrived, the fire was burning out of control on the third and fourth floors, and the main stairway, the most likely escape route, had filled with searing, acrid smoke.

As a crowd on the street looked on in horror, heavy black smoke began pouring out of every opening in the building. People crowded to the windows and began screaming and begging for help. To avoid being burned alive, dozens climbed out of the windows and hung onto the sills, sometimes three to a window. When their grip on the ledges weakened, they jumped, aiming for snowdrifts. But in every case they missed and were smashed to pieces on the pavement.

Firemen tried to rescue two women from a ledge on the fourth floor using a ladder that reached only to the third floor. The fireman who went up the ladder was about a yard from the window. As he extended his arm to the women, one of them lost consciousness from the smoke, fell to the ground, and was killed. The second jumped and was caught.

Soon red flames rose fifteen feet above the building's roof. Ammunition and computers exploded. The inferno melted the guns in the police arsenal, charred metal safes, cracked the windows of nearby apartment buildings, and sent thousands of police documents spiraling in hot updrafts into the night sky.

For hours the fire raged while poorly equipped firemen fought to bring it under control. At 5:00 A.M. the building collapsed. When the last pockets of flames had been extinguished, rescuers searched for bodies in the smoking rubble. An early tally showed fifty-seven dead and twenty missing, all of them presumed dead. The fire had also destroyed virtually all the local documents of the Ministry of Internal Affairs, including records of the investigation of organized-crime groups in the city of Togliatti.

Togliatti is the site of the Volga Automobile Factory (Avtovaz) and the criminal capital of the Samara region. The factory, which was founded in the 1960s, employs 110,000 people, and its mile-long assembly line turns out a new car every twenty-two seconds.

Even under the Soviet regime, Togliatti attracted criminal elements. But with the advent of privatization bandits began to join together to organize large, structured criminal gangs.

The privatization of Avtovaz was accomplished via a sequence of complex financial maneuvers that a whole series of subsequent government commissions found impossible to penetrate. Its result was that large stakes in the factory were acquired by the factory directors. A short time later, 380 firms were created for the resale of cars. These firms received the cars at giveaway prices and sold them at a huge profit. The founders of many of these firms were also the directors of the factory. It quickly became known in Togliatti that the factory had been carved up among its "generals" and "colonels" (as the executives were called), and residents watched with quiet fury as huge dachas for factory management began to appear on the shores of the Zhigulevsky Sea. Soon, however, the gangs in the area had grown strong enough to force corrupt factory managers to "share" their newfound wealth. The most powerful of the gangs was that of Vladimir Vdovin (Mate), a martial-arts specialist who began his career stealing spare parts. One of Vdovin's lieutenants, as well as his driver and best friend, was Dmitri Ruzlyaev (Big Dima). But Vdovin and Ruzlyaev quarreled, and Ruzlyaev left to form his own gang. Allied with Vdovin was a Tatar gang headed by Shamil Danulov (Shomok); allied with Ruzlyaev were two Chechen gangs headed by Shamada Bisultanov and Suleiman Akhmadov.

By 1992 the bandits began to meet the car dealers outside the factory gates and demand payments of up to 10 percent of the cost of each vehicle. The tribute was invariably paid, because anyone who refused risked being killed. As a result, the bandits were soon making sums of money that would have been unimaginable in the Soviet Union.

Togliatti soon became one of the most gang-ridden cities in Russia as well as one of the most violent. In 1994, forty-one people were killed in Togliatti as the opposing gangs fought over spheres of influence. The local newspapers covered the killings as if they were reporting on sporting events. Residents woke up to headlines such as "Two More Are Smashed!!!" The cemetery filled up with ornate black gravestones interspersed with marble tables and chairs. On one side of a pathway were members of the Vdovin group. On the other were the graves of members of the Ruzlyaev group.

In the mid-1990s the gangs reached an agreement on dividing up the Avtovaz production. The production of the factory's "A" shift was divided between the gangs of Ruzlyaev, Bisultanov, Akhmadov, Igor Ilchenko, and Miron Mokrova, as well as a private security bureau, Forpost, which consisted of former police officers, and Kontinental, a supposed fund for the support of law enforcement. The involvement of the last two organizations gave credence to accusations that the police were working with the gangsters. Cars released during the "B" shift were controlled by the Vdovin gang, Danulov, the Kupeev brothers, and the Krestovsky group.

The peace, however, was not destined to last. The Avtovaz factory concluded contracts with the dealers calculated on production of 5,000 automobiles a day, although it was equipped to produce only 2,500 a day. Conflicts arose over which orders would be fulfilled first. To enforce his claim, Ruzlyaev hired killers to liquidate members of the Vdovin group. Vdovin's group retaliated in kind. In an attempt to stem the bloodshed, Radik Yakutian, the head of the investigative department of the oblast prosecutor's office in Samara, began an investigation. He, too, was killed.

In the meantime, the gangs were trying to find a way to penetrate the 1,500-acre factory complex in order to steal spare parts and cars right off the assembly line. This became possible when, in 1995, the gangs gained access to the Avtovaz computers, which gave them a new instrument of pressure on factory management.

Soon the factory directors allowed representatives of organized crime onto the territory of the factory. They feared that otherwise the gangsters would sabotage the main computer and the conveyor. "Businessmen" connected to the bandits were given annual passes that allowed them to enter the factory and, with the help of midlevel bosses who received regular cash payoffs, organize the theft of spare parts and cars, in many cases hiding them on the factory grounds. Managers who tried to defend the interests of the factory took a huge risk. Yuri Bolotov, the head of the transport shop, was killed for refusing to allow the theft of spare parts.

By October 1997 there were 230 people with ties to criminal organization operating in the factory. In 1997 the gang wars began again, and in the course of twelve months nearly 200 people were murdered in Togliatti while losses from the theft of cars and spare parts ran into the billions of rubles. The factory, which should have been highly profitable because of low labor and raw materials costs, lost hundreds of millions of dollars a year. The losses were translated into huge tax arrears.

Law enforcement authorities in Moscow proposed a crackdown on the criminal elements, but the directors of Avtovaz warned that firms dominated by the bandits controlled nearly all the automobile-carrying trucks, and a refusal to unload the cars could halt the work of the entire factory.

Nonetheless, on October 1, 1997, the Ministry of Internal Affairs carried out "Operation Cyclone" against organized crime at Avtovaz. Three thousand operatives from the MVD, the prosecutor's office, and the tax police converged simultaneously to block the factory's exits and seize its computer files. In the first stage, all the representatives of organized crime were expelled from the factory, and more than sixty special passes giving the bearer the right to drive cars out of the factory without inspection were withdrawn. It was later learned that these cars had frequently been used for removing stolen details and spare parts. In hiding places on the factory grounds, the police found 500 locked cars whose keys and documents were missing. Information about these cars had been erased from the factory computers.

The raid also unearthed evidence that gangsters connected to Avtovaz had carried out sixty-five murders of company managers, car dealers, and business rivals and that at least fifty-seven of the firms created to sell the factory's production had either been founded by directors of Avtovaz or employed their close relatives.

The information gained as a result of the raid led to the opening of nearly a hundred criminal cases. This documentation, however, was lost when fire broke out in the MVD headquarters in Saratov.

The relatives of Tatyana Polushkina, a forty-nine-year-old police colonel, were able to identify her body only by the ring that had melted around her finger and a small onyx pendant that had baked into her body. The burned remains of Vadim Gordeyev, a thirty-eight-year-old investigator with the Economic Crimes Unit, were identified among those of other officers because of his broken toe. Irina Kolesnikova recognized a fragment of the charred body of her friend Galina Smenyakina, a thirty-nine-year-old criminal investigator, from scars from recent surgery.

Funeral ceremonies were conducted with twenty closed caskets, rimmed with red and black ribbons, that were placed in the playing field of the municipal stadium on February 13. Seventy thousand people attended. Nurses in white overcoats were on hand to care for distraught relatives gathered around the coffins, in some cases giving them injections to calm them.

On February 18, investigators announced that the cause of the fire was a lighted cigarette that had been thrown into a receptacle full of papers. This explanation was greeted with disbelief in Samara. Numerous witnesses had seen the fire break out in three different places at once. All three sources of the fire were on the third floor, but at least two were isolated from each other by a thick brick wall that divided the entire building, including the roof, into two parts. At the same time, the unprecedented speed with which the fire spread through the building (an earlier fire in the building in 1980 had been successfully contained) suggested that it had been carefully planned. It was also suspicious that the fire alarm system had not been working at the time of the fire and that although film from the surveillance cameras in the building's courtyard captured the height of the fire, an earlier portion of the film that would have shown how the fire began was hopelessly ruined.

The fire put an end to the serious prosecution of organized crime in Togliatti. The criminals resumed control of the factory, and no charges were brought against the overlords of Avtovaz as a result of "Operation Cyclone," the biggest anti–organized crime operation of the Yeltsin era.

The situation in the Avtovaz factory reflects a central fact of Russian life, the power and savagery of organized crime. Gangsters in Russia are not a marginal phenomenon confined to such areas of the illegal economy as narcotics, prostitution, and gun running. They control large parts of the legitimate economy, and neither a powerless public nor the organs of law enforcement have the means to bring them under control.

In 1997, 9,000 criminal groups in Russia with nearly 600,000 members controlled an estimated 40 percent of the Russian economy.[1] The U.S. Central Intelligence Agency estimated that more than half of Russia's twenty-five largest banks were either directly tied to organized crime or engaged in other illegal activity.[2] Criminals dominated the market in oil products, aluminum, real estate, restaurants, hotels, and alcohol, and they controlled the wholesale and collective farmers' markets. In large parts of the country, they subordinated the local government and, through it, received support for their businesses and direct access to government funds.

The influence of gangsters is so powerful that they dominate the culture. Their language—"fenya," a form of labor camp slang—is used by government officials, entertainers, and media personalities.[3] Their songs are sung at social gatherings, and they are the heroes of novels, films, and television series.

Organized crime created a world of limited freedom in which millions of Russians live under constant threat of violence to replace the total lack of freedom that existed under communism.[4] The success of the gangs in establishing their domination was in turn a result of police corruption, ties with political leaders, and a total disregard for human life. These factors made the gangs ruthless machines of coercion, ideally suited to the conditions of a society without law.

The gangsters' first project was to corrupt the police. Russian bandits enriched by extortion contributed part of their gains to the *obshchak,* or criminal treasury, and used another part to pay off police officers, particularly the chiefs of the police stations in whose districts they operated.[5]

The usual strategy was to make payments through a firm that the police official had registered in the name of a relative or friend. The firm was paid for some mythical service provided to an enterprise controlled by the gang. In return, the police official ignored the gang's activities, particularly extortion from businessmen.

In cases in which a police official could not be bribed, the gangs sought ways to blackmail him. The Solntsevo gang in Moscow was well known for collecting compromising material on police officials and members of their families. One technique was to organize a lover for a police official's wife so that she could then be blackmailed into pressuring her husband. Another, more widely used method was to involve the officers' children in compromising situations, such as enticing them to run up large gambling debts that they could not repay.

The result was that the police were largely neutralized. In fact, if a businessman went to the police and complained that bandits were demanding money from him, the response was often to begin an investigation of the businessman. This inevitably showed that he had been doing business off the books, and the complainant was arrested for tax evasion.

Sometimes the police act as enforcers for the gangs. A police officer will often walk past a row of booths in a city market, shaking hands with the vendors until he sees someone he doesn't recognize. At that point, the following scene may unfold:

"Who do you work for?"

"For Vasya."

"What?!"

The policeman then brings his boot down on the table, sending the vendor's goods flying in all directions. From this, it is clear that the bandits controlling the market have not received any payoff from Vasya or have not received enough.

Besides corrupting the police, Russian gangsters establish high-level political connections. This is possible because, when the reform period began, gangsters were treated as a legitimate economic interest group, and it quickly became understood in political circles that friendship with bandits was potentially lucrative.

One gangster who established close ties to the political authorities was Otari Kvantrishvili, who, until his assassination in April 1994, combined the careers of criminal boss and civic leader.

Kvantrishvili was a talented wrestler and candidate for the wrestling team of the Soviet Union in the Olympics. In 1966, however, he was convicted of rape. In the 1980s he got a job as a wrestling coach for the Dynamo sports complex, where he trained many boxers, wrestlers, and weight lifters who would later become leaders of Moscow's most powerful criminal organizations. He also established relationships with a number of thieves professing the code, including Vyacheslav Ivankov (Yaponchik).[6] When Ivankov was arrested and sentenced to fourteen years in prison for banditry, Kvantrishvili assumed guardianship of his children.

While working at the Dynamo stadium, Kvantrishvili organized his own gang and made money from currency speculation, gambling, and extorting protection money from prostitutes in Moscow's leading hotels. Having amassed his first capital, Kvantrishvili turned to entrepeneurship, founding a holding company, Association Twenty-first Century, which sought to engage in the export of oil, timber, and nonferrous metals. For this, however, Kvantrishvili needed political contacts. He developed these with the help of a close friend, Iosif Kobson, a singer with ties to political leaders and the Russian underworld. Kobson became the association's "vice president for humanitarian questions," and through Kobson, Kvantrishvili established connections with members of Yeltsin's entourage, with Moscow mayor Yuri Luzhkov, and with high-ranking officials in the Ministry of Internal Affairs and the FSB.

Through widespread bribery Kvantrishvili soon benefited from a flow of lucrative export contracts. To bolster his respectability, he organized the Lev Yashin Fund for the Social Defense of Sportsmen, which funded sports programs and provided aid and job training to impoverished athletes.[7] "Sport is the only means of saving the nation," he explained. "That's why I am building sports schools—to divert young people away from drugs and from screwing each other up the ass."[8]

The Yashin Fund helped make Kvantrishvili a Moscow celebrity. He appeared frequently on television discussing the situation of athletes and became a frequent guest at beauty pageants, sporting events, and celebrity parties.

As Kvantrishvili's wealth grew, his web of connections steadily widened. With Luzhkov's assistance, he began to import tax-exempt vodka, a huge source of income. He also established interests in automobile dealerships, oil trading firms, and an oil refinery. At the same time, he arbitrated criminal disputes and intervened for prisoners with high-ranking officials of law enforcement, gaining a reputation of never refusing a request for assistance.

Kvantrishvili was soon the criminal world's unofficial emissary to society, and vice versa. Criminals turned to him to lobby their interests with high officials, and officials and businessmen relied on him to intercede for them with the gangs.

In the summer of 1993, Kvantrishvili's connections produced their most impressive result. Yeltsin signed a document authorizing Kvantrishvili to organize a sports center. The center's expenses were to be covered by the sale abroad of aluminum, oil, and cement from the state reserves, and it would be exempt from taxes and customs duties through 1995.

The agreement over the sports center, however, was to prove dangerous for Kvantrishvili. The center was a monopoly that, by making deals between foreign firms and domestic producers, was capable of generating huge profits. Kvantrishvili's criminal competitors resented the fact that they would have to do business through the center and, as a result, suffer financial losses.

At the end of 1993, Kvantrishvili decided to enter politics. To this end, he created his own political party, Sportsmen of Russia. On April 5, 1994, however, he was killed by three shots from a sniper as he left a bathhouse in Stolyarny Lane surrounded by bodyguards.

At Kvantrishvili's funeral in the Vagankovskoye cemetery, the crowd consisted in almost equal parts of members of the political and cultural elite and representatives of the criminal world. Among the well-known public figures attending were Luzhkov, Gusinsky, Kobson, Shamil Tarpishchev, Yeltsin's tennis coach, and Alexander Rosenbaum, a popular singer. As Kvantrishvili was laid to rest next to the grave of the venerated Russian bard Vladimir Vysotsky, Rosenbaum said, "The country has lost—I'm not afraid of this word—a leader."

Another example of the close ties that gangsters establish with the political authorities is the relationship between the Solntsevo brotherhood and the city of Moscow.

The Solntsevo brotherhood is believed to collect tribute from 30 percent of the commercial structures in Moscow, and it is closely connected to the city government and particularly to Sistema, the financial holding group run by people close to Luzhkov.[9]

The Solntsevo gang was organized by two former waiters, Sergei Mikhailov (Mikhas) and Viktor Averin (Avera-Senior), who decided to create a gang of a new type modeled on the American mafia. The gang's principles were discipline and unquestioning subordination, including readiness to carry out any order of the gang's leaders. Punishments ranged from dismemberment to execution, and the gang's new approach, combined with business acumen and a disregard for the thieves' traditions, produced results. In a short period the gang took over the entire southwest side of the capital, collecting protection payments from taxi drivers, kiosk owners, and the operators of small businesses and controlling gambling, prostitution, and the trade in stolen automobiles.

By 1995, in the opinion of specialists, the Solntsevo gang controlled hundreds of firms and banks in Moscow, Samara, Tyumen, and abroad.

Sistema was founded by Vladimir Yevtushenkov, a Luzhkov family friend, who combined the Moscow Committee on Science and Technology (MKNT), a former city agency; a group of highly profitable Moscow trade and financial firms; the Moscow Bank for Reconstruction and Development (MBRD), which managed city funds; and Region, a security firm run by former Soviet KGB chief Vladimir Kryuchkov, to form a new conglomerate that began to do an enormous volume of business with the city.

Although city-owned businesses, despite the advantages they received from the municipality, generally had to face tough commercial challenges, Sistema's subdivisions were granted near monopolies practically without competition.

Today Sistema is a $2 billion financial industrial conglomerate with more than 150 companies and 55,000 employees. Sistema's insurance company, Lider, insures the Moscow metro. The Sistema-controlled Kedr-M is the largest company authorized to sell gasoline in Moscow. Sistema's information companies make the metro's magnetic cards; its construction arm is involved in the city's mortgage program and a city-funded program to renovate large apartment buildings.

Yevtushenkov sits on a twenty-four-member Moscow municipal board and holds an official position as Luzhkov's economic adviser. In November 1998 he was a principal organizer of Fatherland, the political movement created to support Luzhkov's bid for the Russian presidency.

The Solntsevo gang's ties with Sistema go back to the early 1990s. Yevgeny Novitsky, the current president of Sistema, started in business as the chairman of the board of the IVK company, which was later partially owned by the Solntsevo gang's SV-Holding.

On May 31, 1995, Novitsky was held and fingerprinted after being discovered among the guests during a police raid at Averin's birthday party at a restaurant in Prague. A confidential report citing sources in the Ministry of the Interior and the FSB, a copy of which was received by *Le Monde,* affirmed that Novitsky, since becoming president of Sistema, had not taken a single decision without the agreement of the Solntsevo brotherhood.[10] The high-level connections of the Solntsevo gang were reflected in the gang's seeming invulnerability in Moscow. At the end of 1993, a massive hunt was organized to arrest suspects in the murder of Valery Vlasov, the director of the Valery casino, who had paid tribute to the Solntsevo group. Mikhailov was one of those arrested, but he was released that evening.

Mikhas was subjected to searches on several occasions, after which he left Russia and established himself for a time in Israel. In his absence, some efforts were made to crack down on the Solntsevo group. The most serious was "Operation Zakat," which was carried out by the Moscow RUBOP with the assistance of the police Economic Crimes Unit at the end of August 1995.[11] Nearly 500 police took part in the operation, and from 6:00 A.M. to 11:00 P.M. they detained bandits all over Moscow. In the course of the operation, the police checked more than three dozen addresses, forcing doors or breaking them down.

But in the end, only 23 of the 2,000 members of the Solntsevo gang were detained, and, of these, only one, Alexei Kashaev (Cyclops), was a significant figure. Kashaev, however, had quarreled with Mikhailov and had been in hiding in the Kaluga oblast. It was obvious that the leaders of the gang had been informed in advance of the raid and that only those bandits were arrested whom the gang either did not succeed in warning or did not want to warn.

In fact, the Solntsevo gang had no shortage of allies at the highest levels of law enforcement. One night, Igor, a leading Moscow journalist, was celebrating an award he had received for reporting with a group of officers in the headquarters of a federal law enforcement agency. Shortly before midnight, after they had been drinking for nearly five hours, the chief of the investigative division said, "I know a place. Let's go." Igor, the chief, and a lower-ranking investigator got into a car and began traveling across Moscow.

"Where are we going?" Igor asked.

"It's a secret. You'll find out," the chief said.

They left Moscow, entered a dark forest, and arrived at a clearing where there was a two-story house surrounded by a large fence. They went to the door. "Lads," the chief said, "we are now in the lair of the Solntsevo criminal organization."

Igor immediately became sober. He and the investigator looked at each other in disbelief.

The door opened, and the chief was greeted and embraced by a man in his thirties. All four then went up to the second floor, where there were a billiard table and a long table laden with vodka, beer, black caviar, sausage, and salads. The men at the table invited the new arrivals to sit down, and there were toasts to getting acquainted and friendship.

After the drinking had gone on for some time, Igor and the investigator were invited to use the sauna. They were escorted there by a thick-necked, completely bald man of about sixty in a purple robe. In the sauna, Igor and the investigator were alone. Igor asked, "Can you explain this?" The investigator shook his head.

After their sauna the two men took a swim and went back to the banquet room, where the chief seemed to be among old friends. Finally, after a round of billiards, they left. The next morning, Igor met the investigator. "I'm in shock," he said. "I am too," the investigator said.

The Solntsevo gang had its own group of professional assassins and was suspected of participation in every one of the most notorious contract killings in Moscow, but arrests were never made. After that evening, Igor was convinced that one of the reasons was the gang's intimate relations with the highest levels of the police.

The effectiveness of the Solntsevo gang's high-level connections was also reflected in its protection from investigations by foreigners. The best-known case involved Mikhailov.

In 1995, under pressure from Israeli intelligence, Mikhailov left Israel and moved to Switzerland, where he lived illegally, much of the time in the city of

Boreks. Upon flying into Geneva from a family shopping trip to Antwerp, however, he was arrested by the Swiss police and charged with violating the Swiss passport regime.

With Mikhailov in custody, there began to be attempts to keep him there. The U.S. Federal Bureau of Investigation sent a dossier on Mikhailov to Geneva, including information about his ties with Ivankov; and the Swiss began to investigate him in connection with international prostitution, the narcotics trade, and money laundering. On the basis of the evidence, the prosecutorial chamber of the Geneva court ordered Mikhailov held in the Champ-Dollon prison, and in January 1997 his confinement was extended. (As it happened, Mikhailov's arrest suspended a $350 million contract that Sistema was preparing to sign with him for the renovation of the underground systems of water supply and communications in Moscow.)

The Swiss finally settled on a charge of belonging to a criminal organization, which carried a potential prison sentence of eight years. To convict Mikhailov, however, the Swiss needed cooperation from Russia. But the material arriving from the Russian side was all in favor of the accused.

The first statement received in Geneva was signed by the prosecutor of the Solntsevo raion and said that Mikhailov had never been convicted. The second, from the general prosecutor, said that there was no pending case against Mikhailov and no information about him in the files of the MVD, FSB, tax police, or general prosecutor. These reports directly contradicted information from the Interior Ministry and RUBOP, according to which Mikhailov had been convicted of swindling and had been under investigation in 1989 and 1993. When the Swiss asked Yuri Skuratov, the general prosecutor, about the discrepancy, he promised to order an investigation; but there was never any information about his investigation and no further help was ever provided.

The Swiss ran into similar trouble when they tried to learn about complaints from victims. It turned out that, in ten years, there was only one complaint against the Solntsevo gang, made by the cooperative Fund in 1988. The directors of Fund later retracted their statement, and the head of the cooperative, Vadim Rosenbaum, emigrated to Holland. He was murdered there in 1997 when the Swiss prosecutors began to gather material on Mikhailov.

At the trial, Nikolai Uporov, a former major in RUBOP who had been granted political asylum in Switzerland, testified that when the Swiss prosecutors asked him, as the chief specialist on the Solntsevo gang, for information about the gang, his superiors insisted that he write that the gang was a journalistic myth.

A former official of the firm Almaz testified in Geneva that Mikhailov and his associates had looted the firm of $2 million, but the co-owner of the firm, who was living in Russia, sent a statement to the court saying that he had never heard of any Solntsevo criminal organization.

In the end, ninety witnesses from six countries described Mikhailov's participation in murders, the narcotics trade, money laundering, and prostitution for the Geneva court. Nonetheless, in December 1998 Mikhailov was acquitted, a decision attributed to the difficulty of establishing his direct responsibility for the crimes and to the lack of cooperation from Russian law enforcement. Mikhailov was freed in Switzerland to continue his criminal activities in Russia.

The corruption of the police and the ability of gangsters to establish high-level political connections are complemented by gangsters' use of contract killers, usually veterans of the police, FSB, and special forces who are ready to kill on demand. The methodical cold-bloodedness with which hired killers carry out their work is demonstrated every day.

36 SHARIKPODSHIPNIKOVSKAYA STREET, MOSCOW, NOVEMBER 1, 1995

Sergei Plyatskovsky, the director of Diana, a food-product wholesaling firm, was in his office with his wife when the lights went out at 10:00 P.M. Assuming that a fuse had blown, he went out to the fusebox in the corridor. At that moment, however, someone standing on the landing shone a light into his eyes, blinding him.

As Plyatskovsky covered his eyes, the stranger began firing. Trying to save himself, the wounded man ran back to his office, but his terrified wife instinctively slammed the door. According to the police, this move saved her life.

Bleeding heavily, Plyatkovsky ran down the corridor to the other wing of the building. The killer ran after him, caught him at the end of the corridor, and shot him repeatedly. He then fired a shot into his head. At the place of the killing, experts found seven cartridges and five bullets.[12]

10 KUTUZOVSKY PROSPEKT, MOSCOW, APRIL 27, 1998

At 10:00 P.M. two businessmen entered an elevator and punched the button for the tenth floor. In fact Dotsenko, the twenty-nine-year-old commercial director of the firm Rapid-1, and Bushev, the thirty-four-year-old general director of the company Prom-fin, did not know each other. They merely rented apartments in the same building.

When the elevator reached the tenth floor, the two men walked out together. At that moment, a killer waiting on the landing began firing repeatedly at both of them. The businessmen staggered in the corridor and then fell. The criminal successfully fled. An ambulance was called, but Dotsenko was already dead. Bushev was taken to the hospital in extremely grave condition. Afterward investigators speculated that the assassin had shot both men because he was not sure which was his target and was afraid to make a mistake.[13]

KUSTANAISKAYA STREET, MOSCOW, DECEMBER 18, 2000

At noon a young man in a work uniform with a small suitcase in his hands went up to the seventh floor of an apartment building and picked the lock of the outer door leading to the apartment belonging to Alexander Strebykin and two of his business associates. He then disconnected the apartment's telephone and electricity.

When an occupant of the apartment came out to check the fusebox, the killer took two pistols out of his suitcase, forced the victim to return to the apartment, and shot him. A second occupant ran out of the apartment to the rear stairway. The killer found him there and shot him in the head. The killer then left grenades on the stairway, which he had apparently planned to use in case the other methods failed.

Strebykin ran a private real estate business and, according to his acquaintances, knew that something might happen to him. The day before his death, he told one of his neighbors, "If they decide to kill me, there is already nothing I can do."[14]

NEVSKY PROSPEKT, ST. PETERSBURG, AUGUST 8, 1997

At 9:00 A.M. a car carrying Mikhail Manevich, the chairman of the city property committee, turned off Rubenstein Street onto Nevsky Prospekt. At that moment there was a burst of sniper fire from the attic of the building at 76 Rubinstein Street.

The sniper could not see Manevich. The shots were aimed to kill whoever was sitting to the right of the driver. The car was traveling at high speed, and the shots were fired from a distance of 100 meters (330 feet), but five of the eight bullets hit their target. Manevich died in the Marinskaya Hospital an hour later.

On the day of the killing, Manevich was preparing to leave for Moscow to meet Anatoly Chubais, who, according to some reports, wanted to name him deputy chairman of the State Property Committee (GKI). According to investigators, a group of four or five persons followed Manevich's entire route by radio. It was even taken into account that when turning onto Nevsky Prospekt, Manevich's car would have to brake. The skill of the assassination suggested to experts that the killing was organized at the highest national level.[15]

Russian gangs corrupt the police, establish alliances with politicians, and inspire fear and punish noncompliance with the help of contract killers. The power that this gives them makes it possible to overwhelm ordinary citizens with a sense of their own vulnerability, and the response is a degrading submission so widespread that it assumes the attributes of normality.

The nature of this acquiescence was demonstrated in the experiences of individuals—many less than perfect themselves—as they struggled to survive.

On a quiet Sunday morning in early winter, Yefim Kuznetsov (a pseudonym) entered the waiting room of his office on Leningradsky Prospekt and greeted four gangsters connected with Valery Dlugach (Globus), a thief professing the code, who were waiting for him. The gangsters had accused Kuznetsov of betrayal as a pretext for seizing his share of their joint business.

"We both know the real situation," Yefim said to Misha Myasnik, the group's leader. "I'm not guilty of anything. You just want to get rid of me."

"That's right," Myasnik said. "You're not necessary to us any more."

After a moment of hesitation, he asked, "Will you be satisfied if I leave myself?"

"Yes," Myasnik said. "Just leave."

In 1987 Yefim had organized a cooperative for the remodeling of apartments. At first his enterprise prospered, but after the reforms began he was ruined by hyperinflation and developed a new business, exchanging rubles illegally for hard currency.

After the Baltic republics left the ruble zone, Russia signed agreements with them to destroy their supplies of rubles. But the rubles were not destroyed, and the resulting trove gave rise to various schemes to return them to Russia.

At this time Yefim had contacts in the Baltics capable of supplying him with rubles, and he established connections with officials at Rostorg, a state-run trading organization, who had large quantities of dollars. The officials organized a private firm whose "roof" (an organization providing protection) was Globus and the Kazansky criminal organization. Yefim and his associates began illegally importing the rubles, legalizing them in their own account and then selling them at far below the exchange rate to their partners, who used them to purchase real estate in Russia as well as more dollars.

The deal went well, and Yefim and Armen Arutunyan (a pseudonym), the head of the firm created by the Rostorg officials, suggested that they establish a new, joint company to work on future projects.

In addition to the currency exchange scheme, Yefim, like many Russian businessmen, was searching for a way to gain access to oil. There was a huge difference between the internal and the world prices of oil, and he was using all his contacts to try to find officials who could be bribed to facilitate the sale of oil at the internal price for subsequent resale abroad. Finally, in May 1992, he met an official from Novosibirsk who had ties to a number of refineries and agreed, in exchange for a generous cut of the profits, to organize the sale of oil to Yefim's organization for subsequent resale to Ukraine, which at the time was in the grip of a severe energy crisis.

Yefim managed to locate this official, but it was only the beginning of the operation. The most complicated aspect of the arrangements was to put together documentation that would conceal the fact that ten million tons of oil had disappeared. This meant that Yefim's contact had to give bribes to officials in the refineries and in Transneft, the agency in charge of the pipelines. The money for the bribes came from Yefim's partners from Rostorg.

During the preliminary stages of the deal, Yefim and the officials from Rostorg met every day, either in Yefim's office or in the office of Rostorg on Tverskaya Street. At these meetings, three or four bandits from Arutunyan's roof, including Myasnik, were always present. Myasnik was relatively friendly, and he, Yefim, Arutunyan, and others often went out to dinner together or to the banya (steam baths) in the Sevastopol Hotel.

Once a contract between Ukraine and the joint firm was signed and the first payment for oil was made, however, the bandits became curt and peremptory. One day Yefim's deputy called him at home and said, "Something bad is happening. They are developing something against you." Kuznetsov went to his office, where he met Myasnik, who said, "Yefim, you are selling us out to Mikhailov." Yefim had never had contact with the Solntsevo gang. He realized that this was a pretext for seizing his share of the business.

Yefim called Arutunyan and pointed out that he had been the originator of the whole project. Arutunyan was sympathetic but said that there was nothing he could do. His roof was insisting that Yefim be cut out. He added that Myasnik had once killed someone in his presence and hinted that Myasnik was ready to come to Yefim's office and kill everyone there as well.

In desperation, Kuznetsov called Vladislav Vinner (Babon), another criminal boss in Moscow, and arranged a meeting with him in the Peking Hotel. As a car full of armed bandits waited on the street outside, Yefim explained his dilemma and asked for Babon's help. Babon was attracted by the amount of money involved, but he was not as powerful as Globus. He told Yefim that he could offer some short-term protection but that in the long run there was little he could do. The amount of money involved was large enough to get Yefim killed but not enough for him to start a gang war over it.

Yefim realized that he was helpless. His ulcer flared up, and for several days he was in great pain and stayed in bed. As soon as he could get up, he went to the office and told Myasnik that he would walk away from the deal that would have made him a wealthy man.

With the loss of the oil deal, Yefim lost his faith in Russian business. He closed his firm and began to work as an unofficial cab driver. During this period Globus was assassinated along with his driver outside the discothèque U Lis'sa, and Babon was assassinated in Tushino. Yefim decided to study Eastern medicine and embark on a new career as a healer.

The minutes ticked away as Yuri Kurkov (a pseudonym) waited in the reception area of the empty office of his friend Vladimir Subbotin (a pseudonym), who had asked to meet him. At length, four men entered the waiting room from the street. They walked past Yuri, stepped into Subbotin's office, and told Kurkov to follow them.

After Yuri entered, they closed the door behind him. The oldest member of the group, who was about forty-five and dressed in a suit and tie, said, "Give us the money."

"I don't have the money. I lost it in Vlasteline."

"You couldn't think of anything more stupid to do? Bring the money in a week or prepare a noose for yourself."

"I'm not going to prepare a noose for myself."

"We'll help you."

Yuri Kurkov ran a set of street kiosks in Moscow, and in 1994 his friend Vladimir Ilyich, who worked in a bank, told him about Vlasteline, which was paying 100 percent a month on investments. Kurkov understood that this was some type of a swindle. A return of 100 percent a month was possible only from narcotics, the arms trade, or prostitution. But Vladimir Ilyich explained that their investment would be protected. He had a friend, Vladimir Balagansky, who knew A. V., the deputy director of a government agency. In return for a 10 percent commission to Balagansky, A. V. would guarantee that he and Vladimir Ilyich received their 100 percent a month regardless of what happened to the other investors.

The idea appealed to Yuri. Fortunes were being made and lost every day, and he did not want to lose a chance to guarantee his own future and that of his children and grandchildren.

Vladimir Ilyich took Kurkov to see Balagansky, who lived in the countryside, eight and a half miles outside Moscow. Balagansky introduced them to A. V., and they went to the banya, where, sitting in the steam, they agreed to make the investment. "Boys," said A. V., "be calm. You'll get your money."

Yuri and Vladimir Ilyich raised 1.46 billion rubles ($649,000). They invested 90 percent in Vlasteline and gave 10 percent to Balagansky to guarantee their investment. Kurkov's share of the money amounted to $179,000, $22,000 from his savings and $157,000 that he had borrowed from Subbotin.[16] The rest of the money came from Vladimir Ilyich, $330,000 from members of the Uzbek embassy in Moscow and $70,000 in unregistered cash from the bank where he worked as head of the hard currency department.

The money was invested on September 12, 1994. The first payment was due on October 16, thirty-five days later. On October 15 Kurkov and Vladimir Ilyich went to Podolsk, where Vlasteline had its headquarters. They were given tokens to use the next day to collect the return on their investment. On October 16, however, they were told that payments had been temporarily suspended. Every day for the next four days they went to Podolsk and were given the same message. Finally, on October 20, they were told that Valentina Solovieva, the director of Vlasteline, had disappeared and that without her signature no one could be paid anything.

With the apparent failure of Vlasteline, Yuri and Vladimir Ilyich went to see Balagansky. He promised to return their money but said it could not be done immediately. Kurkov accepted his promise, but until the day Balagansky disappeared, he drove out regularly to his home, a distance of thirty miles, to remind him of his obligation.

In the meantime, the Mozhaisky criminal organization, Subbotin's roof, called Kurkov, warning him to return the money he had borrowed from Subbotin, and the Uzbeks began to demand their money back from Vladimir Ilyich.

Kurkov and Vladimir Ilyich decided that they had to see A. V. Vladimir Ilyich met with him in his government office. His manner was friendly and reassuring. He told Vladimir Ilyich that he and Kurkov would definitely get their money. Several weeks later, Vladimir Ilyich went to see him again. This time, however, he said, "You did not give the money to me, you gave it to Balagansky. You should direct all questions to him." Finally, Kurkov went to see A. V. and was told that he no longer worked at that agency.

Yuri now became seriously worried. The Mozhaisky gang was calling him every week. He knew that their patience would not last forever.

To avoid being killed, Yuri began borrowing money from everyone he could think of—relatives, friends, and acquaintances, including the salesgirls in his own kiosks—and bringing it to Subbotin. Six months after Vlasteline collapsed, he had returned $64,000 of the $157,000 he had borrowed. This, however, was not enough for the Mozhaisky gang. Subbotin called Yuri and asked him to come to his office. It was there that he was met by the bandits who told him to pay the rest of the money or prepare himself a noose.

Kurkov now began drinking heavily and praying at home and in church. He thought about suicide, but he told himself that God gave life and he did not have the right to take it. Finally, he contacted his own roof, the Tagansky gang. To his surprise, they were reassuring. "This is all theater," they said. "To kill a person is more difficult than you think; everyone knows to whom you owe money. No one is going to kill you, but you have to give them something to let off steam. What do you have?"

Yuri said he had a dacha that was under construction.

"OK," said the bandits, "you can give them that."

A week later, Kurkov returned to Subbotin's office to meet with the Mozhaisky bandits, accompanied by bandits from the Tagansky group. "He fell into this situation," one of the Tagansky bandits argued. "It wasn't his fault." Yuri offered them his dacha, and they took it as further partial payment. This, however, was not the end of Kurkov's troubles. The businessmen who lent Yuri money to repay Subbotin had their own roofs, and these bandits, principally from the Solntsevsky and Balashikhinsky gangs, began to call Yuri at home about these debts and demand that he return the money.

Yuri continued to see Balagansky, often taking along Vladimir Ilyich as well as Vladimir Ilyich's wife, who considered herself a parapsychologist and capable of defending them. After a few months, Balagansky no longer promised to return their money. Instead, he appealed for sympathy. "I was taken in, just like you," he said. Under increasing pressure, Yuri lost his temper during the visits. "Come on, goat!" he shouted. "Give me the money."

Finally, Balagansky suggested that they invest in a scheme to sell gas to Ukraine. Balagansky said he would use his share of the profits to pay the debt. The only thing that was required was a line of credit. Vladimir Ilyich had left his own bank, which was waiting for him to repay the $70,000 he had borrowed to invest in Vlasteline. But he still had ties to officials at other banks, which had their own "black cash," and he organized a credit of 500 million rubles at 180 percent a year in exchange for a payment of 5 percent of the value of the loan to his contacts at the bank. In February 1995 the first tranche was ready, and Yuri and Vladimir Ilyich drove out to tell Balagansky, only to learn that he had vanished.

Kurkov sold four of his seven kiosks and began driving a cab at night, working twelve hours a day, seven days a week. He earned $2,500 a month, of which he kept $500 to live on. The remaining $2,000 went to monthly payments on his debt.

For a time, the attention of the Mozhaisky gang was diverted to Subbotin, who had fallen behind in his payments in part because of Yuri. Subbotin was beaten at his dacha by six members of the gang, who left him in a pool of blood after threatening to douse him with gasoline and set him on fire. Other gangsters, however, called Yuri constantly with demands for money.

Over the next two years, Yuri met nearly every week with bandits from the Solntsevsky, Mytischinsky, Balashikhinsky, and Mozhaisky gangs, never knowing whether he would return home alive. Whenever he left for a meeting with bandits, which often took place either in an office of one of his creditors or in a café on the street, he instructed his wife to call him on his pager at a specific time. He told her that if he did not call back, it meant that the bandits had abducted him and she was to call the Tagansky gang and ask for their help.

The encounters were always brutal. The bandits threatened to break Yuri's legs or his head. They told him that he was dead without money. But Yuri tried to remain calm. If he did not have the required sum, he always tried to pay something and to ask for more time. (Yuri had no assurance that his tactics would work. One of his friends, Sergei Golovin, was beaten to death over a debt of $15,000; Mikhail Khmelevskoi, a businessman who had a black belt in karate, was beaten and shot to death in his garage over a debt of $45,000; Andrei Bondarenko, a former employee of Kurkov's, was thrown out of a fourth-floor window.)

In cases in which Yuri felt there was a grave danger, he asked for members of the Tagansky gang to accompany him. In such cases, the bandits explained that Yuri had been deceived and intended to repay his debts. But Yuri could not be sure that the Tagansky bandits would protect him forever. He knew of many cases in which bandits washed their hands of a businessman, particularly if he had debts and could not repay.

On one occasion, three bandits from the Solntsevo gang came to Yuri's home. He had borrowed $15,000 from a friend, and they said he owed $25,000. Yuri said that he owed $15,000 not $25,000, plus $2,000 interest. He offered to pay the interest and then, when he got the money, pay the principal. One of the bandits said, "We had a businessman who also did not pay. We hung him upside down for two hours, and after that he found the money."

"You can put me in a crematorium," Yuri said. "I don't have the money."

In the end, the bandits agreed to allow Yuri to pay just the interest.

Yuri dreamed of opening a restaurant, but he dared not put any money aside because he knew that only his ability to give almost all the money he earned to the bandits was keeping him alive.

Yuri did not take much solace from the fate of his friends. Subbotin had lost everything and was now unemployed, living off his wife's salary. He feared that he would be killed once the head of the Mozhaisky gang was released from prison. Vladimir Ilyich ran a small consulting firm, earning $120 to $200 a month. After the Uzbeks threatened to kill his family, he suffered a heart attack, was hospitalized, and then fled from the hospital.

On August 17, 1998, however, the situation changed. The ruble collapsed, and there was a wave of contract killings of businessmen who could not repay their debts. In the resulting confusion, however, some relatively small old debts were quietly forgotten.

To Yuri's surprise, many of the bandits to whom he still owed money stopped calling. Bandits from the Solntsevo gang called once, and he told them that he had nothing to give them. They did not call again.

The months went by, and Yuri quietly began putting money aside for a new enterprise. More than four years after he lost money in Vlasteline, he dared to hope that his long period of slavery to the gangs was finally coming to an end.

POKROVKA STREET, MOSCOW, AUGUST 1996

"Doug," said a voice, "Get in the car."

It was 7:45 A.M. Doug Steele, the owner of the Hungry Duck Bar, was about to walk home after a long and busy night. He turned and saw a parked black limousine with three men in it and recognized Ali, a Chechen gangster, and his former business partner in the back seat.

Doug shouted to Hannibal, a Cuban bartender at the Duck, who was on the street about 100 feet ahead of him, and Hannibal ran back to where he was standing. Doug asked him to translate.

"Let's take a ride," Ali said. "We've got some business to discuss."

"If you want to discuss something," Doug said, "talk to my security."

As Doug turned toward the courtyard, Ali, a second Chechen, and his driver jumped out of the car and grabbed him from behind. Hannibal tried to help, punching the driver while a friend who had also just left the Duck ran to get the bar's security guards. The Chechens tried to force Doug into the back seat of the car, but he struggled, holding on to the frame of the door. He was too big to be overpowered easily. A small crowd gathered, and guards from the Duck, running at full speed, emerged from the archway with guns drawn. The Chechens, seeing that they were outnumbered, let Doug go, jumped into the car, and sped away.

An hour later, Doug was at the Duck meeting with the head of the bar's security service, a former KGB general. "Frankly," the security man said, "this has gone to a level we did not expect. They know the bar is doing well, and as far as they're concerned, it's their bar. They would have held you for ransom or killed you. They weren't taking you to have a cup of tea."

Steele, a Canadian from Halifax, had first come to Moscow in September 1992 with a Canadian friend who had been invited by a Russian acquaintance. As he walked the streets, it struck him that Russia was embarking on a democratic transformation with no bars, restaurants, or foreigners. He immediately hit upon the idea of opening a bar.

On the evening of his second day in Moscow, Doug met a Belgian businessman in one of the few foreign bars in Moscow. He told the Belgian his plan, and the Belgian said that it was a good idea but Doug would need a "roof." The Belgian explained that a roof was an organization that provided protection. It could either be an official structure or a mafia structure. His roof was a mafia structure, the Solntsevo gang. He recommended them because, he said, in the event of trouble with the mafia, it was necessary to have a mafia group to talk to a mafia group. "Get a roof first and then open your bar," he advised. "They can help you to find locations, and you can negotiate with them. Once you're in place, you have to negotiate on their terms."

Doug returned to Moscow in November and set about trying to make contact with a potential roof. The Russian lawyer introduced him to a Canadian lawyer whose translator, Sasha, had a friend, Vasya, whose brother was a leader in the Kuntsevo criminal organization. Vasya agreed to set up a meeting between Doug and the gang.

Doug had no experience of the criminal world in Canada, where he had worked for a food company, but he banished his doubts about becoming involved with the Russian underworld.

The meeting took place in early December. Doug and Sasha were met at

6:00 P.M. in front of the Oktyabrskaya metro station by sixteen men in four cars and driven to a restaurant in the Kuntsevo district. A long table was laden with food and drinks, and a tall bandit with a long scar on his neck sat down next to Steele. This was the brother of Vasya.

During the next few hours, Doug and the bandits discussed the terms for extorting money from him as if this was a normal business practice.

The apparent leader of the gang asked Doug what kind of business he wanted to establish. Doug said he wanted to set up a bar.

"Why do you want to set up a bar?" he asked.

"The country will evolve," Doug said. "The bar scene will boom." The bandits indicated that they understood this.

The leading bandit said, "We'll help you find a location and protect your person and your business interests. Your partners will have their own security. We'll deal with them. It will cost $5,000 a month."

Doug said that he would consider their offer and call when he was ready to open his bar.

A short time after the meeting with the Kuntsevo group, Doug met a Russian in the Shamrock Bar who suggested a meeting with his gang. A rendezvous was arranged, and Doug was met on Komsomolsky Prospekt by nine bandits and the Russian, who translated. The group got into three Volvos and drove to a restaurant.

The bandits told Doug, "If anyone gets in your way, we'll kill them." Steele said, "I don't want to kill anyone. I just want to open a bar." There was something in their manner that made him think that they would not hesitate to kill him too.

A short time later, Doug met again with Sasha, who mentioned that another friend of his, a former driver, now had his own criminal organization. Doug agreed to meet him. He was picked up in front of the Tren-Mos restaurant by bandits in two Volvos who had cell phones and were wearing workers' caps. They took Doug to a restaurant near the Moscow Zoo.

Doug discussed his plans for a bar, and the bandits listened intently. As he spoke, however, they continually took out their guns and placed them on the table. A week after the first meeting, Sasha told Doug that the group had been involved in a shootout in central Moscow, and Doug broke off contact with them.

Doug returned to Canada and, for the next eighteen months, traveled back and forth between Moscow and Halifax, gathering information for investors and trying to find a location for his bar. Finding a good location, however, proved more difficult than he had expected. Every time he found a property that interested him, it proved impossible to determine the rightful owner. One empty building had nine different, unrelated persons registered as the owner. In late 2000, it was still empty.

One evening in September 1993, Doug was drinking in Rosy O'Grady's Bar in Moscow when a friend introduced him to two Oriental women who spoke Russian. The women explained that they were Kalmyks and invited him to a birthday party, where he was introduced to Geisha Ting Li, a Buddhist monk who was also the Dalai Lama's spiritual representative to the CIS and Mongolia. At the party he also met Dmitri Kichikov and Yuri, two Kalmykian businessmen, and Dmitri offered to help him set up his bar.

The next day, Kichikov took Doug to 54 Bolshaya Polyanka, a building owned by two Chechen brothers, Akhmed and Sharip. The Chechens had a restaurant in the building, and they offered it as the location for a bar. Doug called his partners, John and Jim Whelan, in Canada, and they agreed. Terms were drawn up. Doug and the Whelans would put up $160,000 and pay rent, Kichikov would put up $160,000, and the Chechens would put up the restaurant.

Akhmed and Sharip already had a Chechen gang as their roof, and they urged Doug to share it, arguing that it was senseless to pay double. Doug, however, said that he needed someone to defend his and his partners' interests. He called Vasya and told him to tell the Kuntsevo gang that he was finally ready to open his bar.

The next step was a meeting between Akhmed and Sharip's roof and the Kuntsevo gang. The meeting took place in a private room at the Moskvichi restaurant. There were eight Chechens and six Kuntsevo bandits, and the meeting lasted for forty-five minutes. Finally, the bandits emerged and announced that they had found "a common language." At the last minute, however, Kichikov, who was supposed to arrive with his share of the money, disappeared. The Chechens agreed to work with Doug anyway. They put up their own money, and the deal was clinched.

With the contract signed, the parties moved quickly. Doug flew in an architect from Canada who designed the bar, and it opened in January 1994 with Doug as manager. The demand for entertainment in Moscow far outstripped the supply, and by its second month of operation, the new bar, called the Moosehead, was making $20,000 a month in profits on the strength of huge markups and large crowds.

From the moment the Moosehead opened, however, Doug began to have trouble with Akhmed and Sharip. The Chechens did not understand concepts like retained income or putting money aside for taxes.

Two months after the Moosehead opened, Kichikov reappeared in the bar and invited Doug to look at a location for another bar. Doug agreed, and they went to a building near the Kuznetsky Most metro station. Doug said that it was an excellent location. Kichikov offered Doug 15 percent of the profits to run the new bar with no investment necessary. Doug prepared to manage the new enterprise while Jim Whelan flew over from Canada to run the Moosehead.

Whelan's arrival marked the beginning of serious conflicts with Akhmed and Sharip. Whelan, a former military policeman, was anxious to make big profits quickly and was not interested in local mores or the Chechens' way of doing business.

Trouble began over a conflict that was relatively petty. The Chechens often ate at the Moosehead with their friends. It was an informal arrangement, and the Chechens paid half of the charge. On one occasion, however, Akhmed arrived with his mother and a large group of other family members. Jim said through a translator that Akhmed could eat for half price but his mother and the others had to pay full price. Akhmed became furious, and the argument quickly escalated into threats of violence. Whelan called the Kuntsevo gang for help. In explaining the situation, he said, "If it was my fucking mother, I'd make her pay too." A member of the gang then called Doug and said that anyone who did not respect his mother did not deserve their respect.

In another incident, Jim refused to give Akhmed part of the rent three days in advance. There was also a dispute over expenses. Although Doug and his partners paid rent, Akhmed and Sharip were supposed to pay for utilities. The Chechens, however, demanded that Doug and his partners pay for electricity. They said that electricity was not a utility.

The tensions grew to the point that there were rumors that Akhmed and Sharip had contracted with their Chechen roof to kill Whelan. Finally, there was a meeting of the two sides with their respective roofs, and the Chechens offered to buy the Canadians out. By October 1995 the bar's profits had reached $40,000 a month. The Chechens agreed to pay the Canadians $20,000 a month for twelve months and then make a payment of $360,000. Sasha urged Doug not to agree, warning that they would never be paid. Nonetheless, Doug and Jim decided to go through with the sale. Jim called his brother, John, in Canada. John sent a power of attorney, and they signed over the bar.

For the next three months, the Chechens paid $20,000 a month to Jim. At the beginning of the fourth month, however, the Chechens informed Jim that they had to stop paying. They said that the bar was not doing as well as before and they had other debts, including electricity.

The explanation enraged Whelan, and a meeting was held in Akhmed's office near the Moosehead. Whelan began berating Akhmed and Sharip, and they demanded a translation. Doug, fearing violence, called a halt to the meeting. Two hours later, he received a call from the Kuntsevo gang to arrange a meeting at a sports club near Victory Park.

Doug had been paying the gang $5,000 a month in cash for protection, and he now needed their help to force the Chechens to honor the terms of the contract. When he went into the sports complex, he saw almost all the bandits that he knew. An older member of the gang, a weight lifter whose picture hung on the wall of the gym, approached Doug.

"Everyone speaks highly of you," he said. "Your partner is the reason you've been called here. The Chechens have taken out a contract on his life, and we had to pay to stop it. Frankly, he's an asshole. Any man who doesn't respect his mother does not deserve our respect. We must withdraw from the Moosehead project."

Doug realized that his investment was lost. The Kuntsevo gang either was afraid of Akhmed and Sharip's Chechen roof or had made a deal with them. Either way, no one would take on the Chechens now.

"But Akhmed has to pay us for the bar," Doug said.

"I'm sorry," the Kuntsevo bandit said, "$5,000 a month is not worth having someone killed for."

Doug left realizing that he and his partners had invested $160,000 in the bar, made it profitable, and then handed it to the Chechens. The meeting with his roof spelled the end of his involvement with the Moosehead.

On December 8, 1995, Steele's new bar, the Hungry Duck, opened its doors. The space was rented from the Central House of Workers in the Arts (TsDRI), whose director had signed the lease with Dmitri in return for a $20,000 bribe. The roof for the bar was another Chechen gang.

The Duck's principal innovation was that it allowed dancing on the bar, and its opening was a huge success. Shortly after midnight, however, a group of ethnic Kalmyk police carrying automatic weapons came in looking for Kichikov. A group of Chechens took them aside, and after some discussion the police left peacefully.

This incident was not the end of the problems with Kichikov, who, Doug learned, had ties to Kirsan Ilyumzhinov, the president of Kalmykia. Just as the bar was beginning to attract crowds of patrons, the electricity was turned off in the building because Kichikov had not paid the rent; the staff was not being paid; and Doug learned from a translator that Kichikov was arriving every day and taking money from the cash register.

Doug next discovered that the bar did not even belong to Kichikov. He had sold shares in the bar representing 160 percent of the cost of opening it to two groups, Kalmyks and the Chechen roof, each of whom considered themselves the 100 percent owners. In the meantime, the federal tax police also began looking for Kichikov. On New Year's Eve, Kichikov stopped in briefly at the Duck and then disappeared.

After Kichikov's disappearance, Doug was visited at the Duck by Ali, a Chechen from Grozny and a member of the gang that was the bar's roof. The gang claimed that Dmitri had opened the bar with their money and the bar belonged to them. They promised Doug a 15 percent interest and a salary if he would keep working. Doug agreed, and Ali told him to call them if there were any problems.

A short time later, however, Stanislav Panich, the director of TsDRI, told Doug that Kichikov owed the building $110,000. He said that if Doug would take over the debt, he would sign a new lease, this one with Doug. He also introduced Doug to the members of his security firm, which was linked to the FSB. The head of the firm, a former KGB general, said that Ali and his associates were midlevel Chechen gangsters and, given the war in Chechnya, they would not be able to control their holdings in Moscow. He proposed creating a structure that would make it look as if his firm had bought the bar, although in fact the Duck would belong to Doug. If anyone asked, Doug could say that the bar belonged to the security firm and he had been kept on as a manager.

Doug agreed to the plan. The bar was closed for two days and then reopened under "new management."

Chechen gangs had carried out a reign of terror in Moscow, and pulling a bar out from under a Chechen gang was a high-risk proposition, but at first the reaction of the Chechens and the Kalmyks was muted. Large groups of Chechen bandits came to the Duck and stood around menacingly, and a few drunken Kalmyks came and danced on the bar tops.

One afternoon, however, Doug was visited by a Chechen arms dealer who spoke fluent English. "I am a representative of the true owners of the bar," he said. "No one has any claims against you. But the bar belongs to us. Now I want to ask you: are you on our side, their side, or your side?"

Doug repeated that the bar had been taken over by the security firm and he had only been hired as manager.

At first the Chechens seemed to accept Doug's explanation. In April 1996 Ali entered the building, went up to Panich's office, grabbed him by the collar, and tried to slit his throat. Panich was saved because two security guards ran into his office, forcing Ali to flee. Doug, however, moved around freely, behaving as if he had nothing to fear. This ended when the Chechens tried to kidnap him on the street in front of the Duck in August 1996.

In the wake of the kidnapping attempt, Doug was guarded twenty-four hours a day. When he drove, there were three guards in the car; when he walked, the same three guards surrounded him. An armed guard sat in front of his apartment all night long. Nonetheless, it was during this period that Doug showed his greatest creativity. He introduced "ladies' night," which featured free drinks for women and male strippers in the first part of the evening and high prices for the males who were let in later. The gimmick made the bar famous. He also opened another Moscow expatriate bar, the Chesterfield, which was later reorganized as the Boar House, and two restaurants, Tibet Himalaya and Pancho Villa.

Doug received constant threats. He was warned that it was the last day of his life and that the Duck would be blown up. But his bodyguards proved efficient in warding off potential dangers. The only forces that he couldn't deal with were the government agencies that were continually extorting bribes in return for not shutting him down. After a raid by the economic crime police in May 1998 that temporarily closed the bar, Doug dropped the security firm, which had proved relatively helpless against official extortion, and hired RUBOP as his roof. The Duck reopened three days later.

The organized crime unit proved itself more adept than the FSB-linked security services at buying off government officials and preventing harassment. They also provided Doug with physical protection. Gradually he began to move around with fewer bodyguards, although he never went anywhere alone.

In August 1998, however, Doug was approached in the Pancho Villa by Roman, a leader of the Chechen gang that had claimed the Duck. Roman told Doug to meet him at the Moosehead or he would kill him. Doug's protectors from RUBOP intercepted Roman at the Moosehead. Two weeks later Steele learned that Roman had died of a heart attack. He asked a contact in RUBOP why no one had told him that Roman was dead.

"He won't bother you anymore," the contact said. "Whether he's dead or not is not your concern."

Nonetheless, the signs were not auspicious for the Duck. It had become Moscow's best-known foreign bar, in part because ladies' night had inspired many Russian women to dance on the bar in their bras, topless, or, in some cases, completely nude. Steele did not ask anyone to take off his or her clothes, but he didn't discourage it either.

The reports of nude dancing at the Duck were soon being discussed in the

State Duma, where the bar's activities began to be described as a threat to the moral fabric of Russia. In March 1999 the board of TsDRI, reacting to the reports of nude dancing at the Duck and under political pressure from Russian deputies, refused to renew Doug's lease, and the bar was closed.

Doug's operations now centered on his restaurants. He continued to receive threats, but despite the insecurity, he gave no thought to returning to Canada. He realized that after his experiences in Moscow, he could never return to a conventional life in Halifax. Instead, from his headquarters in the Boar House, behind a wall of security men and hidden video cameras, he looked forward to new ventures in the country he still considers to be the best place on earth to make money.

Teacher, before thy name, allow me to bend my knee.
—*Nikolai Nekrasov*

9 *Ulyanovsk*

DECEMBER 3, 1998

An icy wind blew in off the steppes as the first mourners filed into the entryway of the building where, until a few days before, Yuri Motorin had lived with his family in an apartment on the fourth floor. Soon the entire stairwell was full.

Inside Motorin's apartment, the mirrors and television were covered with linen, and a candle burned in front of an icon with a silver frame. Bread, a glass of vodka, and a dish of salt were arranged on a small table. They had been placed there for Motorin's soul, which, according to Orthodox tradition, remains with the deceased's survivors for forty days before ascending to heaven. The open coffin was in the middle of the room, and a priest sang prayers and swung a censer, releasing clouds of incense. Motorin's mother-in-law bent over his body and cried, "Why did you leave us when we all loved you so? Do you see how many people have come to accompany you on your last journey?"

As Motorin's wife, son, and daughter watched from benches in front of the coffin, the mourners entered the apartment and moved past the body in a continuous stream, paying their respects to the forty-two-year-old teacher, who had died as a result of a hunger strike to protest nonpayment of salaries. From the windows of the apartment, soccer fields were visible in the distance and, beyond them, the open plain. Thousands of miles away across that plain were the mountains of Afghanistan, where Motorin had fought and received the Order of the Red Star for bravery.

At exactly noon, after hundreds of people had walked past the coffin, six uniformed paratroopers with black bands around their arms entered the room, lifted the coffin, and carried it down the stairs. As they emerged from the entrance of the building, nearly 1,500 people on the street removed their hats in the bitter cold and stood silently. All around them, people on the upper floors of the surrounding buildings watched from their balconies because Russian tradition forbids viewing a dead person through a window.

To many, it seemed that they were witnessing the funeral not just of one man but of education in Russia.

The hunger strike by teachers in Ulyanovsk that cost Motorin his life had its roots in the gigantism of the Soviet military-industrial complex and the failure to restructure the economy after the Soviet Union's demise.

Ulyanovsk, a city on the Middle Volga and the birthplace of Lenin, was built on the crest of a hill along the western bank of the Volga. For years, on the other side of the river wheat fields and meadowland had extended to the eastern horizon.

In the 1970s, however, the Soviet Union embarked on a major military expansion, and to improve the airlift capacity of the armed forces, the Soviet leaders approved plans for production of the Antonov-124 cargo plane, also known as the "Ruslan," which was to be the largest aircraft in the world. To produce the An-124, the Soviet authorities ordered the construction of the Aviastar factory and a new district to house the factory workers. Novy Gorod was built directly across the Volga River from Ulyanovsk and became the Zavolzhsky raion.

At the peak of its operations in the early 1980s, the Aviastar plant had 23,000 workers and was producing up to seven An-124s a year. The complex also began to produce the Tupelov-204 passenger plane, which resembled the Boeing 747. In 1991, however, with the collapse of the Soviet Union, it became harder to produce the An-124 because the factory that manufactured its engines was in Ukraine, now an independent country. At the same time, orders for both planes were sharply reduced.

In 1995 the factory was privatized, and there were delays in paying salaries. In September 1996 Aviastar began a massive firing of workers, and those who could find other ways to earn a living did so. By 1998 only 11,000 workers were employed at Aviastar, and, of those, only 4,000 were actually working.[1]

When production at Aviastar virtually came to a halt, it was the salaries of factory workers' wives working as teachers that enabled families to survive.

The new district had attracted thousands of young families from the surrounding villages. They came because the pay at the Aviastar factory was high and the future for workers there seemed secure. They also came because, at a time when the country faced a serious housing shortage, workers at Aviastar were being given new apartments. The apartments in Novy Gorod were allocated on the basis of the number of children in each family. As a result, people began to have children, in part to increase their living space. The growing number of "apartment children" created a demand for teachers, a demand filled largely by the wives of factory workers. Soon there were forty-nine kindergartens in Novy Gorod with 150 to 200 children in each.

Beginning in 1996, however, there were also delays in paying teachers' salaries. Many families were now left with no source of income. Families began sharing food and pawning their jewelry. In March 1997 the teachers in ten schools in Novy Gorod went on strike. The strike was settled when local officials promised to pay salaries on time, but the agreement was immediately violated.

By May 1998, the city's teachers had not been paid for four months. A small group of teachers mounted a brief hunger strike, and as a result the lag in payments was reduced to two months. In June, when the teachers did not get pay that was due them for the summer break, forty teachers set up a tent city in front of the oblast administration building and mounted a four-day hunger strike. They received their vacation pay in September. In October, they were paid for May but not for September and October. At the end of October the leaders of the Zavolzhsky strike committee, which was based on the strike committees elected in the schools the previous year, threatened another strike. In response, the city officials said they could not pay salaries because they were out of funds.

How much money was in fact available was far from clear. The budget figures for the Ulyanovsk oblast were impenetrable not only to ordinary citizens but also to journalists and deputies in the oblast parliament. One entry in the budget was for "unexpected expenditures." No one knew what this meant. Another was for "support for the information media." No one knew what this meant either.

One of the biggest businesses in the oblast was the firm Prodovolstviye, which owned stores, gas stations, and collective farms and sold products to schools, hospitals, and orphanages that were run by the oblast. The major shareholder in the firm was the oblast government. The firm's director, Oleg Goryachev, was the son of the governor, Yuri Goryachev. The company appeared to be very profitable, but there was no trace of that profit in the oblast budget.

There was also a pattern of not spending budget money for its intended purpose. A debate about fulfillment of the oblast budget for the first half of 1998 revealed that some articles of the budget had not been funded, while others had been overfinanced by as much as 60 percent.[2]

All of this was known to the desperate teachers who, in ten of the seventeen schools in the Zavolzhsky raion, voted to go on strike.

In the schools that decided to strike, the teachers began meeting with parents, explaining that they would not be able to take responsibility for their children while they were on strike and asking them to keep the children home. The only question now was whether the strike should be accompanied by a hunger strike. The teachers feared a hunger strike. The years of hardship had left many with heart disease, gastritis, diabetes, and high blood pressure. But the teachers saw that they could refuse to work forever without achieving any serious result. They also knew that by striking they would be turning 15,000 children out on the street, and they did not want that situation to drag on indefinitely.

On November 17, 465 teachers agreed to begin an unlimited hunger strike on the following day.

On the night of November 17, Motorin was at home with his family preparing to participate in the action. Privately, he believed that a hunger strike was senseless, but as a former military man and an elected member of the strike committee he could not stand aside while his female colleagues were preparing to risk their lives.

On the morning of November 18, the striking teachers gathered in each of the ten participating schools. They brought folding beds, mattresses, and sheets as well as bottles of mineral water and vitamins.

Motorin went to School 20, where he taught personal security (a course that concerns health and how to deal with electricity, accidents, and natural disasters and is often taught by former military men) and was an elected member of the strike committee. The building was cold because in School 20, as elsewhere, the city was trying to save money on the cost of fuel. The teachers, dressed in heavy clothing, established themselves in the warmest rooms, on the third floor. Motorin and the other male teachers prepared to sleep in one room and the female teachers in two others.

Drawing on his military experience, Motorin briefed the teachers on what to expect. He said that on the third day without food, the organism, in its search for sustenance, begins to poison itself, and the best way to survive is to lie quietly and not move around.

Motorin, however, did not follow his own advice. The headquarters of the strike was at School 72, in a different part of Novy Gorod. Motorin walked there with Galina Mukhina, another member of the strike committee, at least once a day. This meant going up three flights of steps in both places. The walk took half an hour in each direction, and Motorin continued to smoke.

The spectacle of almost 500 teachers going on hunger strike both impressed and frightened the city authorities. Representatives of the raion department of education went from school to school trying to persuade the teachers to desist. They said, "Women, spare yourselves, you have chronic diseases. You will get sick. Who will take care of your children?"

When the teachers asked when they would get their salaries, the officials said that they would be paid as soon as there was money.

News of the hunger strike riveted the Ulyanovsk oblast. Local radio and television provided saturation coverage, interviewing many students and parents as well as striking teachers, and throughout the city many people argued that the strike proved that life had been better under communism. At the same time, ORT, the national television network, began to report on events to the whole country.

The teachers hoped that the hunger strike would force a change in the attitude of the local authorities, but despite the publicity, the local political leaders, including the governor, refused to meet with the teachers, apparently counting on wearing them down.

On the second and third days of the hunger strike, the teachers were frequently visited by students. The teachers joked and tried to smile, but the children, seeing the teachers in a weakened condition, were distressed. In one case, a group of students wrote to city officials threatening to go on hunger strike themselves.

During this period the teachers in School 20 kept records of one another's blood pressure. The first readings showed that Motorin's blood pressure was significantly elevated.

The first teachers to show serious symptoms were excused from the strike. In School 20, Nahil Prokurov, a geography teacher, went home after his ulcer opened. Although he seriously needed medical attention, he did not have the 800 rubles to pay for medicines, so he did not go to a hospital. In School 63, Lyudmilla Abramchenko, one of the leaders of the strike, suffered a sharp rise in blood pressure. She could not speak and had very sharp headaches. An ambulance took her home, where she gradually resumed eating.

On Saturday, November 21, the teachers wrote out appeals to the Red Cross and the United Nations Committee on Human Rights; parents who had home computers sent them out. The schools then received calls from these organizations, which boosted the morale of the hunger strikers.

The teachers repeatedly called the offices of the mayor and the governor from strike headquarters in School 72. Both officials refused to meet with them. At a press conference in the oblast administration building, Yuri Goryachev said, "If I give the teachers money, the whole oblast will go on hunger strike." Representatives of the department of education told the teachers that there was no money.

The striking teachers also met in each school with their directors or principals, who urged them to return to work, saying that the authorities needed to resolve the situation for all schools, not just for those that had gone on strike.

The teachers listened courteously, but they realized that neither the directors nor the education officials could decide anything. Everything depended on the governor.

A mood of fatalism settled over Novy Gorod. The district, with its large number of unemployed and unpaid workers, was almost deserted at night, and the lights burning late in the ten striking schools were the only sign of activity amid the rows of nine-story concrete apartment buildings that stood eerily silent on the edge of an unforgiving steppe.

On November 23 the striking teachers and almost 300 parents met in School 20. Although the teachers were already weak and emaciated, they changed out of robes and pajamas into their street clothing and tried to present a normal appearance.

The atmosphere was generally supportive of the teachers. The parents agreed to demonstrate outside the mayoralty on Monday, November 30, if the teachers' demands had not been met by that time; but the chairman of the school parents' committee also said that the parents wanted to know when their children would be studying again.

By the seventh day, nearly all the hunger strikers were lying on their folding beds because they were too weak to stand. Students continued to visit striking schools, and the teachers told them not to worry. But when some of the striking teachers tried to get up, they fainted. Motorin was one of the few who was mobile, and his calm manner comforted the others. But he smoked continually and occasionally suffered chest pains, which led him to rub his chest while he was walking. When other teachers asked him what was wrong, he said, "This sometimes happens."

Gennady Veritenikov, the chief doctor in the oblast, warned in a radio interview that the teachers' lives were in danger because, although a ten-day hunger strike is not normally fatal for a healthy person, "all of Russia has been on a conditional hunger strike for a number of years."

As the days passed without concessions, the teachers began to tell each other that the authorities did not care about the risk to their lives. By the eighth day, unnerved by the official attitude, many were in a state of extreme nervous tension, and at the strike headquarters in School 72, discussion often deteriorated into fits of hysteria.

On the evening of the eighth day, the male teachers in School 20 went as a group to one of the rooms occupied by the women teachers and hinted that it was time to end the hunger strike. "I think we have to ask ourselves whether it makes sense to continue," Motorin said. "I'm a man; I can last another two weeks. But you women, think of yourselves. How much longer do you think you can last?"

In the tense atmosphere, most of the women took Motorin's suggestion at face value. They said that they would continue at least until Friday, November 27. Only Mukhina, who knew Motorin well, sensed that the real reason for his suggestion was that his health was failing and that he was afraid to admit it.

"We aren't achieving anything," Motorin said. "Maybe it makes sense to stop the hunger strike but to continue the [other] strike."

The women teachers replied that no one was being held against his will. If the men were at the end of their patience, they could leave. Motorin said, "You think badly of us," and the men then turned and left.

On Thursday, November 26, the ninth day of the strike, a critical meeting was held in School 72. The weekend was coming, and the teachers knew that for two days the authorities would not decide any serious questions. This meant that the hunger strikers had either to quit now or to hold out until November 30. By the thirteenth day, however, there was a danger that some of the undernourished and chronically ill teachers might die. The teachers debated the question. Some argued that it was time to acknowledge defeat because the strikers were too weak to continue. But many were counting on the hunger strike to make it possible for them to feed their children. In the end, despite the danger, the strike committee voted to continue.

On the night of November 26, however, Alexander Burkin, the head of the raion department of education, came to strike headquarters and informed the teachers that on the following day they would receive an advance on their pay for September and that they would also be paid for November on condition that they began teaching by December 1. The rest of the money for September would be paid in a week.

On Friday a meeting was held in School 72 between the strike committee and local officials, including Burkin and the head of the Zavolzhsky raion. The offer of payment had an effect on the striking teachers. Still to be resolved, however, was the question of whether the teachers would also be paid for the days they had been on strike. They rejected the officials' first offer, to pay the teachers 50 percent of their salaries for this period. When the officials finally agreed to give the teachers full pay for the days they had missed, the teachers agreed to end the strike.

The teachers, many so weak they could barely speak, were relieved that their ordeal was finally over. But the settlement actually gave them very little. After a ten-day hunger strike, they had been promised some of the money that was owed to them, but there was no guarantee that they would be paid in the future. Nonetheless, the teachers collected a portion of their wage arrears and went home. Of the 465 teachers who started the hunger strike, nearly 300 finished it.

Motorin returned home to his family and on Saturday was already eating normally. He was also smoking heavily. The teachers were given the day off on Monday to recover. On Tuesday there was a severe frost. Motorin went to work and then returned home, complaining of not feeling well. He lay down, and a short time later his wife heard a moan. When she went into the room, he was dead.

The pallbearers placed the coffin containing Motorin's body on a platform in front of the apartment building, and the crowd observed several minutes of silence. Nine of Motorin's colleagues from School 20 were crying as they stood over the coffin. Then the pallbearers picked up the coffin and carried it through Novy Gorod. Walking first in the procession were the members of Motorin's family. They were followed by uniformed Afghan veterans who carried his portrait. Then came Motorin's colleagues, students, and friends carrying wreaths with ribbons reading "From Colleagues," "From Relatives," and "To a Beloved Teacher, from Students." In the biting wind, the crowd stopped several more times for periods of silence. Then the coffin was lifted into the hearse.

With word of Motorin's death, teachers all over Russia sent money to help his wife and children to pay for the funeral. Some of these funds were used to hire buses to take the nearly 400 mourners to the Arkhangelsk cemetery three miles away. A military band played Chopin's "Funeral March" as the cortège left for the cemetery. On the way out of Novy Gorod, the buses passed the Aviastar factory and the adjoining engine factory, which had never been completed.

At the cemetery, the mourners walked to the gravesite in the "Avenue of Glory," which contained the graves of those who had died in Russia's recent wars. The paratroopers took the coffin to an area behind a stand of pine trees that protected the mourners from the wind. In the distance, the white trunks of birch trees and a field of white, black, gray, and blue gravestones stood out under the dome of a stark white sky.

Motorin's body was put on stools next to an open grave, and one after another his colleagues spoke, praising Motorin as good, kind, and knowledgeable and promising that he would remain in their hearts and in the hearts of the children he had taught. An Afghan veteran said, "We remember how you courageously went through Afghanistan and endured the difficulties of our life."

With the speeches ended, a guard of honor fired a volley of shots over the grave in a tribute to the former army captain. The paratroopers then nailed the coffin shut, and each mourner threw a handful of dirt onto the coffin as it was lowered into the ground.

In the days after Motorin's funeral, there was a feeling of hopelessness among the teachers of Ulyanovsk. Classes resumed, but the salaries for the second half of September that had been promised as a condition of ending the strike were not paid. Overwhelmed by a sense of defeat, the teachers resumed borrowing from friends and raising their own food on private plots.

It seemed to the teachers that they were totally expendable. And there was a bitter symbolism in the way the strike had ended. The hunger strike had been a supreme effort, mobilizing almost 500 teachers. All of them had risked their lives, but the only salary that was paid in full in the wake of the hunger strike was Motorin's, which was paid posthumously.

Things had better work here because beneath that immense bleached sky is where we run out of continent.
—*Joan Didion,* Play It As It Lays

10 *Vladivostok*

JANUARY 2001

An icy wind blew in off the Sea of Japan, and as temperatures fell to -4 degrees, a driving snow dusted the roofs of apartment buildings. People and cars slipped on the ice that coated Vladivostok's sidewalks and streets.

In an apartment at 13 Chasovitina Street, Faina Kobzar, an elderly pensioner, sat down on the bed where her invalid husband, Ivan Ivanovich, was lying under a blanket, shivering in the cold. A few feet away, the reddish-orange bars of a space heater gave off a small amount of heat. "If there is electricity, the space heater is always on," Faina explained. "With its help, the temperature in the room reaches 46 or 48."

On the previous day the electricity had been shut off for three hours, and the apartment, like thousands all over Vladivostok, became freezing cold. Faina said she had put plastic bottles filled with hot water all around Ivan Ivanovich, who had suffered a stroke and was unable to walk, and covered him with blankets.

Today things were better, but Ivan Ivanovich was wearing a fur hat, sweater, and boots in bed, and Faina placed a bottle of hot water next to his paralyzed legs.

Ivan Ivanovich tried to add something. But describing what it was like to live in the cold was hard for him. No sooner did he begin to speak than he started to cry.

The Kobzars' twelve-story building on Chasovitina Street had been built in 1988 by the Dalzavod shipyards, where the Kobzars had worked for fifty years, she as a tally clerk in the sawmill and he in the repair shop, reconstructing submarines. After the fall of the Soviet Union, the building ceased to be maintained, and the pipes became rusted and clogged with sand. In 1994 the building was transferred to the city, but maintenance did not improve, and in 1996 the heating system broke down completely, leaving the residents, including veterans of the Battles of Kursk and Stalingrad, to warm themselves with electric heaters or the plates of their electric stoves.

The municipal authorities had begun repairing the heating system in December 2000. A few weeks later, temperatures fell to −40, and the work stopped. The city had promised to resume work in the "near future."

"I don't think that we'll survive until the spring," said Faina. "Before, the space heater warmed our room a little, but this year they sometimes turn off the electricity for the entire day, so we're just left here to freeze."[1]

The situation of the Kobzars was shared by most residents of Vladivostok and the Primorsky krai in the winter of 2000–2001. For years the infrastructure of the region had deteriorated, and the situation had reached the point where now many areas were without central heating. In January 2001 electricity cuts in Primoriye became massive, with power turned off for as many as twenty-one hours a day. These cuts, in turn, disrupted the delivery of heat to buildings whose central heating systems were still functioning. Without electricity, hot water could not be pumped by the heating stations, and in the bitter cold, pipes froze and burst.

As large parts of Primoriye found themselves without electricity or heat, schools and medical clinics were closed. Yuri Kopylov, the mayor of Vladivostok, acknowledged that "the energy system of Primoriye has collapsed." His statement was one of the few truthful assessments of the situation to be made by the Primoriye authorities, and it marked the logical conclusion of the wholesale pillaging of one of Russia's richest regions by the forces of organized crime.

The looting was carried out by a criminal oligarchy led by the governor, Evgeny Nazdratenko, who, 6,000 miles from Moscow, established his own system of totalitarian rule.

In August 1992, after enterprises were freed to form economic connections of their own, 213 directors of the largest enterprises in Primoriye, most of them defense plants, organized the Primorsky Corporation of Goods Producers (PAKT), ostensibly to aid the transition to a market economy.

The directors sold the products of their factories to PAKT at minimal prices, and PAKT then resold them at market prices, splitting the difference among the directors. The directors then used the profits to privatize the factories. The founders of PAKT also sought to gain control of the krai's quotas, licenses, and budget. This, however, led to conflicts with Vladimir Kuznetsov, then governor of Primoriye, who wanted to encourage outside investment, not to preserve the existing industrial base for the benefit of a group of supermonopolists.

PAKT, however, established connections with officials in Moscow. In May 1993 it organized the removal of Kuznetsov and the appointment of Nazdratenko, a deputy in the Russian Supreme Soviet and a member of the council of directors of PAKT, as the new governor. He named Igor Lebedinets and Anatoly Pavlov, two other members of the PAKT council of directors, as his deputies.

The factory directors who participated in PAKT saw Nazdratenko as someone who would do their bidding, but once in office he expanded his personal power, eliminating many of his early backers and forming alliances with organized crime.

When it became possible for Russians to travel, residents of Primoriye started going to Japan to buy used cars. Vladivostok quickly became the hub of the trade in Japanese cars, and gangsters began meeting the ferries from Japan and forcing each of the purchasers to pay a "tax" on his newly acquired vehicle.

In the late 1980s Sergei Baulo (Baul), a leading gangster in Dalenogorsk, where Nazdratenko had been president of the Vostok Mining Company before being elected to the Supreme Soviet, moved to Vladivostok and became involved in the extortion racket. When Nazdratenko became governor, Baulo set up an office in the Gorky Theater across from the headquarters of the krai administration and rapidly took over racketeering in the city. In the next few months, nine high-ranking bosses were killed in a bloody redefinition of spheres of authority. By the time the fighting was over, Baulo had become the underworld's unofficial "vice governor" of Primoriye.

Nazdratenko next insisted that the factory directors do business with firms created by the criminal structures, and payoffs from these firms flowed to the krai administration. The administration established a dense network of intermediary firms to make purchases with krai budgetary funds. These firms raised prices to the krai on everything from gasoline and coal to sugar, bread, and electricity, with the "profit" going to officials of the krai. In return for bribes, krai officials also leased strategically located real estate to criminal and semicriminal groups for next to nothing. The krai also issued quotas to criminal groups for the exploitation of Primoriye's natural resources in return for bribes. The most lucrative quotas were for fish; those who received them engaged in uncontrolled fishing, transferring several times the value of their quota to foreign vessels in the middle of the sea. The profits were then deposited in foreign bank accounts.

By early 1994, the krai administration dominated the economy of Primoriye, and with the onset of privatization in Vladivostok, it would have been in a position to appropriate virtually unlimited wealth. In June 1993, however, Viktor Cherepkov, a deputy in the krai parliament, was elected mayor of Vladivostok, defeating eighteen other candidates and taking 67 percent of the vote. A former navy captain, Cherepkov had become famous for his role three months earlier in exposing the mistreatment of sailors at the naval base on Russky Island near Vladivostok, where four sailors had died of starvation and nearly 1,000 had been hospitalized for malnutrition.[2]

Cherepkov's election came at an opportune time. Yeltsin had dispersed the country's parliaments in October 1993, and the krai administration was preparing to privatize buildings, factories, fishing and refrigerator fleets and harbor terminals under circumstances in which there would be no legislative oversight.[3]

Many of these installations, however, were located in Vladivostok, which meant that the privatization process could not go forward without the approval of the mayor. Cherepkov made it clear that he was ready to fight corruption, and he refused to accept gifts of any kind. Most important, he began to transmit to the federal authorities evidence of the abuses of the krai administration, leading to the arrival of the first of many investigative commissions in Primoriye.

The reaction of the krai administration was not long in coming. It was to lead to one of the most bizarre episodes in the history of Primoriye—but one with long-lasting consequences.

As soon as he took office, Cherepkov began to receive ordinary citizens to listen to their requests. In one two-week period 1,115 persons signed up to see him, and he received people from 10:00 A.M. until 3:30 the next morning. On February 6, 1994, Cherepkov was visited by a man named Volkov, who presented himself as an Afghan war veteran and requested an office for a veterans' organization in Primoriye. Cherepkov instructed his staff to look into the matter, and four days later Volkov entered Cherepkov's office and thanked him for his help. He then took off his beret and threw it on Cherepkov's table. He later stated that the beret had contained money.

On February 11, 200 police surrounded the mayoralty and searched

Cherepkov's office. In the course of the search they found a piece of paper that Volkov, who was later revealed to be Valery Bugrov, a senior police lieutenant, claimed was used to wrap the money that he had given to the mayor. At the same time, a search was carried out in Cherepkov's home, where, in the torn pocket of an old coat, police found one million rubles in an envelope and, on the bookshelf, a Swiss Omega watch.

At 5:00 A.M. Cherepkov was removed from the mayoralty at gunpoint and taken to Vyacheslav Yaroshenko, the city prosecutor, who was expected to sanction his arrest. Yaroshenko, however, refused, and in doing so probably saved Cherepkov's life; Cherepkov had been warned that preparations had been made to murder him in jail, with the killing made to look like a suicide.[4]

The expulsion of Cherepkov from the mayoralty was accompanied by a purge of the city administration; 126 people were fired in a single night. Police broke down doors, threw officials down stairs, and confiscated keys and computer disks. Many of the officials were replaced the next morning by appointees of Konstantin Tolstoshein, a krai official with underworld connections, who was named by Nazdratenko to replace Cherepkov.

The forcible removal of the elected mayor, however, led to protests in Vladivostok, and eventually the case against Cherepkov was taken out of the hands of the local prosecutor and transferred to the Office of the General Prosecutor in Moscow, which began an investigation that cleared Cherepkov and led to criminal charges against the investigator, Vladimir Dudin, and three police officers for fabricating a case.[5]

But the general prosecutor's findings made little difference to Nazdratenko. He appealed to the president to fire Cherepkov anyway, and on December 23, 1994, Yeltsin signed a decree removing Cherepkov in connection with the "lengthy nonfulfillment of his duties." The decree was arranged with the help of Nazdratenko's influential backers in Moscow, who included Alexander Korzhakov.

Cherepkov left for Moscow, where he spent the next year and a half fighting for his reinstatement. In the meantime Nazdratenko turned Primoriye into a minitotalitarian state.

With Cherepkov gone, Nazdratenko took steps to control the press. In July 1994 the studio of Primorsky Commercial Television (PKTV), which had been in opposition to Nazdratenko, was invaded by supposed robbers. They destroyed equipment and murdered an engineer; shots were fired through the apartment window of Mikhail Vosnesensky, the local correspondent for

ORT television; and Alexei Sadikov, a young radio reporter who had aired an ironic commentary about Tolstoshein, was kidnapped, taken out of Vladivostok, and beaten and tortured for twenty-four hours.[6]

A cloud of fear familiar from its history spread over Primoriye. Conversations touching on the krai administration began to take place only in private. Critical articles about Nazdratenko disappeared from the local press. Vladivostok residents, if they called in to radio talk shows, gave only their first names or did not identify themselves at all.

The midnight silence of Vladivostok was now frequently broken by the sound of gunfire and explosions. The newspapers filled with reports of the violent deaths of local "businessmen," and the streets became the scene of lavish funeral processions with dozens of expensive cars moving to the accompaniment of police sirens.

The atmosphere of intimidation paralyzed law enforcement. Representatives of the federal government in Vladivostok feared the power of Nazdratenko's protectors in Moscow, while local investigators feared that Nazdratenko was paying off their superiors.

At the same time, the pillaging of Primoriye assumed immense proportions. The following are a few examples of the corruption that was documented by federal investigators:

- On November 5, 1994, the firm Transit, which was founded in Moscow by a relative of Mikhail Savchenko, a deputy head of the krai administration, concluded a contract with a Chinese firm for the purchase of 250,000 tons of coal at a price of $12 a ton. Two days later a second contract was signed between the firm and the krai administration for the purchase of the same 250,000 tons but for a price of $16.49 a ton. The difference of $4.49 a ton produced a payment to Transit from the funds of the krai of $1,122,500.

  The payment was hard to justify on the basis of anything Transit actually did. The Chinese delivered the coal to the Russo-Chinese border, and Transit arranged only for it to be moved to the Russian border town of Poltavka. Payment for the Chinese coal was also made in advance so that Transit could collect interest on the money, and Transit was freed of customs duties on the grounds that the coal deliveries were intended to combat the consequences of flooding in parts of Primoriye in September.

- In April 1994 the krai administration approved an interest-free loan of $1.4 million to the firm Interflot, which had been set up by Alexander Zakharenko (Zakhar), a businessman with close ties to Nazdratenko and organized crime. The ostensible purpose of the loan was to purchase crab and caviar "to feed the poor." The caviar and crab, however, were never delivered, and the money was never returned. When krai officials were asked what had happened to the products, they said they had been lost in the Kobe (Japan) earthquake.

Zakharenko was nonetheless arrested. After two months in jail, he was freed by the Leninsky raion court on a motion by Nazdratenko. A few days later, he was killed by a bomb in the entryway of his apartment building.[7]

- In November 1994 the krai administration began to buy oil products from a refinery in Komsomolsk-on-Amur, where the price was 30 percent higher than that charged by the previous supplier in eastern Siberia. The purchases were made through the firm Representative by Mikhail Chechelnitsky, who was the head of the krai's department of fuel resources— and the firm's part owner. The first payments by the krai to Representative were worth 2.8 billion rubles ($849,000.) An audit of the firm's bank account, however, showed that the firm spent only 1.2 billion rubles on the purchase of oil products. What happened to the other 1.6 billion rubles was never established.

The discovery of the shortfall, however, seemed to presage an investigation of the whole system for the purchase of oil and oil products in Primoriye. Chechelnitsky would have been central to any such investigation, and on December 28, 1995, he was invited to take tea in the office of Nazdratenko. Hours later, he died suddenly, at the age of thirty-eight. According to the autopsy report, he died of a heart attack. It was widely believed, however, that he had been poisoned. A year later, after renewed interest in abuses of power by Nazdratenko in Moscow, Chechelnitsky's body was disinterred and reburied, giving rise to rumors that the body had been cremated to prevent a new autopsy following a court-ordered exhumation.[8]

By late 1994 the bleeding of the krai budget had produced a severe financial crisis. Teachers, doctors, and other state employees were going for months without pay, necessary maintenance and renewal of infrastructure were ignored, and hospitals, schools, and orphanages no longer received essential supplies.

The effects of corruption also spread to the coal-mining regions. As the krai administration took money from the federal government that was intended for Dalenergo, the state power company, and used it instead to plug holes in the krai budget caused by corruption, Dalenergo ceased paying the coal miners. The miners mounted strikes in late 1994 and hunger strikes in 1995. Finally they stopped supplying coal to the power stations. As a result there were cuts throughout Primoriye in electricity, heat, and water.

By early 1996, there were days when power in Vladivostok was off for twenty-three hours out of twenty-four.

On a typical day, most people returned home to find there was no heat or light.[9] The first step was to light candles or a kerosene lamp. The next step was to heat up food in the dark on a butane gas stove. The food, as a rule, had been prepared the previous night. At some point, dots of light would appear in the buildings, and there would be shouts of "It's been turned on!" People then rushed to switch on everything that could be switched on—cooking rings, stoves, teakettles, refrigerators, heaters, washing machines, and televisions—in order to take a shower, do the dishes, wash clothes, and cook for the following day.

The disruption of daily life affected everyone. People were afraid to take an elevator lest they be trapped for hours inside a box suspended nine stories above the ground. It was difficult to wash or launder, carry out elementary business, or provide for oneself and one's family.

Those who could afford them bought generators, which were usually kept on the balcony, but jealous neighbors were likely to complain about the noise. Rumors spread that in apartments owned by "new Russians" the electricity was never interrupted. More infuriating to city residents than anything else, however, was the electric advertising for hotels, restaurants, and casinos, which operated continuously. The cost was seven times the normal rate, but most people were not familiar with the details. Accordingly, it was not difficult to guess what would happen to those signs if the day came when people lost patience and were no longer content to vent their aggression simply by cursing the authorities.

In June 1966, the political situation changed unexpectedly: Yeltsin fired Korzhakov, Mikhail Barsukov (the head of the FSB), and Oleg Soskovets (a deputy prime minister) and named Anatoly Chubais head of the presidential administration. The change was important for Primoriye because Korzhakov was Nazdratenko's principal patron in Moscow, whereas Chubais was his longtime enemy.

Chubais soon took steps to neutralize Nazdratenko. On August 5, a Kremlin spokesman announced to journalists that 60 billion rubles earmarked to pay the salaries of coal miners in Primoriye had been diverted and deposited instead at interest in banks friendly to Nazdratenko.[10]

On August 14, Cherepkov, who for many months had made repeated, futile attempts to contest the presidential decree removing him as mayor, was unexpectedly restored to his post. A Moscow court ruled that Yeltsin, in firing Cherepkov, had violated eight articles of the constitution, three federal laws, and five of his own edicts. A short time later, Cherepkov returned to Vladivostok despite warnings that he would be killed the moment he stepped off the plane.

The return of Cherepkov to Vladivostok made it possible to revive the resistance to Nazdratenko. Guarded twenty-four hours a day, Cherepkov began efforts to end the misuse of city funds, and at first he had some success. He ameliorated the energy crisis in Vladivostok by buying coal from mines and delivering it directly to the power stations in exchange for electricity, bypassing Dalenergo. As a result, the city came through the winter with minimal disruptions.

These initial successes, however, proved to be temporary. The attempt to deal with the power stations directly came to an end when Dalenergo, under pressure from the krai administration, prohibited power stations from receiving coal from the city. Nazdratenko also stopped making all but the most unavoidable payments to Vladivostok from the budget of the krai. In 1997, the money given to the city from the krai amounted to only 14 percent of the krai's revenue although Vladivostok has more than 30 percent of the region's population.

The result was economic hardship throughout the region not seen even during the worst days of World War II.

PARTIZANSK, JANUARY 27, 1998

As the sun penetrated the morning fog that hung over the valley, residents of the city converged on the dilapidated railroad station for an attempt to disrupt traffic on the Trans-Siberian Railroad.

Most of the demonstrators were coal miners, but they were joined by doctors, teachers, and even police officers. By 11:00 A.M. there were 1,000 protestors. At noon they moved onto the tracks of the only railroad linking European Russia to the Far East. The demonstrators remained on the rails for the next two hours, even as it began to snow furiously, with the snow obscuring the electric lines and tracks in the distance.

Finally Viktor Novikov, the leader of the trade union at the nearby Nagornaya mine, spoke through a portable loudspeaker. "The miners are not opposed to reform," he said, "but we want to know where the reforms are leading. Where has our pay disappeared? And what is the contribution of the bureaucrats whose standard of living is ten times higher than that of those who work in the pits?"

The miners had gone for many months without pay. Many were so thin that acquaintances from other cities found it hard to recognize them. Journalists speaking to miners noticed the unusual smell of acetone on their breath, a sign of chronic malnutrition and the dangerous disruption of their metabolism.

Novikov was followed by Yelena Malykhina, a housewife. "I don't know how to feed my children," she said. "There's no breakfast at school anymore. Sometimes children faint from hunger or they get bloody noses from undernourishment and from the cold. What kind of government is it that can't feed its own people?"

The speeches continued for another half-hour while the rapidly falling snow covered eyebrows, fur hats, and the shoulders of threadbare winter coats. One of the speakers threatened a bloody revolt.

The miners had chosen to hold their demonstration when there would be no trains, and many in the crowd argued that, as a result, their action was futile. "There is absolutely no effect to this demonstration," said one woman, "If the train were standing here, we would shake the railroad. Maybe someone important from Moscow would be on the train. Then the message would get through."

But most of the crowd had little will to stop vital rail traffic. With no train in sight and the weather worsening, the meeting ended, and the exhausted miners dispersed to their homes.

On the morning of March 27, 1998, men began fishing through the ice of the Amur Gulf near the village of Sanatornaya. Soon there were 200 fishermen on the ice. Shortly after noon, however, the ice began to break. The emergency was reported to the Coast Guard, which dispatched a Hovercraft to the scene.

When the rescuers arrived, they told the fishermen to leave the ice immediately. Some left, but a sizable minority refused, cursing the rescuers for frightening the fish. While they argued, the ice split, and two fishermen disappeared.

The ice now began cracking everywhere, and the remaining fishermen got up to leave, with the exception of one old man who continued to fish. The Hovercraft maneuvered to within 500 yards of where he was sitting, and a rescuer shouted over a megaphone to him to leave the ice, but he still refused to move. At last, however, the old man got up and returned to shore. Later a rescuer asked him why he had refused to leave.

"I don't have anything to eat," he explained. "My pension is 304 rubles. Here you can catch fish."

"And what if you had drowned?"

"It's better to die than to live like I'm living now," he said.

One evening in March 1998, Vasily Naplyokin, a police officer on duty in the Frunzensky raion in Vladivostok, received a call that an elderly alcoholic man had died in his apartment.

Naplyokin went to the apartment with his partner, registered the fact of death, and then left, assuming that SpetsService, a private firm that transports bodies for the city, would remove the corpse. The next day, however, there was a call from a neighbor. The body was still there; SpetsService had stopped removing bodies because the firm had not been paid.

Naplyokin returned to the scene and tried to decide what to do. None of the police in Vladivostok were equipped to transport a corpse. Finally he went downstairs and stopped a truck on the road. The driver agreed to help. Naplyokin, the driver, and his partner put the body on a stretcher, carried it down, and placed it in the back of the truck. The truck driver then drove it to the morgue.

"In the law on police," said Anatoly Petrusha, a deputy chief of police, "all our responsibilites are defined. Removing corpses is not one of them. But as long as we go out to the scene and respond to a dead body, people think we should remove it. And we have to because there is no one else."

APRIL 9, 1998

As the fog lifted over Golden Horn Bay, revealing the blue outlines of the distant hills, activists began putting up banners in Vladivostok's Central Square, preparing for a demonstration against "the threat of starvation" in Primoriye.

Leaflets announcing the event, which had been organized by the Primoriye Federation of Trade Unions, read: "If you are against the constant degrading of your human dignity and violation of your constitutional right to labor, salary, and social guarantees; if you are fed up living in hunger, cold, darkness, and poverty, YOU SHOULD TAKE PART in the protest against the assault on the rights of workers."

In a corner of the square the demonstrators erected a stand that compared the results of Yeltsin's reforms with Hitler's plan for the enslavement of Russia: "Destruction of the Soviet Union as a state—achieved, 1991; the destruction of the soviets—achieved, 1993; the destruction of Russian industry, science, and culture—achieved, 1991–94; the reduction of the population of Russia—in process; the transformation of Russia into a colony and raw-materials appendage of the West—in process; the establishment of a regime of hunger, violence, and terror—achieved, 1991–98."

By 11:00 A.M., 3,000 people from all parts of Primoriye had arrived in the square. (Many others were stranded in outlying cities because they could not afford the bus fare to Vladivostok.) Most of those attending belonged to the Communist or Liberal Democratic party (LDPR). Some people carried signs reading: "Only Slaves Work for Free."

The first speaker was Nikolai Kostyukov, the deputy chairman of the Federation of Trade Unions. "We gather here today," he said, "to demand light in our apartments, water in the faucets, and money in our pockets. This is a question of physical survival."

There was scattered applause from the crowd.

Ivan Pavlenko, the trade union chairman on a state farm in Ussurisk, said, "What we are witnessing is the genocide of the Russian people.

Yuri Maron, the chairman of the strike committee at a Vladivostok housing trust, said, "The capitalists have taken the third way toward the destruction of Russia. They have moved heavy industry abroad and left us with nothing, only slavery."

Nadezhda Pushkar, a teacher in the Khasmisky raion, said, "Our money is in foreign banks. The reforms led to the impoverishment of the people, and we see the price—rape, degeneration, and murder."

The final speaker was Viktor Potapeko, a member of the radical Communist group Working Russia. He said, "The workers have lost their rights and are now in the position of prisoners in the fascist concentration camps."

When he finished, martial music played over the loudspeaker, and the demonstrators slowly dispersed, returning to indigent lives in a region that should be rich.

On May 13, 1998, the front page of the newspaper *Vladivostok* carried an article titled "Electroshock: Primoriye Becomes a Place of Death." The article noted the following:

Orphanage. The electricity was turned off in the city orphanage on the 6th, 7th and 8th of May at 8 A.M. It went on at noon for two hours and then was turned off until late at night. While the power was on, the personnel washed and fed 90 children between the ages of one month and four years, most of whom were invalids. All attempts by the chief doctor to call to responsible persons in the mayoralty and Dalenergo were unsuccessful.

Psychiatric Hospital. In the city psychiatric hospital, the cutoff of power created serious problems for the personnel. The mentally ill patients demonstrated increased agitation in connection with delays in giving them their meals, and the nurses and orderlies found it difficult to explain to them the reasons for the absence of light in the hospital.

Venereal Clinic... as a result of the absence of power in the refrigeration unit of the clinic, more than 20 quarts of unanalyzed blood spoiled and was poured into the sewage system of the city. In the opinion of doctors, it was therefore possible that infectious venereal agents ended up in the . . . waters of the Amur Gulf.

Ussurisk. The "darkest" days since the beginning of May were the 6th and 7th. During these days, the refrigerators of residents of the raion rumbled for only 40 minutes a day.

A dispatcher in the Vladivostok central ambulance station on Ocean Prospekt got up from her place and signaled to Dr. Lyubov Novikova. "They've called again from Borisenko," she said. "They want to know when they can expect the ambulance."

Eight hours earlier, the station had received a call that a thirty-nine-year-old fisherman had suffered a stroke and was lying paralyzed. His wife and mother had begged the dispatcher to send an ambulance immediately. It was now 1:00 A.M., and there was still no ambulance although the family had called back a dozen times.

Only eleven or twelve of the sixty ambulances needed for a city the size of Vladivostok were operational. Finally, at 1:30, an announcement came over the loudspeaker: "Brigade 20–22, on call." A car had arrived. In less than five minutes Novikova, an orderly, and a nurse were in a minivan on their way to Borisenko.

The team arrived at their destination at 2:00. The patient was on the ninth floor, but the electricity had been cut off after 11:00 to save power, so Novikova, the nurse, and the orderly climbed the stairs. When they reached the patient's apartment, they rang the doorbell and were greeted by an older woman, who said, "Thank God, you didn't abandon us altogether."

The patient was lying on a couch. He said that in the late afternoon his arm had stopped working and then he could not move his side. At that point his wife had decided to call for an ambulance.

Novikova and the orderly lifted the victim off the couch and put him on a blanket they had spread out on the floor. They then lifted the blanket and carried him out of the apartment, into the corridor, and down the stairs, where they put him in the ambulance and took him to the Construction

Workers' Medical Clinic. The delay could have cost the fisherman his life, but this story had a happier ending than usual: the last that Novikova heard, the patient was recovering.

With the cutoff of funding, the city ambulance service organized itself on a wartime basis, treating only the most critical cases.[11]

There was also a severe shortage of drugs. The "line" ambulances, which went out on more-routine calls, were soon traveling with almost nothing at all. One car left the station with two ampules of analgesic, an ampule of saline solution, and less than an ounce of alcohol. There were no heart drugs or drugs to ease breathing, and there was nothing for lowering blood pressure. The analgesic was kept for the most critical cases and, out of caution, was often not given even in the case of severe pain, as with a patient suffering from kidney stones. Ambulance drivers arriving in emergency situations often asked relatives of the sick person to buy necessary medicines at nearby pharmacies, although medicines were frequently beyond their means. The cardiological brigade had one defibrillator, but its batteries were exhausted and needed to be replaced. There was usually enough power for one discharge; a patient in a state of cardiac arrest needed three to four.[12]

The doctors also faced a steady increase in serious illnesses. "The situation leads to acute stress and premature death," recalled Tamara Sitkina, a cardiologist with the ambulance service, one evening at the headquarters. "The social psychology in the country changed, and people cannot adapt to a new way of life. The number of suicides among the elderly has gone up. Earlier, suicide was very rare. Vladivostok was a very patriotic city, and for the people who fought in the war and defended socialism, the idea that we should now build capitalism is very difficult. They remember the enthusiasm, the party, the Komsomol, the postwar reconstruction . . . so now when they are told that it was all unnecessary, it turns out that they lived their lives in vain, and they don't try to survive. It's not for nothing that the ancients said that all disease is from stress."

The doctors lived in fear that any mistake could lead to a death. One night, when Lyudmilla Yakutova was on duty, the cardiological brigade used the defibrillator to treat an eighty-year-old woman. The next call came from the family of a fifty-nine-year-old man who had just had his second heart attack. When the brigade arrived at his apartment, the apparatus could not produce a discharge. Desperate to keep the patient alive, the doctors carried him on a stretcher, massaging his chest as they walked. In the ambulance, they continued the massage, Yakutova radioed the hospital, and doctors were waiting for them when they arrived. They carried him into a ward, massaging his heart as they went, but as they prepared to stimulate his heart electrically, he died. Yakutova was haunted for weeks afterward by the thought that the man could have been saved had the defibrillator in the ambulance been working.

Such incidents led to a practice of not being frank with patients' relatives. In many cases when a patient died after being brought to a hospital, no one discussed the kind of treatment the patient had received before arrival.

In an open letter to Nazdratenko, Svetlana Orlova, a deputy in the State Duma from Primoriye, pointed out that in 1997 the revenue of the krai— consisting of tax income and financial support from the federal government —was 7.2 trillion rubles, but the 3 trillion rubles that was to cover salaries and social payments, including children's subsidies, was not paid on time or in full, although by law these payments had to be made immediately on receipt of the necessary funds.

In most regions of Russia, the share of unitemized expenditures in the budget was 3 percent. In some areas, it reached 10 percent. In Primoriye, "other expenditures" in 1994 accounted for 40 percent of the budget. By 1997 they were 58 percent.

Despite such incidents, Nazdratenko not only was not prosecuted but even began to be mentioned for the post of deputy prime minister.[13]

In these circumstances, Cherepkov was virtually powerless. Nonetheless, he posed a threat that Nazdratenko could not afford to ignore. Nazdratenko controlled the instruments of political power in Primoriye, but sooner or later he would have to run for reelection. If, by some chance, Cherepkov won the election, Nazdratenko could count on prison or worse.

As it happened, a victory by Cherepkov in the election for governor was a serious possibility. New elections for mayor of Vladivostok were imminent, and if Cherepkov were reelected mayor, he would be in a strong position to challenge Nazdratenko in 1999. It was therefore imperative from the point of view of Nazdratenko to organize the final elimination of Cherepkov.

After several postponements, the date for the mayoral election in Vladivostok was set for September 17, 1998. In August, Sergei Markelov, Cherepkov's chief of staff, was informed by a contact in the FSB that there would be an effort to remove Cherepkov from the mayoral race with legal maneuvers but that if these failed, there were plans to have him killed. With this information

Cherepkov registered as a candidate and then disappeared, moving into an abandoned building on a chicken farm in Nadezhdinsk, a village thirty miles from Vladivostok.

Cherepkov's isolation meant that he could not campaign, but he believed that if he remained alive, he would win the election overwhelmingly. Nazdratenko, however, had no intention of letting this happen. On the night before the voting, the electoral commission of the krai, which Nazdratenko controlled, eliminated Cherepkov as a candidate on the grounds that, because he had put up signs reading "From the City and the Mayor" at the site of various city projects, he was guilty of preelection agitation.

The next morning, voters were handed ballots with Cherepkov's name scratched out. The result was an electoral revolt. Many people simply refused to vote. Others tore up their ballots and threw them in the faces of the local voting officials. A few attacked officials, and the police had to be called in to protect them. Soon the words "Vote Against All" were scrawled on buildings all over Vladivostok. The final tally showed that, of 370,000 people who arrived at the polls, the majority either refused to vote or cast spoiled ballots. Of the 142,000 who cast valid ballots, 76,000, a majority, voted against all the candidates, invalidating the election.

With the election invalidated, Cherepkov remained as mayor, but in early December Nazdratenko's allies in the presidential administration prepared a decree for Yeltsin removing Cherepkov on the grounds that his term as mayor had ended. In fact the constitution stipulates that a mayor should remain in office until the election of his successor, but Yeltsin signed the decree, and Nazdratenko named Yuri Kopylov, a deputy mayor who had been fired by Cherepkov and who had received one percent of the vote in the September 27 election, to succeed him.

The removal of Cherepkov as mayor set the stage for a new confrontation. On December 11, after Cherepkov received the news that he had been fired by Yeltsin, he announced that he was not leaving his office. Crowds of his supporters converged on the mayoralty, filling all nine floors of the building and the surrounding square.

On December 14 the krai administration ordered the police, armed with automatic weapons, to surround the mayoralty, blocking the entrances. The electricity and telephones were cut off, and the krai authorities halted publication of the region's only independent newspapers, *Primoriye* and *Arseniye Vesti,* and disconnected the radio station, Forpost Rossiya.

Inside the mayoralty, Cherepkov, working by candlelight and using two telephone lines that still functioned and a cell phone, organized fuel, energy, transport, water, and heat for the beleaguered city.

By evening on December 14, rumors swept the square that the police were getting ready to storm the building. At 9:00 P.M., however, three deputies from the State Duma—Telman Gdlyan, a supporter of Cherepkov; Svetlana Goryacheva, a Communist; and Oleg Finko, of the LDPR—arrived outside the mayoralty and met with the crowd, calming the atmosphere.

The deputies negotiated with the krai authorities until, on December 17, they arranged a truce and the police were pulled back. Nazdratenko then signed an agreement promising not to use force to remove Cherepkov pending new elections, and many of the defenders of the mayoralty abandoned the building, leaving behind only a small group of pensioners to stand guard. On December 23, Cherepkov left for Moscow to try to obtain a reversal of the presidential decree.

On the night of December 27, however, with city officials at work in their offices, the police burst into the mayoralty, breaking down the doors to offices, seizing all money, documents, and equipment and expelling Cherepkov's deputies. Kopylov was then brought to the mayoralty and installed as mayor, eliminating the last base of political opposition in Primoriye.

There was now only one problem for Nazdratenko. New elections for mayor had been set for January 17, and it was certain that if they were held, Cherepkov would win. But on January 11 the Leninsky raion court, which was controlled by the krai administration, canceled the elections on the grounds that Vladivostok first had to elect a city duma.[14]

In an interview with ITAR-TASS, Kopylov expressed satisfaction with the result. Holding the elections would have posed a serious danger, he said. "What if another crazy man had been elected? He could say, 'I have four years, and I can do what I want.'"

When the caravan turns around, the last camel becomes first. —*Russian proverb*

11 *Krasnoyarsk*

A crowd of reporters and cameramen jostled each other in the arrival hall of Sheremetevo-2 airport as they waited for Anatoly Bykov, the former chairman of the board of the Krasnoyarsk Aluminum Factory (KRAZ), who was being returned to Russia from Hungary to face charges of conspiracy to commit murder.

Suddenly, from the service entrance, three special forces soldiers in black face masks and camouflage appeared, pulling a fourth person who had a bag over his head. "Bykov!" shouted the reporters. "Everyone to the side!" said one of the soldiers.

The soldiers and their charge hurried past the cordon of waiting journalists and then crashed into a thick glass door, which did not open automatically, apparently because of a fault in the controlling photo element. The soldiers pushed open the door, stepped out onto the sidewalk, jumped into a waiting car, and, with siren wailing, sped toward Moscow.

A short time later, Dmitri Pavlov, a correspondent for *Kommersant*, interviewed General Alexander Lebed, the governor of the Krasnoyarsk krai.

"Alexander Ivanovich, should I congratulate you on your victory?"

"I'll treat this as a victory when a court dots all the 'i's and it becomes clear who Mr. Bykov is."

"Does Bykov still have influence in the Krasnoyarsk region?"

"He dominated the krai for seven years, and time is needed in order for that system to collapse."

"Do you know the name Tatarenkov? How important is he for the case against Bykov?"

"This is one of the most important figures in the case against him. Bykov used Tatarenkov to eliminate his enemies. Tatarenkov will soon be returned to Russia."

"Is it true that Bykov had a contract on your life?"

"I heard about this, but it doesn't bother me."

"Can it be said that Bykov's empire was built on blood?"

"Let the court say that. I need Bykov alive. He has to be guarded, even pampered. Let's not make him a dead hero, a patriot who wanted to do things but was not able to."

"Can you give a guarantee that Bykov will not be killed in prison?

"Why should I give such a guarantee? I said that I'll do everything possible to prevent that from happening."

With the arrest of Anatoly Bykov, a career that began in poverty and crime and reached the pinnacle of wealth and power came full circle. Using criminal methods, Bykov took over a large part of the Russian aluminum industry. In 1999, however, he began to pay for his crimes after he lost the factor that had guaranteed his invulnerability—the tacit support of the political authorities.

The setting for Bykov's career was Krasnoyarsk, a Siberian industrial center on the Yenisei River, full of tall chimneys emitting rust-colored smoke, log houses sunk to the window frames in the earth, and miles of standard Soviet apartment blocks.

During the Soviet period, the Krasnoyarsk, Bratsk, Sayansk, and Novokuznetsk aluminum factories supplied the needs of the Soviet air force. In 1992, however, with the former Soviet economy in ruins, the Russian aluminum smelters were left impoverished and isolated. The traditional suppliers of alumina were in Kazakhstan and Ukraine, both independent countries, and the smelters could not afford the world market prices and duties to import it.

In this situation, David Reuben, the chairman of Trans-World Metals Ltd., a London metal trading company that had been buying aluminum from the Soviet Union since the late 1970s, came up with the idea of "tolling." Reuben realized that if he provided alumina to the Russian factories, he could get the finished metal at low domestic prices and sell it at world market prices, paying the factories only for processing.

To navigate in the Russian environment, however, Reuben needed a local partner. He recruited the Chernoy brothers (Lev and Mikhail), metal dealers with ties to Oleg Soskovets, the chairman of the Russian Committee on Metallurgy. The Chernoys were also friends of Shamil Tarpishchev, Yeltsin's tennis coach, and they had connections to Anton Malevsky (Anton), the head of the Izmailovsky criminal organization. Later their circle of contacts expanded to include Alexander Korzhakov, Yeltsin's bodyguard and the head of the presidential security service.[1]

In 1992 Reuben set up the Chernoys in a Monte Carlo–based company, Trans-CIS Commodities, which was combined with several other of the Chernoys' companies to form the Trans-World Group (TWG). In August and September 1992, with the active support of Soskovets, the Chernoys concluded tolling contracts with the ten largest aluminum factories in the country, including KRAZ. The Chernoys guaranteed the factories hard currency and imported raw materials, and in return the government exempted them from customs duties and value-added tax. The price of aluminum on the London market was about $1,500, three times the cost of production, so the potential profits were enormous. To obtain the aluminum, however, the Chernoys had to raise tens of millions of dollars to pay for the first round of tolling. They did this by diverting money from the Russian Central Bank.

In the early 1990s, Russian commercial banks did not clear transfers. This was done by the Russian Central Bank. The payer's bank transferred money to the branch of the central bank in its city, and the branch instructed its counterpart in the payee's city to transfer a sum of money to the payee's account. Swindlers, however, learned the ciphers and codes of banking documents and wired phony instructions to the branches, ordering them to transfer specific sums. The branch in the payee's city was required to confirm with its colleagues in the payer's city that it had received the promised sum, but in the case of the false instructions, the answers came from the swindlers themselves. As a result, the branches ended up making wire transfers when no equivalent deposit had been entered. The transfers were then either quickly turned into cash or passed through several commercial banks and in that way legalized.

According to a report of the investigative committee of the Ministry of Internal Affairs, from 1992 through 1994 the Chernoy brothers, using these methods, stole 7 billion rubles, receiving the money in accounts in commercial banks. In this way, they were able to lay the basis for the takeover of Russian aluminum.[2]

Using the profits from tolling, TWG purchased enough shares in Russian aluminum factories to assure itself control. At KRAZ, however, although

TWG's share was 20 percent, the firm had a difficult time asserting its authority. Aluminum intended for TWG was stolen by local bandits working with employees in the shops and warehouses and sold to TWG's competitors. It was this situation that led the Chernoy brothers to form an alliance with Bykov.

Bykov, who had been a high school physical education teacher in Nazarovo, near Krasnoyarsk, was distinguished by his willpower, determination, and energy. In the late 1980s he organized a gang made up of nonsmoking, nondrinking sportsmen to extort money from the owners of the first private businesses. At the same time, Bykov cooperated with the Krasnoyarsk criminal bosses, Vladimir Liphyagov (Lyapa) and Yuri Tolmachev (Tolmach), and became acquainted with Vladimir Tatarenkov (Tatarin), a veteran criminal, who controlled the Sayansk Aluminum Factory in Sayanogorsk.

Bykov's gang soon was collecting tribute from a large number of businesses in both Nazarovo and Krasnoyarsk. The turning point in Bykov's career, however, came in December 1992, when he successfully defended Yuri Kolpakov, the commercial director of KRAZ, in a brawl in a restaurant in Krasnoyarsk. When the fight was over, Bykov told Kolpakov that he could assure security at KRAZ with the same success he had had in defending Kolpakov personally. Kolpakov introduced Bykov to Chernoy, who concluded an agreement with Bykov to protect TWG's interest and guard the factory.

The selection of Bykov to guard KRAZ set the stage for a criminal war. Krasnoyarsk was largely under the control of Tolmach, Lyapa, Chistyak, and Sinii, all of whom were connected to the theft of aluminum at KRAZ and none of whom was willing to hand over the profits from the aluminum business to Bykov. At the same time, Bykov began to challenge the traditional criminal world openly. He started to speak of his hatred for "blues," the tattooed veterans of the Russian penal system; and he refused to submit to the laws of the thieves' world, declining to pay a "severance" to Tolmach and Lyapa for leaving their control or to contribute to the criminal *obshchak*.

As tension between Bykov and the traditional thieves in Krasnoyarsk grew, Bykov established alliances. The first was with Tatarenkov, who had assembled a brigade of professional killers in Sayanogorsk. Tatarenkov's killers became the enforcers for Bykov.[3] The second alliance was with Boris Petrunin, the head of the interior ministry for the krai, who wanted to "fight crime with the hands of the criminals." Petrunin's idea was to select one criminal leader and use him to annihilate the others. Petrunin favored Bykov, in part, because of the absence in his group of career criminals, and as a result the police began to assist Bykov, giving him information about his criminal competition from their network of informants.

Eight months after forming a partnership with Chernoy, Bykov launched a drive to dominate KRAZ. The first to be killed was Chistyak, who was shot on August 10, 1993. He was followed by Sinii on September 22. Bykov and the Chernoys faced resistance from Ivan Turushev, the general director of KRAZ, who objected to TWG's encroachments on his authority. On October 20 two masked men surprised Turushev in the entryway of his apartment building and beat him with iron rods, breaking his legs and fracturing his skull. When he recovered from his injuries, Turushev resigned, and Kolpakov was voted general director with TWG's support.

Suspecting his role in the murders of Chistyak and Sinii, Lyapa took out a contract on Bykov. The assassins, however, informed Bykov, who offered them twice as much to kill Lyapa. The killers arranged a meeting with Lyapa on November 23, 1993, in the center of Krasnoyarsk, and when Lyapa got out of his car, the killers opened fire on him with automatic weapons. According to one description, bullets flew "like sparrows on a garbage dump."[4] Lyapa died from a bullet to the head. His bodyguard was also wounded. It was later determined that the killers had been guests in Lyapa's apartment the previous evening.

In the wake of these killings, Tolmach, the last traditional criminal leader in Krasnoyarsk, became very nervous. He traveled everywhere with dozens of guards, and when he arrived at his nine-story apartment building, he did not leave the car until his guards had checked the entire stairwell. On May 12, 1994, however, Tolmach arrived home and left his car after his guards had searched the stairway. At that moment, a ventilation window leading to the basement was opened, the barrel of a gun was stuck out, and there was a burst of fire from an automatic weapon. Tolmach was hit by twenty bullets. When his guards ran into the basement, all they found was the discarded automatic.

With the killings of Lyapa, Chistyak, Sinii, and Tolmach, Bykov had crushed all traditional criminal networks at KRAZ. He began to build a professional security service at the factory, and at the same time he launched a new wave of killings, intended to help him take over the entire region.

The first victims were businessmen who had paid the recently deceased criminal authorities—Lyapa, Chistyak, Sinii, and Tolmach—and did not want to pay Bykov. In late July and early August 1994, five leading Krasnoyarsk businessmen were killed in ten days. One of the victims was Viktor Tsimik, the former second secretary of the krai Communist party, who had become one of the leading entrepreneurs in the city. He was shot five times in the entryway to his apartment building.

Dozens of killings soon followed. The victims included government officials, such as Yuri Kaletnikov, who was in charge of aluminum in the committee on metallurgy; businessmen like Sergei Skorobogatov and Oleg Gubin; and criminal leaders such as Mustaf Mustafin, who arrived from Moscow to force Bykov to give money to the all-Russian *obshchak*. Also killed were Konstantin Voitenko and Alexander Naumov, who were planning to kill Bykov; and four businessmen from Tyumen whom Bykov mistook for hired killers.

The wave of murders caused panic in Krasnoyarsk. Bykov's killers not only mowed down their victims in full public view; they also shot anyone who got in their way. There was a feeling that law enforcement had broken down completely. By 8:00 P.M., the stores, streets, and bus stops of Krasnoyarsk were deserted.

In this atmosphere, the organized crime groups that still operated in the city submitted to Bykov's control. Bykov's lieutenants divided up the city and were soon exacting tribute from virtually every business in Krasnoyarsk. Bykov, in turn, justified the extortion racket in interviews with the press. The greatest Russian problem, he said, was that "in their lessons in arithmetic, our citizens did not learn how to divide. God ordered us to divide, and it is necessary to divide and not try to be cleverer than everyone else."

By late 1994, Bykov had brought KRAZ under TWG's complete control, and the giant factory became an integral part of an empire that produced 40 percent of Russia's aluminum and had sales of from $5 billion to $7 billion a year. Bykov was not destined, however, to remain subordinated to the Chernoys. TWG usually relied on the leader of a criminal group to run its factories,[5] but the firm was accustomed to dictating the terms. In this respect, TWG underestimated Bykov. Having got what it wanted from him, it proceeded to cheat him. The result was what became known as the "great aluminum war."

In addition to establishing order at KRAZ, Bykov and his partner, Gennady Druzhinin, organized the purchase of factory workers' shares on TWG's behalf. Payment for this service was made to Bykov and Druzhinin in an offshore account controlled by the Chernoys. After payment was made to the account and a receipt was shown to Bykov, however, Lev Chernoy removed a large amount of money from the account, citing a mistake in the receipt.

Bykov's response was to tell Kolpakov to erase 85 percent of TWG's shares in KRAZ from the factory share registry.[6] TWG was left with a 3 percent interest in KRAZ, which was not enough for a management role.

TWG reacted to the cancellation of its shares by sending a brigade of men armed with automatic weapons, as well as two Jeeps, on a special flight to Krasnoyarsk to take over KRAZ by force. At the administration building they were met by hundreds of Bykov's men armed with automatic weapons and by a unit of OMON police. In the tense confrontation that resulted it quickly became clear that the new arrivals were not ready to die for TWG, whereas Bykov's men were ready to open fire. The fighters from TWG finally got back into their Jeeps, drove several times around the factory headquarters, and left for Moscow. TWG, which only a few weeks earlier had been all-powerful at KRAZ, had been barred at the factory's gates.

After the standoff, Bykov received 10 percent of the 17 percent share in the factory taken from TWG and joined the KRAZ board of directors. In that position, he established his personal dictatorship inside the factory, using intimidation, including the beating of managers, to enforce his authority.

Bykov also began to engage in philanthropy. He established a charitable fund, Faith and Hope, and through it gave money to orphanages, schools, and hospitals and set up a network of social organizations designed to involve young people in sports. He also helped war veterans and invalids and gave money to construct an Orthodox church, a synagogue, and a mosque.

On the surface, calm returned to KRAZ. TWG did not send any more special flights to Krasnoyarsk. Instead, inconspicuous assassins arrived in the city, only to be discovered and killed by Bykov's men. Their bodies were left on benches in the city parks. When the police entered the hotel rooms of the deceased, they found rifles with optical sights and other tools of their trade. In the meantime, Bykov moved to a bunker and never sat opposite a window or open door.

The battle between Bykov and KRAZ and TWG and the Chernoy brothers, however, continued in Moscow, where the Chernoys had the support of Soskovets, Tarpishchev, and Korzhakov, who, as head of the presidential security service, had authority over the FSB. The Chernoys were unable to defeat Bykov in Krasnoyarsk, but KRAZ needed financial contacts, and those who tried to work with the rebellious factory were killed.

The first victim was Vladimir Yafyasov, the vice-president of the Yugorsky Bank. He was shot in his car in a courtyard in central Moscow on the night of April 10, 1995. The police established that several days before his murder,

Yafyasov began to be followed everywhere by a red BMW automobile that was registered to an employee of Trans-CIS Commodities. During this period Yafyasov met with the president of the Yugorsky Bank, Oleg Kantor. After the meeting, Yafyasov told his driver, Vadim Tishaev, that he had been sentenced to death and that the following Saturday was to be the last day of his life. As it happened, he erred by only one day.

On July 20, 1995, a little more than three months after the death of Yafyasov, Kantor was found murdered in the foyer of his dacha. He had been stabbed dozens of times, and a knife had been left in his chest. His throat had been cut from ear to ear. Kantor's bodyguard, a heavyweight boxing champion, was found about 200 feet away. He had been stabbed repeatedly and shot twice.

The dacha complex where Kantor was killed was surrounded by a fence and guarded twenty-four hours a day by a special police unit assigned to protect government buildings. Entry to the complex was possible only through a checkpoint where all visitors and their cars were registered. These circumstances created the impression that Kantor's killers had been cleared to enter the complex by someone in a position of political authority.

The Yugorsky Bank, which had been one of the most important in Russia, had recently lost the accounts of its principal clients in the oil business, and Kantor had hoped to compensate by moving into the aluminum business, in particular by obtaining the accounts of KRAZ and the Achinsk Alumina Factory (AGK). This effort appears to have led to his death. In the last few weeks of his life, Kantor seemed anxious and depressed. On the day before his death, he unexpectedly turned to Irina P., a twenty-two-year-old businesswoman, and asked, "Ira, will you lay flowers on my grave?"

Finally, on September 8, 1995, the body of Felix Lvov was found by the side of the Volokolamskoye Highway, about sixty miles from Moscow in a pile of garbage with five bullet wounds. Lvov, the commercial director of the American firm AIOC, had tried to obtain control of 20 percent of the shares in AGK for his firm, which had taken over from TWG as the metal trader for KRAZ. It was hoped in this way to strengthen the position of AIOC in the Russian market. In his pursuit of the 20 percent share of AGK, Lvov, in turn, had relied on the energy and political connections of Yafyasov.

The ensuing investigation established that Lvov, accompanied by guards from his company, arrived at Sheremetevo airport for a flight from Moscow to Almaty. His guards left, and he passed through security. Fifteen minutes before the flight was to take off at 11:30 P.M., two men came to him and introduced themselves as FSB agents, presented identification, and asked Lvov to come with them. He was last seen leaving the airport in their company.

In the end, however, the effort to strangle KRAZ was a failure. The factory established channels for selling its products through offshore firms, and Bykov survived numerous attempts on his life.

After Yeltsin's removal of Soskovets and Korzhakov during the 1996 presidential elections, TWG was seriously weakened and broke up into a number of parts, including Siberian Aluminum, under a former TWG manager, Oleg Deripaska, which gained control of the Sayansk Aluminum Factory.

Bykov's struggle with TWG, however, made him a local hero. The terror that had stalked Kransoyarsk was partially forgotten, and the image of Bykov as a ruthless killer was replaced by that of a young Siberian schoolteacher who had defended the region's leading factory against gangsters, corrupt Moscow officials, and a giant conglomerate run by citizens of Great Britain and Israel.[7]

Bykov was plagued at KRAZ, however, by a financial crisis, one that prepared the way for the return to KRAZ of Lev Chernoy but under conditions in which he acknowledged the authority of Bykov.

The crisis at KRAZ was the result of Kolpakov's incompetence. At a time when the price of aluminum had reached $2,100 a ton, the factory managed, through overpayment to intermediaries, to run up debts of 8 trillion rubles to creditors. In late 1996 Kolpakov concluded a contract through an offshore company to deliver aluminum worth $20 million to an American firm. The aluminum was delivered, but the payment was never received. To extricate himself from this situation, Kolpakov agreed with Vasily Anisimov (Vas Vas), a vice-president of the Rossiskii Kredit bank, that Anisimov would pay $20 million for 48 percent of the shares in KRAZ, including those belonging to Bykov and Druzhinin.[8]

The news that Kolpakov had sold Bykov's and Druzhinin's shares without their permission sent a wave of fear through the aluminum industry. Many expected shooting to break out at any moment. Anisimov, however, flew to Krasnoyarsk and gave back to Bykov and Druzhinin their 10 percent shares in the factory. He then proposed to Bykov that he open negotiations with Lev Chernoy.

The conflict between Bykov and the Chernoys had led to a dozen murders, but the killings had been over money, not principle, and with enough money the hard feelings could be assuaged. Chernoy said he had never intended to cheat Bykov, and he blamed the "misunderstanding" on friends in the Izmailovsky criminal organization. KRAZ was in serious financial straits, and Chernoy was in a position to pay a higher price per ton for the factory's aluminum than any competitor. The result was that the parties agreed to restore to TWG the 17 percent share in KRAZ that had been seized in 1994 and to divide the factory's exports into three parts, a third for Chernoy, a third for Anisimov, and a third for Bykov and his associates. Bykov agreed to protect Chernoy's and Anisimov's interest in Krasnoyarsk, and Chernoy and Anisimov became Bykov's "roof" in Moscow.

Bykov became chairman of the board of KRAZ, and in this capacity he used violence to realize his ambition to join to KRAZ other important components of the Krasnoyarsk energy metallurgical complex.

First, KRAZ bought 17 percent of the Krasnoyarsk hydroelectric station, Russia's second largest, for only $3 million. Shortly afterward there was an additional stock issue, and the station passed under Bykov's control, becoming the first private producer of electricity in Russia. When Chubais, who became the head of United Energy Systems, tried to recover control over the hydroelectric station for the state-run corporation, he was threatened physically.[9]

Bykov also moved to take over TANAKO, a holding company created at the initiative of the krai administration that united the state shares in the largest enterprises in the krai, including not only the Krasnoyarsk hydroelectric station but also the power company Krasnoyarskenergo, the Krasnoyarsk steel mill, the Borodinsky open-face coal mine, AGK, and the Krasnoyarsk railroad. In August 1997 Valery Zubov, the governor, left on vacation, and Bykov called an extraordinary shareholders' meeting at which a vote was taken on a motion to remove the state representative from the board of directors. The agenda for the meeting was passed out by enforcers from Bykov's organizations who advised the shareholders how to vote. The motion passed, transferring the holding company into the hands of Bykov.

Bykov was now the ruler of a regional economic empire. The only thing that he lacked was political power, and in December 1997 Bykov ran for a seat in the Krasnoyarsk krai legislative assembly, depicting himself as an enemy of organized crime.

Bykov's candidacy was a test of moral judgment for the citizens of Krasnoyarsk. It was known that Bykov was implicated in contract killings, and he even admitted that he had taken, in his words, some "illegal chances." But Bykov said he had broken the law to establish order and rid the region of thieves professing the code. Many people in Krasnoyarsk accepted this explanation at face value.

At the same time, Bykov's philanthropy made a big impression.

DECEMBER 1997

As a steady snow fell outside the assembly hall of the House of Teachers in Krasnoyarsk, a gray-haired teacher mounted the podium and began to speak. "Comrades!" she said, "I want to tell you a story that I cannot fail to tell. I was in the office of Anatoly Petrovich!

"Do you know how Anatoly Petrovich began the conversation with me? He began to tell me about his family. If you have not heard Anatoly Petrovich talk about his mother, you haven't heard anything. Comrades, I ask you, do many of us begin a business conversation with a story about our mama? But Anatoly Petrovich does exactly that! Forgive me, I can't speak any more . . ."

The teacher burst into tears and returned to her place.

Behind the podium, in a place of honor, Bykov sat with his hands folded, smiling shyly. The occasion was the announcement of Bykov's decision to finance a memorial book in honor of the deceased former teachers of the Krasnoyarsk krai. A second teacher, who had been sitting next to him, got up and went to the podium.

"Who gives life to a child?" she asked.

"His mama," answered the teachers in the hall.

"And then?"

"The teacher!"

"That's right, the teacher who teaches him to do good deeds. And who in the krai does good deeds?"

"Anatoly Petrovich!" came the chorus from the hall.

A third teacher mounted the podium. "I can speak of Anatoly Petrovich only in poetry," she said. She then recited several poems on the theme of goodness. When she finished, she said, "It seems to me that God has descended from the heavens in the person of Anatoly Petrovich Bykov."

At an orphanage in Nazarovo, Bykov cut a ribbon releasing balloons into the air, then opened a box and began handing out presents to the children. On the wall was a sign with his photograph and the words "Children and their parents are with A. P. Bykov."

After the gifts were distributed, the children, who were dressed in Russian folk costumes, formed a line, each of them holding his or her present, and the director of the orphanage made a brief speech. "I am so grateful for this show of goodness and warmth toward our children," she said. "I know that A. P. Bykov has a big program, and it is necessary that he fulfill it, so I want also to give him a present." She then presented Bykov with a block of salted fat and a jar of berry *varenie* (preserves). The children recited, "Uncle Tolya is like a natural father to us. All of us, without a doubt, belong to Anatoly Petrovich Bykov."

In the end, Bykov won more than 80 percent of the vote. He was named chairman of the industry committee in the legislative assembly, which gave him authority over legislation and increased his economic power still further.

By the beginning of 1998, Bykov had emerged as the head of a parallel structure of power in Krasnoyarsk krai that was more powerful than the legal government. He controlled not only the principal enterprises in the region but also all organized criminal activity. The head of the krai's ministry of internal affairs, Petrunin, was his friend, as was the head of the legislative assembly, Alexander Uss.

The seeds of Bykov's downfall, however, were already being sown. With the forcible takeover of TANAKO, Zubov became alarmed at Bykov's immense power and ordered a tax audit of KRAZ. The audit led nowhere, but he next invited a commission of the interior ministry under General Vladimir Kolesnikov to investigate corruption at KRAZ. This, too, produced no result, in part because Bykov showered the members of the commission with expensive gifts. The experience of being investigated, however, convinced Bykov that he had to do away with Zubov. He then made a mistake that was to prove disastrous for him: he decided to throw his support behind General Alexander Lebed in the election campaign for governor.

In many ways, the Bykov-Lebed alliance was logical. Lebed was running for governor, but his real goal was to run for president. Bykov wanted only to strengthen his economic empire in Siberia. At the same time, he controlled the levers of economic power in the krai, and Lebed knew it would be difficult to win without him. The problem lay in the two men's personalities. Bykov did not like being slighted, and Lebed, accustomed to commanding armies, did not like making allowances for anyone but himself.

Nonetheless, at first the new partnership seemed to be working. Bykov and Lebed agreed that Bykov would support Lebed and, in return, Lebed would allow Bykov to establish a holding company for a single, integrated energy-metallurgical complex, including KRAZ, the Krasnoyarsk hydroelectric station, AGK, and the open-face coal mines. Bykov and Lebed appeared together constantly, and Bykov donated large sums to Lebed's campaign.

After Lebed was elected, however, the partnership fell apart. Lebed refused to authorize the energy and metallurgical holding company that he had agreed to with Bykov, explaining that the company, as envisaged by Bykov, would produce profits of $85 million a year for its directors but only $500,000 a month in taxes to the krai. Lebed's violation of their agreement led Bykov to charge publicly that Lebed was incompetent to administer the krai, and growing tension between the two men exploded into outright war.

Lebed asked Kolesnikov to renew his investigation of Bykov. Soon afterward Kolesnikov returned to Krasnoyarsk, and this time he opened sixty-four criminal cases connected with Bykov and two implicating him directly in violations during the privatization of KRAZ.

The situation became so serious that, in the midst of the investigation, Bykov left Russia, ostensibly for medical treatment, and moved into a villa in Montenegro on the Adriatic Sea.

While Bykov was out of the country, an event occurred that made it possible for Kolesnikov to expand his investigation significantly. This was the arrest of Tatarenkov in August 1999 by the Greek police.

Tatarenkov had been on the run since 1994, when a member of his gang was arrested and implicated him in a series of contract murders, including killings on behalf of Bykov. In October 1996 he arrived in Greece, where he began living under a false name and running a hotel owned by Bykov. Tatarenkov had always been devoted to Bykov, but about a year before his arrest there were signs that these feelings were not reciprocated. Bykov took steps to remove the hotel in Greece from Tatarenkov's control, then summoned him to a meeting in Germany. At the last minute, Tatarenkov decided not to go. He later learned that waiting for him in Germany were professional killers. Shocked by Bykov's betrayal, Tatarenkov began making videotapes on which he described the killings he had carried out for Bykov.

On one of the videotapes, Tatarenko directly addressed Bykov. "Respected Anatoly Petrovich!" he said, "I have prepared many videocassettes in which I speak about how . . . much blood was spilled so that you could become what you are today. Do you not dream about those persons murdered perhaps not by you but on your orders? Maybe you've forgotten them, so I'll remind you: Chistyak, Lyapa, Tolmach, Terekh, Loban, Shorin, Sergei Skorobogatov, Oleg Tubin. Murderers in Russia were never pitied, and you have a long list of victims, enough for life imprisonment. All of this evidence is confirmed by facts and stored with reliable people." In all, Tatarenkov implicated Bykov in thirteen contract killings.

After Tatarenkov's arrest, the videotapes were turned over to the police and new charges were filed against Bykov for money laundering and conspiracy to commit murder.

With Bykov under investigation and out of the country, the aura of menace that had always surrounded him began to weaken, and a coalition of his enemies mounted an attack on his economic empire. The enemies included Chubais, who resented the tactics used by Bykov in taking over the Krasnoyarsk hydroelectric station; the Alfa group, which seized control of AGK with the help of OMON police acting on orders from Lebed; and Deripaska, who had not forgotten how Bykov's partner Tatarenkov had called him regularly on his mobile phone and threatened to kill him.

The coalition began to act against Bykov's sources of income. Deliveries of aluminum to KRAZ from AGK and from the Nikolaevsk Aluminum Factory in Ukraine, which was under the control of Deripaska's firm, Siberian Aluminum, were curtailed and then stopped. The United Energy System filed two suits against KRAZ for 3.3 billion rubles and 500 million rubles. At the same time, the police received orders to detain Bykov's "soldiers" for any infraction, including crossing the street on a red light. In the city markets, persons describing themselves as Trans-Dniester fighters began going from stall to stall recommending to vendors that they give to the Lebed Youth Movement the payments that they had previously given to Bykov's henchmen.[10]

On October 29, 1999, Bykov was arrested on the Hungarian-Yugoslav border. He was extradited to Russia and imprisoned in Moscow. On Lebed's insistence, he was then transferred to Krasnoyarsk.

Lebed wanted Bykov to be tried in Krasnoyarsk to show local residents that Bykov was a criminal, not a "Robin Hood." The krai legislative assembly, however, gave Bykov nearly unanimous support, and leading citizens rose to his defense. In a collective letter to the krai prosecutor, editors, teachers, and duma deputies spoke of the dangers of a witch hunt and a return to Stalin-era terror. They promised to guarantee Bykov's "appropriate behavior" in the event that he was released on bond.

Bykov was also active. He sent letters from prison in which he expressed his concern for the moral direction of the nation. In one, he wrote: "I believe in the triumph of reason. Our salvation lies in only one thing—the spiritual and moral resurrection of the personality."

Finally, at the end of August 2000, Bykov was freed on bail and announced that he intended to create a broad-based political movement. There were rumors that he planned to run for governor. Bykov was too dangerous, however, to be allowed to stay free.

While Bykov was in prison in Hungary awaiting extradition, the situation of KRAZ, under seige from the combined forces of Lebed, Deripaska, the Alfa group, and Chubais, significantly worsened, and Chernoy and Anisimov sold their shares in KRAZ to Sibneft, the oil company controlled by Roman Abramovich, a major oligarch. These and shares in AGK and the Bratsk Aluminum Factory were subsequently combined with Deripaska's Siberian Aluminum to form Russian Aluminum in the biggest merger in the history of post-Soviet business. The new firm soon produced 10 percent of the world's primary aluminum.

Bykov, however, continued to control his share of KRAZ, and if he were elected governor, Russian Aluminum would face an extremely powerful opponent.

Because of Lebed's alliance with Bykov's economic competitors, what had originally been a personal conflict between Bykov and Lebed had grown into a conflict with Abramovich and Deripaska, two of the most favored oligarchs under the new Putin regime. It was this "correlation of forces" that weighed on Bykov's fate.

A little more than a month after Bykov was freed on bail, the wristwatch of one of his lieutenants, Vilor Struganov (Pasha Tsvetomuzyka), was found during a search of Bykov's dacha, and Bykov was charged with Struganov's murder. A few days later, however, it was established that Struganov had not really been killed. His "death" had been staged with the help of a body covered with a sheet that was carried out of a building on Kutuzovsky Prospekt.[11] Nonetheless, despite the protests of his lawyers, Bykov was not released. The prosecutor insisted that although the murder had been faked, Bykov had really ordered Struganov killed.

The incident involving Struganov allowed the authorities to bring Bykov to Moscow. "To act on all of the material that has been gathered on Bykov," a source in the prosecutor's office told *Kommersant*, "in a city that is under his control would have been impossible."[12]

Six weeks after the "murder," Bykov was taken to an interrogation room where investigators from the prosecutor's office were waiting for him. Given the fact that Struganov had not been murdered, Bykov assumed that he would be freed. But the prosecutors announced that he was going to be held on charges of conspiracy to commit murder.

Bykov now understood that, eight years after beginning his ascent from street racketeer to master of one-sixth of Russia, there was a formidable group of forces arrayed against him. This, not the evidence, threatened to cut short the trajectory of his life, and in the presence of his attorney and the prosecutors he became disoriented and showed signs of despair.

"All right," he said, "lock me up. But you won't hear anything more from me." Bykov's eyes then filled with tears and he turned sharply to the wall, trying with all his strength to keep from crying.

There are ants down there somewhere swarming. Who is going to raise objections if accidentally one of them is crushed?—Novaya Gazeta, *August 16, 1999*

12 *The Value of Human Life*

DISTRICT HOSPITAL, POGRANICHNY, RUSSIAN FAR EAST, FEBRUARY 12, 1997, 6:00 P.M.

Floodlights illumined the operating room as Galina Suvernyeva, the thirty-one-year-old wife of a Russian army major, gave birth to a baby girl by caesarean section. Dr. Valentina Lysenko handed the newborn to a pediatrician, relieved that the operation had gone well.

Ever since power began to be cut off in the Far East, Lysenko had tried to avoid operating at night. In this case, however, a night operation had been unavoidable. Suvernyeva's pregnancy had been difficult, and once she started to have contractions, a caesarean needed to be performed immediately.

Lysenko started to sew up the incision. At that moment, Suvernyeva began bleeding heavily from the uterus. Lysenko tried to stem the bleeding, but it only intensified, and she realized that if she did not act quickly, Suvernyeva was in danger of bleeding to death. Lysenko decided to remove the uterus, but just as she began the operation, the electricity in Pogranichny was cut off, plunging the operating room into total darkness.

Pogranichny is a town on the Russo-Chinese border consisting of weathered wooden houses, a central square dominated by a statue of Lenin, and pastel-colored, three-story concrete apartment blocks on potholed streets.

Beginning in late 1994, as a result of the energy crisis in the Far East, power was cut off regularly in Pogranichny. The cuts of from four to six hours usually took place in the morning, when people got up and prepared for work, and in the evening, when they returned home. As a rule, only half of the village was cut off at a time. On some occasions, however, electricity was shut off for the whole town, with no exception made for the hospital.

For many months, the power cuts that affected the hospital did little damage because they occurred during daylight hours or at a time when no operations were in progress. In the summer of 1996, however, the town's reserve generator burned out, greatly increasing the risks of a power cutoff. The chief doctor, Vadim Kizey, raised the issue of a new generator at meetings of the raion government, but officials said the raion could not afford one. A short time later, Kizey left Pogranichny to take a course in St. Petersburg.

On December 14, the medical personnel in the hospital had their first reminder of the growing risk. The lights in the hospital went out for twenty minutes while a woman was undergoing a caesarean. The woman's blood pressure fell to zero, but she was saved because the doctors were able to put clamps on her major blood vessels. A few days later, the hospital's electricity was again turned off while an operation was in progress. This time the doctors sewed up a patient's intestine in the dark, solely on the basis of touch.

Despite these incidents and the panic they caused, there was no effort to replace the generator or to prepare for a possible future emergency. The doctors tried to operate only when there was daylight—and with the onset of winter, the days were progressively shorter—but the risk of a patient's dying on the operating table during a cutoff of power was treated like the risk of a natural disaster rather than as something preventable, and an atmosphere of torpor and helplessness settled over the hospital.

In the pitch darkness, Lysenko squeezed Galina Suvernyeva's aorta to slow the bleeding. This had some effect, but soon Lysenko faced another problem: the medicines regulating Suvernyeva's breathing had stopped working. Suvernyeva needed additional medicine, but it was impossible to find the vein for an intravenous feed without light.

Svetlana Vodneva, a nurse, left the operating room and begged her colleagues to search for a flashlight. She then ran to a telephone and began dialing for help. Her first call was to Sergei Cherkasov, the acting chief doctor. His line was busy. She next called the office of the head of the raion administration, Anatoly Rozhenko. There was no answer. She called Rozhenko's home, but his wife said he had just left.

In the corridor outside the operating room, the nurses were going through drawers and cabinets in the hope of finding a flashlight. During the six months that the hospital had been without a reserve generator, no one had thought to buy flashlights. One nurse finally found a flashlight in a supply cabinet, but it was broken. Later, flashlights were found in other parts of the hospital, but they, too, were broken.

Lysenko held tight to Suvernyeva's aorta and prayed that the hospital generator would begin working. But as the minutes passed and Suvernyeva continued to lose blood, the electricity did not come on. A nurse ran into the operating room with a kerosene lamp, but the anesthesiologist, Arkady Marilov, told her to get out; the room was crowded with canisters of oxygen and nitrous oxide, and ten feet from the operating table an oxygen canister was leaking. There was a danger that introducing a flame into that environment would blow up the whole hospital.

Vodneva called the duty officer at Communenergo, the power company for Pogranichny. "Turn on the lights," she said. "A woman is dying!" The duty officer said that Dalenergo in Ussurisk had ordered the cutoff.

Vodneva asked how to call Ussurisk. The duty officer said, "I don't know."

No one at the hospital had bothered to compile a list of emergency telephone numbers.

A nurse gave Vodneva the home number of a colleague whose husband worked for Communenergo. When Vodneva reached him, he told her that the generating station at Lipovtsy had probably cut off the electricity. He then gave her the number. Vodneva called Lipovtsy and said, "This is the central raion hospital in Pogranichny. Our patient is dying. We need light." Forty minutes had passed since the power had been cut off. The person at the other end of the line said, "OK," and moments later the lights in the hospital came back on.

Lysenko removed Galina Suvernyeva's uterus in six minutes, and the bleeding stopped. Suvernyeva was moved into intensive care and given massive blood transfusions. Her husband, Nikolai, drove back and forth to Vladivostok for drugs because the hospital was short of basic supplies, including saline solution. The efforts, however, were futile. Seven days after going into the hospital to give birth to her second child, Suvernyeva died without regaining consciousness.

Soon after Suvernyeva's death, the newspaper *Izvestiya* investigated the incident. A reporter who tried to phone Dalenergo in Vladivostok was told that the number had been disconnected, apparently to avoid calls from irate citizens. But the newspaper did reach Vladimir Alexeev, an employee of

Dalenergo in Ussurisk, who had been working the night that Suvernyeva died. He said that he had received an order from Vladivostok to turn off the electricity to consumers, including the village of Pogranichny, at 6:05 P.M. in order to reduce the demand for electricity. By 6:50 the goal of saving 35 megawatts had been achieved. It was in this interval that Suvernyeva lost her last chance of survival on the operating table in Pogranichny.

Not long after Suvernyeva's death, there were some changes in Pogranichny. Money was found to repair the hospital generator. At Nikolai Suvernyev's request, a criminal case was opened against hospital personnel and then dropped for lack of evidence of a crime. The hospital refused to accept blame for Suvernyeva's death, although Lysenko, haunted by feelings of responsibility, suffered a minor stroke.[1]

In Pogranichny, people discussed Suvernyeva's death for a long time. Some blamed the raion government, others the doctors or the hospital administration. The general opinion was that a young mother had died because no one had cared enough to make sure that a dangerous situation was avoided. "This is the way it always is in Russia," said Raisa Glapshun, who was in charge of social questions in the raion administration. "A person is dead, but no one is guilty."

The fate of Galina Suvernyeva was not an aberration. On the contrary, her experience reflected a basic reality in contemporary Russia: the low value attached to human life.

Lack of respect for human life is traditional in Russia. Like the other negative aspects of Russian life—corruption, criminality, and lack of moral discrimination (as well, indirectly, as the positive characteristics, compassion and deeper wisdom)—it stems from the fact that society and its institutions are not anchored in an appreciation of ethical transcendence, defined by Carl Jung as the "reciprocal relationship between man and an extramundane authority which acts as a counterpoise to the 'world' and its 'reason.'"

The lack of a sense of ethical transcendence, in turn, derives in part from the destructive effect of two ideas, the so-called Russian Idea and economic determinism, an outlook that Russia shares with many in the West.

The Russian Idea is the distinctly national ideology with which Russia traditionally justified its lack of freedom vis-à-vis the West. Proponents of this idea rejected the notion that Russia differed from the West only in its backwardness and argued instead that Russia had a culture of a different type that was based on Orthodoxy and dedicated to the development of the spirit.

This spiritual culture was superior to the materialism of the West, and, in recognition of this verity, it was the mission of the Russian state to bring godliness in the form of (the Russian) religion to the whole world.

Although the Russian Idea was originally developed to defend tsarism, it came to characterize Russian thought generally. The Slavophiles saw the state's mission in terms of religion, the Westernizers in terms of socialism, but, according to Berdyaev, both believed that it was the role of the Russian state to save humanity on the basis of a totalitarian ideology that combined "philosophy with life" and "theory with practice."

The Russian Idea gave to the state a role in salvation that, in the Western tradition, is reserved for God. It followed from this that there could be no true role for values that were over and above the state and to which the state itself was also subject. The lack of a transcendent point of reference was reflected in the arrogance of the officials of the state and the lack of concern for the fate of the individual.

In addition to the influence of the Russian Idea, the lack of a sense of transcendence in Russian society is the result of the impact of economic determinism. For seven decades, the Soviet Union inculcated the notion that moral factors in society have no independent existence but are a function of underlying economic relations, and the lesson was well learned by generations of Russians, including the future young reformers.

As a result, when the Soviet Union fell, the reformers were not guided by moral considerations but concentrated on the mechanics of capitalist transformation. The reformers assumed that once a class of private owners was created, it would manage resources rationally and, de facto, in the interests of society. What they took to be universal economic behavior, however, was only normal economic behavior within a specific legal and moral context. They failed to consider that in Russia that context had been destroyed and the country's most urgent need was its restoration.

The lack of a sense of transcendence left its mark on Russian history. During Russia's more than seven decades of Communist rule, human beings were treated as raw material in the service of some "higher" social goal. Hundreds of thousands of slave laborers died to build the White Sea Canal, and millions were sacrificed to win World War II.[2] The lives of individuals did not matter. What mattered was the system.

The hope of the reform period, under these circumstances, was that Russian society would accept the authority of transcendent values that recognized the sanctity of the individual and that those values would provide the guiding principles for a state based on law.

Unfortunately, however, this did not happen. The reformers did not think in terms of transcendent values. Their goal was also to create a system—in this case, a market economy. But practices derived from a socioeconomic system reflect the requirements of that system, which is concerned first of all with its own functioning. The absolute priority that the new government gave to the transformation of economic structures was reflected in the choice of policies that had deadly consequences for the population.

In the first place, to facilitate the reforms, the government removed all restrictions on the sale of alcohol. The result was that Russia was flooded with cheap vodka, and while the purchasing power of the average Russian was cut in half, his salary in relation to the cost of vodka increased threefold. The period of unrestricted sale of alcohol coincided with the rapid privatization of state property. Tranquilizing the population with cheap vodka made it easier to carry out privatization, even at the cost of thousands of lives.[3]

Another example of the new government's disregard for human life was the failure to finance the system of public health. For the first time, Russians found that they had to pay for many medical services, from necessary medicines to lifesaving operations, and inability to pay led many to give up on their own health. The failure to finance adequately even such hospitals of "last resort" as the Vishnevsky Surgical Institute in Moscow, which was underused despite a surge in the death rate, came at a time when well-connected insiders were acquiring giant Soviet enterprises for next to nothing.[4]

The most important sign of the priority of political change over the need to protect lives, however, was the tolerance shown for corruption and organized crime. The absence of legal safeguards during the privatization process led to an increased level of conflict in Russia and destroyed the possibility of introducing elements of moral idealism in postcommunist society. For many people who had been raised under the Communist system, the resulting spiritual void was intolerable. It led to a sharply higher murder rate, a spiraling suicide rate, and an epidemic of heart attacks and strokes.

The "shock therapy" approach to reform resulted in a tidal wave of premature deaths. In the period 1992–1995, deaths exceeded births by 2 million, a demographic catastrophe not experienced in Russia in peacetime except during the famine of 1932–33 and the Stalinist terror of 1937–38.[5]

Just as the life of the individual had had little importance under communism, so it continued to have little importance during the period of reform—the chief difference was that the system for which the individual now had to be sacrificed was based on private ownership instead of ownership by the state.

The expendability of the individual was the dominant reality of postcommunist Russia, and it was reflected in individual fates.

MINSK HIGHWAY, DECEMBER 12, 1997

The weather was cold and clear. Ivan Lapshin and his family were driving home from Moscow to Odintsovo with Ivan's future son-in-law, Vyacheslav, at the wheel. In the back seat were Ivan's wife, daughter, granddaughter, and five-year-old grandson, Denis.

Suddenly, when the Lapshins' car was about 10 miles outside Moscow, a Jeep Cherokee crossed the median strip to pass a long truck. But there was a second truck in front of the first. The Jeep could not return to its lane. It swerved to avoid a head-on crash with an approaching car, turned sharply to the left, and hit Ivan's car, propelling it across the highway into a pillar. Ivan lost consciousness. He awoke to hear his wife screaming, "Deniska is dead."

A few minutes later, someone pulled Ivan out of his car. In front of him, flanked by men in dark coats, was the driver of the Jeep. A few feet away stood Vladimir Putin, the head of the Control Directorate in the presidential administration. The Jeep was his official car. Ivan did not know his name, but he recognized him as someone he had seen on television.

Ivan was forced into an ambulance and taken to a nearby hospital. At the hospital, the surgeon who examined him told Ivan that the Jeep had crossed the median strip 80 meters (about 250 feet) from where it hit Lapshin's car and collided with a car driven by a soldier named Alexeev. Alexeev had been brought to the hospital but was not seriously hurt. Ivan spent the night in the hospital.

While Ivan was being driven to the hospital in an ambulance, a car arrived at the accident scene. Men in dark coats got out, lifted the body of Denis from the side of the road, hailed a cab, and took the body to the 71st Moscow Hospital. Passengers in Alexeev's car who remained at the scene later told Ivan that the same men had kicked the fragments from the first accident to the other side of the median strip to give the impression that it was Alexeev's car that had crossed the median strip, not Putin's.

In the following months, Ivan tried in vain to have criminal charges brought against Putin's driver, Boris Zykov. Zykov had not been tested for alcohol at the time of the accident, but there were repeated attempts to build a case against Alexeev, whose car was inspected three times.

In response to his repeated protests, Ivan was finally received by the deputy interior minister, Y. N. Olkhovnikov, who showed him a police report stating that Alexeev's car had been hit 8 meters, not 80 meters, from the scene of the collision with Ivan's car. This gave the impression that the Jeep had caromed off one car into another. Ivan said that the report was false. He also said that Zykov, having hit the first car, had not stopped but, on the contrary, accelerated, and in the process caused a crash that killed his grandson.

Ivan appealed to the prosecutor of the oblast to open a case against the police for not having prevented the removal of the body of his grandson from the scene of the accident, for having allowed the Jeep to be removed from the scene (it was immediately repaired and sold), and for having removed him from the scene of the accident for medical care that he did not need. After additional long delays, Ivan was told by the MVD that Zykov would be tried in the death of his grandson.

Ivan waited uneasily for the judicial process to begin. Repeated statements by the police that the case was "complicated" made him fear that no one would answer for the death of Denis. In the end, his fears were borne out. In July 1999, shortly before Putin was named acting prime minister, Zykov was amnestied without trial.[6]

Denis Lapshin was not the only person to fall victim to the reckless driving habits of Russian officials, their relatives, or their chauffeurs.[7] On the evening of February 27, 1999, three pedestrians were struck and killed by Alexei Soskovets, the son of Oleg Soskovets, as they walked along the side of the Rublevo-Uspenskoye Highway. One of the victims was caught on the bumper and dragged 200 feet before being cut off and thrown in a ditch. There was no attempt to offer help. Instead, the driver fled. In Kursk, the Jeep of the son of Governor Rutskoi struck and killed a pedestrian, but the criminal case against the younger Rutskoi was closed after an employee of FAPSI stated that he had been the driver at the time. On the night of February 2, 1999, the car of Viktor Gerashchenko, the chairman of the Central Bank, struck and killed eighteen-year-old Roman Yudakov as he crossed the Yaroslavskoye Highway. Evidence at the scene showed that Gerashchenko's driver had not even braked.[8]

DUBKY STREET, MOSCOW, FEBRUARY 22, 1998, 5:00 P.M.

Through the window of a police car, Galina Mkrtumyan saw two ambulances parked in front of the grocery store where she normally did her shopping. About twenty people were gazing at a pool of water as dense clouds of gray steam billowed up from its surface.

Galina got out of the police car, hurried to the first ambulance, and opened the door. Inside, her husband, Vladimir, was being given an injection.

"What happened?" she asked.

"I'll tell you later," he said. "Take care of our son."

Galina closed the door and started toward the second ambulance, but a doctor blocked her way. At that moment the door of the ambulance opened, and Galina caught a glimpse of her ten-year-old son, Artyem. To her horror, she realized that he had lost his skin.

Shortly after dawn that day, residents of buildings on both sides of Dubky Street had noticed steam rising from the ground next to the neighborhood grocery store. They began making calls to warn the maintenance office for the area that underground pipes were probably leaking hot water.

At 1:00 P.M. Oksana Teryokhina, the manager of the grocery store, also saw steam rising from the ground near the store. When she called the maintenance office, an employee said it was their day off. Teryokhina next called the department of communal services for the raion. "There is a hole with hot water," she said. "The earth is disintegrating. Someone could fall in there." The dispatcher called the raion headquarters of Mosteploset, the organization responsible for the Moscow heating pipes. At 3:45 an inspector from Mosteploset arrived, saw that steam was rising from the ground, and left to report the incident to his superiors. By this time the earth was bubbling and periodically belching clouds of steam.

Shortly after 4:00 P.M. Mkrtumyan and his son left their apartment to buy bread at the local grocery store. It was a mild and sunny day. The snow was melting, and the sidewalks were clear. As they approached the store, Artyem dropped his father's hand and started to run across a grassy lot to the entrance of the store. At that moment, the earth gave way, and as his father watched helplessly, Artyem disappeared into a pit of boiling water.

Vladimir jumped into the pit to rescue his son, but clouds of steam blinded him. Hot water was pouring out of the pipe, and, submerged to his waist, Vladimir could not find the edge of the constantly expanding pit. It took fifteen minutes for him to lift Artyem out of the pit and then climb out himself. When he emerged, Vladimir placed his son carefully on the ground and then ran into a building to call an ambulance. His decisive actions created the impression that he was not seriously hurt.

People in nearby buildings who had witnessed the accident began calling for help, and minutes after the first calls, members of the "salvation service," a volunteer rescue organization, arrived. The rescuers cut slits in Artyem's trousers and removed them. His skin came off with his trousers. The boy began screaming in agony and calling for his mother. A salesgirl from the grocery store who witnessed the scene almost fainted. The crowd grew, and everyone waited anxiously for an ambulance, which, despite dozens of hysterical calls to the dispatcher, took half an hour to arrive.

When Galina saw her son in the ambulance, she realized that he and her husband, who an hour before had left the house to buy bread, were now in danger of dying. The ambulances left, and Galina listened in disbelief to witnesses' descriptions of what had happened. A policeman told her to go to the Third Hospital.

As the crowd dispersed, Galina collected her husband's and son's soaked clothing and left the site of the accident. The clothes were heavy, and Galina walked the 500 yards back to her apartment with great difficulty. When she washed out Artyem's shirt, the water ran red with blood. When she spread the other clothes on the floor, she saw they were full of human skin.

Galina called the Third Hospital and spoke to a hospital official, who told her that Vladimir had been taken to the burn center at the Sklifosovsky Institute and Artyem to the Ninth Children's Hospital. Galina called the Ninth Hospital and asked if they needed anything. They said no. When she called the Sklifosovsky Institute, however, a nurse gave her a long list of items to bring, including vodka and shampoo to treat the burned tissue, and elastic linen wrapping. Galina went to the market, bought the supplies, and took them to the institute. She was told that her husband was in intensive care and advised to return in the morning.

Galina went home but could not sleep. The horror overwhelmed her, and she could not stop crying.

On the following day, she resigned from her job as a construction engineer and went to the Ninth Hospital, where Artyem was lying unconscious. He had suffered fourth-degree burns over 100 percent of his body. The attending doctor refused to let her see Artyem. "This is not a sight for a mother," he said. "We see this every day. For you, it would be very difficult."

Galina next went to the Sklifosovsky Institute. The doctors there told her that Vladimir had suffered fourth-degree burns up to his waist and was in great pain but that his main concern was for his son. They said they had told him that Artyem's condition was satisfactory. Galina was not allowed to see Vladimir, but they passed notes to each other. He asked about Artyem. Galina, not wanting to upset him further, also said that Artyem's condition was satisfactory.

After she left the hospital, Galina went to the scene of the accident, where workmen were desultorily draining the pit. She saw that the pipes at the bottom of the pit had been laid without concrete protective casings, which would have prevented water from saturating the ground in the event of leaks. As an architect and construction engineer, she knew that this was a violation of the most basic rules of technical safety.

On Tuesday, February 24, articles about the incident appeared in the Moscow press. Almost immediately afterward, advanced medical equipment was brought to the hospital for Artyem, and doctors began to cover his body with imported, self-breathing, moistening bandages.

Galina, however, did not take this show of concern seriously. After the first articles appeared, she met with Anastasia Bolshakova, a reporter from *Komsomolskaya Pravda*. Bolshakova told her that there had been many cases in Moscow of people dying after falling into pits of boiling water. Ten months earlier a woman had been walking with her three-year-old son in the area near Marshala Vassilevskogo Street when the boy had fallen into a sinkhole. The mother had jumped into the pit and tried to rescue him, but both had died from burns over 100 percent of their bodies. Bolshakova said that while investigating the incident she learned from doctors in the Ninth Hospital that in the past few years at least four children a year had died after falling into sinkholes filled with boiling water from leaking hot-water pipes. There were no reliable figures for adult victims because Bolshakova did not have information from other hospitals.

On Wednesday, while at the Ninth Hospital, Galina was called to the telephone. An official from the office of Boris Nikolsky, the deputy mayor, told her that Nikolsky wanted to speak to her. A short time later, a car arrived at the hospital and took her to Nikolsky's office, where she was met by Nikolsky, Ruslan Balikoyev, the general director of Mosteploset, and Nikolsky's deputy, Vladimir Masyuk.

Balikoyev said that the incident involving her husband and son had been a monstrous accident but that, in general, his organization did high-quality work. Galina replied that she was a construction engineer and had seen that the pipe on Dubky Street did not have a concrete casing. "This means the work was done with massive violations."

"How can we help?" asked Nikolsky. "You have large expenses. How much money do you need?" Galina did not know how to reply. "My son is apparently going to die," she said. "But there is still a chance that my husband can survive. Do what you can to help my husband."

He said, "We'll help you. Whatever you need, call my deputy."

Galina went to the Ninth Hospital and the Sklifosovsky Institute every day. At the Sklifosovsky Institute, the doctors explained that because of his age and the severity of his burns, Vladimir had only about a 15 percent chance of survival. At the children's hospital, however, Artyem's condition improved slightly. The doctors maintained his vital functions at a stable level, and after several days he began to regain consciousness. When the doctors saw this, they gave him medication to keep him comatose out of fear that if he woke up and saw what had happened to him, the shock would kill him.

For the next few days, there was no change in Artyem's condition, and Galina marveled sadly at the strength of his young organism. On the morning of March 5, however, eleven days after the accident, Galina arrived at the hospital and was met by the attending doctor, who told her that Artyem was dead.

Galina had understood that there had never been a chance to save Artyem, but she was still overwhelmed by her loss. She resolved not to say anything to her husband and to have the funeral the next day.

Organizing the funeral, however, posed problems. The funeral would cost money, and she was now unemployed. She called Nikolsky's office to ask about his promise of help. An assistant told her, "Call again later. We're preparing for the holiday." (March 8 was International Women's Day.)

"You have a holiday, and I have a funeral," Galina said. She then put down the phone and left for the cemetery to get a plot for her son.

In the hospital and later at the morgue, Galina was warned not to open her son's casket. Instead, a photograph of Artyem was placed on his coffin. There were relatively few mourners—only Galina, several relatives, and Artyem's teacher. As they lowered the casket, Galina recalled that her son had always been afraid of pain and had always held his father's hand.

After the funeral, Galina returned home and called the Sklifosovsky Institute. She was told that Vladimir had lost consciousness. For two weeks, Vladimir lingered in a coma; then his heart stopped. The doctors resuscitated him, and Galina was invited into the intensive care unit for a last look at her husband. His face was swollen, and he did not seem to be alive. She left the hospital and called a short time later. Vladimir's doctor told her that he was dead.

On March 21 there was a funeral and Vladimir was cremated. Galina hired a lawyer and prepared to file suit against the city of Moscow. While doing so, she learned of the fate of Marina Yarova, a forty-three-year-old mother of two, who had been boiled alive after falling into a sinkhole in a field near her apartment while walking her dogs on March 11, seventeen days after the accident involving Galina's husband and son. With this news, she lost all hope for the future of her country. It seemed to her that there was no tragedy sufficiently horrible to shake the indifference of the authorities or their disregard for human life. She later told a reporter that her son had died a death that would not have been imposed on even the most hardened recidivist in the most barbaric and uncivilized country in the world. Because of the criminal carelessness of the city authorities, her life had been ruined. "What I feel now is terrible emptiness," she said, "and I am standing on the brink of an abyss."[9]

MILITARY HOSPITAL, ROSTOV, FEBRUARY, 3, 1995

The bodies were stacked three high along the sides of the refrigerator car, and as Anna Pyasetskaya went from stretcher to stretcher, shining a lantern on each set of remains, she saw that many of the soldiers who had been killed in Chechnya were little more than boys. Some had not even begun to shave.

Anna looked first at each dead soldier's hair, then at the face and then at the clothes. If the body had no head, she looked at the hands and feet.

In all, Anna went through twelve refrigerator cars looking for the body of her son, Nikolai. She then went out to the tent city on the grounds of the hospital, which was also filled with the corpses of young men as the North Caucasus military district tried to cope with the overwhelming flow of death. Nikolai's body, however, was not in the cars or in the tents. Anna's search would have to continue.

Anna's ordeal began on New Year's Eve, 1994–95. She was at home with friends when the celebrations on television were interrupted by the first reports of the slaughter of Russian soldiers in Grozny. Only days before, Anna's son, a nineteen-year-old member of the Ryazan Paratroop Regiment, had been sent to Chechnya.[10]

On January 2 and 3 the press reported details of what had happened in Grozny. According to NTV, the 81st Samara Regiment and the 131st Maikop Brigade, two of the first units to enter the city, had been annihilated. There was no mention of the Ryazan Paratroop Regiment, and Anna clung to the hope that Nikolai was unhurt.

On January 5, however, Anna received a call from the headquarters of the paratroop regiment. Her only son had been killed in Grozny.

For five days, Anna was unable to eat or drink. The thought of Kolya and the other boys who had been killed on New Year's night tortured her, and she cried for all of them.[11] On January 11, Anna brought herself to call the staff of the paratroop forces of the Tula Division, which included the Ryazan

Regiment, and ask for the body of her son. A duty officer told her that Kolya had been killed when a grenade hit his tank but his body had not been found.

Anna now fell into deep despair. There were reports that thousands of bodies were lying in the streets of Grozny being eaten by dogs and cats; all she could think of was her son's corpse being devoured by animals. She called the regiment and division repeatedly but was told only that her son's body would be recovered and was asked to be patient. There began to be reports that local residents were burying the bodies of Russian soldiers so that dogs would not eat them.[12]

On January 15 Anna decided not to wait any longer for the army to recover the body of her son. Having heard on the radio that members of the Committee of Soldiers' Mothers would be going to Grozny, she went to the group's headquarters. There she met members of a BBC film crew that was leaving for Chechnya and described her situation. They offered to take her with them, and she accepted the offer and prepared to search for her son's body on her own.

On January 26 Anna arrived in Nazran, the capital of Ingushetiya. She was destined to spend most of the next seven months in the war zone.

Anna had never been to the Caucasus, and in the chaos of war she did not know where to begin her search, but on arriving in Nazran she learned of a striking coincidence that seemed to help her. A BBC film crew had interviewed a Chechen woman named Zarema who was helping to transport people wounded in Grozny to Stary Atagi. She had shown them the military identification cards of four Russian soldiers who had been killed. The BBC correspondent, Andrew Harding, had written down the last names, and by some miracle one of them was Pyasetsky. Anna viewed the footage and left with the BBC crew for Grozny, intending to search for Zarema.

In Grozny, Anna was told that Zarema frequently helped in a hospital that had been set up in a basement in the city center. Local residents found Anna an apartment, and each day she made her way through heavy fire to the hospital. On the evening of January 31, as the film crew was getting ready to leave Grozny, Zarema appeared. She had the military identification card and gave it to Anna, but she would not say how she had got it or where Kolya had been killed. She mentioned three different places: the press building, the former headquarters of the state deliveries bureau, and the Khankala military airport.

Anna left Grozny with the BBC crew and returned to Nazran, where hundreds of Russian mothers had now come to search for their sons. Hearing there that unidentified bodies were being gathered in Rostov, on the night of February 1–2 she flew in a military plane from Nazran to Rostov.

In Rostov Anna went to the military hospital, where she read through registration books containing the names and units of 1,800 soldiers whose bodies had been identified. Kolya's name was not among them. These, however, constituted only 40 percent of the total number of soldiers who had been killed in Chechnya. So Anna gathered her courage and went to look for her son among the unidentified bodies being kept in the twelve refrigerator cars.

When she had viewed all the bodies in the tents and cars, Anna wrote down the numbers of the cars she had inspected and then flew from Rostov to Vladikavkaz. From there she took a train to Prokhladny and a bus to Mozdok.

By now Mozdok was also inundated with parents seeking their sons. They gathered each day outside the Mir movie theater, where officers dealt with the parents of soldiers from each unit. Anna spoke to an officer who handled paratroopers and was given permission to view the bodies in the four refrigerator cars in Mozdok. There were forty-seven bodies, but Kolya's was not among them. A few cars had been sent to Rostov while Anna was on her way to Mozdok, but rather than go back to Rostov, Anna decided to leave Mozdok for Grozny. This was to prove a fateful omission.

In Mozdok, Anna took an electric train to Chervlennoi and proceeded to Tolstoy Yurt on foot. Fighting was continuing, so she started walking to Grozny. Soon ethnic Russians in a passing truck picked her up, took her into the city, and gave her the keys to the apartments of relatives who had fled.

Back in Grozny, Anna began walking as many as twelve miles a day to the locations that had been mentioned by Zarema. She left at 8:00 A.M. and returned no later than 4:00 P.M. to avoid the random shelling that began after dark.

At first Anna spent most of her time in the area around the Khankala airport, speaking to people who buried soldiers and showing them a photograph of her son. From their accounts of the fighting, however, she realized that she was looking in the wrong places. She next went to the area around Prospekt Kirov but was also unsuccessful there. Finally, on February 19, a week after arriving, she went to the press building on Mayakovsky Street.

The weather was damp and overcast, and the scene of devastation captured the horror of that New Year's night. Everywhere there were soldiers' boots, pieces of uniforms, tank treads, and craters. Along the streets there were shattered trees, dead dogs, and ruins instead of buildings. The only thing standing was a monument to "friendship of peoples," depicting a Russian, a Chechen, and an Ingush with their arms around one another. Chechens referred to it as "three fools."

Anna went with a photograph of her son to the buildings where people were still living. She asked residents if they had buried anyone who looked like Kolya. But they said that it had been impossible to bury anyone because of the shelling. Residents said that the Ryazan Paratroop Regiment had fought there and nearly 600 Russian soldiers had been killed.

Finally, Anna met an Ingush woman who told her that a blond soldier who looked like Kolya had been buried on the grounds of the Ninth City Hospital. She took Anna to the Chechen family who had buried him, but they told her that the soldier they had buried was a Tatar from Kazan. The Chechen family had taken him in after he was severely wounded, and he had died two hours later. Before he died, he told them his name. Anna later contacted his parents and told them how their son spent his last hours.

At the end of February Anna returned to Mozdok, and on March 3 she flew to Rostov, where she again went through the refrigerator cars but without finding the body of Kolya.

On March 6 Anna returned to Moscow. She was exhausted, depressed, and did not know how to continue her search. But the need to find her son's body and give him a decent burial gave her no peace. If her son's military identification card had been saved, it was hard for her to believe that his body could simply have disappeared.

During the next two weeks, Anna asked the military prosecutor to begin a search for Kolya and went frequently to the office of the Committee of Soldiers' Mothers. The committee was organizing a "Mothers' March for Peace" from Nazran to Grozny for March 25. Unable to remain idle in Moscow, Anna decided to join the march. She took a train to Nalchik and from there a bus to Nazran, where she met the marchers. On March 25 the marchers walked from Nazran through Russian territory. When they crossed into Chechnya, however, they were forced into buses by Russian internal troops and driven back to Mozdok.

After the breakup of the march, Anna returned to Nazran, where she spent seven days. There she met Svetlana Belikova and Tatyana Ivanova, whose sons had served in the 81st Samara Regiment, and the three women left together by bus for Grozny, where local residents helped them to settle in vacant apartments.

Having returned to Grozny, however, Anna was not sure what to do. She had already visited the scenes of the battle in which her son's regiment had been involved without finding anyone who had seen him. And she knew that unidentified bodies were being buried all over the city and Kolya's body could be anywhere. She began to visit the Grozny cemetery, which had become an open-air morgue, with bodies gathered from all over the city spread out in rows for possible identification. Despite hours of grim searching, however, Anna did not find anything that looked like the body of her son.

Finally, Anna decided to search for her son as if he were alive and had been taken prisoner. She left Grozny with Svetlana and Tanya and went by bus and car to Vedeno, a village in the mountains, in the hope of making contact with Chechen military leaders. When she arrived, she learned that Vedeno was the headquarters of the Chechen commander, Aslan Maskhadov.

Anna spent the months of April and May in Vedeno. Local Chechens helped her, Svetlana, Tanya, and Olga Osipenko, whose son, Pavel, had also been in the 81st Samara Regiment, to find a place to live. Anna talked to Russian soldiers who were being held prisoner in the village and to Chechen officers who had fought in Grozny near the press building, where Kolya had apparently been killed. But no one could give her any information about her son.

In May, as the front advanced, Vedeno began to be bombed. During one attack, the house where Anna was living became a target. A bomb exploded about a hundred feet from the house, blowing out the windows. As the women ran to the door, there was a second explosion. When the thick cloud of dust had cleared, Anna saw that the entire second floor had been sheared off. The women ran out into the street and then ran back and hid in the basement. As explosions rocked the area, they feared they would be buried alive. The attack on the village continued for half an hour. When the bombing ceased, the women emerged and saw an enormous crater fifteen feet from where they had hidden.

Flying glass had cut Svetlana, and Anna and Tanya persuaded her and Olga to leave for Shali, which was at a lower elevation. Anna and Tanya, however, asked to be taken to Shatoi, where a large group of Russian prisoners was being held. The trip could not be arranged immediately, and while they waited the two women slept in the open air. Each night they studied the sky, trying to distinguish Russian aircraft. If a star began to fall, it meant that a plane was descending to bomb a target.

Finally Anna and Tanya left for Shatoi with a group of Chechen fighters. The group traveled on a mountain road linking Vedeno and Shatoi, moving at night without lights because the road was constantly bombed.

In Shatoi the Chechen fighters inquired about Anna and Tanya's sons, but neither was among the prisoners. On June 10 Russian forces approached Shatoi, and Anna and Tanya left the village with a unit of Chechen fighters and moved higher into the mountains to Borzoi. On June 15 they left Borzoi for Itum Kale.

The trip to Itum Kale, which was even higher in the mountains and almost on the border with Georgia, the spine of the Caucasus, was the most hazardous of the whole journey. Although it was June, there was snow on the ground. At night, the moon was an enormous ball over the edge of the mountains. They had to pass through an area that was exposed to Russian fire. The Russians had night-vision equipment, so the trip was dangerous at all hours. The group crossed the area at dusk, when vigilance was reduced, driving in a small Jeep without lights on clay roads running alongside chasms.

As Anna and Tanya arrived in Itum Kale, however, a group of Chechen fighters under the command of Shamil Basayev invaded the southern Russian city of Budennovsk, seizing more than 1,000 hostages and holding them prisoner in a hospital. On June 17, two attempts by Russian special forces to storm the hospital failed. Under intense pressure to save the hostages, Prime Minister Viktor Chernomyrdin agreed to a ceasefire, safe passage for the Chechen fighters, and the opening of peace talks. This led to a break of several months in the fighting.

In early August, Anna and Tanya, accompanied by Chechen fighters who had changed into civilian clothing, left the mountains for Grozny. By the time they arrived, peace talks were under way, and Anna and Tanya joined other Russian and Chechen mothers outside the building on Mayakovsky Street where the talks were taking place. It was there that the mother of another soldier told Anna that her daughter, Evgeniya, had been involved in an auto accident near Moscow.

On August 25 Anna left for Moscow. By the time she arrived, her daughter had been operated on and was in intensive care. On the night of September 5, with Evgeniya scheduled for another operation the following day, Anna got a call from Tanya Ivanovna. She said she had found Kolya's body in Rostov.

After Anna left for Moscow, Tanya went to Rostov, hoping to find the body of her son. By this time, there was a video record of the bodies, and mothers no longer had to enter the refrigerator cars. Tanya began watching the video. At number 157, she asked the operator to stop the film. The face of Kolya was clearly recognizable. The experts took out the file on number 157 and told Tanya that the body was that of Evgeny Gilyev and that he had been buried in the village of Stepnoye Ozero in the Altai region, 200 miles from Barnaul.

Anna had shown Tanya photographs of her son, and Tanya was absolutely sure that number 157 was Kolya. She immediately called Anna. Kolya's father traveled to Rostov and, after viewing the videotape, confirmed that it was his son. He brought a copy of the videotape back to Moscow, where Anna also confirmed that the body was that of their son.

Kolya's body had been identified as that of Gilyev by a soldier who had served with Evgeny even though Pyasetsky and Gilyev did not resemble each other, had different hair color, and were wearing the uniforms of different units. After the soldier made the identification, there was no effort to confirm its accuracy. In fact, the slightest effort would have revealed the mistake. An emblem taken from Kolya's uniform and included in the file for number 157 was for a member of the Ryazan Paratroop Regiment. Gilyev was a member of the motorized regiment of the Yurga Division, so number 157 could not have been Gilyev.

While Kolya's body was being prepared for shipment to Gilyev's family, Gilyev's body was in one of the refrigerator cars registered as number 162. Evgeny, sensing that he would die, had written a note with his name and address on it, put it in an empty cartridge, and put the cartridge in his shirt pocket. For months, however, no one checked his shirt pockets, and his body was listed as "unidentified."

The corpses of Russian soldiers were returned to their families in coffins that were covered with a sheet of zinc. The families of the dead soldiers were instructed not to open the coffins. When Kolya's body arrived in the village of Stepnoye Ozero, Evgeny's parents disobeyed the instructions and sheared open the zinc covering, but after the 2,000-mile journey from Rostov, the body was unrecognizable.

Evgeny's mother later told Anna, "When I buried the boy, I feared that it was not my son."

As Anna later learned, Kolya's body had been in one of the two refrigerator cars that arrived in Rostov while she was en route to Mozdok after her first visit. Her lapse might have led to her losing her son's body altogether, because until mid-February hundreds of bodies had been sent from Rostov for burial on the basis of careless or incomplete identification procedures. After six weeks of intense warfare, however, the Russian military authorities began videotaping the bodies of unidentified dead soldiers, taking clothing samples and dental records, and recording birthmarks and distinguishing characteristics. They videotaped Kolya's body on February 21.

Kolya's body was sent to Barnaul for burial on March 2, a day before Anna returned to Rostov to continue her search. When she described for an officer Kolya's birthmarks and a small tattoo during the second visit, the officer mistakenly said that there was no one with those characteristics in the computer.

The parents of Gilyev gave their permission for the exhumation of Kolya's body, and the Ryazan Regiment agreed to transport the body to Moscow. For six weeks, however, Kolya's body remained in Barnaul because the regiment had no fuel. Finally, on October 15, the body was flown to the Burdenko military hospital in Moscow.

While Anna waited for her son's body to be transported to Moscow, Tanya Ivanova at last found the body of her son, Andrei, which was also in Rostov. His body was one of a set of charred remains, and she was able to identify it only with the help of experts on the basis of the shape of her son's skull and rib cage and information about his blood type.

In the months after Kolya's final burial, Anna devoted herself to helping other mothers find their missing sons. Nearly 4,400 Russian soldiers were killed in Chechnya during the first Chechen war, 1,400 of whom were still missing in late 1997. There were 400 unidentified bodies in Rostov.

In the first weeks of the war, word began to spread of numerous cases of bodies being shipped to the wrong families. This inspired fear in hundreds of parents, who were no longer sure they had buried their sons.

Under these circumstances, the unidentified bodies in Rostov began to have particular importance. They needed to be identified not only for the sake of the families of the soldiers whose remains were being kept there but also to help reassure other parents that the soldier they had buried was really their own and to exclude the soldiers in Rostov from the list of the missing.

In most cases, however, positive identification of the unidentified soldiers in Rostov, many of whom did not have blood types or X rays in their files, required techniques available in only the most advanced genetic testing laboratories. The Russian government, which spent $40 billion on the war in Chechnya, insisted that it did not have the money to establish a genetic testing laboratory in Rostov, and the mothers of missing soldiers, many of whom were not receiving their salaries, did not, as a rule, have the money to pay for private genetic testing of remains in the laboratories of the Health Ministry in Chelyabinsk, Tyumen, or Moscow, where the findings, in any case, were frequently unreliable.

In this way, the carelessness about the identity of the dead became a source of anxiety for the whole country, and many of the mothers whose sons were killed in Chechnya, deprived of the assurance that their sons' graves actually contained the remains of their sons, were robbed of their children a second time.

On a cloudless day, as Moscow sweltered in the 95-degree heat, Galina Andreeva left her apartment in the Yugozapadny district to run the grimmest errand of her life.

Galina had just gotten off the phone with a laboratory assistant in the Morozov Children's Hospital who told her that the body of her daughter's child had been cremated. Neither she nor her daughter, however, had seen the child's body or knew the reason for the child's death.

Galina took the metro to the Dobryninskaya station, walked to the hospital, and crossed the courtyard to the pathology department on the first floor. A laboratory assistant and two pathologists, one of whom had performed the autopsy, greeted her. The pathologist opened a journal and began to read. She said that the child was a male and weighed 5.5 pounds.

"But what did our child die from?" Galina asked.

To Galina's surprise, the doctor spread her hands and said, "I don't know."

"You don't know? How can you not know after an autopsy?"

Galina then turned to the laboratory assistant, who was sitting at a nearby desk. "When was he cremated?" she asked.

"I don't remember exactly," the assistant said.

"I work in a dormitory," Galina said, unnerved by the response. "When we send out a load of laundry, we list every piece of clothing and record the date when it was sent. Is it possible that you sent the body of a child to the crematorium without the consent of his parents and didn't even note when you sent it?" Moments later, Galina left the hospital. With each step she took, it seemed to her that the mystery surrounding the fate of her daughter's child only deepened.

On the night of June 13, Galina's daughter, Svetlana Bizimana, was nine months pregnant, and Moscow was already suffering in the unseasonable heat. Svetlana drank a lot of fluids, which caused her legs to swell. At about midnight, she went out for a walk and felt her baby moving. At 7:00 A.M. her water broke, and she and her mother went in a taxi to Maternity Hospital Ten.

At the hospital, Svetlana was examined in the admitting room and transferred to a ward on the second floor. Almost immediately, however, she began to have strong contractions, and at 8:45 A.M. she gave birth. A nurse took the baby in her arms, and Svetlana saw that the baby's head and hands were blue. The nurse cut the child's umbilical cord and took it to the nursery.

Seconds later, there was a cry of "Oxygen!" and doctors and nurses ran into the nursery. Dr. Yudeeva, the admitting physician, appeared and hurried to join them. A short time later, she came out and began screaming at Svetlana, "You're a murderer. You killed the baby."

A pediatrician came out of the nursery and said to a midwife in Svetlana's presence that the child had been dead for three days.

Galina was waiting downstairs. Suddenly she was called to the admitting room. Nadezhda Kucher, a midwife, said, "Sveta had swollen legs, and the child died." Several hours later, Galina talked to Yudeeva and asked her for the child's body. But Yudeeva said that in such cases the child was not buried. The body had already been sent to the Morozov Children's Hospital for an autopsy. Galina then asked for a death certificate, but Yudeeva said that death certificates were issued only for children who were buried.

Svetlana now felt absolutely helpless. Her child had been taken from her before she could even see it, and she had lost all control over his body.

On Svetlana's second day in the hospital, she was moved to a ward on the first floor. In the late afternoon a woman was brought in crying. The woman said that her child was stillborn. Svetlana asked her how she knew. She said the doctors had listened to the baby's heart before she gave birth and told her that the baby was dead. They then induced labor and, after the birth, showed her the body of the child.

The woman's story convinced Svetlana that the story about her child being dead for three days was false. The doctors had listened to the child's heart after she was admitted, and when her husband, Jean, a Rwandan studying in Moscow, had called to inquire about her, hospital personnel had told him that everything was proceeding normally and she would give birth soon.

For the next few days, Jean repeated the family's request for the body of their child, but the chief doctor for the first floor, A. D. Zelentsova, said only that their request was "being considered." The response suggested that, for some reason, the hospital authorities did not want them to see the body of the child. During this period Svetlana, uncertain of her ability to control her emotions, spoke as little as possible to the doctors.

On her fifth day in the hospital, Svetlana prepared to be discharged, and Galina again asked Zelentsova for the child's body. This time, however, she said, "You yourselves refused. Go to the Morozov Hospital. The body is there."

Galina realized that for some reason the maternity hospital personnel were lying to her, and instead of going to the Morozov Hospital she went to the prosecutor for the Zuzinsky raion, where Maternity Hospital Ten was located, to ask for their help in finding her daughter's child.

Galina wrote out a statement in which she said that the hospital had refused to show the family the child's body, provide them with a death certificate, or turn over the body for burial. All this, she said, raised doubts as to whether the child in the morgue of the Morozov Children's Hospital was really theirs.

Moscow, at this time, was rife with rumors of children being kidnapped from maternity hospitals, and verified cases of the kidnapping of newborn infants from maternity hospitals in other cities in Russia and in Ukraine had been reported in the press. Galina and her daughter were working people, and Jean was an African. She knew that no one would spend a lot of time worrying about their child's fate.

For a month, Galina repeatedly called the prosecutor's office and was repeatedly told to wait. Finally, Sokolova, the prosecutor who was handling the case, said that her investigation showed that the child's body was not in the maternity hospital, the raion cemetery, or the Morozov Children's Hospital.

Galina sensed that something terrible was happening, but this news also inspired a slim hope. Perhaps, Galina thought, if they cannot find the child, he is alive.

Galina called the burial bureau for the Zuzinsky raion. All deaths in the raion are registered in their computer. In the case of stillbirths, officials register the names of the parents. The officials in the burial bureau said that nothing was listed for Svetlana's child. Finally she called the Morozov Children's Hospital, even though the prosecutor had said that the child was not there, and was told that the body of the child had been cremated.

Three days after her visit to the Morozov Children's Hospital, Galina called the Nikolo-Arkhangelsky crematorium, which handles the remains of children. She called at 2:00 P.M. and was told that the body of Svetlana's child had been cremated only moments earlier.

Desperate for a trace of her daughter's lost child, Galina went to the crematorium to ask for the child's ashes. She spoke first to a secretary, who said that the ashes had been put in a common grave. She then spoke to the director, who said, "What common grave? There is no common grave. Nothing remains of the children, only steam."

It now seemed that the only way to learn the fate of Svetlana's child was to open a criminal case against the maternity hospital, and Galina put all her hopes in timely action by the prosecutor. A few days after her visit to the crematorium, however, she received an answer to her complaint from the raion prosecutor stating that the personnel at Maternity Hospital Ten had not violated the law, despite the fact that the practice in Russian hospitals is to show stillborn children weighing more than a kilogram (a little over 2 pounds) to their parents and even though the Russian law on burial and funeral arrangements states that the disposition of the body of a dead child is up to the child's parents.

Several months later, Galina went to see a private detective. The detective said that if the child had been stolen, a well-organized criminal gang was involved, and if he took the case, he would be risking his life. Nonetheless, he said he was willing to investigate the matter for $600 a day. This, however, was far beyond what Galina and Svetlana could pay.

Galina appealed the ruling of the raion prosecutor to the prosecutor for the okrug. She said that the raion prosecutor had not taken action on her complaint, that the maternity hospital had refused to give up the body of her daughter's child and had not provided a death certificate, and that she feared that a stillborn child could have been cremated as her daughter's child while her daughter's child was sold.

After her statement was taken, a prosecutor promised Galina that there would be an investigation. When Svetlana later went to the prosecutor of the okrug to give her statement, however, an investigator asked her, "By the way, don't you stand on the psychiatric inventory?" Svetlana was stunned by the suggestion that she was mentally ill, but she kept her nerve. "No matter what, I'll find out what happened to my child," she said.

Several months after Svetlana gave her statement to the okrug prosecutor, Galina went to the maternity hospital to collect her daughter's medical documents. She was received by Zelentsova, who treated her efforts to learn the fate of her daughter's child as a form of hysteria.

"Have you calmed down?" Zelentsova asked.

"No," Galina replied, trying to ignore the insolence of the question. "I cannot calm down. This will be with us for the rest of our lives."

For the Russian it is not sufficiently understood that honesty is obligatory for every person, that it is tied to the honor of a person, and that it forms the personality.
—Nikolai Berdyaev, Sudba Rossii (Russia's Fate)

13 *The Criminalization of Consciousness*

Sergei Mikhailov rose from his desk to greet his visitor, Laurent Nicolet, the Moscow correspondent for the Geneva newspaper *Le Temps*. "I'm preparing for an important meeting," he said, "but for a newspaper such as yours, I can always find time for an interview."

Nicolet was taken by surprise by Mikhailov's remark. Either Mikhailov had not read what *Le Temps* wrote about him during the two years when he was an inmate in Geneva's Champ-Dollon prison, or he was extremely forgiving.[1] A group of men in business suits looked on. They were waiting to take their places around a conference table in Mikhailov's office that was laid out for a banquet. Several beautiful young women stood nearby, apparently waiting to entertain the guests once the meeting was over.

Mikhailov led Nicolet to a room next to his office, accompanied by two lawyers and his press spokesman. They were soon joined by Oleg Lurye, a journalist for *Novaya Gazeta*.

"What have you been engaged in since your return from Switzerland?" Nicolet asked.

"Business," said Mikhailov.

"Could you be a little more specific?"

"Let's put it this way," he said, "the purchase and sale of goods."

The press spokesman interrupted the interview to say that Mikhailov was also involved in charitable work. He was referring to Participation, created by Mikhailov in 1993, an organization that gave help to destitute families, victims of the war in Chechnya, and orphanages, and provided funds for the restoration of churches. Participation donated money to erect a belfry with nine bells in a church in the village of Fedosino. The principal bell carried an inscription stating that it had come from the fund Participation and the Solntsevo brotherhood. Among other charitable bequests were gifts to the investigative detention section at the Sailors' Silence Prison (food products, electrical goods, and 500 pairs of jeans) and the 176th district police station (furniture for a children's room). Russians were also surprised to learn that Participation had sponsored a documentary film about an MVD unit in Chechnya. Glancing at his lawyers, Mikhailov explained the last by saying, "I understood the importance of Russian public opinion's knowing the truth about what happens in the hot spots in the country."

"Why do you think the Swiss authorities made such enormous efforts to gather evidence against you?" asked Nicolet.

"The Swiss legal system has a distrustful attitude toward Russian citizens," said Mikhailov, "but this type of behavior hurts not Russians so much as it does Switzerland itself . . . Large sums arriving from Eastern Europe are being removed from Swiss accounts because it is impossible to be certain that someone won't be sticking his nose into your affairs."

After they had finished speaking, Mikhailov escorted Nicolet down one floor and showed him around the office of Participation. On the bookshelves were numerous photographs, including shots of Mikhailov among smiling orphans and a photo of Mikahilov about to receive the Order of Sergei Radonezh, the highest award of the Russian Orthodox church, from Patriarch Alexei.

"The Swiss, like the Americans," said Lurye, "acted out of the conviction that all their economic problems are the fault of Russia and its mafia and also out of a desire to prevent Russia from becoming a participant in global business."

Mikhailov is one of the most important gangsters in Russia, but he also has considerable prestige in polite society. He not only has avoided prosecution and gained acceptance but is viewed by many as a figure of authority.[2]

The tolerant and even admiring attitude toward explicit criminality in Russia is a product of the post-Soviet era. The roots of the present situation, however, are deep. The notion of laws equally applicable to everyone and based on transcendent principles had little sway in prerevolutionary Russia, where laws were framed to defend the property rights of landowners. This situation gave rise among the Russian peasantry to the idea of law as something distinct from justice, which, for them, was often determined on the basis of the economic status of the parties.

When the tsarist regime was overthrown, the peasants' class-based approach to the law was enshrined as official ideology, and during the years of revolutionary upheaval an arrested person's economic status was more important in determining his fate than whether he had broken the law. Later the Stalinist regime drew a sharp distinction between prisoners who were "socially friendly," in effect common criminals, and those who were "socially hostile," for the most part political prisoners arrested for belonging to a specific class. The common criminals were treated with leniency and used in the labor camps to terrorize the politicals.

The result of this evolution was that, in Russia, the notion of law as a universal standard had little strength in the face of society's desire for "justice." It could therefore offer little resistance when, after the fall of the Soviet Union, society was overwhelmed by a wave of crime.

Against this background, three factors made it possible for gangsters to achieve legitimacy and even a form of respectability. The first was the gangsters' depiction of themselves as Robin Hoods who forced corrupt businessmen to "share" their wealth and, to a degree, redistributed it.[3]

The second factor was the general belief that the gangsters, by using force to appropriate wealth, were not that much different from anyone else. Russians were raised on a depiction of capitalism as a jungle in which only the most ruthless survived, and they saw how, in Russia, huge enterprises were stolen and fortunes made on the basis of political connections. Accordingly, it often did not seem that the activities of the gangsters were particularly blameworthy.

Finally, Russians accorded gangsters legitimacy because, with the collapse of Communist ideology, which, to a degree, gave people a sense of meaning, the population was left without moral orientation.

The resulting moral vacuum often had murderous consequences. In the years 1992–1997 in Moscow alone, 20,000 people sold their housing and then disappeared. In the country as a whole, the number for the period was many times higher. A significant percentage, if not the vast majority, of these people were believed to have been murdered for their apartments.

Once housing was privatized in Russia, it became valuable, and apartment gangs formed in cities all over the country. They bribed building superintendents to give them the names of alcoholics or elderly persons living alone without close relatives. They then, under various guises, made contact with these persons, forced them to sign over their apartments, and then killed them. The "sale" was then registered with the help of cooperative notaries and officials of the passport department of the local police.

The success of the apartment gangs was, in part, a tribute to their ruth-lessness. But it was possible because of the cooperation of ordinary citizens. The building superintendents, police officials, and notaries knew, or at least strongly suspected, that nothing good would come to the persons whom they identified or certified to have sold their apartments, but they did so anyway because the fate of these people was not their concern.

Similar moral indifference was demonstrated by high-ranking officials. In 1992 the Kremlin Palace of Congresses was rented out for an unusual specta-cle. Members of Aum Shinri Kyo, the Japanese doomsday cult, dressed in tinsel-colored leotards danced around in clouds of dry ice in a musical written by the cult leader, Shoko Asahara, to mark the beginning of Aum's "Russian Salvation Tour." It was during this tour that cult members made the acquaintance of Oleg Lobov, the secretary of the Security Council and a close associate of Yeltsin, inaugurating an era of close cooperation between Aum and the Russian authorities.

With Lobov's help, members of the sect, described as "Japanese business-men," trained at the bases of the Taman and Kantemirov Divisions near Moscow in the use of machine guns, rifles, and tanks; shopped for advanced weapons, including MiG-29 fighter jets, Proton rocket launchers, and nu-clear warheads; and attended lectures at the Laboratory of Thermodynamics of the Academy of Sciences, where they studied the circulation of gases.

In 1995 members of the sect launched a sarin nerve-gas attack on the Tokyo metro that killed 12 people and injured more than 5,000. At the trial of the leader of the sect, Aum's chief of intelligence testified that the produc-tion designs for the sarin had been delivered to Aum by Lobov in 1993 in return for $100,000 in cash. (Yeltsin's response was to promote Lobov to be his envoy to Chechnya.)

The situation demanded the ability to draw clear moral distinctions, but in a society that had lost one worldview without having gained another one, many Russians found those distinctions impossible to make.

The consequences of the loss of a worldview were evident everywhere.

SUICIDE PREVENTION CLINIC, IZMAILOVSKY RAION, MOSCOW

"During the last few years, everything changed—the name of the country, the emblem, the national anthem, and the prices," said Stella Sharmina, a psychiatrist at the clinic. "People had lived almost their entire lives with stable prices. Suddenly, prices were different for the same product. People went from store to store, and they could not get used to the idea that in each place the prices were different. They were afraid that if they went searching for the best prices, the product would be sold out in the store where they had started.

"In the early 1990s, many children refused to study in school. They thought that to get an education was expensive and unprestigious. The parents put pressure on them, and this often ended in suicide attempts.

"A woman came to us because she was concerned about her sixteen-year-old son. He was involved in commerce. He and his friends bought goods and went by electric train to the outlying villages, where they sold them. The mother felt absolutely helpless. He adapted better to the new conditions than she did. The result was a change in roles. He became the head of the family. The woman said, 'I don't know what to do. I don't want to live anymore.'

"There was an older woman, over sixty years old, who worked as a designer of costumes in a theater. She was on a pension when perestroika began, and the changes left her in a state of constant fear. She began to be afraid to go out on the streets, to watch television, or to read the newspapers. She stayed in her apartment alone and shouted, 'What am I to do?' We visited her and brought her groceries. As soon as she began to receive a little help, her condition improved.

"Another woman, who was recommended to the clinic by one of my friends, said, 'I don't want to live. My religion does not allow me to take my own life, and that is all that stops me.' She was alone, and, with everything changing around her, she feared that if something happened to her, no one would know.

"People in Russia were conditioned to worry about family problems and about the global situation, particularly the struggle for peace, but not about crime, accidents, catastrophes, or the struggle to earn a living. When these problems began to intrude on them, the reaction was often fear and hysteria. Many people wanted to commit suicide because they were overcome with fear, but it was an undefined fear."

MOSCOW EMERGENCY RESCUE SERVICE, "02"

The emergency rescue system is organized according to the same principles as similar services in the West, such as "911" in the United States. The calls are taped, and the information is communicated to a local police station, which is expected to dispatch someone to the scene within minutes.

In reality, however, the time involved in sending help can be much greater. Galina Dyuzheva, the shift boss at service 02, said that the service had no direct line to thirteen police stations and poor connections to twenty-two others. This often led to serious misunderstandings.

One night, 02 received a report that someone had found a dead body. A duty operator called the relevant police station but reached an apartment by mistake. A man answered and the operator said, "There is a dead body at such-and-such an address." She then asked, "Have you written this down?" The man answered, "I've written it down." After a few minutes, however, he called back and asked, "What am I supposed to do with this dead body?"

Dyuzheva has a special control panel that allows her to listen in to the calls received by the other employees and, if necessary, to help.

Robbery of an apartment: "When were you robbed?"

"In the morning."

"And why are you only calling in the evening?"

"There is always such a mess that I didn't notice right away that something was missing."

Gang rape: "When did this happen?"

"Yesterday."

"Why are you calling today?"

"I rested."

There are also calls about "suspicious" packages (which usually turn out to be filled with various types of garbage) and about alcoholics lying on the street. Sometimes one alcoholic will inspire numerous calls.

On a typical day in Moscow, people all over the city leave their apartments and realize that they cannot find their cars. During the day, it is relatively quiet. In the evening, an ordinary worker learns that his apartment has been robbed, a husband beats his wife, and a man attacks his neighbor with an ax. Throughout the night there is a flood of calls from drunks and the mentally ill that demonstrate clearly surrealistic thought processes.

"Calm yourself, man."

"I'm not a man, I'm a war veteran."

"Tell me, is he your husband?"

"A little."

"How was the robber dressed?"

"Fashionably."

"In what did he escape?"

"The elevator."

"What happened?"

"A corpse is lying here and singing songs."[4]

On the fourth floor of a dilapidated apartment building, the heavy double doors are opened and a woman in a black gown leads a visitor down a dark corridor past a crucifix on the wall and a large hand holding a translucent purple ball. It is here that Ruzanna and Natalya, two witches, receive their clients.

"The magician," says Ruzanna, "is a doctor who deals with spiritual energy. In this respect, religion and magic are closely related."

Natalya says that most of their clients are businessmen who have experienced financial problems and people unhappy with their love life.

Financial crisis tears a hole in a businessman's biological field, and Ruzanna and Natalya try to restore it by performing ancient rituals, including the singing of magic songs at regular intervals. On one occasion, the president of a firm that was on the verge of collapse arrived with his commercial director. They wanted to make sure that a court case would be decided in their favor. Ruzanna asked for the firm's documents and official stamp. She cast a spell on the stamp and cleaned the documents ritually. She then sang the song of success. Ruzanna then used the stamp and documents in a separate ritual and made the firm an individualized talisman.

The persons seeking help with their love life were usually experiencing some degree of sexual dysfunction. Financial worries caused women to become frigid and men to lose the ability to perform. To help such people, Ruzanna and Natasha performed a ritual for the harmonization of families and prescribed the ingredients of a "sweet bed" for sexual partners, including rose petals and special sexual perfumes for women.

In some situations, clients asked the witches to change the behavior of their partner, usually by instilling a fixation. To achieve this, the witches, using a photograph, made a wax figure of the person whose emotions were to be changed. They inserted a needle into the figure's sexual parts and then removed the needle. Requests to perform the ritual came from women suffering from unrequited love or wives whose husbands had left them for other women. When the witches received these requests, they tried to persuade their clients that instilling a fixation was a serious step that could affect the subject for the rest of his life. Nonetheless, the witches sometimes agreed to interfere. For example, they sometimes saw by studying the subject's photograph that a fixation had already been instilled by another witch. A wife usually asked the witches to remove that fixation and instill a fixation for her. In such cases, according to Ruzanna, the witches removed the first fixation but did not necessarily replace it with one for the subject's wife. They performed only the ritual for the harmonization of family relations so that the man could decide himself with whom he wanted to live.

Besides businessmen and persons with romantic problems, the witches were sometimes approached by bandits for protection against being killed in a shootout or for help in collecting debts. Sometimes bandits wrote to the witches from prison for help in arranging their financial affairs.

On one occasion, a professional killer visited Ruzanna and Natalya. He explained that he wanted to change his fate because he feared he would meet a violent end. He had killed many people and he saw his victims in his sleep. The witches gave him the opportunity to speak his mind but said they had no right to change his fate. "There were too many lives on his shoulders, too many children without fathers. If we changed his fate, then we could have been punished," Natalya said.

Ruzanna and Natalya are in demand in Moscow and receive three or four letters a day from the provinces. Their success has inspired a certain amount of jealousy. "There are many magicians in Moscow," Ruzanna said. "But how can there be competition in helping people?"[5]

On March 18, 1998, a reporter for the newspaper *Komsomolskaya Pravda* published an advertisement that consisted of two words—"Killer. Inexpensive"—and then gave a telephone number. The reporter intended the ad as a joke and prepared to publish the responses on April Fool's Day. The number of people who responded seriously, however, was far more than would have been expected in the case of an ordinary advertisement.

The first call came at 9:00 A.M. A man said in a half-whisper, "I'm calling regarding the advertisement. What is this, some kind of joke?"

"The time for jokes has long passed," said the reporter, speaking in a peremptory tone.

"And what kind of orders do you accept?"

"Any kind."

"OK, good. I'll definitely call you back."

Half an hour later, the bureau received another call.

"I'm interested," the caller said. "Killer, this is what?"

"This is a person who eliminates inconvenient people."

"And how much do you charge for your services?"

"Two thousand dollars."

"Independent of the person who is to be killed?"

"We don't accept orders on politicians and officials."

"Why not?"

"We don't want to get involved with them. They have bodyguards and so on, and this can cost us a lot of money."

"But if people are prepared to pay for this, why not?"

"Tell me, who is bothering you?"

"Who is bothering me? I don't know. It's just that 2,000 for a killing, in principle, is a reasonable price. And after this, you don't betray the person who gave you the order."

"Not under any circumstances."

"So everything is on the quiet."

"Yes."

"And what kind of methods do you use?"

"Traditional methods."

"And how quickly can you fulfill an order?"

"As quickly as you need it. For example, in a week. It depends on the order, on whom and how."

"What is this, a small business?"

"Yes."

"What do you call it? 'Kill An Enemy?' "

"Something like that."

"Thanks. I'll call back."

From that point on, calls came in every half hour. Several callers explained that they were calling out of "sporting interest." And several threatened the supposed businessmen. "You aren't afraid for your life?" one of them asked.

"No, I'm not afraid," the reporter answered.

"Well, well," was the reply.

But the majority of calls were attempts to arrange an assassination. Many potential clients were calling long distance, which the reporter took as a tribute to the broad circulation of *Komsomolskaya Pravda*. And most of the motives for the prospective killings were of a domestic character. One woman called to arrange the killing of her husband's lover. Another wanted to eliminate a neighbor who constantly flooded her apartment with water. One person was interested in killing someone who had not repaid a loan.

There were no requests to kill major political figures, but one caller wanted to kill a local official who lived about 300 miles from Moscow. The reporter declined the job on the grounds that this was too far to travel.[6]

One afternoon in October 1997, Alexander Milokosty, a well-known Russian actor, was picked up on the street and taken to the headquarters of the

Moscow Criminal Police, where he was informed that someone had ordered his assassination.

After ten years of marriage, Milokosty had fallen in love with a younger woman, and his wife, Natasha, demanded that he leave their large three-room apartment to her. When he refused, she decided to have him killed.

To organize the murder, Milokostaya, a gynecologist, turned to Nina Antipkina, one of her acquaintances. She paid Antipkina $5,000 to organize the killing, and Antipkina gave the job to Vladimir Gavrilov, a vagrant, offering him $300 to carry it out.

As it happened, Antipkina's desire to make as much money as possible off the murder of Milokosty did not serve Milokostaya's goal. Gavrilov shadowed Milokosty. But the more he saw of him, the less he wanted to kill him. He finally decided that he could not go through with the killing and turned himself in to the police.

Shortly afterward, Milokostaya and Antipkina were arrested and jailed. Milokostaya's patients, however, including many judges and prosecutors, rallied to her defense. The prosecutor handling her case came under intense pressure to treat her with leniency, and she was released from jail after three days.

Nonetheless, she did not avoid trial. Milokostaya, Antipkina, and Gavrilov all were tried on June 15, 1998. Natasha denied her guilt, but Antipkina admitted hers and implicated Natasha. Gavrilov was drunk and fell asleep in the court. When he rose to testify, however, he described the plot with such lucidity and eloquence that it was hard to believe that he had been drinking. At the end of his remarks, he said, "Imprison me together with them." The judge, however, did not imprison anyone. The defendants received eight-year suspended sentences and were freed directly from the courtroom.

In a country in spiritual chaos, gangsters began to exemplify capitalism in the eyes of many people, and their drive not only to make money but also to establish their legitimacy enjoyed striking success, seriously undermining Russia's already shaky moral foundations. Both emerging from and contributing to an atmosphere of moral and ideological confusion, the gangsters were viewed by many as forerunners of a new ruling class.

On a cold and rainy November night, Andrei, a Moscow cab driver, met with four bandits who had agreed to be his protectors outside a large auto service center on Kutuzovsky Prospekt. It was a cold night, and the lights of the traffic refracted in the haze. The five men entered the service center and went to a damaged Mercedes parked in the lot. Standing next to the car were five members of a Dagestani criminal organization. About fifty feet away, a Korean stood and watched. He was being represented by the Dagestanis.

One of the Russian bandits asked Andrei to wait some distance away. "Don't interfere," he said. "If we call you, come. Otherwise, remain silent." The two groups of bandits then began to talk among themselves.

At length, the Russian bandits called Andrei over and, as the Dagestanis looked on, the leader of the Russian group, who was six and a half feet tall, handed him a piece of paper. "Tomorrow," he said, "take the car to this service station and tell the director that I sent you. In two weeks, the car will be like new. They want 5,000 for the hospitalization of their client. You have to give them 2,000 because he really was in the hospital. But you won't pay for the whole Mercedes, only for what was damaged." He then asked Andrei, "Do you understand?" Andrei said yes. The bandit then turned to the Dagestanis and asked, "Do you agree?" They said yes. "When the work is done," he said to Andrei, "call the Korean and tell him to get his car."

On a night two weeks earlier, Andrei had been driving down Leningradsky Prospect on his way to the Sheremetevo airport. At a point about a mile ahead of him, a drunk wandered into the far left northbound lane, causing a BMW to stop suddenly to avoid hitting him. A Mercedes traveling behind him crashed into the rear of the BMW. The driver of the BMW and the driver of the Mercedes and his Korean passenger got out of their cars and stepped between the cars to inspect the damage. Meanwhile, Andrei tried to pass a microbus. Suddenly the same drunk appeared in front of him. Swerving to avoid him, Andrei crashed into the rear of the stopped Mercedes, pinning the legs of the Korean and his driver against the BMW.

Andrei, whose chest hit the steering wheel, was removed from his car by the police and taken to Botkin Hospital, where the doctors took several X rays and found that nothing was broken. He was released and driven by several friends back to the scene of the accident, where four GAI traffic police were standing around near his car, which had been moved to the right side of the road.

Andrei asked what had happened. One of the police said the Korean had lost both legs. When Andrei heard this, he went to the side of the road and threw up. He knew that if the Korean had lost both legs, the police would find a guilty person regardless of the circumstances. Soon one of police left to check on the condition of the Korean. He returned with a grim expression. "The situation is very bad," he said. "The Korean is unconscious in intensive care. They can't bring him to the phone. The doctors won't let us talk to him."

"Nonetheless," said a second officer, "we wrote up the accident report in your favor." He then added, "You should be grateful." Andrei's friends asked the police how much they wanted. They said $800 would be sufficient. Andrei was too stunned to give a bribe, but his friends collected the money, and the $800 was paid.

Andrei later learned that the Korean had suffered only a couple of bruises. He also learned that while the traffic police had guarded his car, the tape recorder, electric pump, and antiradar device had been stolen.

Several days after the accident, Andrei was summoned to the raion office of the GAI traffic police. Arriving a half-hour before the assigned time, he noticed a late-model gray Mercedes with darkened windows parked on the street. Standing around the vehicle were some Caucasians.

At 3:00 P.M. Andrei entered the office and introduced himself. A Russian and the Korean who had been injured in the accident were talking to the GAI inspector, who asked Andrei to wait outside. When he stepped out onto the street, two of the Caucasians grabbed him and led him to their car.

Once they were in the car, the apparent leader of the group said, "I'm Garik. The people you hit are my people. Because you put one of them in the hospital, I lost a $5 million contract."

"What do you want from me?"

"First of all, I don't want any police or hearings. You should pay for the repair of the Korean's car and for his period in the hospital and for his medication."

"If they find me guilty, I'll do that." Andrei said.

"You *are* guilty."

As they talked, the Korean and Russian emerged from the building. Garik pointed at them. "You see those people," he said. "All questions should be settled with them. If they're dissatisfied, they'll call me, and then I'll take care of you."

The Caucasians let Andrei go, and he went in to see the investigator. The office was rather small, and for a long time the investigator ignored him. Finally she put down some papers and looked at him with an air of total indifference. "I've reviewed the case, and it's clear that you're guilty," she said.

"But there was a drunk . . ."

"He was only a pedestrian."

"The Mercedes did not have on its warning lights."

"So what?"

Andrei understood that a bribe to the investigator had neutralized his bribe to the police.

Andrei left the office and met Oleg, the Russian who had accompanied the Korean, on the street. They agreed to meet the following day at the central GAI holding lot, where the Mercedes had been taken. Andrei understood that he was defenseless, but he spoke calmly and tried to maintain a businesslike façade.

The following day Andrei met Oleg at the lot, and they had the damaged Mercedes towed to a service station. An attendant there estimated that repairs would cost $4,000, plus the cost of spare parts. Oleg reported the estimate to the Korean's boss, another Korean, named Bak Sang-u (pseudonym). Both men worked in the Moscow office of a Korean electronics firm. Bak, however, was not satisfied. Andrei went to his office to meet with him.

Speaking in broken Russian, Bak said, "I don't want to work through the service station. Give me the money. I'll take care of it."

"How much do you want?"

"Give me $8,000. The estimate of $4,000 is too little. They'll do a bad job."

"I think $4,000 is reasonable," Andrei said.

"Actually, $8,000 is very little," Bak said. "When the accident took place, our employee lost consciousness, and during his hospitalization, $3,000 was stolen from him and $1,500 was stolen from the driver. In fact, you should be paying $12,000. But this is not the final sum. I will get some advice and give you a final figure."

Andrei realized that the "advice" would come from the bandits.

"I don't have that kind of money," he said. "The most I can do is sell my car and hand over the proceeds, but that would be $6,000."

"What do you have besides a car? A dacha? An apartment? My friends will take everything you own. When I heard that there was an accident, I hoped that you were rich. I would have taken every penny. But I see that you're just a worker, and since I like Russians, I want to do this in a nice way. You owe $12,000, but this is not exact."

"No matter how much you like Russians," Andrei said, "I don't have the money."

"If you want to live peacefully, you'll sell your apartment and anything else that you have."

Two days later Bak called and said that Andrei now owed $18,000 because the victim had spent an extra $5,000 for treatment. A short time later, Andrei met Bak at the service station. Andrei repeated that he did not have that much money. Bak said that he would pay it whether he had it or not. "We know your address and the school and the kindergarten where your children are in school," he said. From this, Andrei realized that Bak knew that he had two children.

Andrei returned home and told his wife what had happened. When he finished, she began to cry. The newspapers were full of stories of people murdered by gangsters, and she feared Andrei would be next. Several years earlier, however, another driver had introduced Andrei to some bandits at the Sheremetevo airport. Andrei's friend said that they could resolve any problem. At the time, it was obvious from their appearance what kind of problems his friend was referring to.

Andrei sent his wife and children to stay with relatives in the countryside and arranged a meeting with the bandits. They met in an office in the city center. To his surprise, they listened to his story with sympathy. When he told them how Bak said he liked Russians, they became angry.

"If he loves Russians so much, I'll put him in the sack and love him," one of the hulking bandits said.

"He asked for $5,000 for treatment?" asked another.

"Yes."

"For that kind of money, I'll take off his legs."

The bandits asked Andrei about his family and debts. Andrei explained that he supported his wife, two young children, and his elderly mother.

"He's alone, supports a family, and these cattle wanted $5,000."

Reflecting on the situation, however, one of the bandits added, "Of course, we do the same thing. But we take the money from businessmen, not from a simple workingman. This Korean with these Caucasians is trying to establish his own rules. What can you take from a worker? People don't earn anything."

The bandits asked about the meeting with the GAI investigator. Andrei said that the investigator had found him guilty. They said that, in that case, Andrei would have to pay something. But he would pay only for the repair of the car, not one kopeck more. "Call the Korean and have him come with his boys. Bring your wife and kids back home. This is not your worry anymore. Relax."

Andrei had lived in fear ever since the accident. Now, for the first time, he felt a sense of relief. He called Bak and told him that he wanted a meeting. He said he might have some money for him but he wanted any discussion to take place in the presence of the Dagestanis. Bak agreed to meet him at the service station in an hour. Andrei then called his bandits. They told him to wait for them at the entrance to the garage. Andrei arrived at the garage, and the Russian bandits showed up moments later in two cars.

Andrei walked into the service station accompanied by the four bandits. When they entered, the station's security guards disappeared. Andrei and the bandits walked out to the Mercedes. They saw Bak and Oleg but not the Dagestanis. The Russian bandits told Bak to call the Dagestanis. He began calling on his mobile phone. Finally, he made contact, and they said that they would be there in half an hour.

Andrei and the bandits went to a nearby bar. There was a lot of commotion, but as the group entered, the bar quickly became silent, and many of the customers lowered their heads. A woman who had been watching television immediately got up to take their order. The group waited for half an hour. Finally, Oleg came in and summoned them. They returned to the service station, where they reached a settlement with the Dagestani gang and Bak.

After they left the service station, Andrei asked the bandits how much he owed them. "Nothing," they said. "You're already paying a lot. We know where you work and what you do. We know you're not a businessman. We did this for our mutual friend. This wasn't such hard work. Besides, you're better off using the money to buy something for your children."

In the end, Andrei gave the bandits gifts of gold chains worth $1,500 and they parted as friends. "You know our numbers," they said. "Call any time, and in fifteen minutes we'll be there. If you have work for us, we'll even divide the money. Just send us the work."

NIZHNY NOVGOROD, MARCH 1998

Andrei Klimentiev, a former convict, faced an overflow crowd in the Ordzhonikidze House of Culture. On the table in front of him was a big pile of papers with questions from the audience. People craned their necks to see the man who might be their next mayor.

The first question: When will they build a circus?
KLIMENTIEV: This will never happen. There is already a circus in everyday life. You don't have to go far.
A BUSINESSWOMAN: Why is it that a place in the Meshchersky Market that used to cost three dollars now costs six dollars?
KLIMENTIEV: This is because I was put in prison.
AN ELDERLY MAN: Many officials are saying that if you are elected mayor, the city will become just as criminal as you are.

KLIMENTIEV: You see how they talk about me. This is because they don't do anything and I do something.

In the 1980s, Klimentiev, whose underworld nickname was "Prishch" (Pimple), served an eight-year prison sentence for pornography and card sharping. In 1995 he was convicted of stealing a $2.4 million credit given by the Ministry of Finance under a guarantee from the oblast for the Navashino docks, of which he was a major shareholder. He appealed the decision to the Supreme Court, which, although it found no grounds for acquittal, in 1997 returned the case for review. As a result Klimentiev, after serving eighteen months, was freed pending a new hearing, preparing the way for him to run for mayor.

This was not Klimentiev's first attempt to run for political office. In 1995, after being arrested in the Navashino case, Klimentiev campaigned for a seat in the State Duma by recording speeches from his prison cell that were then played at election rallies. He received 10 percent of the vote. In December 1996 he ran for the city duma, again from prison, and would have won had not the prison administration insisted that all the inmates vote in the districts where they lived rather than in the district where the prison was located. Klimentiev, who had strong support among his fellow inmates, lost by six votes.

Klimentiev was believed to be the richest person in Nizhny Novgorod. He owned the city's most expensive food stores, restaurants, Rokko, the city's only night club, and banks. Because of his criminal reputation, however, his candidacy was at first not taken seriously; an early poll showed he was favored by only 13 percent of the voters. The two principal candidates appeared to be Dmitri Bednyakov, a former mayor of Nizhny Novgorod, and Vladimir Goryn, the acting mayor.

Klimentiev, however, proved to be a natural campaigner. He spoke simply and colorfully, answering every question that was put to him, in marked contrast to Goryn, who spoke in bureaucratic phrases, and Bednyakov, who referred constantly to the city's "greatness."

At the same time, Klimentiev did not hesitate to make outlandish promises. He promised to cut the cost of gas and electricity by 20 percent and the cost of motor fuel by 10 percent, although the cost of gas and electricity is determined by Moscow and the cost of motor fuel by the market. He promised to reduce by 30 percent the cost of food products in three stores in every raion of the city, a measure that, as mayor, he could have enacted but at the price of cutting all other social expenditures. He also promised that within

50 days after his election he would raise salaries and within 100 days he would raise pensions. If he did not accomplish these things, in 150 days he would resign. After watching Klimentiev at various meetings, Yekaterina Yegorova, a Moscow political consultant who was advising Bednyakov, concluded that Klimentiev had a serious chance of winning the election.

The campaign began in late January. By mid-February Klimentiev's support in the polls had nearly doubled, and his campaign rallies in factories, hospitals, and schools were attracting big crowds. This success inspired him to expand on his promises. At a construction site for the city metro, Klimentiev promised $1 million for the project. At neighborhood meetings, he promised to create a program to enable young people to obtain housing on credit.

Whenever Klimentiev's criminal record came up at the rallies, he focused on his conviction for pornography, ignoring the one for card sharping. At a meeting in School Number 30 in the city's central district, Klimentiev answered a question about his criminal record by saying, "My misfortune was that my father bought me a videocassette player, and I saw these [pornographic] films a little earlier than you did." When asked whether he intended to steal if he became mayor, Klimentiev said, "I am already under the triple control of the prosecutor of the oblast, the ministry of internal affairs, and the FSB. Who is going to give me a chance to steal? To think about it is impossible."

As support for him increased, Klimentiev intensified his efforts, holding as many as five rallies a day. In early March he began to lead in the polls, provoking a panicked reaction from city authorities. The newspapers and television asserted that if Klimentiev were elected, the city would be ruled by a *pakhan* (criminal boss). His opponents pointed out that he had come from prison and that his contacts in business were criminal.

Klimentiev responded by emphasizing his supposed spiritual qualities. A campaign video showed him standing in the falling snow in front of the ancient Pechorsky Monastery. In the background was the sound of choral singing. "We need a strong, spiritual person as the head of our city," Klimentiev said. "Most of all, our children need an internal spiritual base. From the moment I come to power, I'm going to work for our moral resurrection." He pointed to the peeling walls of the monastery and said, "Within fifteen days after my election, I will create decent living conditions for the monks, and in two years the restoration of the monastery will be finished."

Klimentiev participated in phone-ins and answered readers' letters in the newspaper. The view began to be widely expressed that if Klimentiev had made so much money, even illegally, it was a sign that he was clever enough to do something for the city.

In mid-March Yegorova asked the members of one focus group if it worried them that Klimentiev had a criminal background. The participants answered that the other candidates were no better and that since Klimentiev was rich, he had already stolen his share and would not need to steal further. The comments included: "The only difference is that Klimentiev was convicted and the others were not" and "He at least does something. The others steal and don't do anything."

It began to appear that, if the ballots were counted honestly, Klimentiev would win. But the citizens of Nizhny Novgorod assumed that there would probably be attempts at falsification in favor of Goryn. On election day, the managers in some factories collected the workers' internal passports and drove them in buses to the polling places, where they were handed their passports and told to vote for Goryn.

The attempts at coercion, however, made little difference. The results showed that 24 percent of the votes went to Bednyakov, 31 percent to Goryn, and 34 percent to Klimentiev, with the remaining votes split among minor candidates and those who had voted "against all."

The election of Klimentiev as mayor of Russia's third-largest city threw local leaders into a state of shock. The local election commission annulled the results of the election on the basis of "numerous violations" of the election rules, which, on closer examination, were either insignificant—for example, in several polling places people who voted ahead of time were not listed as having done so in the register—or committed not by Klimentiev but by his defeated opponents.[7]

The annulment of the election, however, provoked a wave of outrage even among those who had opposed Klimentiev. The mood was expressed in the local headlines: "The Imitation of Democracy Is Finished," "Chronicle of a Stolen Victory," and "We'll Vote Until We Vote the Way We're Supposed To."[8]

The oblast court, under pressure from the presidential administration, then canceled Klimentiev's conditional liberty, and he was returned to the investigative prison where he had been held before running for mayor. He was put on trial a short time later, and on May 27 he was found guilty in the theft of the "Navashino millions" and several related offenses and sentenced to six years' imprisonment minus time served. He began working out his sentence in a labor camp outside Nizhny Novgorod.

In the wake of the invalidation of the election results and his imprisonment, however, Klimentiev became a popular hero. Public opinion polls showed that Klimentiev was the leading political figure in Nizhny Novgorod; if allowed to participate in new elections, he would be swept into office with two-thirds of the vote.[9]

As bright sunshine bathed the brick walls of the Uralmash machine-building factory, thousands of people strolled through the factory grounds, enjoying the fair commemorating the "Day of the Child," an event organized by the Uralmash gang, Yekaterinburg's leading criminal organization. Parents and children carrying balloons and banners stopped at puppet shows and shooting galleries; children took part in drawing contests on the asphalt. There were also a children's theater and nonstop performances by acrobats, clowns, and rock bands in the factory's main stadium. There were free ice cream and exotic fruit for children and free beer for adults courtesy of the gang.

Long known to the police as the Uralmash organized criminal group (OPS), the gang had recently founded a political movement called the Uralmash Social Political Union (also OPS).[10]

Members of the gang in gym suits spoke over cell phones but did not interfere with the crowd. A journalist who covered crime in Yekaterinburg noticed a police officer whom he believed to be on the payroll of the gang and approached him.

"It looks like our friends are becoming respectable," he said.

"Why not?" said the policeman. "They have become normal businessmen. In ten years they'll be a force in the oblast and even in Moscow. If they come to power, it will be better. A person who has money and only wants to satisfy his ambition is impossible to buy. They will impose their own will instead of lobbying the interests of others."

The Uralmash gang's sponsorship of the Day of the Child was part of an attempt to depict itself as a group of socially concerned citizens. This required a substantial effort because, in ten years, the gang had gained a reputation for ruthlessness not only in the Urals but throughout Russia.

The Uralmash gang was founded by former athletes in the Uralmash raion of Yekaterinburg.[11] It began by extorting protection money from kiosks and small businesses and soon brought many of the city's markets and gas stations under its control.

The group's principal competitor was the Central gang, which was founded by former black-market operators and also concentrated on extorting protection money. At first the city was divided among Uralmash, the Central gang, and the "Sinii" (Blues), a group of former convicts under the control of five thieves professing the code. This division of the city into spheres of influence, however, was not destined to last.

In June 1991 Grigory Tsyganov, the leader of the Uralmash gang, was shot by a sniper when he appeared for a moment in front of a window in his kitchen. With his death, leadership of the Uralmash gang passed to Grigory's brother, Konstantin, who organized a "special forces" unit and declared war on the Central gang.

The special forces unit, a gang within a gang, was run by Sergei Kurdyumov, a thrice-convicted career criminal who worked under the overall direction of Sergei Terentiev, one of the Uralmash gang's founders. The unit had forty members who were trained by instructors from the army special forces. The members were subjected to iron discipline, and any serious failure or leak of information from the unit was punished by death.

The unit quickly went to work. On October 26, 1992, Oleg Vagin, the leader of the Central gang, and his three bodyguards were murdered by masked gunmen as they stepped out of the entryway of Vagin's apartment building in the center of Yekaterinburg. Vagin and his bodyguards were shot in the legs and then finished off with bursts of automatic weapons fire. Nearly ninety bullets were found at the scene; Vagin's body had between twenty and thirty bullet wounds. Eduard Roussel, the governor of the Sverdlovsk oblast, lived in the same building.

The murder of Vagin was followed by a wave of killings that effectively destroyed the Central gang as a competitor. Members of the Central gang and its business partners were killed by snipers, mowed down in broad daylight on the street, or blown up in their cars. The Kurdyumov unit even reached its victims abroad, killing Nikolai Shirokov, one of the founders of the Central gang, in Budapest. In a two-year period, Uralmash execution squads killed a minimum of thirty people connected to the Central gang. Throughout this time the Central gang's own execution squad under Georgy Arkhipov hunted in vain for Konstantin Tsyganov.

As the Central gang disintegrated, the Uralmash gang took over the city, annihilating other criminal groups or subjecting them to its control. Soon the vast majority of businesses in Yekaterinburg were paying protection money to the Uralmash gang.

As its execution squad destroyed all real and potential competitors, the Uralmash gang also assembled a far-flung economic empire. It soon controlled ten commercial banks; every copper smelter in the region, including Uralelektromed, one of the largest copper-producing complexes in Russia; all the region's hydrolytic plants; and all its jewelry manufacturing. It also engaged in the export and sale abroad of ferrous and nonferrous metals, including silver and gold.

The gang's most profitable undertaking, however, was the sale of vodka made with technical spirits, which are normally used for cleaning and are legally forbidden for consumption. The gang owned three factories that produced technical spirits, and they placed forged labels of known brands on the bottles of false vodka. The false vodka was sold for about one-third the usual price. The biggest customers were the region's alcoholics, many of whom died from it.

As the Uralmash gang increased its power, it corrupted officials until the only government structure that offered any opposition was the oblast's organized crime unit.

Konstantin Tsyganov was arrested by RUBOP on April 29, 1993, and charged with attempted extortion. A short time later he was freed on a bond of 150 million rubles ($120,000) by a judge in Perm and promptly disappeared. (The gang responded to Tsyganov's arrest by firing a grenade through the window of the organized crime unit's headquarters on May 2, 1993. On June 10 a grenade was fired at the building of the oblast administration.) The unit had more success in suppressing the Kurdyumov group. On December 5, 1995, law enforcement agencies arrested Kurdyumov in Nizhny Tagil. At that time Kurdyumov was a suspect in at least ten murders. On April 8, 1996, a judge in Nizhny Tagil freed him on a 70 million ruble bond ($13,000), ostensibly because he was suffering from prostate cancer. He, too, promptly disappeared.[12]

In August 1995, however, a search began for Terentiev, reputedly the brains behind the Kurdyumov group. For more than a year, Terentiev avoided arrest, living in various cities in Russia as well as in Sweden, Greece, and Bulgaria. But in November 1996 he was arrested at Vnukovo airport in Moscow, where he was carrying three foreign passports, and sent back to Yekaterinburg. Arrests of other members of the combat unit quickly followed. Ultimately, eighteen members of the Kurdyumov group were charged in connection with twenty-eight murders.

One witness in the case, an electrical engineer who was lured into the Kurdyumov group with work assignments and then forced to work as a bombmaker, described the atmosphere in the unit in an interview with Sergei Plotnikov, a television journalist in Yekaterinburg.

Q: Were people afraid of Kurdyumov?

A: Yes, they were, because there was a serious danger that at any moment Kurdyumov could decide that a person was not necessary to the organization and it was time to get rid of him.

Q: To unite people in such a group you need some kind of incentive . . .

A: At first there were incentives. People were well paid for not very demanding work. In this way, they became obligated to Kurdyumov. At that point the rewards were reduced, and people began to work not for money but out of fear.

Q: I know that you tried to leave the group. How did this conversation go?

A: I made two attempts. The first time, Kurdyumov told me that all my movements were being watched and I should report all my plans to him. The second time when I said that I wanted to end our relationship, he pointed to the floor and said that the only way to leave the group was through the earth. He told me that if I made the slightest move to leave the group, there would be trouble not just for me but for my relatives.

Q: At this time, you already knew of several persons who had been killed in this way?

A: There were a large number of people who at one time participated in the organization and then for some unknown reason disappeared. In the group there were conversations that someone left and did not come back and that another left and did not come back, and this introduced an element of nervousness, as each person, sitting in the front seat of an automobile, feared that at any moment he could be strangled by someone throwing a cord around his neck.

Q: Were there attempts to revolt against Kurdyumov?

A: This was impossible. You revolt today, and tomorrow your body will be lying in the woods. The terror was like in 1937 [the first year of Stalin's Great Terror]. Sentence was passed by Kurdyumov, and there was no shortage of potential executioners.

Q: Did Kurdyumov indicate anything when he decided to have someone eliminated?

A: No, he was absolutely cold-blooded in these matters.

Q: Did the members of the group make plans for the future?

A: There were no plans. Everyone lived for the present. Today, you bought a car or repaired your apartment, and with this you were satisfied.

Q: What did the members of the gang spend their money on?

A: In the first place, there was an apartment, then remodeling, and then a car and then another car. They compensated for the fear by buying themselves all these things. Everyone knew that gunmen were treated rather savagely, and the members of the group hurried to enjoy life while they could.

Q: Kurdyumov acted on the model of the secret services. Do you think he had some type of special knowledge in this area?

A: No, there was no special knowledge. Everything was shown in films.

Q: Did anyone simply flee the gang and not appear again?

A: No. If they had fled, many people would have saved themselves. People did not leave for many reasons. The majority had relatives, wives, children. Anyway, where are you going to run? And from whom? In the end, you're nonetheless going to return home to your family, to see your relatives; this is human nature . . .

Q: What is worse, the Kurdyumov who sits opposite you or the Kurdyumov who sits inside you?

A: That's an interesting question. People are mostly afraid not for themselves but for those close to them.

Q: But isn't there some kind of . . . ?

A: Code of honor? No, there is no code that relatives should not be touched. For them, on the contrary, the more they could hurt a person, the better.

Q: What about social conditions? Do you think that for the majority of the members of the [Kurdyumov group] being hungry affected their orientation?

A: Moral principles dissolved, of course. It became a question of self-preservation, save yourself, save your family, support your parents who don't receive their pensions . . . Of course, you can reach a person through a variety of means.

The arrests of the members of the Kurdyumov group, however, did not affect the fortunes of the Uralmash gang as a whole. By the beginning of 1997 its annual income was believed to exceed the yearly revenue of the city of Yekaterinburg, with a million and a half inhabitants.[13] The only thing the gang lacked was political power, and in 1997 it entered politics in order to take over the region completely.

The Uralmash gang had several advantages in going into politics. Commanding vast wealth and controlling hundreds of enterprises, it could draw on large reserves of manpower, equipment, and facilities. To compete in politics, however, it needed to neutralize the negative feelings it inspired as a result of its criminal activities. To this end, the gang began to engage in philanthropy.

The gang concentrated first on the Ordzhonikidze (Uralmash) raion, which has a population of about 300,000. It organized a network of sports clubs for children and teenagers, and gang members began to work without pay as guards in schools, where they kept order and prevented smoking. The gang also delivered food parcels and televisions to old-age homes. The result was that the gang's popularity rose, even among those who had not forgotten its murderous beginnings.

In 1997 Alexander Khabarov, who had become the leader of the gang after Tsyganov's disappearance, ran for a seat in the State Duma. He lost the election. In 1998, however, he ran again and received more votes than the other candidates. The election was invalidated only because fewer than half of the eligible voters participated.

The strong vote for Khabarov was a sign that the gang's public relations campaign had been a success and the population was ready to vote for the Uralmash leaders.

In the spring of 1999, twenty-three leaders of the gang announced the formation of the Uralmash Social Political Union. They stated that the goal of the new group was to participate in the elections. According to the organization's charter, its income was to come from lectures, exhibitions, sporting events, and "voluntary contributions."[14]

With the formation of the Social Political Union, the charitable activities of the gang moved to a new stage. The first event it organized was the celebration of the Day of the Child. Other fairs, exhibitions, and sporting competitions followed. In anticipation of the 1999 elections to the State Duma, the gang embarked on another project to establish itself firmly as a moral force in the community. This was a drive to rid the city of narcotics.

The center of the narcotics trade in Yekaterinburg is the "Gypsy village," a region of wooden one-story houses and brick mansions behind iron fences where it was possible to buy drugs at any time of day or night.

On September 22, 1999, the peace of the Gypsy village was disturbed by the arrival of a cavalcade of imported cars in front of Telman 12, one of the most notorious selling points for narcotics in the city. While frightened residents quickly locked their doors and watched from behind drawn curtains, dozens of members of the Uralmash gang got out of their cars and began milling around. Khabarov addressed the crowd, which was quickly augmented by a large number of television reporters.

"In the beginning of the 1990s," he said, "we did not allow the Chechens into Yekaterinburg, and we say the same thing today. We're going to wage a merciless war against the representatives of the narcomafia and expel them from the city." As Khabarov spoke, dark-haired children jumped out from behind weathered wooden fences and extended a third finger to him and the members of the crowd. On the fringes of the village, addicts who had come to buy drugs wandered around in anxious circles, waiting for the visitors to leave.

Khabarov pointed to the building at 12 Telman Street and said, "We have to destroy the retail drug market in the city. If we close all the sales points, no one will bring this poison here. It won't be profitable." After Khabarov finished, Sergei Vorobyev, another leader of the Uralmash gang, promised that he would personally make sure that the sale of drugs in the city was stopped. The members of the gang stood around for twenty minutes looking menacing and then got back into their cars and left, promising to return in the near future with more than just words.

The show of force in Gypsy Village was the beginning of the antidrug campaign.

A group called City Without Narcotics had fought against narcotics addiction, principally through educational efforts, for several years. But in September 1999 Igor Varov, a businessman with close ties to the Uralmash gang, became the leader of the fund and announced to the employees that thereafter they would fight against narcotics together with the Uralmash Social Political Union. Most of the employees promptly resigned, but their protest passed unnoticed.

With new personnel, City Without Narcotics advertised its pager number and asked citizens to report the locations where drugs were being sold. About 300 sales points were reported, almost all of them already known to the police. At the same time, some drug dealers had their legs broken or their homes set on fire. One suspected dealer was tied to a tree with a sign saying that he was poisoning the city's youth. Skeptics began to joke, "The people and the mafia are united."[15]

In the final analysis, however, the antidrug campaign was not very effective. There was increased public attention to the city's drug problem, but dealers staggered deliveries, and the price of heroin doubled. Varov said that what was important was the fact that it had been possible to create "social intolerance for evil."

City Without Narcotics also opened up two "rehabilitation centers." The rehabilitation consisted in taking a young addict, strapping him to a narrow bed, pulling his pants down, and beating him with leather belts on the buttocks as many as 300 times. The addict, unable to walk, spent his first few weeks handcuffed to a bed, left to face withdrawal symptoms with nothing but bread and water. Andrei, a twenty-year-old who was treated at the center, said he had been beaten so badly that he spent three weeks in the hospital and was scarred for life. After being beaten unconscious, he was left to hang handcuffed for three days from a wall. "They are sadists," he said. "They love the power—that's what it is all about. You can hardly call it therapy."[16]

Many people in Yekaterinburg did not take the Uralmash gang's claim to be crusaders against narcotics seriously, noting that the narcotics sales points exposed by the gang were all outside the Uralmash raion. Some journalists speculated that the gang simply wanted to organize pressure on its competition in order to take over the drug trade at some point in the future.

The antidrug campaign, however, was a political success. The general belief in Yekaterinburg that it was impossible to resist the Uralmash gang inspired a desire to believe that they had turned themselves into normal businessmen. The gang, in turn, cultivated this image with the help of journalists who were either intimidated or paid off.

In the December 1999 elections to the Duma, Khabarov's competitor was the head of the Yekaterinburg branch of the Ministry of Internal Affairs, Nikolai Ovchinnikov. In this contest between the city's chief police officer and its leading bandit, Khabarov lost by only 1 percent. He drew strong support from older people, who were convinced that the government did not care about them, and from young people, who viewed the Uralmash leaders as successful businessmen who devoted themselves to charity and whose criminal activities—"if they existed at all"—were in the distant past.

The fate of a drowning man is in his own hands.
—*Russian proverb*

Conclusion: Does Russia Have a Future?

In 1999–2001, after a decade of steady decline, Russia experienced its first years of economic growth, spurred by a tripling in the price of oil and the effects of the devaluation following the August 1998 financial crisis.

Michael Binyon, the correspondent of the London *Times,* reported: "Many Russians have never had it so good . . . Putin has reaped a reward from his determination to change Russia. Once again, he has been voted Russia's man of the year."[1]

Leon Aron, a biographer of Yeltsin, wrote in the *Weekly Standard*, "The revolution Yeltsin led has become irreversible . . . There were 18 cars per 100 households in 1990; 42 in 2001. The produce shortages and ubiquitous lines of the Soviet era have been forgotten. Fresh and delicious food is available everywhere. For the first time since the late 1920s, Russia not only feeds its people and livestock but is a net exporter of grain."[2]

Anders Aslund, an economic consultant and author, wrote in the *Moscow Times*, "As the rest of the world sinks into recession, Russia booms . . . It is time to realize that Russia is a country that solves its problems with an efficacy and speed that the West can only envy."[3]

In fact there was some basis for the effusive praise. Russia's economic situation did improve significantly, though relative to a very low base. Output in light industry, for example, rose from 12 percent of its 1990 level to 18 percent, investment from 22 percent of its 1990 level to 27 percent; and the average national wage reached $100 a month, a significant increase, though only two-thirds of the wage level before the August 1998 financial crisis.

The state of Russia, however, did not lie in any of these figures. Regardless of what they said—and the possibility that they would look better if war in the Middle East sent oil prices soaring—Russia still faces serious fundamental problems that threaten its stability and call into question its long-term survival.

The reform process took place without the benefit of higher values, and it bequeathed to Russia a moral vacuum. The result is that Russia faces three dangers—dictatorship, economic collapse, and depopulation—that define the circumstances of the country's existence and, despite fluctuations, threaten to do so for the foreseeable future.

The danger of a dictatorship in Russia stems from the fact that although elections take place and Putin currently enjoys wide popularity, democracy is a matter of convenience, not of values. Russia could revert to dictatorship immediately if the present oligarchy considered itself seriously threatened.

The potential for future dictatorship was demonstrated by several of Putin's actions since assuming office, all of them reflecting a police-state mentality.

In the first place, Putin took steps toward establishing his own cult of personality. A children's alphabet book appeared in Russia illustrated with photographs of Putin as a boy. This was followed by the production of sculptures of Putin and paintings of the president gazing out from the Kremlin over the Moscow River in the visionary manner of Stalin or Kim Il Sung. At the same time, officials in the presidential administration founded Walking Together, a pro-Putin youth movement that announced its existence with a pro-Putin rally at the Kremlin wall. At the rally, young people in T-shirts emblazoned with Putin's picture carried signs declaring, "Together with the president" and "Youth follows the president."

The members of Walking Together were instructed to read at least six Russian classics a year and to visit the sites of battles where the Russians had been victorious. They also embarked on an effort to "purify Russian literature." The group condemned modern works that contained frank descriptions of contemporary Russian life and offered to exchange them for a collection of stories recounting the victories of the Red Army during World War II.

In addition to the creation of an incipient cult of personality, the Putin leadership limited free speech in Russia by closing down the independent management of NTV and TV-6, the only two national television stations free of government control. In both cases, state-owned energy companies used financial pressure to eliminate the stations' management.

In the case of NTV, the motive for the action may have been the broadcast on the eve of the presidential elections of the discussion program regarding the Ryazan "training exercise." The broadcast was believed to have led to a reduction in Putin's margin of victory, and action against Vladimir Gusinsky, the station's owner, quickly followed. In May 2000, armed and masked federal agents raided the headquarters of Media-MOST, the holding company that owned NTV, and accused Gusinsky's security service of eavesdropping. In June, Gusinsky was arrested and confined in Lefortovo Prison on embezzlement charges arising out of the privatization of the firm Russky Video. After his release from Lefortovo, Gusinsky signed over Media-MOST to Gazprom in return for $473 million owed to Gazprom and $300 million in cash. The agreement was linked to the dropping of the corruption charges against Gusinsky and his freedom to travel and was cosigned by Mikhail Lesin, the minister of the press in Putin's government.[4]

After the takeover of NTV, Evgeny Kiselyev, the station's former director, and a group of journalists loyal to him went to TV-6, which was 75 percent owned by Boris Berezovsky. There they continued reporting that was critical of the government. In May 2001 Lukoil-Garant, the pension fund of the Russian oil giant Lukoil, which owned 15 percent of TV-6 and was itself minority owned by the Russian state, filed a bankruptcy suit demanding that the station be liquidated because its debts outweighed its assets. TV-6 maintained that it was profitable according to Western accounting standards. In the meantime, the law allowing minority shareholders to bring bankruptcy proceedings against a company lapsed on January 1, 2002.

Nonetheless, on January 11, 2002, the Supreme Arbitration Court, overruling an appellate court decision that had overturned the decision of a lower court, ordered the station liquidated. On January 14 a TV-6 talk-show host was interrupted in midsentence and replaced with test-pattern stripes and the message "We have been pulled off the air."[5]

The action against the two stations left national television, the principal information source for the majority of Russians, monopolized by the government for the first time in the post-Soviet era.

The most important indication that Russia remains in danger of becoming a dictatorship, however, is the evidence that the apartment-house bombings in September 1999 were the act not of Chechen terrorists but of the FSB.

The view that the bombings were the work of the Russian government is based on the logic of the political situation at the time of the attacks and what is known about the bombings themselves.

In September 1999, the members of the corrupt oligarchy that gained power and wealth in Russia during the years of reform were in danger of arrest. According to Yuri Skuratov, the disgraced former prosecutor general, every one of them could have faced criminal charges.[6] The bombings, however, galvanized public support for a new war against Chechnya, and the prosecution of the war made possible the election of Putin, who preserved the Yeltsin-era oligarchy virtually intact. Gusinsky, who backed Luzhkov in the 2000 elections, and Berezovsky, who overestimated his own power, were forced into exile, but otherwise none of the oligarchs was called to account.

Among the members of the Yeltsin "family" who continued to exercise power under Putin were Voloshin, the chief of staff; Kasyanov, the prime minister; Grigory Kutovoi, the head of the federal energy company, which according to experts regulates 65 percent of the Russian economy; and the three current leading oligarchs, Roman Abramovich, Alexander Mamut, and Oleg Deripaska, the son-in-law of Valentin Yumashev, who is Yeltsin's son-in-law and former chief of staff.[7]

This group, which at one time included Berezovsky, had been most directly threatened by the possibility that after the 2000 presidential elections, power in Russia would pass to someone other than Yeltsin's handpicked successor. In the last years of the Yeltsin era, these men were in a position to give orders to the FSB.

The evidence from the bombings themselves and the claim of an "exercise" in Ryazan point to the involvement of the FSB. In the cases of the bombings in Moscow, Buinaksk, and Volgodonsk, the speed, organization, and expertise required imply the participation of an intelligence agency, as does the fact that the explosive agent used in the bombings was originally announced to be hexogen, which is produced in Russia in a single factory guarded by the FSB. The evidence, however, is limited because the sites were obliterated by the explosions and the rubble quickly cleared away.

The key to whether the FSB carried out the bombings lies in Ryazan. It is difficult to draw firm conclusions about what happened in Moscow, Buinaksk, and Volgodonsk, but in Ryazan one fact is undeniable: the FSB placed a bomb in the basement of an apartment building and was caught in the act.

The FSB maintains that the Ryazan incident was an exercise. The evidence that the operation in Ryazan was not an exercise, however, but rather a failed provocation, is nothing short of overwhelming.

The modus operandi in Ryazan—a bomb containing hexogen set to go off at night and destroy a residential building in a working-class area—was identical with that of the bombings in Moscow, Buinaksk, and Volgodonsk.

The detonator used in the bomb was real. This fact was confirmed by local police, bomb experts, and a date-stamped photograph of the bomb components. The three sacks attached to the detonator and placed next to the principal supports of the building contained hexogen. This fact was determined by bomb experts who perform more than 100 defusing operations per year.

In response to questions about these seemingly unexplainable inconsistencies, the government has insisted that the gas analyzer that detected the presence of hexogen in Ryazan was in error, the bomb placed in the basement of 14/16 Novosyelov was a dummy, and the substance in bags attached to the detonator was sugar.

These statements appeared to be directly contradicted by the physical evidence, but the government did have a way to substantiate its claim. It needed only to produce the people who carried out the training exercise, the records of the exercise, and the dummy bomb itself. The FSB, however, refused to do this on grounds of secrecy, and evidence relating to the Ryazan incident was sealed for seventy-five years.[8]

Both the logic of the political situation and the weight of the evidence lead overwhelmingly to the conclusion that the Russian leadership itself was responsible for the bombings of the apartment buildings. This was an attack in which many of the victims were children whose bodies were found in pieces, if at all. There can be little doubt that persons capable of such a crime, regardless of how they present themselves, would not give up power willingly but would react to a threat to their position by imposing dictatorial control.

Besides the danger of reverting to dictatorship, Russia faces the possibility of economic collapse.

In the first place, Russia is critically dependent on the world price of oil. Every dollar difference in the price of oil translates into roughly $1 billion in budget revenue and directly affects the government's ability to balance the budget, pay state employees, and repay Russia's foreign debt.[9]

At the same time, Russia faces the breakdown of its economic infrastructure. It has been estimated that the modernization of the Russian economy would cost $2 trillion. Russia needs to modernize everything, from housing and telephones to roads, factories, atomic power stations, and dams. More than half the equipment of the Russian electrical system is in need of replacement, as are up to half the rolling stock of its railroads and up to 60 percent of the equipment used by its oil industry.[10]

Under these circumstances, if commodity prices fall and critical elements of Russia's infrastructure begin to collapse at the same time, there is little to guarantee Russia's continuing economic stability.

In a report on the socioeconomic situation in Russia, the Swedish Defense Research Institute in Stockholm described a possible Russian economic collapse. Although the sequence of events presented is a worst-case scenario, it needs to be kept in mind.

In the Swedish scenario, a fall in raw material prices on the world market triggers an economic crisis. The economic situation grows progressively worse. A series of Chernobyl-type disasters hampers the ability of the government to maintain basic infrastructure.

> Under these circumstances, the budget deficit increases to unmanageable proportions, and inflation grows accordingly, so that the IMF refuses to grant new credits. Both foreign and Russian capital flees from Russia, which reduces investments drastically.
>
> Imports drop steadily . . . and the country's food supply is threatened, since production by the agro-industrial sector continues to drop.
>
> . . . A new Duma and a conservative and authoritarian president try to salvage the situation by a partial return to the command economy. This makes the economy and the ruble fall even more.
>
> This causes an explosive increase in the export of currency, and a virtually completely demonetarized economy arises, in which 90 percent of the stagnating trade is in the form of barter. Poverty becomes increasingly widespread, and 70 percent of the people are living below the subsistence level.
>
> Those who are able to emigrate to the West do so. The situation in Russia affects other economies in transition and growing countries in Asia and South America, which are hit by new crises. International preparedness to deal with Russia's problems is steadily eroded as a result.
>
> Finally, after a catastrophic harvest and emptied reserves, there are widespread food shortages, and the people move in increasing numbers toward the center of Russia and gradually to surrounding countries as well. The world finally reacts by closing its borders and sending a limited amount of disaster relief—measures that have only a limited effect.[11]

The third, and in some ways most serious, danger facing Russia is that of depopulation.

Russia has one of the lowest birthrates in the world and the death rate of a country at war. According to Igor Gundarov, the head of Russia's State Center for Prophylactic Medicine, if current trends continue, the population of Russia will be reduced by half in eighty years, to about 73 million, making the Russian state as it now exists untenable.[12]

With a few exceptions, the reform years in Russia outside of Chechnya were not characterized by massacres. Nonetheless, the period did not pass without victims. The increase in the death rate during the reform period led to 5 million premature deaths, a grim testimony to the toll inflicted by "shock therapy."

In 1992–1994 there was an almost vertical rise in the death rate. Mortality rose one and a half times by comparison with the second half of the 1980s, and at the same time the birthrate fell by half. The largest increase in the death rate was among the working-age population, especially men between the ages of twenty and forty-nine. In 1994 the death rate reached 15.7 persons per 1,000. The difference between births and deaths became 700,000 to 900,000 persons as Russians died at a rate of 1 percent a year.

At first the sharp increase in the death rate was explained as the result of the sudden impoverishment of the population. Poverty alone, however, could not have accounted for the rise in deaths. The economic level in the 1990s fell to that of the 1960s, but in the 1960s the death rate in the U.S.S.R. was the lowest in the developed world. In Moscow, where the standard of living in the 1990s was one and a half times higher than in the rest of Russia, the death rate was two times higher (10 per 1,000 in Moscow, compared with 6 per 1,000 in Russia as a whole). The death rate was also higher in Russia than in former Soviet republics that were poorer, such as Georgia, Uzbekistan, and Turkmenistan.

Gundarov concluded that poverty, state-encouraged alcoholism, and the deterioration of the system of public health accounted for only 20 percent of the reduced longevity in Russia. The remaining 80 percent was attributable to the spiritual condition of the population in the wake of the failure, after the fall of communism, to offer any new ideal for Russian society. "There proceeded an attempt to 'transplant souls' and replace the old, nonmarket soul with a new, pragmatic businesslike approach to life," Gundarov said. "This change was unaccompanied by an effort to provide . . . a reason for which this change should be undertaken. For many people, who needed something to live for, this change was intolerable, and they lost the will to live because life no longer had any meaning."[13]

In fact, the decisive influence of spiritual factors on the rate of mortality was nothing new for Russia.

In the years immediately following World War II, the death rate in the Soviet Union for civilians rose by 20–30 percent. In contrast, in 1943, despite the hardships of the war, the death rate among civilians was only half what it had been in 1939. The reason was that after the Battle of Stalingrad, there began to be faith in ultimate victory.

After World War II the rate of mortality was cut in half even though there was economic chaos. People's spirits were lifted by hopes for a new life. The death rate began to rise only after the end of the Khrushchev thaw, when disappointment spread through Soviet society. In the 1970s, when the economic situation was relatively favorable but there was no prospect of change, mortality rose.

When Gorbachev came to power and initiated his policies of glasnost and perestroika, the death rate fell by 40 percent. Even though the economic situation was difficult, with shortages and long lines, there was an emotional surge in response to the advent of freedom of speech and the opening of borders.

The catastrophic rise in death rates that began in October 1991, a rise so dramatic that at first Western demographers did not believe the figures, continued until 1994. In the mid-1990s the death rate fell, but only temporarily. After the August 1998 financial crisis, the death rate again reached the 1994 levels, with a net population decline in 1999 of almost 800,000. The Russian population fell by 750,000 in 2000 and by 458,400 in the first six months of 2001.

At the Mitinsky cemetery in Moscow, gravestones have taken over the neighboring fields all the way to the horizon. A reporter from *Moscow News* spoke to a gravedigger who said, "Even to the eye it's obvious that the deaths are not standard, there are constantly more young people, less than 50 years old."[14]

Because of the high mortality rate among men of working age, the Russian population is increasingly weighted toward those incapable of working —children, invalids, and pensioners. If existing trends continue, by 2005 the country will begin to close schools, and soon there will not be enough conscripts to fill the army.

The issue of Russia's population also has geopolitical significance. Population density in European Russia is 8.5 per square kilometer, 3 times lower than in the United States, 14 times lower than in China, 17 times lower than in Western Europe, and 38 times lower than in Japan. In Siberia the population density is 2.5 per square kilometer. If the population of Russia continues to fall, surrounding countries will find it difficult to resist the temptation to take over empty territories; and even without an overt takeover, Russia might be forced to invite foreign nationals to help man vital industry.[15]

The danger of a new dictatorship, the possibility of economic collapse, and the looming demographic catastrophe shadow visible changes in the Russian economic situation that are, in fact, directly connected to the price of oil.

These threats are the product of the moral vacuum in Russian society, and as long as that vacuum exists, the future of the country will be in danger.

Both in Russia and in the West, there has been a tendency to interpret success in Russia strictly in economic terms. Unfortunately, Russia's problem is that Russian society lacks moral foundations, and those in power often interpret liberty to be the freedom to do whatever they want, regardless of the welfare of others. Under these conditions, ordinary citizens are helpless to defend their dignity, and the degraded condition of the individual is the root cause of Russia's systemic malaise.

Much of the discussion of the Russian reform experience concerned the relative merits of "shock therapy" versus government regulation. But as long as 145 million people are repeatedly shown that the best way to acquire property is to steal it, such disputes make little sense. Any economic measure introduced into this atmosphere will be immediately deformed by the underlying immorality of the society and the political system.

In the final analysis, the individual in Russia can reclaim his status as a moral actor and aid his country's transition only if he is supported by society's recognition of the authority of universal, transcendent values. Unfortunately, it was this element that was missing in the whole reform process.

Nikolai Berdyaev, the Russian religious philosopher, wrote: "In the soul of the Russian people, there should appear an immanent religiosity and immanent morality for which a higher spiritual beginning creates internally a transfiguring and creative beginning."

In this, he saw the hope for the future. The Russian people, he wrote, need to enrich themselves with new values and replace a "slavish religious and social psychology" with a "free religious and social psychology." They need to recognize the godliness of human honesty and honor. "At that point, the creative instincts will defeat the rapacious ones."[16]

Notes

INTRODUCTION

1. Quoted in Lawrence Elliott and David Satter, "Three Days That Shook the World," *Reader's Digest,* January 1992.
2. Quoted in Alexander Danilkin, "Mafia—nash rulevoi," *Trud,* December 10, 1994.
3. According to a survey of businessmen, several thousand bribes are given and received in Moscow every day; Yuri A. Voronin, "The Emerging Criminal State: Economic and Political Aspects of Organized Crime in Russia," in *Russian Organized Crime: The New Threat?* ed. Phil Williams, special double issue, *Transnational Organized Crime,* 2, nos. 2/3 (summer/autumn 1996): 53–62.
4. Solonik was famous in the Russian underworld for his ability to shoot accurately with both hands and for an unprecedented escape from the Sailors' Silence Prison. He came to Moscow, usually on "business," and is believed by law enforcement officials to have assassinated fifteen people during these visits; Georgy Rozhnov, "Osobye Primety: Krasivaya i Molodaya," *Kriminalnaya Khronika,* March 1998.
5. Solonik was believed to have been killed in retaliation for an attempt to kill Asatryan, the head of the Kurgan mafia. The full story of the fate of Svetlana became known after agents of the organized crime unit arrested seventeen leaders and operatives of the Kurgan mafia, several of whom told authorities what they knew about her death. According to an official in the organized crime unit, Svetlana was strangled after the killing of Solonik in order to eliminate a possible witness. Killers like those from the Kurgan mafia never leave witnesses and also kill wives and girlfriends as an act of terror that will make an impression in the Russian underworld; Rassledovanie, "Poslednyaya Zhertva Solonika," *Express Gazeta,* no. 20 (1997); and Rozhnov, "Osobye Primety."

CHAPTER 1. THE *KURSK*

1. *The Exile,* September 28, 2000. In an interview on February 1, 2000, with the newspaper *Kurskaya Pravda,* the commander of the *Kursk,* Gennady Lyachin, gave the following

account of the *Kursk*'s capabilities: "Our ship is, in fact, unique, having a whole series of advantages over the submarines of our adversaries. They do not have such a class of ships, combining torpedoes and rockets. Our weapons surpass their models in both power and range and in terms of their possibilities. If it is necessary, we can simultaneously attack many objects from the ocean depths—for example, hit targets on land, single ships, or convoys. Besides this, the ship has good maneuverability and high speed while underwater." Excerpts from the interview were reprinted in "After an Autonomous Cruise, I Reported to Vladimir Putin," *Komsomolskaya Pravda*, August 12, 2000.

2. This account is based on Georgy Sviatov, "Death of Kursk," *Submarine Review*, October 2000, 47–52; "K-141 Is Down," *The Exile*, September 28, 2000; and Alexander Yemilyanov, "'Kursk' ne Stalkivalsya s Innostrannoi Podlodkoi," *Novaya Gazeta*, February 15, 2001.

3. Valery Matlin, "Oni Ukhodyat iz Zhizni, Dazhe ne Ponimaya Etogo" (transcribed by Alexander Kots), *Komsomolskaya Pravda*, August 14, 2000.

4. Oktai Ibragimov, "Massovogo Psikhoza na Lodke Net" (transcribed by Alexander Kots), *Komsomolskaya Pravda,* August 13, 2000.

5. Such suspicions gained support from some of the answers of high-ranking naval officials as to why Russia was not accepting foreign assistance. Vice Admiral Yuri Kvyatkovsky, the director of the Russvoencenter, a government organization, said that the *Kursk*'s communications system, apparatus, and ciphers were all of interest to foreign intelligence but that the "tastiest morsel" was the submarine's winged rockets and their guidance systems, including the data-processing equipment for the directing of rocket strikes and the self-guiding systems of the warheads. Other state secrets included the torpedo apparatuses and their electronic stuffing. "The divulging of these and other secrets," Kvyatkovsky said, "would allow our adversaries to work out methods of defending against Russian submarines." See Viktor Baranets, "Komandovanie VMF Zasekretilo Vse Krome Svoei Nerazvorotivosti, " *Komsomolskaya Pravda*, August 13, 2000.

Many aspects of the *Kursk* tragedy were reminiscent of the tragedy of the Soviet submarine *Komsomolets*, which sank on April 7, 1989, with a loss of forty-two lives. In that case, a fire broke out as a result of a short circuit and quickly spread throughout the submarine. The *Komsomolets* surfaced, and the order was given to evacuate. Only one raft capable of holding twenty-five men was inflated. Fifty crewmen tried to climb aboard. Efforts to inflate other emergency rafts were unsuccessful. The submarine started to sink. Many crewmen clung to the raft, freezing to death in 36-degree water. The Soviet authorities, for reasons of secrecy, did not allow the Norwegian coast guard to rescue the dying men. In the end, twenty-nine men were rescued alive, two of whom later died from shock. Of the forty-two who lost their lives, only four died from the fire and subsequent explosions. The rest drowned or died from immersion in the icy water while awaiting help.

6. Paul Beaver, "Darkness, Dampness, and Cold," *The Times* (London), August 16, 1999.

7. Only a few journalists were allowed to attend the meeting, and the use of tape recorders was forbidden. Only one television camera (that of RTR, the official Russian television station) was present, and the footage that was subsequently broadcast was carefully selected by RTR's general director. Andrei Kolesnikov of *Kommersant Vlast*, however,

managed to tape the meeting, and its proceedings were published in the August 25, 2000, issue of the magazine. Without this proscribed recording, the full story of what happened at the meeting would not have reached the public.

8. In reality, contact with the sub was lost at roughly 1:00 P.M.

9. This account of the memorial service is based on Ulyana Skoibeda, "Vsem Nam Khvatit Vody, Vsem Nam Khvatit Bedy," *Komsomolskaya Pravda*, August 24, 2000.

10. Since the first Chechen war began in 1994, the Committee of Soldiers' Mothers has initiated 350 "wrongful death" lawsuits against the Russian government on behalf of parents of soldiers killed in what they considered to be incompetent or unnecessary military operations. The courts agreed to hear 19 of these cases, and the parents lost all of them. There are still an estimated 3.4 million Soviet soldiers missing in action from World War II, and there have been few efforts to learn their whereabouts or to assist their families. In Russia, "missing in action" implies possible cowardice or desertion, and the families of those men suffer from that taint to this day. See Fred Weir, "On Kursk, a New Caring Kremlin," *Christian Science Monitor*, November 2, 2000.

11. Pavel Felgenhauer, "Time to Let Go of the Past," *Moscow Times*, November 9, 2000.

12. Ulyana Skoibeida, "Rassledovanie po Pismu Vdovy," *Komsomolskaya Pravda*, February 24, 2001.

13. Tylik's mother, Nadezhda Tylik, said at a news conference that her son just smiled at her when she told him that everything would be fine; "Russia Is Said to Have Known of Sub Flaw," *New York Times*, February 23, 2001.

14. See Sviatov, "Death of Kursk," 51–52. Another, not unimportant consideration may have been the personal ambitions of Klebanov, who was rumored to be a leading candidate for the post of Russian defense minister as part of a move by Putin to restructure and "civilianize" the post. Obviously, any indication that his personal negligence was involved in the *Kursk* tragedy would have undermined his chances; "Kursk Recovery Mission Ended, Many Questions Unanswered," Jamestown Foundation *Monitor*, November 10, 2000.

The views of Klebanov and Kuroyedov were not shared by a group of retired Russian naval officers. At a Moscow seminar, two former submarine commanders—one of whom had commanded the *Kursk* itself and the other of whom had commanded another like it—said categorically that the *Kursk* could not have been sunk by a collision with another submarine. Another Russian naval officer, former Baltic Fleet commander Admiral Eduard Baltin, said that although there could have been such a collision, "it would not have had such tragic consequences." He said that a crash would have probably dented the submarine's outer hull but would not have crippled the vessel. The former officers suggested that a combination of several external and internal factors was probably at the root of the disaster. However, they refused to elaborate on their conclusions, out of fear, they said, that they might face prosecution by the FSB for revealing classified information; "Lost Russian Submarine Continues to Generate Controversy," Jamestown Foundation *Monitor*, December 4, 2000.

Supporting the view that a collision could not have sunk the *Kursk* is the fact that the hull of an Oscar-II submarine has ten separate waterproof compartments and was designed to be able to float even after a direct torpedo hit.

15. Yemilyanov, " 'Kursk.' "

1. Anna Savina, who spent all night on the street, described the atmosphere of panic surrounding the Ryazan incident. "At 11:00 P.M., the police went from apartment to apartment asking people to leave the building immediately. I was in my nightgown, but I threw on a raincoat and ran out. It was only on the street that I learned that our building had been mined. But my mother remained in our apartment. She is completely bedridden. In horror, I ran to the police and said, 'Let me back into the building so that I can remove my mother!' But they did not let me go back in. Only at 2:30 A.M. did they begin gradually to take residents back to their apartments to check if there was something suspicious. When my turn came, I pointed to my sick mother and said to the police officer that I was not leaving without her.

   "The officer quietly wrote something in a notebook and then disappeared. I then realized that I was probably alone with my mother is a mined building. It became horrible . . . But suddenly, there was a ring at the door. In the entrance stood two senior police officers. They asked me severely, 'Have you decided to bury yourself alive?' My legs were giving way out of fear but nonetheless I insisted that without my mother, I was not leaving. At that point, the police officers softened. 'All right,' they said; 'the building has already been cleared' . . . At this point, I myself ran out onto the street." Alexander Litvinenko and Yuri Felshtinsky, *FSB Vzryvaet Rossiyu*, excerpted in *Novaya Gazeta*, August 27, 2001.

2. The Ryazan FSB went to great lengths to assure the residents of Ryazan that it had had no foreknowledge of the supposed exercise. After Patrushev's announcement, Yuri Bludov, the press spokesman for the Ryazan FSB, said that the local FSB had not been informed in advance that there would be an exercise in the city. Sergeev said in an interview with the television studio Oka that he had not known anything about the exercise. When asked if there was any document confirming that what had taken place in Ryazan was an exercise, he answered through his press secretary that he considered a televised interview with Patrushev to be proof that the events in Ryazan had been an exercise.

   The governor of the Ryazan oblast, B. N. Lyubimov, said that he had known nothing about the planned exercise, and Mamatov said that the residents of Ryazan had been treated like guinea pigs. "I'm not against exercises," he said. "I served in the army and participated in them myself, but I never saw anything like this."

3. Voloshin was in Ryazan to cover the awards ceremony organized by the FSB. At that time, he treated the incident as an example of the FSB's penchant for conducting experiments on human subjects. "The residents of Ryazan . . . became participants in extended Moscow exercises. Their experiences were in the spirit of the great Academic Pavlov, who came from Ryazan, and they occurred in time for his 150th birthday. The residents of the city . . . were used by the central apparatus of the FSB in the capacity of Pavlov's famous experimental dogs"; Pavel Voloshin, "Chelovek Cheloveku—Sobaka Pavlova," *Novaya Gazeta*, October 4–10, 1999. Later, after examining the evidence, Voloshin concluded that the Ryazan incident was an unsuccessful attempt to commit mass murder.

4. The FSB insisted that the people who took part in the "exercise" were clandestine agents and could not appear in public. However, there is no legal barrier to making agents available to journalists. Article 7 of the law on state secrets of the Russian Federation,

adopted July 21, 1993, states that among the things that cannot be considered state secrets and declared to be secret evidence are evidence about "extraordinary accidents and catastrophes threatening the security and health of the citizens and their consequences . . . facts about the violation of the rights and freedoms of citizens . . . [and] facts about the violations of the law by state organs and officials." Zdanovich said that if the agents were necessary for the investigation, they would be produced. Since, however, the case that was opened (and which, despite the FSB's explanation of the Ryazan events, the general prosecutor refused to close) was one of terrorism, the needs of the investigation were determined by the FSB.

5. Members of the Ryazan bomb squad said that explosives are not packed and transported in 50-kilogram (110-pound) sacks because it is too dangerous. To blow up a small structure requires only about 18 ounces of the right type of explosive. Fifty-kilogram sacks of an explosive like hexogen are necessary only for terrorist acts. It thus seems logical that the three sacks placed under the main supports of the building in Ryazan came from the warehouse guarded by Pinyaev.

6. The participants in the Nikolaev broadcast included, from the FSB, Zdanovich, Sergeev, and Stanislav Voronov, the first deputy head of the FSB's investigative directorate. Other participants included Duma deputy Yuri Shechochikhin, former KGB general Oleg Kalugin, and Evgeny Sevastyanov, the former head of the Moscow directorate of the FSB, as well as residents of 14/16 Novosyelov, investigators, independent experts, jurists, human rights advocates, and psychologists.

During the broadcast, Nikolaev carefully avoided any connection with the bombings in Moscow, Buinaksk, and Volgodonsk. When one of the participants raised this issue, he said, "We won't discuss this," and cut off the microphone. Voloshin was later told that the FSB had insisted, as a condition for participating in the broadcast, that all discussion of the other bombings be excluded.

Nikolaev invited residents of the building to question representatives of the FSB.

An older, mustached man in a red shirt said, "This was not an exercise. An exercise lasts only a few hours. No one was allowed to go to their apartments. The next morning, they were allowed to return only to dress but could not wash or shave. Sick people were left in their apartments."

The microphone was brought to Zdanovich, who answered, "This was an exercise. There was no real danger. Afterward, I apologized to the residents of the building for any inconvenience, and Patrushev did the same. We can prove that this was planned in advance."

Residents asked where the people were who had placed the bags in the basement of the building.

Zdanovich responded, "We use people who are clandestine agents, and we do not show them. There is presently a judicial case that has been started around these exercises. If necessary in connection with the investigation, they will be shown. But for now we can allow them to be filmed only from behind."

"What's the reason for the heightened attention to this incident?" asked Nikolaev.

"For months," Zdanovich said, "there was no interest and there were no publications. The theme was activated on the eve of the presidential election with the most fantastic details in order to accuse the FSB of planning a real explosion with the death of people. This is actively used in the political struggle."

A white-haired man asked, "Who gave you the right to carry out these exercises and humiliate people?"

"We carry out the 'alarm bell' exercises to practice seizing airplanes," Zdanovich said. "Such exercises are carried out with the abuse of the rights of citizens. They were carried out and they will be carried out. How much are citizens' rights abused when some mentally ill person makes an anonymous call? We are forced to evacuate buildings, hospitals, factories, stores. This also violates the rights of citizens, but it protects the most important right, the right to life."

Sevastyanov, who was participating as an independent expert, said, however, "The residents of the building should not have been part of the exercise. We carry out 'alarm bell' but never with people in the plane."

Nikolaev next asked Raphael Gilmanov, an independent explosives expert in the hall, if it was possible to mistake sugar for hexogen.

"No one who saw hexogen in life would ever confuse it with sugar," Gilmanov said.

"Do you allow for the possibility of a false reading by the gas analyzer?" Nikolaev asked.

"No."

Nikolaev next asked how it was possible that Sergeev had mistaken a dummy for a real bomb.

"General Sergeev," Zdanovich explained, "is not a sophisticated expert in the matter of explosive devices."

Sergeev, however, was only communicating what had been told him by Tkachenko, who had deactivated the bomb. Zdanovich was therefore suggesting that the members of the bomb squad were incompetent.

An expert from the FSB said that the first analysis had been mistaken: some hexogen that was on the top of a suitcase brought to the scene by one of the bomb squads had fallen on the litmus paper used in the testing of the contents of the bags, producing a trace of hexogen.

Finally, the microphone was given to Colonel Churilov, the commander of the base where the sacks of hexogen were found. He said that there was no such soldier as Alexei Pinyaev. Nikolaev, however, then called on Pavel Voloshin, who was in the audience. Voloshin played an audio tape of his interview with Pinyaev and showed the audience photographs of the soldier.

With the conclusion of the first part of the broadcast, it was obvious both to the residents of 14/16 Novosyelov Street who were in the hall and to viewers throughout the country that the FSB had not been truthful in its account of the mechanics of the "training exercise." The discussion then proceeded to the possibility of a coverup.

Sevastyanov said that he was prepared to believe that the FSB had organized a training exercise to test the population's "vigilance" but he was troubled by the fact that the MVD, which had responsibility for the fight against terrorism, had been informed about the exercise only two days after it had taken place. "Why was there such a time lag?" he asked.

"You have to remember," Zdanovich said, "that the events were carried out late at night. They continued to develop the next morning. We needed time to study the whole chain and the search for terrorists. This is why the operation was carried out from the center and the MVD and the Ryazan FSB were not informed."

"The real reason," said a man in the audience, "was that the FSB needed two days to come up with an explanation."

"The FSB organizers of the exercise are criminals," said another male resident of the building. "This was a monstrous, immoral experiment. Even if this was sugar, which is extremely doubtful, they are still criminals."

Nikolaev next raised the question of the legality of the supposed "training exercise."

Pavel Astakhov, a lawyer representing a group of residents of the building who were considering filing suit, said that the law on operational investigative activities that covers the holding of military exercises did not give the FSB the right to mine a residential building and endanger the lives and health of citizens. Moreover, article 5 of the law explictly mentions the necessity of observing civil rights during the carrying out of exercises. In this respect, the incident in Ryazan did not fall within the framework of Russian laws.

A military man in the audience said that the circumstances of the exercise were extremely suspicious. He said that the organization of military exercises is always accompanied by the preparation of ambulances, medicine, bandages, and warm clothing and even the most important exercises, if they involve the civilian population, are always agreed upon with the local authorities and the concerned agencies. In the present case, nothing had been agreed on or prepared for.

Nikolaev then asked why the investigation into the incident was continuing.

"The FSB is assigned to investigate cases of terrorism," said Astakhov. "But there is a prosecutor who can close the case. If it was sugar in those bags, the case should have been closed a long time ago."

Zdanovich tried to answer the charges directed against the FSB. "We are ready for discussion," he said. "This is why we are here. The exercise was intended to guard the security of citizens. We did this because we had no choice. We never acted against the people."

As the meeting ended, however, and the Ryazan residents and FSB officials filed out of the hall, it was obvious that the FSB had suffered a major setback. That the FSB officials realized this was clear from their grim expressions. Zdanovich, Voronov, and a group of other FSB officials met Voloshin at the place where coats were checked and said, "You're working for the West. Prepare for unpleasantness."

The broadcast of the meeting on March 23, a week before the presidential election, over NTV, the independent Russian television network, had a huge effect. People everywhere were struck by the ineptitude of the FSB representatives' attempt to defend the organization's actions, and the overwhelming impression left by the program was that the incident in Ryazan resembled not a military exercise but a failed provocation.

One morning in September 2000, NTV received a collective letter from the residents of 14/16 Novosyelov Street in Ryazan addressed to Nikolaev. The program "Ryazan Sugar— A Test by the Secret Services or an Unrealized Bomb" had been aired six months before and was still controversial. The pro-presidential television channel, ORT, accused NTV of organizing a preelection provocation, and there were estimates that the broadcast had reduced the victory margin of President Putin in the presidential elections by several percentage points.

The broadcast had now been nominated for a high journalistic award, and the appearance of the letter seemed to be tied to this nomination.

The first paragraph read: "We, residents of Ryazan, living at 14/16 Novosyelov Street, decided to express our disapproval of the television broadcasts directed by you, which again and again touch on the events of last year connected with the exercise carried out by the FSB."

The letter next expressed the residents' gratitude to the FSB, sentiments that the residents were not known to have expressed earlier. "We with all our hearts thank the leadership of the Ryazan oblast directorate of the FSB, which reacted in a humane manner to all our requests, providing help in the refurbishing and improvement of our home . . . We state to you with all responsibility that the employees of the FSB save hostages and every second risk their lives in the struggle with terrorists in the cities of Russia."

The letter then concluded in a manner that left little doubt about its intended audience. "We are informing you that a copy of this letter is being sent to the minister of press and information . . . and the head of the presidential administration."

When the letter was presented to Nikolaev, he was astonished by its contents. Nothing in it resembled anything that the residents of the building had ever said before. At first glance, it seemed to be one more mystery in an incident that had been sinister from the start. A closer examination of the letter, however, revealed that most of the signatures were on the reverse, clean side of the sheet of paper. When residents of the building were questioned by journalists about their signatures, they said that they had never signed a letter denouncing NTV. It transpired that the signatures had been collected for payment for the answering system on the front door by Viktor Kuznetsov, a former policeman and resident of the building who in the past had performed minor tasks for the FSB. Those signatures which Kuznetsov did not collect, he simply falsified. Pavel Voloshin, "I Vnov FSB Geksogen Ryazan: Istoriya odnoi falshivki," *Novaya Gazeta*, September 21–24, 2000.

7. There was considerable evidence that at the time of the Ryazan "training exercise," the population needed to be calmed down, not incited further. The weekly newspaper *Versiya* reported that in the period September 13–22, special Ryazan police units responded to more than forty reports by residents of the placement of explosive devices.

On September 13 the residents of 18 Kostyushko Street and adjacent buildings were evacuated in twenty minutes while the building was inspected from basement to attic. Similar operations were carried out in apartment blocks on International Street and Blyuzov Street. In this period it was also necessary to evacuate the editorial office of the newspaper *Vechernyaya Ryazan* and the pupils in school number 45. In all of these cases, the alarms were false. In the same period a military shell was discovered in a building at 32 Stankozavodsky Street. It had been left there as a joke by schoolchildren but could have exploded. Nikolai Bakhroshin, "Kto Vzorval Rossiyu: Zachem FSB Pytalas Vzorvat Sakhar?" *Versiya*, February 22–28, 2000.

8. The buildings that were bombed in Buinaksk, Moscow, and Volgodonsk were also located

in outlying working-class areas. This was one more indication that the "exercise" in Ryazan was planned by the same people who perpetrated the earlier bombings.

CHAPTER 3. THE YOUNG REFORMERS

1. Chubais was the chairman of the State Property Committee (GKI) and, after June 1992, deputy prime minister; Maxim Boiko was an adviser to Chubais and, after 1993, chief executive officer of the Russian Privatization Center; Pyotr Mostovoi was the deputy chairman of GKI and, later, head of the Federal Bankruptcy Commission; and Alexander Kazakov was the director of the privatization effort in the regions and, later, deputy head of the presidential administration.

2. " 'Dvoika' po povedeniyu?" *Komsomolskaya Pravda*, November 18, 1997.

3. Chrystia Freeland, *Sale of the Century: Russia's Wild Ride from Communism to Capitalism* (New York: Crown Business, 2000), 295–96.

4. Because Yeltsin had combined the offices of president and prime minister, Burbulis, as first deputy prime minister, was the effective head of government.

5. "Promotion in the Soviet system was reserved for the children of workers and peasants," a woman who had worked and studied with many of the young reformers told me. "This produced deep resentment and the attitude 'If I had a chance, I'd show the world.'

   "The future young reformers usually were specialists in Western society, which it was their duty to criticize. There was no serious study of the Soviet Union. When we did serious analysis, it was of life in the West. When the young reformers were unexpectedly given power, they actually had no knowledge of their own country. They knew far less than the members of the old nomenklatura, who at least were familiar with their areas of expertise. The reformers borrowed from foreign experience—Korean, Latin American, American—but they had no idea how the economy worked in Russia. Their failure to move up in the Soviet system had alienated them totally from the old elite, and they were ready to build a society based on 'every man for himself.' "

6. As was the case with the Bolsheviks, the reformers' faith in the predictive value of their theoretical assumptions made them indifferent to the suffering they were causing. When the first reform measures led to a sharp drop in living standards and a rise in the death rate, the attitude in government circles was that this was a revolution, and in a revolution people got hurt.

   Gaidar, Chubais, Mostovoy, and other reformers traveled around the country speaking to large audiences. Wherever they went, they behaved as if they were addressing an economic club and proved incapable of expressing themselves in intelligible language. In response to questions such as "Why are pensions not being increased?" or "Why are the factories being closed?" they gave lengthy economic analyses filled with words like *indexation*, *default*, *denomination*, *dollarization*, and *devaluation*. People invariably came away from the meetings with the impression that the speaker was ridiculing them and trying to show how little they knew.

   On one occasion Gaidar went to Magadan, where local leaders pleaded for credits to buy food products and pay for energy. Gaidar's response was that the Far North was over-populated and could support a population only half its current size. On another occasion, when Gaidar, who had an unfortunate tendency to smack his lips in a professorial style when he was speaking (he later corrected it), was warned that the reforms were devastating Russian agriculture, he replied, "It doesn't matter; we'll buy food in the West."

7. During the Stalin era, common criminals were regarded as "socially friendly" and as a result received better treatment in the labor camps than the political prisoners, who were considered to be ideological enemies.

8. The reformers were convinced that the population would not accept for long the hardships connected with the economic reforms, but their awareness of the hardships that the reforms would cause did not lead them to feel any sympathy for the population. They did, however, feel great sympathy for themselves. They referred to themselves as "kamikazes" and bent every effort to reach the "point of no return" beyond which it would no longer be possible to restore the institutions of socialism regardless of the will of society.

In an appearance on the television program "Details" on June 29, 1994, Chubais said, "The goal of privatization is to build capitalism in Russia, in fact, in a few strenuous years, doing that work which in the rest of the world was accomplished over centuries"; Roy Medvedev, *Kapitalizm v Rossii?* (Moscow: Prava Cheloveka, 1998), 172. Chubais' words bear an eerie resemblance to Stalin's declaration in 1929 that the Soviet Union had to build an industrial base in ten years and, in that way, accomplish in a decade what the rest of the world had done in a century.

9. During the Soviet period, any appointment to a senior administrative post had to be approved by the party apparatus at the raion, oblast, or Central Committee level. The people filling these positions were referred to collectively as the nomenklatura.

CHAPTER 4. THE HISTORY OF REFORM

1. Anders Aslund, "Tri Osnovnye Istochniki Bogatstva Novykh Russkikh," *Izvestiya*, June 20, 1996.

2. For an account of the events leading up to the dissolution of the Supreme Soviet and the massacre at the Ostankino television tower that followed it and provided a pretext for the shelling of the parliament building, see David Satter, *Age of Delirium: The Decline and Fall of the Soviet Union* (New Haven: Yale University Press, 2001).

3. See Olga Kryshtanovskaya, "V Chikh Rukakh Sobstvennost?" *Argumenty i Fakty*, no. 15 (1997).

4. The failure of voucher privatization was one of the reasons for the widespread hatred of Chubais, who was considered to have deliberately deceived the population. His promise in 1992 that a voucher, representing each citizen's share of the national wealth, would be worth the value of a Volga car and possibly two, is still remembered. Roy Medvedev, *Kapitalizm v Rossii?* (Moscow: Prava Cheloveka, 1998), 176.

5. Svetlana Glinkina, "The Criminal Components of the Russian Economy," working paper no. 29, Berichte des Bundesinstituts für Ostwissenschaftliche und Internationale Studien, 1997.

6. Stanislav Lunev, "Russian Organized Crime," Jamestown Foundation *Prism*, May 30, 1997, 10.

7. Glinkina, "Criminal Components."

8. Svetlana Glinkina, Andrei Grigoriev, and Vakhtang Yakobidze, "Crime and Corrup-

tion," in *The New Russia: Transition Gone Awry*, ed. Lawrence R. Klein and Marshall Pomer (Stanford: Stanford University Press, 2000), p. 247.

9. Between 1990 and 1998 Russia sold more enterprises than any other country in the world, but it was in twentieth place in terms of revenue. Brazil earned $66.7 billion, Britain earned $66 billion, Italy $63.5 billion, France $48.5 billion, Australia $48 billion, and Russia $9.25 billion. Even Hungary, where the state controlled much less than in Russia, earned $2.1 billion more than Russia did. In Russia privatization revenue was $54.60 per capita compared with $2,560.30 in Australia and $1,252.80 in Hungary. "Privatization, Russian-Style," *Nezavisimaya Gazeta—Politekonomiya, Johnson's Russia List*, April 17, 2001.

10. Anna Politkovskaya, "Norilsk Gotov Poiti v Bank," *Obshchaya Gazeta*, March 6–12, 1997.

11. Jonas Bernstein, "Watergate: Day at the Beach," *Moscow Times*, November 22, 1996.

12. Svetlana Glinkina, "Kharakteristiki Tenevoi Ekonomiki v Rossii," *Nezavisimaya Gazeta —Politekonomiya*, no. 5 (March 1998).

13. According to the Russian Statistics Committee (Goskomstat), during the period 1992– 1998 Russia's gross domestic product fell by about 44 percent. During World War II it shrank by 24 percent. During the Great Depression the U.S. gross domestic product fell by 30.5 percent. Industrial production in Russia during 1992–1998 fell by 56 percent. Peter Reddaway and Dmitri Glinski, *The Tragedy of Russia's Reforms: Market Bolshevism against Democracy* (Washington, D.C.: United States Institute of Peace Press, 2001), 249.

14. Fred Weir, "A Slow Descent," www.intellectualcapital.com, September 25, 1997; and Stephen Shenfield, "On the Threshold of Disaster: The Socio-Economic Situation in Russia," *Johnson's Russia List*, July 2, 1998.

15. Natalya Amanova, "Rossiya—Strana Universalnogo Vzyatochnichestva," *Razbor* (supplement to *Agumenty i Fakty*), no. 6 (1998): 2.

16. Shenfield, "On the Threshold of Disaster"; and Murray Feshbach, "Russia's Population Meltdown," *Wilson Quarterly*, in *Johnson's Russia List*, January 11, 2001.

17. Reddaway and Glinski, *The Tragedy of Russia's Reforms*, 606.

18. Ibid., 611. The information leaks about the plans for the "Storm in Moscow" operation were not the only indication that the Russian leadership was planning terrorist acts. On June 6, 1999, three months before the bombings of the buildings on Guryanova Street and the Kashirskoye Highway, the Swedish journalist Jan Blomgren reported in the newspaper *Svenska Dagbladet* that one option being considered by the Kremlin leadership and its associates was a series of "terror bombings" in Moscow that could be blamed on the Chechens. Konstantin Borovoi, an independent Duma deputy, said that he had been warned by an agent of Russian military intelligence of a wave of terrorist bombings before the blasts took place.

19. In the first poll after the previously unknown Putin became prime minister, his approval rating reflected that of Yeltsin. Of those polled, 2 percent said they would vote for Putin for president.

20. Beginning in September, press reports alleged that Berezovsky, Alexander Voloshin (by then the head of the presidential administration), Anton Surikov (a former member of the GRU), and Basayev had met in France in June or July to plan the incursion into Dagestan. On September 13–14 the newspaper *Moskovsky Komsomolets* published parts

of the transcript of a conversation between a man with a voice similar to Berezovsky's and a man with a voice similar to that of Movladi Udugov, the unofficial spokesman for the radical Chechen opposition, including Basayev and Khattab, in which they appeared to be on friendly terms and appeared to discuss the transfer of money from the person resembling Berezovsky to the radicals. Pavel Gusev, the chief editor of *Moskovsky Komsomolets,* said that he had confirmed that the FSB officer who had taped the conversation was later murdered "on the orders of those who had been recorded."

The combination of these publications may have inspired Tretyakov, the trusted chief editor of Berezovsky's most important publication, to offer a version of events that, if it did not absolve Berezovsky, at least suggested that he was not the only person involved in organizing the fateful incursion into Dagestan. Tretyakov wrote: "It is perfectly obvious that the Chechens were lured into Dagestan . . . in order to provide a legitimate excuse for restoring federal power in the republic and beginning the offensive phase of struggle against the terrorists grouped in Chechnya. Clearly it was an operation by the Russian special services . . . that was, moreover, politically authorized from the very top.

"In light of all this, here is my own personal hypothesis: at worst, Berezovsky may have been used without his knowledge by the Russian special services or, more than likely, he acted in coordination with them . . . My hypothesis is far more realistic than the theory that 'Berezovsky set everything up,' which presumes his absolute influence on the two warring sides simultaneously"; Vitaly Tretyakov, editorial, *Nezavisimaya Gazeta,* October 12, 1999.

21. Reddaway and Glinski, *The Tragedy of Russia's Reforms,* 614.

22. This was not the first time in Russia that the prospect of elections had led to acts of terror in Moscow. In June 1996, on the eve of the first presidential elections, a bomb went off in the Moscow metro, killing four people and injuring twelve, and two trolley explosions injured thirty-eight. These events worked in favor of Yeltsin's candidacy by creating fear of instability. In the case of the August 31, 1999, Manezh bombing, an obscure anticonsumerism group called the Union of Revolutionary Writers left leaflets at the scene in which they appeared to take credit for the explosion. The leaflet read, in part, "A hamburger not eaten to the end by the dead consumer is a revolutionary hamburger." In the past, inane claims of responsibility by previously unknown or little-known groups have been a way of signaling that the real parties responsible were the intelligence services.

23. In the end, many remains were never found.

"I buried my daughter, Yulenka, my darling," said Tamara Gorbileva. (Yulia Chernova lived in apartment 141 on Guryanova Street.) "She was just twenty-eight years old. In the explosion were also killed my son-in-law, Andrei, and my grandson, Tyemochka, but their remains have not yet been identified, although I have personally visited every morgue. I can't tell you the horrible things I saw. We were able to identify Yulenka only because of her luxuriant hair . . . Our Tyemochka in a few days would have been four years old. I swore on the grave of my daughter that I will find Tyemochka and bury him next to her, even if it is only a piece of him."

In the Borovsky-Rykhletsky family, which lived in apartment 123 on Guryanova Street, the grandmother, two children, and mother and father were all killed. Their relatives were unable to identify the body of a single one of them.

In all, seventeen residents of the building on Guryanova Street disappeared after the explosion in the building; Lyudmilla Volkova and Tatyana Ressina, "Dochenka, Ya Prinesu Tebye Tyemochku . . . ," *Moskovsky Komsomolets*, October 19, 1999.

24. High-ranking officials were informed of a bombing in Volgodonsk several days in advance. On September 13, Gennady Seleznyev, the speaker of the Duma, at a meeting of the Duma Council received a note from the Duma Secretariat that he read to those present. It said there had been an explosion in Volgodonsk. Vladimir Zhirinovsky, the leader of the Liberal Democratic party, said that after this statement, those present waited for a report of the bombing on television. The bombing, however, did not take place until three days later, on September 16. On September 17 Zhirinovsky reminded Seleznyev of his statement on the thirteenth and asked him why he had not warned the authorities. Seleznyev told *Noviye Izvestiya* in March 2002 that he had been referring to an explosion organized by criminal gangs which took place on September 15 and which did not claim any victims. The fact of the latter explosion was confirmed by the local Volgodonsk press, but Seleznyev's explanation left several questions unanswered. If the explosion in Volgodonsk referred to in the note to Seleznyev was part of a petty criminal conflict, why was it necessary urgently to inform both the speaker of the Duma and—according to information in the hands of Sergei Yushenkov, a member of an independent commission to investigate the 1999 bombings—Putin? Was it only a coincidence that Seleznyev and Putin were informed about an explosion in the same city where a massive explosion took place on the following day? Why did Seleznyev, who has close ties to Putin, not mention the "routine" explosion in September 1999 when questions about his foreknowledge were first raised? And, finally, if the note that Seleznyev read concerned a low-level criminal conflict in Volgodonsk, why was Seleznyev informed about it two days in advance?

25. Putin's expression in Russian was "mochit ikh v sortirakh." The word *mochit*, which means "to wet," is criminal slang for liquidating someone. In October, when it was suggested that Russia negotiate with the rebels, Putin said that they were bandits and that anyone trying to do so would most likely receive a "kontrolny vyistrel" (control shot) in the head. The term *kontrolny vyistrel* also comes from the criminal world.

   In the months after the bombings, Putin showed poise and equanimity in responding to questions on a wide variety of questions, with the exception of questions about Chechnya. When the subject of Chechnya was raised, he invariably became abusive and insulting. This fact, in combination with his use of thieves' language, has led some to suggest that, for some reason, he is affected by criticism of the second Chechen war not just politically but also personally.

26. Maskhadov accused the Russian secret services of carrying out the apartment bombings to distract attention from the corruption scandals engulfing the Kremlin, and he expressed his condolences to the victims. Basayev and Khattab denied involvement after all three attacks, saying that their rule was always to claim credit for their "acts of war" and that if they had wanted to bomb buildings in Moscow, they would have chosen a military garrison or the Kremlin, because they condemned blind attacks against civilians, which they had not carried out even during the first Chechen war; Sophie Shihab, "Attentats: La piste vite oubliée des services russes," *Le Monde*, January 12, 2000.

27. See David Satter, "Anatomy of a Massacre," *Washington Times*, October 29, 1999.

28. See "Silence after the Explosions," *Moskovsky Komsomolets*, January 19, 2000. It was also noteworthy that a Russian military buildup on the border with Chechnya began in June with the transfer of significant numbers of artillery and aircraft, followed in early July by the arrival of a multiple-rocket-launcher battalion that was capable of destroying entire areas, and thus was suitable for an invasion but not for chasing terrorists. These movements were followed by a slow, linear buildup of forces. OMON units were steadily brought in from all parts of the country until there was the equivalent of a Russian division, about 7,000 men, on the border. The divisions and regiments that were transferred after the September bombings therefore joined an already significant force.

29. Beginning in Buinaksk on September 4, the bombings occurred at three- or four-day intervals, assuring that each new bombing took place while funerals were being held for the victims of the previous one. The fact that the "training exercise" in Ryazan took place six days after the bombing in Volgodonsk was another indication that it was intended to be part of the same series.

30. Hours after the second apartment blast in Moscow, the police arrested Timur Dakhkilgov, an ethnic Ingush textile worker, after he was found to have on his palms traces of hexane, a chemical widely used in dyeing fabric. He spent weeks in jail, where he was repeatedly beaten. See Simon Saradzhyan, "After One Year, Blast Probe Still Drags On," *Moscow Times*, September 15, 2000.

31. The rubble from the bombings was cleared almost immediately despite the objections of the MVD and the Ministry of Emergency Situations. The haste with which the crime scenes were destroyed was all the more striking in light of the fact that, in the cases of the bombings of the American embassies in Kenya and Tanzania in 1998, suspects were identified and eventually arrested as a result of months of careful sifting through the rubble. At the same time, the FSB prevented investigators from the Emergency Situations Ministry from gaining access to the sites at Guryanova Street and the Kashirskoye Highway and interfered with the attempts of rescue personnel to take care of victims. The Russian authorities declined offers of forensic assistance from the United States and other Western countries.

32. Harold Lasswell, *Propaganda Technique in the World War* (New York: Garland, 1972), 190. The sense that the explosions had been stage-managed was reinforced by the reaction of the authorities afterward. Following the explosion on Guryanova Street, extreme emergency security measures were implemented in Moscow. Huge lines of trailer trucks and cars formed at the checkpoints on the roads leading into the city. The 15,000-man MVD Dzerzhinsky Division was put on the street, adding to an already huge police presence. Four or five days after the explosion in Kashirskoye Highway, however, the situation had returned almost to normal, creating the impression that the authorities realized there was no further danger. Western diplomats who tried to gain information from sources in the government or think tanks found that their usual contacts were unable to provide any information about the security situation and that attempts to raise questions about the bombings were a sure way to end a conversation.

33. Two people who were not ethnic Chechens were tried in Stavropol in the fall of 2001 for participation in the Moscow bombings, but both were acquitted. Although they were convicted of other serious crimes, the evidence that they had any connection to

the Moscow bombings was too obviously falsified even for a normally obedient Russian court.

In December 1999, shortly after the FSB announced that the explosive used in the apartment bombings was ammonium nitrate and aluminum powder rather than hexogen, Russian forces in Chechnya claimed to have discovered a laboratory where explosives had been prepared for the bombings in Urus Marten, the center of the kidnapping trade, during Chechnya's brief period of independence. In the laboratory, not surprisingly, were bags of ammonium nitrate and aluminum powder.

34. "Fit for Carrying Out the 'Family' Service," *Russia Today* press summaries, *Segodnya*, May 18, 2000. The newspaper also speculated that the Kremlin had invested too much in Ustinov to change him for someone else. In 1998, it reported, Borodin had bought an apartment for Ustinov that cost $500,000. Moreover, the presidential property department had provided luxurious housing in Moscow for ten other highly placed prosecutors.

35. Voloshin succeeded Nikolai Bordyuzha, the chief of staff in 1998–99, and Valentin Yumashev, who was chief of staff in 1997–98.

CHAPTER 5. THE GOLD SEEKERS

1. Polina Solovei, "Raziskivaetsya ubiitsa," *Trud*, September 13, 1995.
2. For three years, as their pages filled with advertisements for the pyramid schemes, the Russian newspapers made little attempt to warn citizens of the dangers of the new financial companies. Instead, they were full of advice that implicitly validated them. Russians were urged not "to let money lie dormant," which inspired them to rush to invest, and counseled not "to put all their eggs in one basket," which led them to diversify their holdings, with the result that they lost money in many places.

The advertising played on the tendency of Russians to live in a world of their imagination. In the Soviet Union, the paradise they were building received its confirmation in false official statistics, and after the Soviet Union fell, banks and financial companies presented charts showing how their money would grow in much the same way that the Soviet authorities had used charts to illustrate the steady rise of production over successive five-year plans.

3. There were a number of factors that induced Russians to take the bait of promised high returns and give up their money to swindlers. First, the hyperinflation that began after January 2, 1992, wiped out the population's savings and pushed Russians to search for ways to preserve the value of their salaries.

Second, Russians did not understand the risks they were taking. The swindlers operated in a completely lawless environment. To create an investment company in Russia, all that was necessary was starting capital of 10,000 rubles. It was possible to register at any address, and dozens of companies were often registered at an address where none of them was actually located. There was no effort to check the criminal backgrounds of persons who began to solicit investments from the population. When officials interfered with the operations of the companies, it was principally to collect bribes.

4. The advertisements for the Chara Bank were tailored to the situation. In one of them a man standing on a table marked "Chara" rose out of the middle of a whirlpool and said,

"We are the only ones who can save you." In another, a man dying of thirst in the desert collapsed. A large wooden mug marked "Chara" appeared in front of him, and he drank from it and revived.

5. The term *new Russians* is applied to those who have amassed fortunes under the new economic conditions. They are generally considered to differ psychologically from "old Russians."

CHAPTER 6. THE WORKERS

1. During the Soviet period the director was the key link between the party and the workforce. He worked under intense pressure, constantly harassed by higher-ranking officials who berated and humiliated him for any failure. At the same time, he quickly suppressed any challenge from below. This was not difficult, because the workers had no political or legal rights and consequently little or no recourse in the event of violations.

   The result of this system of concentrated power was that directors became accustomed to viewing workers as raw material to be used for fulfilling the objectives of the plan. They addressed workers with profanity and almost always with the familiar form of "you," forced them to work long hours if that was necessary, and humiliated individuals if they posed a problem.

2. Another means of stripping the assets of a factory was to rent out everything possible, with a small part of the rent specified in a formal agreement and the rest paid in cash to the director. The directors also began to organize barter between factories, using their workers as free labor to unload railroad cars for each other. Another strategy was to stock stores in their enterprises. Goods in the stores were sold on credit for prices higher than in neighboring stores. Once the workers stopped being paid, they had no choice but to buy in these stores. The quality of the goods was lower than elsewhere and the prices 10 to 15 percent higher. In these circumstances, Russian producers could rest comfortably in the knowledge that their low-quality and virtually unusable products could be distributed to hungry workers who had not been paid and had no choice but to accept them.

3. "Provintsialnaya Khronika," special issue, *Informatsionnoe Rabochee Agentsvo—Soyuz Obshchestvennikh Korrespondentov (IRA-SOK)*, October 1996, 2.

4. Mordashov's comments inspired bitterness among the workers. Work in the factory was hazardous; there were at least two serious accidents and one death a month. The building had little ventilation, and filters had not been improved for five years. The steelworkers felt the coal dust and coke dust in their teeth, and the heat and noise aged them prematurely; they retired at fifty-five, but few lived long enough to enjoy their retirement. At the same time, it was well known that Mordashov owed his effective ownership of the plant to financial machinations.

5. Invariably the banks that organized the loans-for-shares auctions were the winners at those auctions. The purchase of Yukos was consistent with Khodorkovsky's history of using government connections to amass wealth. In 1987, as a high-ranking official of the Moscow Komsomol, Khodorkovsky organized a trading cooperative financed with party money. In the following year he organized the Menatep Bank. From 1990 through 1993 Khodorkovsky served in the Russian government as an economic adviser to Gaidar and

as deputy minister of fuel and energy. During this period the Menatep group continued to grow. In 1992 Menatep was tapped to handle funding for a host of federal programs, including supplying the military with food, funneling cash for the Chernobyl cleanup, and later rebuilding Chechnya, in the course of which, according to the Russian Accounts Chamber, $4.4 billion sent to Chechnya disappeared. In 1992, when the price of oil in Russia was about one three-hundredth of the world market price, Menatep gained permission to export oil; and in 1993 Menatep was empowered to handle federal budget money and used the funds for short-term interbank lending, reaping enormous profits on the state's money. See Matt Bivens and Jonas Bernstein, "The Russia You Never Met," *Demokratizatsiya: The Journal of Post-Soviet Democratization* 6 (fall 1998): 613–47.

6. In late 1997 Khodorkovsky had bought the Vostochny Oil Company, which allowed him to unite oil-processing plants and service in contiguous parts of the country. As the price of oil fell, Yukos had to retire debts and pay off foreign credits received for the purchase of the Vostochny Oil Company. Under these circumstances, it became easiest not to pay local taxes, because the cities and raions did not have the punitive power of the federal government, which for nonpayment of taxes could withdraw the right to export oil.

7. Workers were told that either there would be mass firings or the workers would have to agree to pay cuts of 30 to 40 percent. Yugansk Neftigas began not to pay bonuses, which in the past had been virtually automatic. The operator of an oil well had previously received a base salary, a coefficient for work in the north, and 70 percent of the total as a bonus. Under the new pay policies, most workers were soon earning from one-third to 40 percent of their former salaries.

CHAPTER 7. LAW ENFORCEMENT

1. There are specialists who connect the growth in the number of crimes among police officers with the fact that, after the fall of the Soviet regime, the new government removed the department responsible for supervising the police from the structure of the KGB. Whereas earlier the KGB had observed the police with an eye to identifying possible shortcomings, once responsibility for controlling the police was removed from the KGB, matters were allowed to drift. See Sergei Romanov, *Moshennichestvo v Rossii: Kak Uberechsya ot Aferistov* (Moscow: EKSMO, 1998), 455.

2. In a survey conducted by the sociological center Status in 1996, 43 percent of Muscovites said that if they were home alone, they would not open the door to a policeman, and 37 percent said they were equally afraid of gangsters and the police; Vladimir Skosirev, "Kto zhe v Rossii Budet Zashchishchat Grazhdan, a ne Gosudarstvo," *Izvestiya*, April 5, 1997.

3. The police may also extort payoffs from the vendors who trade with official permission in the city markets. A vendor can be closed down because his hands are dirty, because he is using an electric heater in the winter that consumes too much power, or because he is trading in an "unauthorized location." In each case, the problem can be avoided with the help of a bribe. In cases in which a gang controls a market, they may be the ones who pay off the police. In this situation, the police become enforcers for the gang.

4. Maxim Glikin, *Militsiya i Bespridel* (Moscow: Tsentrpoligraf, 2000), 120.

5. Romanov, *Moshennichestvo v Rossii*, 480–81.

6. Shamil Basayev spent $9,000 on bribes to Russian traffic police not to examine his trucks. As a result, his Chechen fighters were able to reach Budyennovsk and to seize several hundred hostages and confine them in the city hospital. After Russian special forces suffered losses in two unsuccessful attempts to storm the hospital, a settlement was negotiated with Basayev which allowed for an immediate ceasefire, the opening of peace negotiations, and the transport and safe passage of Basayev's forces to separatist-held areas in Chechnya. During the truce that accompanied the peace negotiations, Chechen forces were given a critical breathing space of several months before full-scale fighting erupted again. During this period they filtered back into most parts of Chechnya, in effect retaking them without a struggle. See Anatol Lieven, *Chechnya: Tombstone of Russian Power* (New Haven: Yale University Press, 1998).
7. According to some estimates, two-thirds of the Russian population has at some point had this experience.
8. Viktor Shirokov, "Ya Boyus: Militseiskie Priklucheniya Intelligenta," *Novoye Russkoye Slovo*, January 30, 1998; reprinted from *Kriminalnaya Khronika.*
9. Yekaterina Karacheva, "Za Shto Zabral, Nachalnik?! Otpusti," *Novoye Russkoye Slovo*, January 12, 2000; reprinted from *Kriminalnaya Khronika.*
10. Perfilyeva spoke from firsthand experience. When her mother-in-law, who had suffered a heart attack on the street, did not return home after work, she and her husband began calling the Moscow morgues. Nastya eventually identified the body of her mother-in-law in the basement morgue of a Moscow hospital. What horrified her most was not the rows of naked bodies laid out on tables with no effort to make them presentable for identification, but the fact that in some cases the morgue attendants had put two bodies on one table.

CHAPTER 8. ORGANIZED CRIME

1. "Osnovy Borbi s Organizovannoi Prestupnostyu," *Nezavisimaya Gazeta*, June 14, 1997.
2. "TsRU o Svyazakh Rossiiskikh Bankov s Mafiei," *Novoye Russkoye Slovo*, December 12, 1994.
3. Some of the most commonly used words are *mochit, nayekhat,* and *bespredel.* As already noted, *mochit,* meaning "to wet," is used by criminals to mean "to kill." *Nayekhat* means "to collide with" and, in reference to a meeting, describes an attempt by gangsters to put pressure on a client or potential victim. *Bespredel* is labor camp slang. Originally used to describe prison officers who exceeded regulations in their brutal treatment of prisoners, the term is now widely used to mean criminality without limits.
4. The growth of modern Russian organized crime began in the 1970s when the first clandestine factories were set up in the Soviet Union. These factories used available machines and materials to produce goods secretly for the black market. The quality of their products was much higher than in the case of the state factories, and their directors grew rich by satisfying the huge pent-up demand for decent consumer goods.

   The activities of the directors *(tsekhoviki),* however, invariably attracted the attention of local criminals who extorted money from them. Since the factories were illegal, the directors could not turn to the police for help. In order to survive, they instead sought an accommodation with the criminals, and in 1979, at a thieves' assembly in Kislovodsk, which many of the directors attended, it was agreed that they would pay the thieves 10 percent of their income in return for protection and allow the thieves to sell part of their production. This meeting marked the beginning of the connection between organized crime and Russia's emergent capitalism.

In the second half of the 1980s the Soviet Union legalized cooperatives, the country's first private businesses. As the cooperatives took hold and spread, traditional thieves (blatnye) were joined by bandits, often former sportsmen, in extorting money from them. When private business was fully legalized after the fall of the Soviet Union, the trend continued. Anyone opening a business in Russia was immediately visited by bandits offering the services of their gang as a roof (krysha) in return for a cut of the business's earnings.

Two types of criminals organized gangs: zakoniki, literally, "legalists," who adhered to the rules of the criminal underworld and its rituals; and "bandits," for the most part petty hoodlums who took their inspiration from American gangster films and liked to think of themselves as "businessmen."

The thieves were dominant in the prisons and labor camps, and in response to the forcible imposition of Communist ideology they developed their own thieves' ideology, which they counterposed to the ideology of the state. This ideology, which demands that the thief refuse all cooperation with the authorities, was enforced by the elite of the thieves' world, the "thieves professing the code" (vory v zakone). Their role was to manage the affairs of the criminal world and to settle disputes. In the early 1990s there were an estimated 400 thieves professing the code in Russia.

The thief professing the code is chosen by the existing criminal hierarchy on the basis of his personal authority and, until recently, his time spent in the camps. He is empowered to give orders that have to be obeyed. Traditionally, he was not allowed to have a family or to work and had to live exclusively off the fruits of his criminal activities.

Unlike the thieves, many of the bandits did not have previous arrest records. They did not adhere to the thieves' code but formed disciplined organizations that extorted money from businessmen and then used that money to start their own businesses.

As capitalism developed in Russia, however, there was a weakening of the commitment of the thieves professing the code to their traditional laws and a growth in their cooperation with and participation in the bandits' criminal organizations.

By the late 1980s, local gangs had organized into larger groups, usually based on a specific region, such as the Solntsevo raion in Moscow, or a single ethnic group such as the Chechens or Dagestanis. Each gang tried to carve out a sphere of influence for itself, and this competition led to the first wars between the gangs over territory.

The Chechens initially dominated organized crime in Moscow. When the other gangs met in 1988 to divide up the capital, the Chechens did not attend. In response, the Slavic gangsters, particularly the Solntsevo, Lubertsy, and Balashikha groups, tried to purge Moscow of Chechens. The resulting gangland war, fought in cafés, restaurants, and on the street, led to a new division of spheres of influence in Moscow. The Solntsevo gang was left controlling the western and southwestern parts of the city, the Dolgoprudny gang Sheremetevo airport and the northern part of the city, the Luberetsky gang several of the Moscow suburbs, and the Izmailovo-Golyanovsky gang the Izmailovo section and part of the Moscow oblast. The Chechens lacked a specific territory, but they were left controlling hotels, restaurants, businesses, and banks all over Moscow.

5. The *obshchak* is usually maintained by a thief professing the code and is used to bribe prison officials, hire lawyers, buy alcohol and narcotics for the prison community, care for family members of persons who are imprisoned, and aid in the planning and perpetuation of new crimes.

An example of police corruption was given in a closed meeting of the Chief Directorate of the Ministry of Internal Affairs in St. Petersburg. A teenager listening to music while sitting at his window and looking out at the street began to notice that the same car often arrived at a nearby store after it was closed. The passengers in the car unloaded something and then quickly brought it into the store. The teenager soon realized that they were unloading guns. The teenager wrote down the car's license number and for the next few days noted the car's movements. Finally, he went to his local police station and reported what he had seen to one of the officers. The policeman to whom he reported his observations, however, was being paid by the bandits who were unloading the weapons.

Two days later the teenager disappeared. His body, which showed signs of torture, was found in a wooded area beyond the city limits. After a large-scale operation, the murderer was found but was declared mentally ill and not subject to prosecution. His testimony was similarly discounted. The policeman to whom the teenager gave his information remained in his post until he retired from the force voluntarily. See Malcolm Dixelius and Andrei Konstantinov, *Prestupny Mir Rossii* (St. Petersburg: Bibliopolis, 1995), 187.

6. Ivankov is perhaps the best-known thief professing the code. Known throughout the former Soviet Union as the "father of extortion," he went to the United States with the intention of establishing new criminal networks between Russia and the United States but was arrested in New York in 1995 and sentenced to nine and a half years in prison for extortion.

7. The fund was named for a legendary soccer goalie. In fact, Kvantrishvili's claim to be a defender of sportsmen was altogether ambiguous, because by the early 1990s sports clubs and schools were well established as training grounds for criminal organizations.

8. Paul Klebnikov, *Godfather of the Kremlin: Boris Berezovsky and the Looting of Russia* (New York: Harcourt, 2000), 19.

9. Donald N. Jensen, "How Yuri Luzhkov Runs Moscow," *Johnson's Russia List*, November 20, 1999.

10. Agathe Duparc with Vladimir Ivanidze, "Iouri Loujkov et 'Sistema,' ou l'archetype de l'oligarchie muscovite," *Le Monde*, February 26, 1999.

11. The name of the Solntsevo region and therefore of the gang was taken from the Russian word *solntse*, which means "sun." The name of the raid, "Zakat," meaning "sunset," was chosen to indicate the intention to put an end to the Solntsevo gang's reign of terror.

12. "Chtoby Vymanit Zhertvu iz Kvartiry, Killer Vyvernul Probki v Podezde," *Moskovsky Komsomolets*, November 3, 1995.

13. "Chtoby ne Oshibitsya, Killer Rasstrelyal Vsekh Direktorov," *Moskovsky Komsomolets*, April 28, 1998.

14. "Oni Byli Gotovy k Smerti . . . ," *Novoye Russkoye Slovo*, December 22, 2000.

15. Alexander Maksimov, *Bandity v Belykh Vorotnichkakh: Kak Razvorovyvali Rossiyu* (Moscow: EKSMO, 1999), 48–51.

16. Subbotin had money to lend to Yuri Kurkov to invest in the Vlasteline pyramid scheme because he was running his own pyramid scheme in the form of a company that solicited money for construction projects and trade. Subbotin's company promised a return of 35 percent a month, which was modest by the standards of the time and inspired confidence. To advertise the company, Subbotin made a video based on interviews with investors. One of the people interviewed, a man in his sixties, said, "I gave money to one firm, and they fooled me. I gave money to a bank, and I lost money again. I invested in the construction of apartment buildings, and the bosses disappeared; but here I feel that I won't be cheated. The rate is 35 percent a month, and I feel that I'll get my money." This interview was replayed continually on a monitor in Subbotin's office, and people saw it as they came in.

   Subbotin told Yuri: "The people who created these pyramids are swindlers, but we're honest. We'll fuck everyone else, but our own people will get their money."

CHAPTER 9. ULYANOVSK

1. At the time of the firings, those who were dismissed were told that they would receive two-thirds of their back pay. In response, on September 2, 1996, nearly 1,000 of the workers who had been dismissed walked fifteen miles to the single bridge over the Volga River linking Novy Gorod with the city of Ulyanovsk and blocked traffic. The protest lasted for five hours. It ended with a promise by management to review the question of back pay, but many workers never received all of their back salary.

2. A shortage of funds forced a stop in the construction of a new bridge across the Volga River that was vital in order to repair the existing bridge, built in 1956. The old bridge was in such poor condition that heavy trucks were allowed to use it only at night, when there was relatively little other traffic. Drivers in Ulyanovsk believed that there was a danger of the bridge collapsing and of cars ending up in the Volga. In early 1999 the central section of the new bridge was standing in the middle of the river without a beginning section or a concluding section.

CHAPTER 10. VLADIVOSTOK

1. Svetlana Zhukova, "Ledyanoi Dom," *Vladivostok*, January 25, 2001.

2. The events on Russky Island were horrific even by the standards of the Russian armed forces. In February 1993 sailors from the naval base fled to Vladivostok to inform friends and relatives that there was mass starvation on the island. Their relatives contacted Cherepkov, a former naval officer and a deputy in the krai parliament, and he went to Russky Island and filmed the sailors. The resulting videotapes alerted the entire country to the tragedy.

   Conditions on the island were barbaric. New enlistees in two navy radio and communications schools were beaten and starved while food supplies were stolen. The sailors lived in derelict buildings without heat during a bitterly cold winter and suffered from dysentery as a result of a break in the sewage system that contaminated the drinking water. Doctors who treated them said they had never seen such emaciation among members of the armed forces. One surviving sailor remarked that anyone who had been on Russky Island would "not be afraid of Buchenwald."

3. In October 1993 Yeltsin disbanded the Russian Supreme Soviet, and the abolition of the krai, oblast, and city soviets quickly followed. New elections were not scheduled in Primoriye until ten months later, and the absence of legislative oversight created a window of opportunity for Nazdratenko and the krai administration. As privatization got underway, the only person able to stand in the way of massive corruption was Cherepkov.

4. There had already been attempts on Cherepkov's life. Shots were fired at him in June and July 1993, and in August he was attacked on the street by five hoodlums. In November Cherepkov's official car was hit by another car, and in December, while Cherepkov was working late in his office, mercury was spilled on the floor. Cherepkov was later told that this was part of a plan to put him in the hospital and kill him there.

5. Cherepkov's fingerprints were not found on any of the items supposedly used to bribe him. Instead, experts found the fingerprints on the money and paper wrapper of the persons who were conducting the case against him. Two of the civilian "witnesses" present at the search of Cherepkov's office also turned out to be the wife and nephew of Dudin, the investigator.

6. Sadikov, who worked for the radio station VBC, was kidnapped and tortured on June 28, 1994. He was seized, a bag was put over his head, and he was driven to a cemetery where a group of attackers beat him and fired a pistol several times under his ear, demanding to know who had paid him for his broadcast. To avoid being killed, Sadikov told his tormentors what he believed they wanted to hear, that he had been paid by Cherepkov. He was then taken to a basement where his fingers were crushed in a vice. He was beaten for hours with clubs and pipes and burned with lit cigarettes before being forced into the trunk of a car with the explanation that he was going to be thrown into the ocean. His attackers let him out on a deserted beach just before dawn and told him that a decision had been made not to kill him. They warned him never again to criticize Tolstoshein and not to tell anyone what had happened to him. Sadikov reported the incident to the police and gave a detailed account on videotape. News of the attack sent a wave of fear through the city, particularly among journalists. Natalya Barabash, "Svo-bodu Pechati u Nas Vsegda Zazhimali, no ne Zheleznimi Tiskami," *Komsomolskaya Pravda*, July 22, 1994.

7. One of the accused murderers of Zakharenko, Alexander Brekhov, was brought to trial in April 1998. During the trial he stated that the killing had been organized or, at the very least, sanctioned by Nazdratenko. V. A. Nomokonov and V. I. Shulga, "Murder for Hire as a Manifestation of Organized Crime," *Demokratizatsiya* 6 (fall 1998): 679.

8. Nazdratenko's reputation for killing anyone who proved inconvenient to him was strengthened by the death of Baulo.

Baulo's reign as the undisputed boss of organized crime in Vladivostok lasted for roughly two years. It was Yeltsin's decree removing Cherepkov that was believed to have led to his death. According to the version related by, among others, Cherepkov, the decree removing Cherepkov as mayor was prepared in return for a bribe of 4 billion rubles ($1.2 million) to members of the presidential administration. The money was collected from the regional *obshchak* by Baulo. Nazdratenko, however, demanded additional money, and Baulo refused. In the course of an argument about the money, Nazdratenko apparently became convinced that Baulo, who had intimate knowledge of the operations of the krai administration, had become a danger to him. In August 1995, Baulo was scuba diving with friends off Reineke Island when he began making erratic movements and waving his hands. Assassins waiting for him underwater, possibly members of the special forces trained by the Pacific Fleet, had apparently twisted his air pipe. When he was pulled from the water, he said, "Boys, I'm dying." He was put in a car and died on the way to the hospital. The cause of death was never established. The size of the funeral—nearly 4,000 people attended—was unprecedented in Vladivostok, and the enormous cortège of cars and buses paralyzed the city.

9. There was also no water because the city is built on hills, and the cutoff of electricity halted the operation of the pumping stations.

10. That Chubais was engaged in a power struggle was made clear by the arrest in Moscow on July 25, 1996, of Pyotr Karpov, the deputy director of the Federal Bankruptcy Commission, who in 1995 had led a commission investigating corruption in Primoriye. Karpov was charged with accepting a bribe of $5,000 in 1992. Although it was a trivial amount by Russian standards, the charge posed a problem for Chubais. Karpov was the deputy to Pyotr Mostovoi, Chubais's chief deputy during voucher privatization. Evidence given by Karpov could be used to incriminate Mostovoi, who might then be induced to give evidence against Chubais.

Chubais wanted to get rid of Nazdratenko to consolidate his own power, but the arrest of Karpov was believed to have been organized by people close to Chernomyrdin, as a warning to Chubais. "Until recently, Chubais was necessary to Chernomyrdin as a balance to Korzhakov . . . With the routing of the Korzhakov group, however . . . former friends . . . became rivals who needed to be restrained with the help of compromising information on each other"; Leonid Krutakov, "Skazhi Mne Kto Tvoi Drug i Ya Tebye Skazhu Kogda Oni Tebya Arestuyut," *Novaya Gazeta*, August 19–25, 1999.

11. The dispatchers began urging callers either to travel to the hospital themselves or to come to the central ambulance headquarters. They also began giving medical advice over the phone and urging callers to call back if there were further problems. In many cases they diagnosed ailments and gave advice with great accuracy, but in others the caller's condition dramatically worsened and the sick person died before he or she could make a second call.

12. The doctors who worked in the central ambulance station and went months without pay were as vulnerable to the growing crisis as their patients. Alexander Kerdyashkin, a pediatrician with three children, found that he could afford to feed his children only bread, kasha, and tea. He lived twenty miles outside Vladivostok and soon was traveling to work on the electric train as a "rabbit," without paying the fare. When he was stopped by the controller, he said, "I am a doctor with the ambulance service and I haven't been paid in four months." The answer to this was usually "I don't care who you are. If you don't pay the fare, we'll call the police and you'll go to jail."

Alexander Semyonov, an older doctor in the ambulance service, fell into a deep depression and committed suicide. He had said to a colleague, "I can't live in these conditions. I visit my grandchildren, and I can't offer them anything, not even a piece of candy or an apple." A short time after this conversation, Semyonov withdrew his savings from a bank and willed half to each of his two grown children. He bought a dark suit to be buried in and put it neatly on a nearby table. He took off the clothes he was wearing, put a pail under himself for his urine and excrement, and then hanged himself.

13. One secret of Nazdratenko's extraordinary success in maintaining the support of the central authorities, even after the ouster of Korzhakov, was intensive lobbying. Lobbyists from Primoriye were a fixture in the halls of government in Moscow, appealing continually for subsidies, credits, and special exemptions, as well as for political favors, most of which were routinely granted in return for bribes.

14. There were sixteen attempts before January 2001 to elect a city duma, and in every case the krai electoral commission found reasons to invalidate the election, citing the lack of a quorum or violations of election rules. The existence of a city duma would have increased the authority of Cherepkov, who would then have been able to base his actions on laws instead of administrative decisions. Without a duma, Cherepkov ruled on his own.

CHAPTER 11. KRASNOYARSK

1. Mikhail Chernoy met Tarpishchev while serving on the sports committee of Uzbekistan. The Chernoys met Soskovets while he was the Soviet minister of heavy metallurgy, as a result of their work in a trading company that delivered coke to steel mills and received in return rolled metal for sale abroad. Soskovets subsequently became responsible for the metallurgical industry in Russia. Later Tarpishchev introduced Chernoy to Korzhakov. Both Tarpishchev and the Chernoys had ties to Malevsky (Anton) and Alimzhanom Tokhtakhunov (Taiwanchik), a thief professing the code.

The relations between the Chernoys, Tarpishchev, Korzhakov, Malevsky, and Tokhtakhunov were described in a taped conversation between Boris Fyodorov, the chairman of the National Fund for Sports, and three other people, identified only as "journalist," "woman," and "entrepreneur." Fyodorov, a former close associate of Tarpishchev, was the victim of an assassination attempt on June 19, 1996. The tape was made available to *Novaya Gazeta,* and a partial transcript was published in the July 8, 1996, issue of the newspaper. The following are excerpts from the published version of the conversation.

FYODOROV: There is a certain Taiwanchik . . .

ENTREPRENEUR: He's one of the most serious [criminal] authorities in Russia.

FYODOROV: [Tarpishchev] brought him together with Chernoy. Then there appeared the Izmailovsky [criminal] group. Taiwanchik was somehow connected with them. And they received an exclusive on Shamil. What they said, that's what he did . . .

WOMAN: Do you have the opportunity to meet with Korzhakov?

FYODOROV: I call him every day. But what can I say to him? And then, honestly, I'm afraid. I don't know their [Korzhakov's and Tarpishchev's] relations . . .

ENTREPRENEUR: It is not possible that a normal person, having these special services, having an enormous number of informers, did not know . . . that Sham [Tarpishchev] steals colossal money . . .

FYODOROV: Steals!

ENTREPRENEUR: . . . Korzhakov in this situation resembles a bandit, just like Shamil. For details of the Chernoys' careers, see Alexei Mukhin, *Korruptsiya i Gruppy Vliyaniya*, vol. 1 (Moscow: Sluzhba Politicheskoi Informatsii i Konsultatsii "Tsentr," 1999), 61–72; idem, *Rossiiskaya Organizovannaya Prestupnost* (Moscow: Sluzhba Politicheskoi Informatsii i Konsultatsii "Tsentr," 1998), 91–93. For the published text of the recorded conversation, see Alexander Minkin, "Favority," *Novaya Gazeta*, July 8, 1996.

2. The operations with false letters of advice (avisos) were among the most sinister cases of economic fraud in Russian history. According to Sergei Glushenkov, a senior investigator with the Ministry of Internal Affairs, the robbing of the Central Bank of Russia could not have taken place without the connivance of high officials of the Central Bank itself. Without such assistance, the swindlers would not have known the ciphers and codes necessary to take part in the internal communications of the bank. At the same time, in the early 1990s ordinary bank transfers moved slowly, but false avisos worth billions of rubles were processed very quickly.

The most disturbing aspect of the scandal with the false avisos was its possible role in the decision to launch the first Chechen war. One of the promoters of the military operation in Chechnya was Soskovets, the sponsor of the Chernoys, who made a large fortune with the help of false letters of advice. The war, in turn, began when investigators in Moscow started to make progress regarding the origins of the false avisos. One of their findings was that some of the money stolen in Siberia was sent to Grozny. Once the war started, the Russian government should, in theory, have been interested in obtaining documentary evidence of Chechen criminal activity; but the first act of Russian forces in Grozny was to bomb the national bank and Ministry of Finance, effectively destroying any traces of the scandal. See Maxim Andreev, "Gryaznye: Za Chto Chernye Lyubyat Tsvetnye Metally," *Sobesednik*, July 1997; and Alexei Tarasov, "Velikaya Sibirskaya Aluminievaya Voina Prodolzhaetsya," *Izvestiya*, January 27, 1995.

3. Bykov's alliance with Tatarenkov, who had a long criminal record, showed that his supposed hatred of career criminals was purely propagandistic. Bykov, however, attached importance to propaganda. Members of his gang typically wore crosses, claimed to be religious, and took pride in being family men. These professions of morality did not prevent them from organizing contract killings. From 1993 to 1998 in the Krasnoyarsk krai, forty-eight entrepreneurs connected with the aluminum business and twenty-seven representatives of criminal groups attempting to establish control over the sale of aluminum were victims of contract killers. At least twenty-eight of the killings were attributed to Bykov. Igor Ukraintsev, "Poslednii Antigeroi Boievika," *Delovye Lyudi*, no. 124–25 (July–August 2001).

4. Yuliya Latynina, "Krakh Imperii Anatoliya Bykova: Khronika Sobytii," *Sovershenno Sekretno*, May 2000.

5. At the Bratsk Aluminum Factory the Chernoys' affairs were managed by Vladimir Tyurin (Tyurik). According to information presented by Alexander Kulikov, the minister of internal affairs, to the State Duma, "Tyurik and a group of Moscow thieves professing the code making use of ties with the . . . Chernoy brothers are responsible for the delivery of aluminum to the London metals exchange." See Alexei Tarasov, "Neprikosnovennye: 2. Bykov i Gangstery ili Voina i Mir po-Novorusski," *Izvestiya*, November 12, 1997.

6. A listing in the register was often the only proof of share ownership because share certificates did not exist under Russian law. According to regulations, the share registers of companies with more than 1,000 shareholders had to be maintained by an independent registrar. But many shareholders' lists were controlled by factory directors who feared—sometimes with good reason—that independent registrars would prove corrupt. As a result, it was possible for a factory director to remove a shareholder simply by crossing his name off the company's register; in such a situation, the only recourse for the shareholder was the use of armed force.

7. David Reuben was a British subject, and Mikhail Chernoy had become a citizen of Israel.

8. This was possible because Bykov's and Druzhinin's shares were held in trust by Kolpakov.

9. Latynina, "Krakh Imperii Anatoliya Bykova."

10. The Trans-Dniester Republic was proclaimed in 1991 by ethnic Slavs in the part of Moldova east of the Dniester River. The separatists were openly supported by the Russian 14th Army, which was based on the territory and commanded by Lebed. The region became a magnet for extreme nationalists opposed to the breakup of the Soviet Union.

11. Doubts arose almost immediately as to whether Struganov had really been killed. Observers noted that the body had been carried out head first instead of feet first, as is usually done with corpses. Also, the body was driven away in an ambulance instead of the usual morgue vehicle. Struganov's funeral was then inexplicably postponed. Finally, the warrant that was used to search Bykov's dacha said the search had been authorized on the basis of "testimony from the victim."

12. Leonid Berres, "Anatoly Bykov chut ne zaplakal," *Kommersant*, October 14, 2000.

CHAPTER 12. THE VALUE OF HUMAN LIFE

1. Kizey, the chief doctor, in a conversation with me in Pogranichny in April 1998, was not similarly haunted. He said that the circumstances that led to the death of Suvernyeva were caused by mismanagement by the central government. He added, however, that some in the hospital had tried to use the incident as an excuse to get rid of him because he was a "tough boss."

2. The state's readiness to sacrifice its citizens was matched by the citizens' readiness to sacrifice themselves. The disregard of Russian soldiers for their own lives makes them formidable adversaries, a fact that was noted by the Germans at the beginning of World War II. The German newspaper *Volkischer Beobachter* reported: "The Russian soldier surpasses our adversaries in the West in his contempt for death. Endurance and fatalism make him hold out until he is blown up with his trench or falls in hand-to-hand fighting"; "Hitler's Soviet Campaign: A Monumental Military Folly Remembered," Agence France Press, June 17, 2001.

3. Vodka became readily accessible to even the most impoverished. Ten new brands of unknown origin appeared and were sold from boxes on the street and on the sides of highways.

   The World Health Organization considers that if per-capita consumption of alcohol in a country exceeds 8 liters (about 8 quarts), each additional liter subtracts eleven months from the life expectancy of the average male and four from the life expectancy of the average female. In Russia per-capita alcohol consumption reached 16 liters. Among the consequences of the government's unprecedented promotion of alcoholism was a rise in all forms of violent death and a sharp rise in circulatory diseases and cancer. Roy Medvedev, *Kapitalism v Rossii?* (Moscow: Prava Cheloveka, 1998), 205–7.

4. The wards of the Vishnevsky Institute began to empty the moment the government ceased financing. In 1997 a single operation cost, on average, 10 million rubles ($1,725) in addition to the cost of a hospital stay, which was 100,000 ($17) to 200,000 ($34) rubles a day depending on the patient's condition. Average salaries were about $50 a month. Under these circumstances, treatment in the hospital of "last resort" was only for the select few. Vladimir Pokrovsky, " 'Poslednyaya instantsiya' bolshe ne spasaet," *Obshchaya Gazeta*, March 20–26, 1997.

5. In 1993 there were 45,060 murders in Russia compared with 26,254 in the United States, and the Russian figure did not include an estimated 22,000 persons who disappeared or the many Russian murder victims whose deaths were disguised as accidents. There was also a sharp rise in suicides, from 26,796 in 1988 to 46,016 in 1993. In 1992–1996 there were 3 million work-related accidents, 63,500 of them fatal. Medvedev, *Kapitalism*, 201–7; and Alexander Kalinin, "Smert v kapustnom chane. I t.p.," *Izvestiya*, February 14, 1997.

6. Ivan Lapshin told his story to *Novaya Gazeta* after a year of fruitless efforts to get the police to take action in the death of his grandson; Nikolai Fedyanin, "Rassledovanie. Ubiitsy soprovozhdeniya," *Novaya Gazeta*, August 16, 1999; idem, "Ubiitsy soprovozhdeniya—2," *Novaya Gazeta*, February 14–20, 2000.

7. After he became president, Putin averted the danger of killing an innocent person in a crash by closing to all other traffic the roads that he intended to use. In the summer of 2001, he commuted to the Kremlin from his dacha every day, so traffic was halted in the morning and in the evening for as long as two hours, with emergency vehicles tied up and thousands of drivers forced to wait on side streets for his motorcade to pass. When Putin went to Vnukovo airport, the road to the airport was also closed along with the airspace over the airport, which remained closed until well after Putin's plane had taken off.

8. Dmitri Zharkov, "Litsenziya na Ubiistvo," *Kommersant*, March 4, 1999; and Otdel Prestupnosti, "Kak Oni Nas Davyat," *Kommersant*, March 4, 1999.

9. In addition to Marina Yarova, an unidentified forty-five-year-old woman died in Moscow on March 12, 1998, when she fell into a pool of boiling water caused by burst hot-water pipes near 56 Tukhachevsky Street. Neighbors told reporters that steam had been rising from the earth regularly but repair crews had satisfied themselves with pouring sand into the fissures. As early as the end of February, as a result of a break in a hot-water line, the basements of apartment buildings and stores on Rusakovsky Street had been flooded with boiling water, injuring five adults and two children. According to Moscow rescuers, nine people died in the capital in the space of one month in 1998 as a result of breaks in hot-water lines. "Za Mesyats v Moskve Zazhivo Svarilis Devyat Chelovek," *Komsomolskaya Pravda*, March 14, 1998.

10. Nikolai Pyasetsky was drafted into the Russian army in June 1994 and quickly experienced the conditions of an army in collapse. He was sent to a base in Omsk, where he trained on a model tank, threw fake grenades, and dug up potatoes. He was then transferred to Ryazan, where he became part of the Ryazan Paratroop Regiment and worked building a dacha. In late December, with no real military training or experience, he was sent to Chechnya.

His experiences were similar to those of members of other units that were sent into Grozny on New Year's night. Many had prepared for war in Chechnya by working in warehouses, cleaning up construction sites, building houses for senior officers, and repairing vehicles. Weapons training took place with as few as three bullets for automatic weapons, and some soldiers had ridden in armored cars only a few times. In addition, in the case of the 81st Samara Regiment, many soldiers were sent into battle without military identification cards, ostensibly because there had been no time to give them out. Later this omission made it harder to identify the soldiers' bodies.

11. The 81st Samara Regiment and the 131st Maikop Brigade entered Grozny as if on parade. Chechen fighters waited until they entered the city's small and narrow streets, then blocked the front and rear tanks and opened fire from windows, basements, and gates with mortars and grenades. Of 26 tanks of the 131st Maikop Brigade, 20 were incinerated; of 120 armored cars, only 18 were eventually evacuated from Grozny. Viktor Litovkin, "Rasstrel 131-I Maikopskoi Brigady," *Izvestiya*, January 11, 1995.

12. In mid-January the Chechens proposed a ceasefire to allow each side to gather the bodies of their dead, but the Russian commander, Ivan Babichev, flatly rejected the proposal. Stanislav Bozhko, a human rights defender who was working to evacuate civilians, told me that he heard the Russian commander reply over the open radio, "Let the dogs eat them; they are no use to us." The bodies of Russian soldiers lay in the streets for several weeks until the Russians forced the Chechens out of the city center.

CHAPTER 13. THE CRIMINALIZATION OF CONSCIOUSNESS

1. After Mikhailov was acquitted of charges of belonging to a criminal organization, largely because of lack of cooperation from the Russian authorities, *Le Temps* commented: "The trial proved to us that today's Russia is more closed and frightening than ever before. We cannot help but think of all those scared people who hoped, for a fleeting moment, that the terror and chaos they had been living with would come to a close in Geneva." See "Geneva Court Sets Mikhailov Free," *Moscow Times*, December 15, 1998. Nicolet describes his encounter with Mikhailov in "Qu'est devenu Serguei Mikhailov, plus riche de 800,000 francs? Rencontre à Moscou," *Le Temps* (Geneva), November 13, 2000.

2. Arkady Levitov, a scriptwriter and longtime acquaintance of Mikhailov, said of him: "Mikhailov is the same type of person as the rest of us except that he is a billionaire and we're not. He is a successful businessman, excellent manager. People listen to him. He knows how to organize business . . . All his companies . . . unfailingly pay taxes to the government, and it is unknown who does this better: Mikhas or the most noble-looking citizen. If Mikhas became our prime minister (and I don't consider this fantastic), we

would live entirely differently. Of course, better. He is an excellent manager at a world level. He knows how to force people to work, and it is impossible to fool him. And this is not through force of arms but on the strength of his authority"; Alexander Maksimov, *Rossiiskaya Prestupnost* (Moscow: EKSMO, 1997), 342–43.

3. The obligatory "sharing" is facilitated by violations of bank secrecy. A widespread practice is for bandits to plant their agents in banks so that they will know if a client of the bank has received a large sum of money. They then demand a cut of the money regardless of the reason for which it was paid.

4. This night at "service 02" is recounted in Olga Minaeva, "Trupy poyut pesni," *Argumenty i Fakty*, no. 20 (1996).

5. Ruzanna and Natalya advertise in *Moskovsky Komsomolets*. They offer "Romantic magic, all types of fortune telling, removal of fear, anxiety and depression, weight correction in a single séance, and the removal of alcohol dependency."

   Other Russian newspapers also carry advertisements from witches, usually under "services" or "magic." The following ad, which appeared in the newspaper *Megapolis Express* on June 23, 1999, is representative: "The most powerful witch in Russia. Hereditary clairovoyant. Parapsychologist. Once and for all will return your loved one. Inspires fixations without damage to health; guaranteed results in 100 percent of cases. Completely separates husband from lover and returns him home. Removal of any spell regardless of complexity and longevity."

6. The discussions with the "assassination bureau" are from "Killer. Nedorogo!" *Komsomolskaya Pravda*, April 1, 1998.

7. Both Goryn and Bednyakov, for example, were held to have violated the ban on television agitation on the eve of the election. In Goryn's case, this agitation took the form of advertisements for the popular satirist Grigory Goryn, which laid particular emphasis on the surname he shared with the candidate. In the case of Bednyakov, in a televised interview he had denied rumors that he had withdrawn his candidacy and urged everyone to participate in the election. In this connection, a local journalist asked, "Is it possible for the transgressions of the defeated candidates to annul the victory of the victor?" V. Okmyansky, "Sud Tozhe 'Ne Ponyal' Voleizyavleniya Izbiratelei," *Nizhegorodskie Novosti*, March 16, 1998.

8. The headlines appeared respectively in *Crossroads of Russia*, April 10, 1998; *Gazette of the Nizhegorodsky Province*, April 3, 1998; *Moskovsky Komsomolets in Nizhny Novgorod*, April 9, 1998.

9. In fact the outcome was different. Klimentiev was barred from running again for mayor after the Russian Supreme Court upheld his conviction, and Yuri Lebedev, a former deputy governor of the Nizhny Novgorod oblast, defeated Bednyakov in the second round of new elections for mayor, held on October 11, 1998. Turnout in the elections was only 36 percent.

10. The leaders of the Uralmash gang frequently displayed a sense of humor. In choosing a new way to describe themselves, as a social political union (*obshchestvennyi politicheskii soyuz*), they deliberately retained the same abbreviation as the designation given them by the police, organized criminal group (*organizovannoe prestupnoe soobshchestvo*). They presented gold watches to journalists who wrote about them favorably and even

gave a certificate to Sergei Plotnikov, one of the few reporters who called attention to their criminality, with the words "In recognition of his constant attention to the activities of the Uralmash OPS."

11. The official name of the raion is Ordzhonikidze, but it is popularly known as the Uralmash raion. The gang took its name not from the factory, with which it has no connection, but from the popular name for the raion.

12. Prostate cancer was apparently the professional illness of all Yekaterinburg criminal leaders who ended up behind bars. Vladimir Kolupailo (Severenok), Andrei Trofanov, and Igor Zimin all supposedly suffered from this disease, presenting certificates to this effect from the same medical establishment.

13. Vasily Rudenko, the former head of RUBOP, estimated that in 1998 the income of the gang exceeded the city's budget; Viktor Smirnov and Ivan Seslavsky, "Kriminal Sozdal Svoyu Partiyu," *Argumenty i Fakty*, no. 27 (1999).

14. The organization of a political party by the Uralmash gang dismayed some people in Yekaterinburg, but Eduard Roussel greeted it calmly. "[People say] the Uralmash leader . . . is a thief, bandit, and so on," he said at a press conference in which he described his relations with the criminal world, "but I invite [the leader] to me and say: well, sit down, thief, tell me how you live, and I give him an assignment and he fulfills this assignment: spend money on capital construction in the Sverdlovsk oblast."

On other occasions, Roussel said that there was no such thing as the Uralmash organized crime group and that references to it were the invention of journalists. In fact, Roussel, a former close associate of Yeltsin, had a long and close association with the Uralmash gang. The gang contributed large amounts of money to his election campaign and, according to reports in the newspaper *Russky Telegraf*, celebrated his victory for an entire week. When, after Roussel described his relations with the criminal world, Eduard Khudyakov, a local journalist well known for his courage, asked if the recent gift of one million rubles from the Uralmash gang to a fund for the salaries of striking metro construction workers in April was in the category of a contribution by criminals to capital construction in the Sverdlovsk oblast, Roussel began to threaten him. "What are you talking about?" asked Roussel, "You have to live here." A few days later, Khudyakov was slashed by unknown attackers in the entrance of his home.

15. During the Soviet period, one of the most common political slogans was "The Party and the people are united."

16. Andrei was too afraid of reprisals to give his full name; Mark Franchetti, "Russians Thrash Their Drug Takers to Stop Addiction," *Sunday Times* (London), June 17, 2001.

CONCLUSION: DOES RUSSIA HAVE A FUTURE?

1. Michael Binyon, "Booming Russia Has a Happy Christmas," *The Times* (London), January 7, 2002.

2. Leon Aron, "Putin's Progress: Russia Joins the West," *Weekly Standard*, March 11, 2002.

3. Anders Aslund, "The Russian Success Story," *Moscow Times*, February 7, 2002.

4. The takeover of NTV by Gasprom was a story of stunning shifts in loyalty.

On the night of June 19–20, 1996, two Yeltsin campaign aides were caught carrying more than $500,000 in cash out of government headquarters. All that night, NTV broadcast news bulletins stating falsely that agents of the SPB had planted the money on the arrested men. The reports helped Chubais to persuade Yeltsin to fire Korzhakov. Chubais then became Yeltsin's chief of staff and worked closely with NTV.

In September 1996 NTV received a license to broadcast around the clock on channel 4 in what was widely viewed as a payoff for supporting Yeltsin's reelection. NTV faced no competition for the license and paid less than $1,000 for it. In 1997 NTV journalists wrote speeches for Yeltsin.

NTV's attitude toward the corruption of Yeltsin's entourage, however, changed dramatically after Luzhkov launched his presidential bid. NTV was suddenly in the forefront of the Russian media publicizing allegations of wrongdoing against the Yeltsin "family." See Laura Belin, "Ten Ironies of the NTV Saga," *RFE/RL Russian Political Weekly* (Radio Free Europe/Radio Liberty, Prague), April 16, 2001.

5. Peter Graff, "Russian Closure of Independent Television Sparks Wide Concern," Reuters, January 22, 2002.

6. Yuri Skuratov, interview with Ilya Tarasov, *Pravda.ru*, November 5, 2001.

7. Alexander Tsipko, " 'The Family' Takes Control of Domestic Politics in Russia," Jamestown Foundation *Prism*, September 2001.

8. As doubts about the Ryazan incident grew, the Russian government reacted to calls for an investigation by either characterizing suggestions of FSB involvement as outrageous or treating them as unworthy of attention. The government also blocked repeated attempts to open an inquiry into the Ryazan incident, most recently in February 2002. At that time, 161 deputies voted in favor of an inquiry, 7 voted against, and the remaining 296 abstained.

9. Victoria Lavrentieva, "Ministers Fret over Diving Oil Prices," *Moscow Times*, November 20, 2001.

10. Evgeny Anisimov, "Ne Pokhoronit li Rossiyu Vzbesivshayasya Tekhnika?" *Komsomolskaya Pravda*, September 21, 2000.

11. "Is Russia on the Verge of Collapse?" NewsMax.com, August 29, 2000.

12. Igor Gundarov, "Neobyavlennaya epidemiya," interview with Alexander Vasinsky, *Vremya MN*, February 21, 2002.

13. Ada Gorbacheva, "Poka Nadeyus—Dyshu," *Nezavisimaya Gazeta*, January 26, 2001.

14. Alexander Vasinsky, "Vremya Lyudei. Neobyavlennaya Epidemiya," *Vremya MN*, February 21, 2002.

15. Igor Gundarov, *Demograficheskaya Katastrofa v Rossii: Prichiny, Mekhanizm, Puti Preodoleniya* (Moscow: URSS, 2001), 17–18.

16. Nikolai Berdyaev, *Sudba Rossii* (Moscow: Izdatelstvo V. Shevchuk, 2000), 289–94.

Bibliography

Afanasiev, Andrei. "Sled Deneg v Dali Propadaet." *Sovetskaya Rossiya*, December 8, 1998.

Akimov, Valery. "Otkrytoe Pismo V. Petukhovu—Generalnomu Direktoru AOZT 'Debit,' Kandidatu Tekhnicheskikh Nauk." *Za Yuganskuyu Neft*, no. 26 (June 24–30, 1996).

Aleksandrov, Yuri. "Krakh Narodnogo Kapitalizma." *Novoye Vremya*, no. 20 (1997).

Amanova, Natalya. "Rossiya—Strana Universalnogo Vzyatochnichestva." *Razbor* (supplement to *Argumenti i Fakti*), no. 6 (1998): 2.

Andreev, Maxim. "Gryaznye: Za Chto Chernye Lyubyat Tsvetnye Metally." *Sobesednik*, July 1997.

Anisimov, Evgeny. "Ne Pokhoronit li Rossiyu Vzbesivshayasya Tekhnika?" *Komsomolskaya Pravda*, September 21, 2000.

Anistratova, Irina. "Zakon Rastvoreniya Vkladov." *Segodnya*, March 27, 1996.

Annenkov, Vyacheslav, and Rodion Morozov. "Bandity Boyatsya Vorov." *Obshchaya Gazeta*, August 3–9, 1995.

Anuchkin, Aleksandr. "Pogib Chelovek, Derzhavshii v Golove Vse Tainy Banka 'Chara.'" *Segodnya*, May 23, 1997.

Arendt, Hannah. *Between Past and Future: Eight Exercises in Political Thought.* New York: Viking, 1971.

———. *On Revolution.* London: Faber and Faber, 1963.

———. *The Origins of Totalitarianism.* Cleveland: Meridian, 1958.

Aron, Leon. "Putin's Progress: Russia Joins the West." *Weekly Standard*, March 11, 2002.

———. *Yeltsin: A Revolutionary Life.* New York: St. Martin's, 2000.

Askoldov, S. A., et al. *Iz Glubiny: Sbornik Statei o Russkoi Revolutsii.* Paris: YMCA Press, 1967.

Aslund, Anders. *How Russia Became a Market Economy.* Washington, D.C.: Brookings Institution, 1995.

——. "The Russian Success Story." *Moscow Times*, February 7, 2002.

——. "Tri Osnovnye Istochniki Bogatsva Novykh Russkikh." *Izvestiya*, June 20, 1996.

Atomnaya podlodka "Kursk": Khronika Gibeli. Moscow: Pushkinskaya Ploshchad, 2000.

Bakhroshin, Nikolai. "Kto Vzorval Rossiyu: Zachem FSB Pytalas Vzorvat Sakhar?" *Versiya*, February 22–28, 2000.

Banerjee, Neela. "Amid Russia's Turmoil, U.K. Firm Wins Slice of Nation's Aluminum." *Wall Street Journal*, January 28, 1997.

Barabash, Natalya. "Meriya Vladivostoka vzyata shturmom," *Komsomolskaya Pravda*, March 18, 1994.

——. "Svobodu Pechati u Nas Vsegda Zazhimali, no ne Zheleznymi Tiskami." *Komsomolskaya Pravda*, July 22, 1994.

Baranets, Viktor. "Komandovanie VMF Zasekretilo Vse Krome Svoei Nerazvorotlivosti." *Komsomolskaya Pravda*, August 13, 2000.

Beaver, Paul. "Darkness, Dampness and Cold." *The Times* (London), August 16, 1999.

Belin, Laura. "Ten Ironies of the NTV Saga." *RFE/RL Russian Political Weekly* (a publication of Radio Free Europe /Radio Liberty, Prague), April 16, 2001.

Beloivan, Larisa. "Shchupaltsy PAKTa Tyanutsya k Vlasti." *Tikhy Okean*, May 22, 1993.

Belotserkovskii, Vadim. "Kontrolnaya Pokupka: Vzglyad na Ryazanskuyu Istoriyu so Storony." *Novaya Gazeta*, March 30–April 2, 2000.

Berdyaev, N. A. *Dukhovnyi Krizis Intelligentsii.* Moscow: Kanon+, 1998.

——. *Filosofiya Svobody. Istoki i Smysl Russkogo Kommunizma.* Moscow: Izdatelstvo V. Shevchuk, 2000.

——. *Russkaya Ideya: Osnovnye Problemy Russkoi mysli XIX i Nachala XX Veka. Sudba Rossii.* Moscow: Izdatelstvo V. Shevchuk, 2000.

Bernstein, Jonas. "How the Russian Mafia Rules." *Wall Street Journal*, October 26, 1994.

——. "Watergate: Day at the Beach." *Moscow Times*, November 22, 1996.

Berres, Leonid. "Anatoly Bykov chut ne zaplakal." *Kommersant*, October 14, 2000.

Binyon, Michael. "Booming Russia Has a Happy Christmas." *The Times* (London), January 7, 2002.

Bivens, Matt, and Jonas Bernstein. "The Russia You Never Met." *Demokratizatsiya* 6 (fall 1998): 613–47.

Boiko, Ruslan. "Chtoby Vzyat Mera, Militsiya Lomala Dveri." *Novaya ezhednevnaya Gazeta*, March 18, 1994.

Boycko, Maxim, Andrei Shleifer, and Robert Vishny. *Privatizing Russia.* Cambridge: MIT Press, 1996.

Bronshtein, Boris. "Za Chto Klimentieva Sudili v Pervyi Raz." *Izvestiya*, April 7, 1999.

Bukatin, Leonid. " 'Visyaki' pod Lichnym Kontrolem." *Novaya Gazeta*, September 10–13, 2001.

Bukreev, Aleksandr. "Svaritsya Zazhivo Mog Lyuboi." *Komsomolskaya Pravda*, March 2, 1998.

Chaadaev, P. Ya. *Izbrannye Sochinenya i Pisma.* Moscow: Izdatelstvo "Pravda," 1991.

Chernikov G., and D. Chernikova. *Kto vladeet Rossiei?* Moscow: Tsentrpoligraf, 1998.

Chiesa, Giulietto. *Proshchai, Rossiya.* Moscow: Izdatelstvo "Geya," 1997.

"Chtoby ne Oshibitsya, Killer Rasstrelyal Vsekh Directorov." *Moskovsky Komsomolets*, April 28, 1998.

"Chtoby Vymanit Zhertvu iz Kvartiry, Killer Vyvernul Probki v Pod'ezde." *Moskovsky Komsomolets*, November 3, 1995.

Chubais, Igor. *Rossiya v Poiskakh Sebya.* Moscow: NOK, Izdatelstvo "Muzei bumagi," 1998.

Chubarov, Evgeny. "Razobratsya i dolozhit." *Izvestiya*, February 27, 2001.

Cohen, Stephen F. *Failed Crusade: America and the Tragedy of Post-Communist Russia.* New York: W. W. Norton, 2000.

Conquest, Robert. *Reflections on a Ravaged Century.* New York: W. W. Norton, 2000.

Danilkin, Alexander. "Mafia—Nash Rulevoi." *Trud*, December 10, 1994.

Daniszewski, John. "Harrowing 911 Calls Point to a Pitiless Moscow." *Los Angeles Times*, January 26, 2002.

"Diktator Primorya." *Novoye Vremya*, no. 40 (1994).

Dixelius, Malcolm, and Andrei Konstantinov. *Prestupnyi Mir Rossii.* St. Petersburg, Bibliopolis, 1995.

Dmitri Kholodov: Vzryv. Moscow: Eksim, 1998.

Dokuchaev, Dmitri. "Obmanutym Vkladchikam ne Vozvrashchayut Dengi, no Vozvrashchayut Nadezhdu." *Izvestiya*, June 23, 1997.

———. "Raskryty Sekrety MMM i Mavrodi." *Izvestiya*, February 18, 1997.

Domnikov, Igor. "Posle Pozhara." *Novaya Gazeta*, February 22–28, 1999.

Dunn, Guy. "Major Mafia Gangs in Russia." In *Russian Organized Crime: The New Threat?* Edited by Phil Williams. Special double issue, *Transnational Organized Crime* 2, nos. 2/3 (summer/autumn 1996): 63–87.

Duparc, Agathe, with Ivan Ivanidze. "Iouri Loujkov et 'Sistema', ou l'archetype de l'oligarchie moscovite." *Le Monde*, February 26, 1999.

Ershov, Anatoly. "Oni Uzhe v Kremle." *Izvestiya*, March 31, 1998.

Evtushenko, Aleksandr, and Vladimir Velengurin. "Zhivye Fakely Tyanuli k Nam

Ruki iz Ognya, Molili o Pomoshchi . . . A Chto My Mogli Sdelat?" *Komsomolskaya Pravda*, February 13, 1999.

Farah, Douglas. "FBI Chief: Russian Mafias Pose Growing Threat to U.S." *Washington Post*, October 2, 1997.

Fedyanin, Nikolai. "Rassledovanie. Ubiitsy Soprovozhdeniya." *Novaya Gazeta*, August 16, 1999.

———. "Ubiitsy Soprovozhdeniya—2." *Novaya Gazeta*, February 14–20, 2000.

Felgenhauer, Pavel. "Time to Let Go of the Past." *Moscow Times*, November 9, 2000.

Feshbach, Murray. "Russia's Population Meltdown." *Wilson Quarterly*. In *Johnson's Russia List*, January 11, 2001.

Figes, Orlando. *A People's Tragedy: A History of the Russian Revolution*. New York: Viking, 1996.

Filonov, Vladimir, and Oksana Yablokova. "Car Swallowed by Boiling Sinkhole." *Moscow Times*, March 6, 1999.

"Fit for Carrying Out the 'Family' Service." *Russia Today* press summaries, *Segodnya*, May 18, 2000.

Fochkin, Oleg, and Iosif Galperin. "Konets Grecheskoi Smokovnitsy." *Moskovsky Komsomolets*, May 13, 1997.

Fonareva, Nataliya. "K Desyatiletiyu Rossiiskikh Antimonopolnykh Organov." *Konkurentsiya i Rynok*, October 2000.

Franchetti, Mark. "Russians Trash Their Drug Takers to Stop Addiction." *Sunday Times* (London), June 17, 2001.

Freeland, Chrystia. *Sale of the Century: Russia's Wild Ride from Communism to Capitalism*. New York: Crown Business, 2000.

Frolov, Sergei. "Skolko Stoit Vladivostok?" *Argumenty i Fakty*, February 17, 1996.

Gaidar, Yegor. *Gosudarstvo i Evolyutsiya*. Moscow: Evraziya, 1997.

Gall, Carlotta, and Thomas de Waal. *Chechnya: Calamity in the Caucasus*. New York: New York University Press, 1998.

Gansvind, Igor. "Monopoliya—Vrag Rynka." *Kuranty*, January 31, 1992.

"Geneva Court Sets Mikhailov Free." *Moscow Times*, December 15, 1998.

Gevorkian, N., A. Kolesnikov, and N. Timakova. *Ot Pervogo Litsa: Razgovory s Vladimirom Putinym*. Moscow: Vagrius, 2000.

Glazyev, Sergei. *Genotsid: Rossiya i Novyi Mirovoi Poryadok*. Moscow: 1997.

Glikin, Maxim. *Militsiya i Bespredel*. Moscow: Tsentrpoligraf, 2000.

———. "Uzakonennoe Bessilie." *Obshchaya Gazeta*, June–July 1995.

Glikin, Maxim, and Vakhtang Yakobidze. "Krasnoe Koleso na Yuge Moskvy." *Obshchaya Gazeta*, May 15–21, 1997.

Glinkina, Svetlana. "The Criminal Components of the Russian Economy." Working paper no. 29. Bundesinstitut für Ostwissenschaftliche und Internationale Studen, Köln, 1997.

——. "Kharakteristiki Tenevoi Ekonomiki v Rossii." *Nezavisimaya Gazeta—Polit-ekonomiya*, no. 5 (March 1998).

Glinkina, Svetlana. Andrei Grigoriev, amd Vakhtang Yakobidze. "Crime and Corruption." In *The New Russia: Transition Gone Awry*. Edited by Lawrence R. Klein and Marshall Pomer. Stanford: Stanford University Press, 2001, 247.

Gokhman Mikhail. "Primorsky Bespredel." *Russkaya Mysl*, October 6–12, 1994.

Goldman, Marshall I. *Lost Opportunity: What Has Made Economic Reform in Russia So Difficult?* New York: W. W. Norton, 1996.

Golovanova, Galina. "Snachala—Pokushenie, Potom—Ubiistvo." *Nezavisimaya Gazeta*, July, 1, 1998.

Golubovich, Tatyana. "S Plyazha na Nary." *Kommersant*, June 6, 2000.

Gorbacheva, Ada. "Poka Nadeuys—Dyshu." *Nezavisimaya Gazeta*, January 26, 2001.

Gorshkov, Mikhail. "Ubit Mer Nefteyuganska." *Nezavisimaya Gazeta*, June 27, 1998.

Graff, Peter. "Russian Closure of Independent TV Sparks Wide Concern." Reuters, January 22, 2002.

Grant, Alexander. "Delo 'Chary' Zhivet, no ne Pobezhdaet." *Novoye Russkoye Slovo*, March 21, 1997.

——. "Greki Polonili Tatarina." *Novoye Russkoye Slovo*, August 30, 1999.

——. *Protsess Yaponchika.* Moscow: AST, 1997.

Grigorev, Andrei, and Elmar Murtazaev. "Samyi Bogatyi Chinovnik Rossii." *Segodnya*, February 5, 1997.

Gubin, Dmitri. "V Nachale Slavnykh Del. Leonid Bochin." *Konkurentsiya i Rynok*, October 2000.

Gundarov, I. A. *Demograficheskaya Katastrofa v Rossii: Prichiny, Mekhanizm, Puti Preodoleniya.* Moscow: URSS, 2001.

——. "Neobyavlennaya Epidemiya." Interview with Alexander Vasinsky. *Vremya MN*, February 21, 2002.

Handelman, Stephen. *Comrade Criminal: Russia's New Mafiya.* New Haven: Yale University Press, 1995.

Henderson, Keith. "Corruption: What Can Be Done about It? A Practitioner's Perspective through a Russian Lens." *Demokratizatsiya* 6 (1998): 681–91.

Hockstader, Lee. "The Boom That Failed: Russia's Far East Had Everything—but Then the Money Ran Out." *Washington Post*, November 3, 1996.

Ibragimov, Oktai. "Massovogo Psikhoza na Lodke Net" (transcribed by Alexander Kots). *Komsomolskaya Pravda*, August 13, 2000.

"Is Russia on the Verge of Collapse?" NewsMax.com, August 29, 2000.

Ivanov, Sergei. "Sovest ili Tekhnologiya?" *Posev*, no. 12 (1999).

Isakov, Andrei. "Skandalnye Pokazaniya v Zhenevskom Sude." *Nezavisimaya Gazeta*, December 9, 1998.

Ishchenko, Andrei, and Nugzar Mikeladze. "Smert Soldata." *Novaya Gazeta*, August 19–25, 1996.

Jensen, Donald N. "How Yuri Luzhkov Runs Moscow." *Johnson's Russia List*, November 20, 1999.

Jung, C. G. *The Undiscovered Self.* Translated by R. F. C. Hull. New York: New American Library, 1958.

"K-141 Is Down." *The Exile*, September 28, 2000.

Kagarlitskii, Boris. "S Terroristami ne Razgovarivaem, no Pomogaem?" *Novaya Gazeta*, January 24–30, 2000.

Kakovkin, Grigory. "Poka Vlast Spit, Klimentiev Stanovitsya Pobeditelem. Kogda Prosypaetsya, On Vyrastaet v Geroya." *Izvestiya*, April 2, 1998.

Kakturskaya, Maria. "Zhizn bez Sveta i Tepla." *Argumenty i Fakty*, no. 37 (2000).

Kalinin, Alexander. "Plach Yaroslavny s Zavoda 'Beda.'" *Izvestiya*, April 4, 1997.

———. "Smert v Kapustnom Chane. I.t.p." *Izvestiya*, February 14, 1997.

Karacheva, Yekaterina. "Za Chto Zabral, Nachalnik?! Otpusti." *Novoye Russkoye Slovo*, January 12, 2000; reprinted from *Kriminalnaya Khronika*.

Karyshev, Valery. *Aleksandr Solonik—Killer Mafii.* Moscow: EKSMO, 1998.

———. *Silvester: Istoriya Avtoriteta.* Moscow: EKSMO, 1999.

———. *Solntsevskaya Bratva: Istoriya Gruppirovki.* Moscow: EKSMO, 1998.

———. *Zapiski Banditskogo Advokata: Zakulisnaya Zhizn Bratvy glazami "Zashchitnika Mafii."* Moscow: Tsentrpoligraf, 1998.

———. *Zhizn Banditskaya: Istoriya Gruppirovki. Vzklyad iznutri.* Moscow: EKSMO, 1999.

Kharitonov, Vladimir. "Lyudi Gibnut za Metall." *Novoye Russkoye Slovo*, November 17–18, 1999.

Khrushcheva, Nina L. *Cultural Contradictions of Post-Communism: Why Liberal Reforms Did Not Succeed in Russia.* A Council on Foreign Relations Paper. New York, 2000.

"Killer. Nedorogo!" *Komsomolskaya Pravda*, April 1, 1998.

Kiselev, Stepan. "S Primorya na Rossiyu Nadvigayutsya Sumerki." *Izvestiya*, October 8, 1996.

Klebnikov, Paul. *Godfather of the Kremlin: Boris Berezovsky and the Looting of Russia.* New York: Harcourt, 2000.

———. "Joe Stalin's Heirs." *Forbes*, September 27, 1993.

———. "Russia-on-the-Pacific." *Forbes*, March 27, 1995.

Klein, Lawrence, and Marshall Pomer, eds. *The New Russia: Transition Gone Awry.* Stanford: Stanford University Press, 2001.

Knight, Amy. *Spies without Cloaks: The KGB's Successors.* Princeton: Princeton University Press, 1996.

Kochergin, Yuri, and Oleg Fochkin. "Tishina posle Vzryvov." *Moskovsky Komsomolets*, January 19, 2000.

Konstantinov, Andrei. *Korrumpirovannyi Peterburg.* St. Petersburg: Folio, 1997.

Korolkov, Igor. "Krovavy Peredel." *Izvestiya*, no. 79–80 (1995).

———. "Razval." *Izvestiya*, May 27, 1997.

———. "Sovershenno Nesekretno." *Izvestiya*, January 14, 1997.

———. "Syn za Otsa, Otets za Syna." *Izvestiya*, November 11, 1996.

———. "Viktor Cherepkov protiv Borisa Yeltsyna." *Izvestiya*, August 3, 1996.

———. "Virus." *Izvestiya*, July 1996.

Korzhakov, Alexander. *Boris Yeltsin: Ot Rassveta do Zakata*. Moscow: Interbook, 1997.

Korzunskii, Oleg. "Bolshye Igry vokrug Malenkogo Noyabrska." *Rossiiskaya Gazeta*, March 3, 1999.

Kovalskaya, Galina. "Gnev Bessiliya." *Itogi*, February 9, 1999.

Kozlovsky, Vladimir. "U Podnozhya Moskovskoi Piramidy." *Novoye Russkoye Slovo*, August 2, 1994.

Kravets, Vadim. "V Nefteyuganske Nastupilo Zatishie. Pered Burei." *Neft i Kapital*, August 1998.

Krivosheev, Stepan. "Mera Nefteyuganska Zastrelili po Doroge na Rabotu." *Segodnya*, no. 137 (1998).

Krutakov, Leonid. "Skazhi Mne Kto Tvoi Drug i Ya Tebye Skazhu Kogda Oni Tebya Arestuyut." *Novaya Gazeta*, August 19–25, 1999.

Kryshtanovskaya, Olga. "In Whose Hands Is Property?" *Argumenty i Fakty*, no. 15 (1997).

Kuibyshev, Pavel. "Krovavykh Bratyev Bolshe Net." *Kommersant Daily*, no. 35 (February 1998).

"Kursk Recovery Mission Ended, Many Questions Unanswered." Jamestown Foundation *Monitor*, November 10, 2000.

Ladnyi, Vladimir. "Krov i Neft." *Komsomolskaya Pravda*, July 8, 1998.

Lasswell, Harold. *Propaganda Techniques in the World War*. New York: Garland, 1972.

Latynina, Yuliya. "Alyuminievaya Opera." *Novaya Gazeta*, September 4–10, 2000.

———. "Krakh Imperii Anatoliya Bykova: Khronika Sobytii." *Sovershenno Sekretno*, May 2000.

———. " 'Sibneft' Pokupaet KrAZ." *Versiya*, February 16–21, 2000.

Latypov, Dmitry. "Iz Shakhty—na Relsy." *Trud*, January 27, 1998.

———. "Tri Lukovitsy na Shakhterskom Stole." *Trud*, August 1, 1996.

Latyshev, Evgeny. "Kriminalnoe Chtivo po Krasnoyarsku." *Izvestiya*, July 20, 2000.

———. "V Chikh Interesakh 'Likvidatsiya' Bykova." *Novye Izvestiya*, April 25, 2000.

Lavrentieva, Victoria. "Ministers Fret over Diving Oil Prices." *Moscow Times*, November 20, 2001.

Lebedev, Valery. "Volshebnaya Palochka Kokha." *Vestnik*, November 10, 1998.

Lee, Rensselaer. "Recent Trends in Nuclear Smuggling." In *Russian Organized Crime: The New Threat?* Edited by Phil Williams. Special double issue, *Transnational Organized Crime* 2, nos. 2/3 (summer/autumn 1996): 109–21.

Leskov, Sergey. "Kto Poteryal Dengi Shakhterov i Energetikov Primoryia?" *Izvestiya*, August 8, 1996.

Lieven, Anatol. *Chechnya: Tombstone of Russian Power*. New Haven: Yale University Press, 1998.

Limonov, Eduard. "Krovavy Alyuminievy." *Zavtra*, no. 19 (2001).

——. *Rassledovanie Eduarda Limonova. Okhota na Bykova*. St. Petersburg: Limbus, 2001.

Litovkin, Viktor. "Rasstrel 131-i Maikopskoi Brigady." *Izvestiya*, January 11, 1995.

Litvinenko, Alexander, and Yuri Felshtinsky. "FSB Vzryvaet Rossiyu." *Novaya Gazeta*, August 27, 2001.

"Lost Russian Submarine Continues to Generate Controversy." Jamestown Foundation *Monitor*, December 4, 2000.

Lunev, Stanislav. "Russian Organized Crime," Jamestown Foundation *Prism*, May 30, 1997, 10.

Lunev, Stanislav, and Ira Winkler. *Through the Eyes of the Enemy*. Washington, D.C.: Regnery, 1998.

Maksimov, Aleksandr. *Bandity v Belykh Vorotnichkakh: Kak Razvorovyvali Rossiyu*. Moscow: EKSMO, 1999.

——. *Rossiiskaya Prestupnost*. Moscow: EKSMO 1997.

Makurin, Alexei. "Kto Raspravilsya s Merom Nefteyuganska?" *Komsomolskaya Pravda*, June 30, 1998.

Manilov, Yuri. "Svetlana v Dyavolskoi Igre." *Express Gazeta*, no. 20 (1997).

Markelov, Mikhail. "Aliuminievye Bratya." *Sovershenno Sekretno*, no. 8 (1996).

Matlin, Valery. "Oni Ukhodyat iz Zhizni, Dazhe ne Ponimaya Etogo" (transcribed by Alexander Kots). *Komsomolskaya Pravda*, August 14, 2000.

Mazin, Arkady. "Ubiistvennaya Logika." *Novaya Gazeta*, July 7–23, 2000.

Medvedev, Roy. *Kapitalizm v Rossii?* Moscow: Prava Cheloveka, 1998.

Merridale, Catherine. *Night of Stone: Death and Memory in Twentieth-Century Russia*. New York: Viking, 2000.

Milosz, Czeslaw. *The Captive Mind*. London: Penguin, 1981.

Minaeva, Olga. "Trupy Poyut Pesni." *Argumenty i Fakty*, no. 20 (1996).

Minkin, Alexander. "Favority." *Novaya Gazeta*, July 8, 1996.

Miroshnichenko, Olga. "Gibel 'Tibeta.'" *Zhizn i Koshelek*, no. 24 (1996).

——. "Intrigi vokrug 'Chary.'" *Zhizn i Koshelek*, no. 21 (1996).

Mitin, Sergei. "Mer Nefteyuganska Ssorilsya s MENATEPOM, a Zadel Interesy Chechenskoi Mafii." *Izvestiya*, June 27, 1998.

Modestov, Nikolai. *Moskva Banditskaya: Dokumentalnaya Khronika Kriminalnogo Bespredela 80–90-kh Godov*. Moscow: Tsentrpoligraf, 1996.

——. *Moskva Banditskaya: Dokumentalnaya Khronika Kriminalnogo Bespredela 90-kh Godov*. Moscow: Tsentrpoligraf, 1998.

Morozov, Petr. "Tma Ovladela Vostokom." *Argumenty i Fakty*, no. 21 (1997).

Mukhin, Alexei. *Korruptsiya i Gruppy Vliyaniya.* Vol. 1. Moscow: Sluzhba Politicheskoi Informatsii i Konsultatsii "Tsentr," 1999.

——. *Rossiiskaya Organizovannaya Prestupnost.* Moscow: Sluzhba Politicheskoi Informatsii i Konsultatsii "Tsentr," 1998.

Muzaev, Timur. "Ryazantsev Vzryvali po Zakonu?" *Russkaya Mysl*, April 6–12, 2000.

Nagornaya, Tatyana. " 'Skoroi Pomoshchi' Nuzhna Neotlozhka." *Vladivostok*, December 5, 1997.

Nikitina, Elena. "Chetyre serii 'MMMavrodizatsii.' " *Zhizn i Koshelek*, no. 23 (1996).

Nikolaev, Petr. "Kto Zakazyvaet 'Murku'?" *Nezavisimaya Gazeta*, June 11, 1999.

Nokomonov, V. A., and V. I. Shulga. "Murder for Hire as a Manifestation of Organized Crime." *Demokratizatsiya* 6 (fall 1998): 676–80.

Okmyansky, V. "Sud Tozhe 'Ne Ponyal' Voleizyavleniya Izbiratelei." *Nizhegorodskie Novosti*, March 16, 1998.

"Oni Byli Gotovy k Smerti . . ." *Novoye Russkoye Slovo*, December 22, 2000.

"Organizovannaya Prestupnost v Rossii." *Novoye Russkoye Slovo*, March 17, 1995.

"Osnovy Borby s Organizovannoi Prestupnostyu." *Nezavisimaya Gazeta*, June 14, 1997.

Ostrovskaya, Natalya. "Primorsky Pakt." *Izvestiya*, December 1, 1993.

Otdel Prestupnosti. "Kak Oni Nas Davyat." *Kommersant*, March 4, 1999.

Paddock, Richard C. "A Russian Ambulance Is Seldom Chased." *Los Angeles Times*, June 17, 1997.

Pavlaskova, Nelli, and Yelena Vishnevskaya. "Vkladchiki Vsekh Stran, Ob'edinyaites." *Izvestiya*, June 25, 1996.

Petrov, Nikolai. *Aleksandr Lebed v Krasnoyarskom Krae.* Moscow: Tsentr Carnegie, 1999.

Piontkovsky, Andrei. "Rassledovanie. Priznanie Oligarkha Prokuroru Respubliki." *Novaya Gazeta*, January 21, 2001.

Pipes, Richard. *Property and Freedom: The Story of How through the Centuries Private Ownership Has Promoted Liberty and the Rule of Law.* New York: Alfred A. Knopf, 1999.

Plotnikov, Sergei. "Ne Verte 'Pekhote," Kogda Ona Bravye Pesni Poet." *Uralsky Rabochy*, April 24, 1993.

——. "Sletel s Nebes Poslednii Bes?" *Izvestiya-Ural*, December 7, 1996.

——. "Tsenu Smerti Sprosi u Mertvykh." *Uralsky Rabochy*, October 31, 1992.

——. "Ural Kriminalnyi." *Ogonek*, no. 38 (September 1996).

——. " 'Zona' Rvetsya v Biznes." *Trud*, July 28, 1992.

Pluzhnikov, Sergei, and Sergei Sokolov. "Zolotoi Klyuchik dlia Peti Avena." *Sovershenno Sekretno*, no. 9 (1998).

Pokrovsky, Vladimir. " 'Poslednyaya Instantsiya' Bolshe ne Spasaet." *Obshchaya Gazeta*, March 20–26, 1997.

Politkovskaya, Anna. "Chelovek s dvoinoi kryshei." *Obshchaya Gazeta*, August 3–9, 1995.

———. "Norilsk Gotov Poiti v Bank." *Obshchaya Gazeta*, March 6–12, 1997.

Polynsky, Andrei. "Organy Obnaruzhili Tysyachi Mashin v Tainikakh AvtoVazA." *Komsomolskaya Pravda*, November 19, 1997.

"Posle 'Avtonomki' Menya Prinyal dlya Doklada Vladimir Putin." *Komsomolskaya Pravda*, August 12, 2000.

"Poslednyaya Zhertva Solonika." Investigation. *Express Gazeta*, no. 20 (1997).

Pravdolyubtsev, Petr. "Kak Kommercheskie Banki Voruyut Dengi." *Argumenty i Fakty*, no. 48 (1998).

"Privatization, Russian-Style." *Nezavisimaya Gazeta—Politekonomiya*. In *Johnson's Russia List*, April 17, 2001.

"Provintsialnaya Khronika." Special issue, *Informatsionnoe Rabochee Agenstvo—Soyuz Obshchestvennykh Korrespondentov (IRA-SOK)*, October 1996, 2.

Pryanishnikov, Petr. "Sotrudniki FSB Dostavliali Vzryvchatku v Moskvu," *Versiya*, September 21–27, 1999.

"Qu'est devenu Serguei Mikhailov, plus riche de 800,000 francs? Rencontre à Moscou." *Le Temps* (Geneva), November 13, 2000.

Raskin, Aleksandr. "Bit'e Okon s Isklyuchitelnym Tsinizmom." *Kommersant*, March 20, 1996.

Rawlinson, Patricia. "Russian Organized Crime: A Brief History." In *Russian Organized Crime: The New Threat?* Edited by Phil Williams. Special double issue, *Transnational Organized Crime* 2, nos. 2/3 (summer/autumn 1996): 28–52.

Reddaway, Peter, and Dmitri Glinski. *The Tragedy of Russia's Reforms: Market Bolshevism against Democracy*. Washington, D.C.: United States Institute of Peace Press, 2001.

Reznik, Boris. "Ostrov Dzhema." *Izvestiya*, July 11, 1997.

Romanov, Sergei. *Moshennichestvo v Rossii. Kak Uberechsya ot Aferistov*. Moscow: EKSMO, 1998.

Rozhnov, Georgy. "Osobye Primety: Krasivaya i Molodaya." *Kriminalnaya Khronika*, March 1998.

Ruzhina, Olga. "Dengi 1-oi FSK: My pol-Evropy po-Plastunski Propakhali . . ." *Revizor*, January 1996.

"Russia Is Said to Have Known of Sub Flaw." *New York Times*, February 23, 2001.

Ryazhsky, Yuri. "Taina Kladov." *Moskovsky Komsomolets*, September 23, 1995.

Salnikova, Valentina. "Demonopolizatsiya Tormozitsya v Vysshykh Eshelonakh Vlasti." *Delovoi Mir*, February 15, 1992.

Samoilov, Sergey. "Adskii Ogon v Samare." *Moskovsky Komsomolets*, February 14, 1999.

Saradzhyan, Simon. "After One Year, Blast Probe Still Drags On." *Moscow Times*, September 15, 2000.

Satter, David. *Age of Delirium: The Decline and Fall of the Soviet Union.* New Haven: Yale University Press, 2001.

———. "Anatomy of a Massacre." *Washington Times*, October 29, 1999.

———. "The Darkness Spreads from Primoriye." Jamestown Foundation *Prism*, December 1996.

———. "The Failure of Russian Reform." Jamestown Foundation *Prism*, May 31, 1996.

———. "The Rise of the Russian Criminal State." Jamestown Foundation *Prism*, September 4, 1998.

———. "Russia's Lost Sense of Morality." Jamestown Foundation *Prism*, April 18, 1997.

———. "Yeltsin: Shadow of a Doubt." *National Interest*, no. 34 (winter 1993–94).

Savin, Alexei. "ZaCHARovannye Kvartiry." *Izvestiya*, July 19, 1997.

Sergeenko, Sergei. "Litso, Kotoroe Sovershaet Zakaznoe Ubiistvo, Segodnya Nichem ne Riskuet." *Argumenty i Fakty*, no. 9 (March 1996).

Serio, Joseph. "Threats to the Foreign Business Community in Moscow." In *Russian Organized Crime: The New Threat?* Edited by Phil Williams. Special double issue, *Transnational Organized Crime* 2, nos. 2/3 (summer/autumn 1996): 88–108.

Shakina, Marina. " 'MMM': Sergei Mavrodi kak Otets Rossiiskoi Mechty." *Novoye Russkoye Slovo*, August 10, 1994.

Shelley, Louise I. "Post-Soviet Organized Crime: A New Form of Authoritarianism." In *Russian Organized Crime: The New Threat?* Edited by Phil Williams. Special double issue, *Transnational Organized Crime* 2, nos. 2/3 (summer/autumn 1996): 122–38.

———. "The Price Tag of Russia's Organized Crime." *Johnson's Russia List*, February 1997.

Shenfield, Stephen. "On the Threshold of Disaster: The Socio-Economic Situation in Russia." *Johnson's Russia List*, July 2, 1998.

Shevchenko, D. *Kremlevskie Nravy.* Moscow: Sovershenno Sekretno, 1999.

Shevelev, Dmitry. "Zolotaya Moya Stolitsa." *Novoye Vremya*, no. 31 (1998).

Shihab, Sophie. "Attentats: La piste vite oubliée des services russes." *Le Monde*, January 12, 2000.

Shirokov, Viktor. "Ya Boyus: Militseiskie Priklucheniya Intelligenta." *Novoye Russkoye Slovo*, January 30, 1998; reprinted from *Kriminalnaya Khronika.*

Shleinov, Roman. "FSB. Geksogen. Ryazan." *Novaya Gazeta*, March 30–April 2, 2000.

———. "Rassledovaniya. Sekretnost Trebuet Zhertv." *Novaya Gazeta*, March 18, 2002.

Shragin, Boris, and Albert Todd, eds. *Landmarks: A Collection of Essays on the Russian Intelligentsia.* New York: Karz Howard, 1977.

Shulman, Sol. *Vlast i Sudba*. Moscow: Ostozhye, 1998.

"Silence after the Explosions." *Moskovsky Komsomolets*, January 19, 2000.

Skoibeda, Ulyana. "Rassledovanie po Pismu Vdovy." *Komsomolskaya Pravda*, February 24, 2001.

———. "Vsem Nam Khvatit Vody, Vsem Nam Khvatit Bedy." *Komsomolskaya Pravda*, August 24, 2000.

———. "Yuru iz 'Adyutanta Ego Prevoskhoditelstva' Dolzhny Byli Ubit Zhena, Koldunya i Bomzh." *Komsomolskaya Pravda*, July 9, 1999.

Skosirev, Vladimir. "Kto zhe v Rossii Budet Zashchishchat Grazhdan, a ne Gosudarstvo." *Izvestiya*, April 5, 1997.

Skukin, Evgenii. "Dobrosovestny Monopolist?" *Rossiiskaya Gazeta*, January 21, 1992.

Skuratov, Yury. *Variant Drakona*. Moscow: Detektiv, 2000.

Smirnov, Viktor. "'Uralmash' v Semi Tomakh." *Kommersant*, November 3, 1999.

Smirnov, Viktor, and Ivan Seslavsky. "Kriminal Sozdal Svoyu Partiyu." *Argumenty i Fakty*, no. 27 (1999).

Smith, Adam. *The Theory of Moral Sentiments*. Edited by D. D. Raphael and A. L. Macfie. Indianapolis: Liberty Fund, 1984.

———. *The Wealth of Nations*. New York: Modern Library, 1937.

Sokolov, Veniamin. "Privatization, Corruption, and Reform in Present Day Russia." *Demokratizatsiya* 6 (1998): 664–75.

Solovei, Polina. "Razyskivaetsya Ubiitsa." *Trud*, September 13, 1995.

Solovyova, Yulia. "Urals Politics Linked to Organized Crime." *Moscow Times*, June 18, 1999.

Solzhenitsyn, Alexander. *Rossiya v Obvale*. Moscow: Russky Put, 1998.

Solzhenitsyn, Alexander, et al. *From under the Rubble*. Translated under the direction of Michael Scammell. Boston: Little, Brown, 1975.

Sorokin, Pavel. "Sibirsky Genii ili Zlodei?" *Argumenty i Fakty*, no. 41 (1999).

"Soyuz Aktsionerov 'MMM' Provodit Aktsii v Zashchitu Sergeya Mavrodi." *Novoye Russkoye Slovo*, August 1994.

Speransky, Albert. "Khozyain i Rabotnik." Manuscript. Moscow, 1998.

Steele, Doug. "The End of an Era: The Hungry Duck Story." *The Exile*, March–April 1999.

Streletsky, Valery. *Mrakobesie*. Moscow: Detektiv, 1998.

Subbotin, Vyacheslav. "Chistye Dengi v Gryaznykh Rukakh." *Delovye Lyudi*, June 3, 1994.

Sviatov, Georgy. "Death of Kursk." *Submarine Review*, October 2000, 47–52.

Szamuely, Tibor. *The Russian Tradition*. London: Secker and Warburg, 1974.

Taina Gibeli Podlodki "Kursk": Khronoka Tragedii i Lzhi 12–24 Avgusta 2000 Goda. Moscow: Komsomolskaya Pravda, 2000.

Tarasov, Alexei. "Bitva za Aliuminii s Kriminalnym Podtekstom." *Izvestiya*, no. 244 (1994).

——. "Intelligentsiya Nakonets Nashla Natsionalnogo Geroya." *Izvestiya*, April 2, 1999.

——. "Neprikosnovennye: 1. Bykov i Ego Okruzhenie ili Kriminalnye Tainy Taezhnogo Zamka." *Izvestiya*, November 11, 1997.

——. "Neprikosnovennye: 2. Bykov i Gangstery ili Voina i Mir po-Novorusski." *Izvestiya*, November 12, 1997.

——. "Neprikosnovennye: 3. Bykov i Vlast ili Sumerki Gosudarstva Rossiiskogo." *Izvestiya*, November 13, 1997.

——. "Neprikosnovennye: 4. Bykov i Obshchestvo ili Molchanie Yagnyat." *Izvestiya*, November 14, 1997.

——. "Nevynosimaya Svoboda." *Izvestiya*, March 10, 1994.

——. "Novye Zhertvy Aliuminievoi Voiny." *Izvestiya*, April 21, 1995.

——. "Ostavshiesya v Zhivykh Geroi Oborony KrAZa." *Izvestiya*, July 29, 1997.

——. "Rossiiskoe Gosudarstvo Ubilo Uchitelnitsu." *Izvestiya*, January 30, 1997.

——. "Velikaya Sibirskaya Aluminievaya Voina Prodolzhaetsya." *Izvestiya*, January 27, 1995.

——. "Vzrivpaket Aktsii." *Izvestiya*, no. 221 (1994).

Timofeev, Lev. "Vokrug Skandala s 'MMM.'" *Russkaya Mysl*, October 6–12, 1994.

Tretyakov, Vitaly. Editorial. *Nezavisimaya Gazeta*, October 12, 1999.

Tsipko, Alexander. "'The Family' Takes Control of Domestic Politics in Russia." Jamestown Foundation *Prism*, September 2001.

"TsRU o Svyazyakh Rossiiskikh Bankov s Mafiei." *Novoye Russkoye Slovo*, December 12, 1994.

Ukraintsev, Igor. "Poslednii Antigeroi Boevika." *Delovye Lyudi*, no. 124–25 (July–August 2001).

Uztyuzhanin, Vasily. "'Dvoika' po Povedeniyu?" *Komsomolskaya Pravda*, November 18, 1997.

Vasinsky, Alexander. "Gorod, Gde Golodayut Stariki i Deti." *Izvestiya*, February 20, 1997.

——. "Vremya Lyudei. Neobyavlennaya Epidemiya." *Vremya MN*, February 21, 2002.

Vekshin, Vladimir. *Biznes i Bezopasnost v Rossii*. Moscow: Selskaya Molodezh, 1996.

Vershov, Yuri. "Zhiteli i Syshchiki Nefteyuganska Ishchut Ubiits Mera." *Vremya*, no. 17 (1998).

Virkunen, Valery. "The Battle for Russia's Aluminum Comes to a Head." Jamestown Fondation *Prism*, January 2000.

——. "Likhaya Afera 'Vlasteliny.'" *Zhizn i koshelek*, no. 22 (1996).

——. "Podaite Deputatu Gosudarstvennoi Dumy." *Argumenty i Fakty*, March 1995.

V. M. "Deputaty ne Khotyat Uznat Pravdu?" *Novaya Gazeta*, April 3–9, 2000.

Volkova, Lyudmilla, and Tatyana Ressina. "Dochenka, Ya Prinesu Tebye Tyemochku . . ." *Moskovsky Komsomolets*, October 19, 1999.

Vologodsky, Sergei. "Udavka dlya Avto." *Sovershenno Sekretno*, no. 2 (1998).

Voloshin, Pavel. "Chelovek Cheloveku—Sobaka Pavlova." *Novaya Gazeta*, October 4–10, 1999.

——. "Chto Bylo v Ryazani: Sakhar ili Geksogen?" *Novaya Gazeta*, February 14–20, 2000.

——. "Geksogen. FSB. Ryazan." *Novaya Gazeta*, March 19, 2000.

——. "I Vnov FSB Geksogen Ryazan: Istoriya Odnoi Falshivki." *Novaya Gazeta*, September 21–24, 2000.

Voronin, Yuri A. "The Emerging Criminal State: Economic and Political Aspects of Organized Crime in Russia." In *Russian Organized Crime: The New Threat?* Edited by Phil Williams. Special double issue, *Transnational Organized Crime* 2, nos. 2/3 (summer/autumn 1996): 53–62.

Voronova, Valentina. "Polny Zaboy Golodayushchikh Shakhterov Obvinili vo Vreditelstve." *Obshchaya Gazeta*, August 8–14, 1996.

Wedel, Janine R. *Collision and Collusion: The Strange Case of Western Aid to Eastern Europe, 1989–1998*. New York: St. Martin's, 1998.

Weir, Fred. "On Kursk, a New Caring Kremlin." *Christian Science Monitor*, November 2, 2000.

——. "A Slow Descent." www.intellectualcapital.com, September 25, 1997.

Williams, Phil. "How Serious a Threat Is Russian Organized Crime?" In *Russian Organized Crime: The New Threat?* Edited by Phil Williams. Special double issue, *Transnational Organized Crime* 2, nos. 2/3 (summer/autumn 1996): 1–28.

Working, Russell. "City's Dead Rest in Streets." *Vladivostok News*, March 20, 1998.

Yakubov, Oleg. *Mikhailov ili Mikhas? Tainy Zhenevskogo Protsessa*. Moscow: VEChE-AST, 1999.

Yanov, A. A. *Rossiya protiv Rossii: Ocherki Istorii Russkogo Natsionalizma 1825–1921*. Novosibirsk: "Sibirskii khronograf," 1999.

Yemilyanov, Alexander. " 'Kursk' ne Stalkivalsya s Inostrannoi Podlodkoi." *Novaya Gazeta*, February 15, 2001.

"Za Mesyats v Moskve Zazhivo Svarilis Devyat Chelovek." *Komsomolskaya Pravda*, March 14, 1998.

Zharkov, Dmitri. "Litsenziya na Ubiistvo." *Kommersant*, March 4, 1999.

Zhukova, Svetlana. "Ledyanoi Dom." *Vladivostok*, January 25, 2001.

Zinoviev, Aleksandr. *Gibel Russkogo Kommunizma*. Moscow: Tsentrpoligraf, 2001.

——. *Russkaya Sudba: Ispoved Otshchepentsa*. Moscow: Tsentrpoligraf, 1999.

——. *Zapiski Nochnogo Storozha*. Lausanne: L'Age d'Homme, 1979.

Acknowledgments

This book was made possible by the support of the Sarah Scaife Foundation, the William H. Donner Foundation, and the Earhart Foundation. I would like to thank Daniel McMichael, the secretary of the Scaife Foundation; Curtin Winsor, Louise Oliver, and the board members and staff of the Donner Foundation; and David Kennedy, the president, and Antony Sullivan, the secretary, of the Earhart Foundation.

During the writing of *Darkness at Dawn,* I have been affiliated with the Hudson Institute and the Johns Hopkins University Nitze School of Advanced International Studies (SAIS). I would like to thank Herbert London, the president of Hudson, and Edwin Rubinstein, the research director; and Thomas Keaney, the director of the Foreign Policy Institute at Johns Hopkins, for their encouragement and support. Some of the material in this book first appeared in essays published in the Jamestown Foundation *Prism.* I thank Bill Geimer, the president of the Jamestown Foundation, for permission to use it here.

Andrew Nagorski and Nancy Lippincott read earlier versions of the manuscript and provided many helpful suggestions. Bob Otto gave generously of his time in helping me to find published material. In Russia, I benefited from the help of Albert Speransky, a leader of the independent trade union movement, and from other Russians who prefer not to be named.

Finally, I would like to thank my children, Raphael, Claire, and Mark, for their tolerance, and my wife, Olga, for her careful reading of the manuscript and other invaluable help.

Index

Abramovich, Roman, 196, 251
Achinsk Alumina Factory (AGK), 189, 193, 195
advertising, false, 72–92, 271nn2,4
Aeroflot, 53, 56–57, 71
Afghanistan, 156, 164
agriculture, 98, 131, 253
alcohol and alcoholism, 49, 107, 115, 131, 134, 203, 242, 254, 282–83n3
aluminum: corruption and, 182–97; "tolling," 183–85
Andreeva, Galina, 218–21
Anisimov, Vasily, 190, 191, 195, 196
Antimonopoly Committee, 40–43
apartment buildings, 88, 89, 136, 283n9; bombings, 24–33, 64–69, 250–52, 260–65nn1–8, 268–69nn22–26, 270–71nn33–34, 287n8; division-of-property issues and corruption, 124–26, 140, 224, 231, 234; energy cuts and corruption, 165–67, 171–73, 177, 198–201, 277–80nn1–14; organized crime in, 224–25; privatization of, 224–25; in pyramid schemes, 88–92
"apartment children," 158
armed forces, 20, 46, 51, 157, 255, 278n2, 282n10; air force, 183; in Chechen wars,
31, 60, 64, 210–18, 259n10, 270n28, 284nn10–12; identification of dead soldiers, 210–18, 284nn10–12; Red Army, 249; Yeltsin and, 58–60
arms trade, 131, 143, 153
Arseniye Vesti, 180
Aryapov, Rashid, 21, 22
Averin, Viktor, 135, 136
Aviastar factory, 157–59, 164
Avtovaz factory, organized crime in, 128–31

babies, kidnapped from hospitals, 218–21
Baltics, 141
banks: corruption, 46–54, 74–92, 96, 100, 107–8, 131, 135, 172, 184, 272–73n5, 285n3; dummy firms and pyramid schemes, 47, 74–92, 102, 271–72nn2–5, 277n16; gangsters for debt collection, 53–54; hyperinflation, 46–48, 74, 76, 88; loans-for-shares scheme, 51–53, 63, 107, 272–73n5; money transfers, 184, 281n2; organized crime and, 53–54, 131, 135; savings accounts wiped out, 37, 47, 87–92, 97
Barents Sea, 5, 7, 12, 18, 20
Basayev, Shamil, 63–65, 274n6

Baulo, Sergei, 167, 278–79n8
BBC, 221
Berdyaev, Nikolai, 202, 256; *From the Depths*, 34; *Russia's Fate*, 1, 222
Berezovsky, Boris, 54, 56–57, 63, 64, 250, 251, 267–68n20
Bible, 5, 93
Bizimana, Svetlana, 218–21
black magic, 228–29
black market, 337, 241, 274–76n4
Black Sea, 40
Boldirev, Oleg, 85–86
bombings, 267n18; apartment-house, 24–33, 64–69, 250–52, 260–65nn1–8, 268–69nn22–26, 270–71nn33–34, 287n8; Buinaksk, 25, 26, 32, 64–65, 67, 251, 264n8, 270n29; FSB and, 24–33, 65–68, 250–52, 260–65nn1–8, 270n31, 271n33, 287n8; Moscow, 64–68, 251, 264n8, 268nn22,23, 269n26, 270–71nn30–34; Ryazan, 24–33, 67–69, 250–52, 260–65nn1–8, 270n29, 287n8
Borodin, Pavel, 56
bribery, 2–3, 233; and criminal oligarchic system, 45–71; economy and, 38–44, 54–55; organized crime and, 127–55, 167–68, 224–25; police corruption and, 112–26, 273–74nn1–10; to save Yeltsin presidency, 58–59, 61, 62. *See also* crime
Burbulis, Gennady, 36, 39, 40, 42, 265n4
Bykov, Anatoly, 182–97, 281n3

capitalism, 1, 224; gangsters as capitalists, 231; transition from communism, 35–44, 55, 95–96, 166, 202, 225–26
card sharping, 237, 238
Central Bank, 91, 184, 205, 281n2
Central gang, 241–42
Chara Bank, 87–92, 271–72n4
Chechelnitsky, Mikhail, 171
Chechnya, 254, 271n33, 273n5, 275n4; gangsters, 147–55; identification of dead soldiers, 210–18; Ryazan bombing and, 25, 29, 31; terrorism, 29, 63–70, 250; wars, 25, 31, 58–70, 85, 210–18, 222–23,

251, 259n10, 267–68n20, 269n25, 270n28, 274n6, 281n2, 284nn10–12
Chelyabinsk Metallurgical Combine, 50
Cherepkov, Viktor, 168–69, 172–73, 179–81, 278–80nn3–14
Chernogorodsky, Valery, 40–43
Chernomydrin, Viktor, 55–56
Chernoy, Lev, 184–91, 196, 280–82nn1–7
Chernoy, Mikhail, 184–91, 196, 280–82nn1–7
China, 170, 255
Chubais, Anatoly, 34, 41, 42, 43, 141, 172–73, 191, 195, 196, 265nn1,6, 266n8, 279n10, 287n4
City Without Narcotics, 246
coal, 170, 191; unpaid miners, 171–74
Committee of Soldiers' Mothers, 10, 213, 259n10
communism, 132, 275n4; fall of (1991), 1, 58, 224, 254; society and, 3, 37, 38, 202, 203; transition to capitalism, 35–44, 55, 95–96, 166, 202, 225–26
Communist party, 47, 59, 69, 70; dissolved (1991), 1, 58, 96
consciousness, criminalization of, 222–47, 284–86nn1–16
contract murders, 53–54, 99, 124, 126, 139–55, 191, 194, 229–31, 283n5
cooperatives, 41, 47, 53, 275n4
copper, 242
corpses: identification of, 210–18, 274n10, 284nn10–12; removal, 175, 227
Credprombank, 100
crime, 1–4; babies kidnapped from hospitals, 218–21; contract murders, 53–54, 99, 124, 126, 139–55, 191, 194, 229–31, 283n5; criminalization of consciousness, 222–47, 284–86nn1–16; disregard for human life and, 282–84nn1–12; dummy firms and pyramid schemes, 47, 72–92, 102, 271–72nn2–5, 277n16; economy and, 37–44, 46, 53–55, 72–92, 131, 166–81, 182–97, 222–47, 284–86nn1–16; factory, 41–44, 47, 49–51, 93–111, 166–68, 182–97, 272–73nn1–7, 274–76n4,

280–82*nn*1–12; oligarchic system, 45–71, 166, 251; police corruption and, 112–26, 204–5, 273–74*nn*1–10; privatization and corruption, 41–44, 46, 49–55, 93–111, 129–31, 165–81, 182–97, 231, 272–73*nn*1–7, 280–81*nn*1–12, 284–86*nn*1–16; tolerance of, 37–38, 222–47, 284–86*nn*1–16. *See also* bribery; organized crime

Crimea, 39–40

currency exchange, 141–42

Czech Republic, 84–87

Dagestan, 63–64, 66, 67, 232, 267–68*n*20

Dalenergo, 171, 173

Danulov, Shamil, 128, 129

daughter firms, 41, 42, 96, 98–99, 102

Day of the Child, 240, 245

death: Chechen war soldiers, 210–18, 259*n*10, 284*nn*10–12; contract murders, 53–54, 99, 124, 126, 139–55, 191, 194, 229–31, 283*n*5; corpse removal, 175, 227; false reports of and baby kidnappings, 218–21; identification of corpses, 210–18, 274*n*10; *Kursk* incident, 5–23, 257–59*nn*1–15; leaking hot-water pipe accidents, 205–10, 283*n*9; moral indifference in Russian society and, 2, 36–38, 132, 198–221, 254, 256, 282–84*nn*1–12; rate, rise in, 60, 88, 175, 176, 203, 249, 253–56, 283*n*5; suicide, 73, 74, 98, 102, 178, 203, 225–26, 279–80*n*12, 283*n*5; in Vladivostok, 175–79

Debit, 108

Defense Ministry, 8, 23

del Ponte, Carla, 56–57

democracy, 1, 35, 249

depopulation, 60, 88, 175–76, 203, 249, 253–56, 283*n*5

Deripaska, Oleg, 195, 196, 251

diamonds, 41

divorce, 118–19, 122, 124

Dolgova, Aliza, 2

Dorofeev, Vladimir, 97–102

Dotsenko, 139–40

drugs, shortage of, 178

Duma, State, 3, 32, 55–56, 58–62, 80, 110, 155, 179, 181, 237, 245, 247, 269*n*24

dummy firms, 72–92, 271–72*nn*2–5, 277*n*16

Dyachenko, Tatyana, 56–57, 63

economic determinism, 37–38, 201, 203

economy, 267*n*13; crime and, 37–44, 46, 53–55, 72–92, 131, 166–81, 182–97, 222–47, 284–86*nn*1–16; dummy firms and pyramid schemes, 47, 72–92, 102, 271–72*nn*2–5, 277*n*16; energy cuts and corruption, 165–67, 171–73, 176–79, 198–201, 277–80*nn*1–14; future of, 248–49, 252–53, 256; hyperinflation, 46–49, 74, 76, 88, 97, 141, 271*n*3; modernization, 252–53; *1998* crisis, 55, 147, 248; organized crime and, 131–55, 222–47; price controls lifted, 37, 38, 46–48, 203; privatization and corruption, 41–44, 46–55, 93–111, 128–31, 157–59, 165–81, 182–97, 231, 272–73*nn*1–7, 280–82*nn*1–12, 284–86*nn*1–16; reform, 1–3, 34–44, 46–55, 157, 166–68, 203, 248–49, 251–52, 256, 267*n*9; socialist structures, 3, 37, 38, 202, 203; transition to market economy, 1–3, 34–44, 55, 166–68, 202–3, 225–26, 252–53, 256; in Vladivostok, 165–81; young reformers and, 34–44, 265–66*nn*1–9

education, 156–64, 171, 226, 238; future of, 255; Ulyanovsk teachers' hunger strike, 156–64, 277*nn*1–2

electricity, 191, 237, 252; cuts and corruption, 165–67, 171–73, 176–79, 198–201, 277–80*nn*1–14

emergency rescue services, 226–27

energy, 48, 51; cuts and corruption, 107–11, 142, 165–79, 191, 198–201, 277–80*nn*1–14

exports, 38–40; raw materials, 48

factories, 238, 239; aluminum, 182–97; daughter firms, 41, 42, 96, 98–99, 102;

advertising, 75–77, 88–89, 271nn2,4; on hospital deaths, 200–201; killers advertised in, 229–30; Russian faith in, 75; on Ryazan bombing, 29–32, 261n6. *See also* specific publications

nickel, 52

Nizhny Novgorod, 61, 236–40

Norilsk Nickel, 52

Northern Fleet, and *Kursk* incident, 5–23, 257–59nn1–15

Norway, 8, 11–18, 20

Novaya Gazeta, 23, 29–32, 198, 222

Novitsky, Yevgeny, 136

Novy Gorod, teachers' hunger strike in, 157–64

NTV, 32, 87, 249–50, 263n6, 286–87n4

nuclear accidents, 253

oil, 39–40, 41, 51, 54, 63, 131, 133, 134, 142, 167, 248, 249, 273n6; corruption, 107–11, 171; price of, 252, 256

Okulova, Yelena, 56–57, 63

oligarchic system: crime and, 45–71, 166, 251; hyperinflation and, 46–48; of late *1990s*, 46, 55–71; of *1992–98*, 46–58, 251; privatization and, 49–53; Putin-era, 70–71, 249–52

Olympics, 132

Oneximbank, 34, 52, 54

Operation Cyclone, 130, 131

OPS (Uralmash gang organization), 240

organized crime, 2–4, 37–38, 53–55, 56, 74, 127–55, 203, 221, 274–77nn1–16, 284–86nn1–16; apartment buildings, 224–25; Chechen, 147–55; contract murders, 53–54, 99, 124, 126, 139–55, 191, 194, 229–31, 283n5; economy and, 131–55, 222–47; in factories, 128–31, 185–97, 240, 274–76n4; government and, 133–39, 141, 154, 169, 193, 237–47; in Krasnoyarsk, 185–97; Operation Cyclone, 130, 131; police corruption and, 132–33, 137–39, 141; in Primoriye, 166–73; privatization and, 128–31,

167–68, 224–25; tolerance of, 37–38, 222–47. *See also* gangsters

orphanages, 171, 176, 192

ORT television, 160, 170

Orthodoxy, Russian, 201

Osipova, Svetlana, 87–92

Ovchinnikov, Nikolai, 247

Pacific Fleet, 9

parliament, 48–49, 55–62

Participation, 222–23

Partner, 103

Patruschev, Nikolai, 28

perestroika, 36, 41, 46, 49, 53, 74, 226, 255

Perm Motor Factory, 41, 53

Peterikov, Igor, 82–85

Petrunin, Boris, 185–86, 193

Petukhov, Vladimir, 107–11

Pinyaev, Alexei, 30–32

Pirozhkov, Alexander, 99–102

Plyatskovsky, Sergei, 139

Pogranichny, 198–201

police corruption, 112–26, 273–74nn1–10; identity checks and, 114–18; vulnerable society and, 118–26

Popov, Gavril, 41

Popov, Admiral Vladislav, 13, 14, 15, 16

population decline, 60, 88, 175–76, 203, 249, 253–56, 283n5

pornography, 237, 238

Potanin, Vladimir, 54

poverty, 1, 46, 48, 100, 254

power, cuts and corruption in, 165–67, 171–73, 176–79, 198–201, 277–80nn1–14

Pravda, 36

presidential elections, 63; of *1996*, 53, 190; of *2000*, 55, 69–71, 251

Primakov, Yevgeny, 55–56, 58, 62, 63, 69

Primoriye, 166–81, 277–80nn1–14

Primoriye, 180

Primorsky Corporation of Goods Producers (PAKT), 166–68

privatization, 34, 38–44, 71, 202–4, 250, 266n7, 267n9; and corruption, 41–44,